High Hopes
The Rise and Decline of Buffalo, New York

MARK GOLDMAN

High Hopes
THE RISE AND
DECLINE OF
BUFFALO, NEW YORK

State University of New York Press

ALBANY

Published by
State University of New York Press, Albany

© 1983 State University of New York

All rights reserved

Printed in the United States of America

For information, address State University of New York
Press, State University Plaza, Albany, N.Y., 12246

Library of Congress Cataloging in Publication Data
Goldman, Mark, 1943-   .
   High hopes before the fall.

   Bibliography: p. 000
   Includes index.
   1. Buffalo (N.Y.)—History. 2. Buffalo (N.Y.)—Social life and customs. I. Title.
F129.B857G64   1983   974.7'9704   82-19629
ISBN 0-87395-734-2
ISBN 0-87395-735-0 (pbk.)

To my mother, Tillie, who introduced me to history;
to Kitty, who introduced me to Buffalo;
to Charlie and Lydia for being themselves.

Contents

Acknowledgments

For helping me develop my ideas about American cities in general and Buffalo in particular, Michael Frisch, Professor of History at the State University of New York at Buffalo; for creating a climate conducive to research and writing, Peter J. Ristuben, Dean of the Niagara Frontier Regional Center of Empire State College, SUNY; for helping me with my research, Dr. Herman Sass, Head Librarian at the Buffalo and Erie County Historical Society. In addition, other members of the staff of that marvelous institution have been extremely helpful. They are Clyde Helfter, Mary Ann Hickey and Pat Gabor. Shonnie Finnegan, Director of the Archives at SUNY Buffalo, was very supportive in offering valuable suggestions throughout the course of this project. I would also like to thank Helene Watson and Pat Losey who typed the manuscript. Finally, I would like to thank my children, Charlie and Lydia, who waited patiently for me while I finished this book on the third floor of our house.

Introduction

In 1901, the year Buffalo hosted the Pan American Exposition, the city was buoyant and rapidly expanding. With over 350,000 people its population was growing rapidly while its economy was strong and diversified. Commerce, Buffalo's traditional source of wealth, gave every sign of remaining prosperous. The city's port, its railroad facilities, its grain elevators, and its livestock yards were among the largest of any in the United States. Meanwhile, the development of heavy industry, particularly of steel, pointed to still more growth and greatness. Buffalo's growth had already been remarkable and its future seemed filled with promise. It was within this atmosphere of achievement and expectation that the Pan American Exposition was held.

The Pan American Exposition reflects much of the history of the city of Buffalo. It is an appropriate metaphor and a fitting place to begin telling the story of Buffalo's rise and decline. Like the city at the beginning of the century, the Pan American Exposition, a world's fair supported largely by local subscribers, opened with the brightest hopes for success. Not only would it succeed financially, its backers believed, but more significantly it would serve to rivet the attention of the world on the city of Buffalo. Events proved otherwise, however. The large crowds never materialized and when towards the end of the exposition President McKinley was assassinated on the fairgrounds, the Pan American turned quickly into a nightmare. Likewise, Buffalo's promise of greatness in the twentieth century was also destined for disappointment. The signs had begun to appear early in the century. Soon they were unmistakable. By the 1970s and early 1980s all of the high hopes that the people of Buffalo had once had for the city

1

had been dashed. Buffalo, like the exposition, faced what many people were convinced was disaster.

High Hopes is an attempt to analyze and interpret the historical phenomena that have shaped this city. In it I have examined the larger, external historical shifts that have affected the city. The book charts the evolution of Buffalo from a small frontier community through its development as a major commercial center and its emergence and eventual decline as a significant industrial metropolis. Within this larger context, the book examines the detailed patterns of local daily life and covers a wide range of subjects including work, ethnicity, family and community life, class structure, architecture and city planning, education, politics, social and cultural life, and values and beliefs. By bringing to bear on these events and developments a broad and disparate range of subjects and ideas, the book attempts to analyze, synthesize, interpret, and understand the vast array of complex forces at work in the historical development not only of Buffalo but of all American cities.

CHAPTER 1

The Pan American Exposition:
World's Fair as Historical Metaphor

William McKinley liked world fairs. They were, he said, "the timekeepers of progress. They record the world's advancement." He had been to the Columbian Exposition in Chicago in 1893 and the Cotton States Exposition in Atlanta two years later. He did not want to miss the Pan American Exposition, to be held in Buffalo during the summer of 1901.

McKinley had hoped to be in Buffalo for the opening of the exposition in May. However, his wife, Ida, was ill, and because he never traveled without her, he postponed the trip. In his place he sent the vice-president, Theodore Roosevelt. Upon Roosevelt's return to Washington, McKinley pressed him for details of the exposition. Roosevelt raved about it. He especially liked the Electric Tower.

McKinley had never been known for his decisiveness. Indeed, there was a joke current that compared the president's mind to his bed: both, it was said, had to be made up for him before they could be used. But now McKinley displayed uncharacteristic resolve and, against the advice of both his wife and his personal secretary, George B. Cortelyou, he insisted on going to the Pan American. Mrs. McKinley did not want to leave their home in Canton, Ohio, where they were spending the summer. She had never really enjoyed her official role as the nation's first lady and lately she found it more distasteful than ever before. For years she had suffered from phlebitis, and since the day in 1873 when her five-month-old daughter died, she had been an epileptic, subject to regular attacks of *petit mal*, brief losses of consciousness, and prolonged seizures followed by bouts of depression. Now, at age fifty-eight, she required constant sedation and medical attention. She would have much preferred to stay home and crochet the slippers and sew the black cravats that gave her husband so much pleasure.

Cortelyou had different reasons for opposing the president's plan to visit Buffalo. He was obsessed with the president's safety and was convinced that the crowds at the Pan American presented a danger that best should be avoided. However, the president insisted on going, and on September 4, 1901, the presidential party, planning to spend three days at the exposition, pulled into Buffalo.

As a result of America's stunning victory in the Spanish-American War and the territorial acquisitions which followed, William McKinley, the leading spokesman of a newly discovered national strength and brazen self-confidence, was extremely popular. His appeal, particularly in Buffalo, the city whose international exposition embodied and glorified the goals of the president's expansionist foreign policy, was vast. It transcended class and party lines, making him the most popular president since Lincoln. The Pan American had been planned during the heady days following the conclusion of the war against Spain, and now as hundreds and thousands of Americans descended on Buffalo to pay homage to Pan Americanism, the city became the national symbol of the country's pride and braggadocio. Never had American power been more apparent. In March 1901, Emilio Aguinaldo, the leader of the insurrection against American occupation of the Philippine Islands, was captured by the United States Marines. In May, the Supreme Court ruled that the Constitution of the United States and the Bill of Rights did not follow the American flag to the territories recently captured from Spain and were not applicable there. In June, the Cuban Senate adopted an amendment to their constitution which authorized the United States to intervene at any time in order to preserve law and order in Cuba. And in July, William Howard Taft was sent to Manila to become the first American governor of the Philippine Islands. Like most Americans, the people of Buffalo were proud of these achievements. They were proud of themselves as well, for the Pan American Exposition had tapped the same source of inspiration in Buffalo that McKinley's foreign policy had inspired in the nation at large. McKinley's visit affirmed their achievement and they waited eagerly for the opportunity to welcome their president. Their chance came on September 4, 1901.

President McKinley's arrival in Buffalo at 5:00 P.M. on Tuesday, September 4, 1901, was clouded by what some would later call an ominous happening. As the presidential train pulled into the Terrace Railroad Station overlooking Lake Erie, it was greeted by a twenty-one-gun salute. In his eagerness to honor this most popular president, the cannoneer, a Coast Guard officer and veteran of McKinley's Civil War regiment, had placed the cannon so close to the railroad tracks that when the salvo began the presidential car shook violently. Although there were no injuries and only minimal damage was done to the train, the presidential party was worried about Mrs. McKinley, who was greatly unhinged by the incident. As the train left the station and headed north to the exposition grounds, a dozen or more people, screaming "anarchist" as if it were a swear word, pounced on a short, swarthy man who had been standing near the cannoneer.

Several minutes later the train pulled into a special platform built at one of the entrances to the exposition grounds. Wearing a black frock coat and a high, black silk hat, President McKinley, his right arm tightly around his wife's waist, disembarked. Following a short and ceremonious greeting by John Milburn, the head of the exposition's board of directors, President and Mrs. McKinley, watched by a crowd of more than sixty thousand, stepped into a low-wheeled victoria drawn by four exquisite trotters, and made a quick tour of the exposition grounds. The McKinleys were then driven to John Milburn's home on Delaware Avenue, about one mile south of the exposition. They were scheduled to return to the exposition the next day.

The Milburns were accustomed to entertaining important visitors. Earlier that summer the Roosevelts had stayed with them, as had the French ambassador and his family. But clearly the president was different, and in anticipation of the visit Milburn had completely renovated his large wooden home. The Milburns were concerned about their guests—not the president, an affable, easy-going man who liked nothing more than smoking a cigar (he smoked over twenty per day) in the company of robust men—but rather Mrs. McKinley. For in spite of the president's best efforts to hide it from the public (and even his best friends), the Milburns knew, as did the rest of the country, about the first lady's epilepsy. While no mention was ever made in the press about Mrs. McKinley's illness, there were constant references to her fortitude, her ability to withstand the rigors of being the nation's first lady, and endless paeans to the president, whose solicitude of his sickly wife embodied, it was said, the most admirable of husbandly virtues.

Because of Ida McKinley's illness the Milburns were not permitted to entertain as lavishly as they would have liked (when ambassador Cambon had stayed with them in July, the Milburns hosted an all-night costume ball that people were still talking about in September).

There was a story circulating about Mrs. McKinley that at one luncheon given in honor of the president and his wife, the centerpiece was a large, stuffed American eagle. When the guests sat down, the thing began to bob its head and move up and down in jerky, lifelike movements. The effect on Mrs. McKinley was shocking. She had a fit on the spot. Thus, because of her unpredictable behavior and her discomfort around people (to avoid shaking hands, she always held a bouquet in her lap when in public), the Milburns planned no public receptions for their honored guests. There wasn't much time anyway, because the president wanted to see as much of the exposition as possible.

While President McKinley heard about the Electric Tower from Theodore Roosevelt, the rest of the country, in detailed descriptions printed in newspapers around the country, had been reading about it all summer long. At the base of the tower were two colonnades forming a semicircle around a huge set of fountains called "The Court of Fountains." Grouped symmetrically around the court were six buildings dedicated to "Manufactures," "Liberal Arts," "Machines," "Transportation," "Agriculture," and "Electricity." Most of the buildings at the exposition were designed in what was referred to as "Spanish Renaissance Style," yet everywhere an incongruous mixture was evident: the New York State Building was a duplicate of the Parthenon, the Midway boasted a number of Islamic minarets and Italian loggias, and Luchow's Alt Nuremburg restaurant had over two dozen medieval turrets.

Unlike the Chicago World's Fair of 1893, nicknamed the "White City," color was used everywhere at the Pan American. It was planned carefully so that buildings at the edge of the exposition were pale while those towards the center became more colorful, so that the Electric Tower at the very heart of the exposition was, as one witness noted, "a riot of color."

There was also an abundance of sculpture. Over two thousand pieces—some historical, others symbolic and allegorical—were placed all over the 350 acres of the exposition: on the ground, on balconies, at bridge heads, and at the entrances to all of the buildings.

Then there was the Midway. In a personal report from John Milburn, President McKinley had heard all about the Midway. Milburn was proudest of the educational features of the Midway, especially the "transplanted native villages with real natives in them." The most popular was "The Old Plantation." The *Buffalo Evening News* described it thus: "Genuine southern darkies, two hundred of them, ranging in years from wee, toddling pickininies to negroes, grey and bent with age, can be seen each day at the Exposition at their different occupations and pastimes. Lovers of negro melodies will have a feast. Many of the darkies will be selected because of their special talents as singers and banjo players and they will dance and sing to the seductive tinkling of instruments exactly as the Negroes of the South used to do in the long, long ago." The *News* reported that the "negroes were selected from the best class of southern darkies, for Skip Dandy, the concessionaire, has the reputation for not tolerating anything shiftless or degrading about him."

The Midway featured the animal show of Frank C. Bostock, "the animal king, a man of unbounded courage and resources, before whom all animals cower"—even Jumbo, Bostock's star attraction. Bostock had recently acquired this nine-ton elephant from the British Army, where it had been decorated by Queen Victoria for bravery in the Afghanistan Wars.

But above all else it was electricity and the Electric Tower that attracted the attention of the millions of people who visited the Pan American Exposition during the summer of 1901. Every building was outlined in incandescent lights, and at dusk, peak time at the exposition, when over two million light bulbs were turned on simultaneously, the effect was staggering. Walter Hines Page, the editor of the *Atlantic Monthly* and an enthusiastic booster of the exposition, described the scene: "Here is nocturnal architecture, nocturnal landscapes, nocturnal gardens and long vistas of nocturnal beauty. At a distance the Fair presents the appearance of a whole city in illumination." But for Page, as for all the visitors to the exposition, nothing rivalled the Electric Tower itself. "The Tower is a great center of brilliancy. There are perhaps not a half million electric bulbs, but there are hundreds and thousands of them and you are willing to believe that there may be millions. It shines like diamonds, a transparent, soft structure of sunlight." Page, an ardent supporter of the imperial foreign policy that the exposition celebrated, saw the Electric Tower as an "epiphanous achievement, a masterpiece of human skill, a monument to the genius of man." "Out of the city of beauty rises a massive pillar, like an overlooking flower in a gorgeous garden, a centerpiece in a cluster of gems, a venerable fabric of jeweled lace. There it stands, glowing with the lights of many thousand bulbs flashing its image in the basin at its feet, showing its gleaming dome to the people in neighboring cities. Its beauty is transcendent." William McKinley couldn't wait until the next day, September 5, to see it, and after his wife had gone to bed, he strolled leisurely around the porch of the Milburn house staring at the Electric Tower.

On September 5, the crowd at the exposition—over 116,000 peoples—broke all records. The great rush came after supper. "Every street-car was loaded and passengers clung to the steps. The whole city, it seemed, was travelling to the Exposition. After 6:00 about thirty thousand people were admitted through the various gates. The grounds had never looked so crowded. Buildings were visited by throngs. The shows were packed at every performance. The restaurants were overwhelmed. From every quarter a flood of humanity bore down upon the esplanade until it was difficult even to worm one's way through the crowd."

First came a concert by John Philip Sousa. Sousa had played at the Bicentennial Exposition at Philadelphia in 1876, the Chicago World's Fair in 1893, the mid-winter California Fair in 1894, the Atlanta Cotton States Exposition in 1895, and the Paris Exposition in 1900, and had been brought in specifically from the Boston Food Fair to play for the president. Then came Henry J. Pain, the "Fire Works King," whose name was synonymous with pyrotechnics. At the Paris Exposition, Pain had launched a three-figured display symbolizing the ideals of the French Revolution. At the St. Louis Fair he used fireworks to create an embodiment of the Louis and Clark Expedition. For Buffalo, he promised the "largest pyrotechnical display ever seen."

At sunset the exposition grounds were illuminated by fifty powerful fires in five different colors. A large number of lighted ballons were next, followed by the discharge of a hundred three-pound rockets fired simultaneously from different sections of the fairgrounds. Ten batteries of mines were then put in motion. Next came five hundred colored lights discharging electric comets in a continuous stream and a salvo of ten thirty-inch bombs with five colors each. Next came a series of ten national streamers, and ten huge shells which each detached one hundred parachutes and fifty silver umbrellas. Then came a display called "The American Empire." At one thousand feet, four large bombs exploded together. The first formed the outline of the United States, the second and third the outlines of Cuba and Puerto Rico, and the fourth splattered into a series of small shells representing the Philippine Islands. But the best was saved for last. For the finale, thousands of tiny fire balls exploded at once, creating a gigantic, sparking likeness of William McKinley. The sky filled with shining letters: "Welcome President McKinley, Chief of our Nation and our Empire."

The president, his aides noted happily, seemed to have enjoyed every minute of Pain's display, and after personally thanking the master of pyrotechnics, the president returned to the Milburn home. Meanwhile, there was violence on the city's East Side. A black woman shot her husband, and a Polish railroad employee stabbed his neighbor seven times in the face and forehead in a place called Pasczek's saloon on Broadway. Leon Czolgosz, who was staying at Walter Nowak's Hotel on Broadway, had seen the stabbing and was, according to later testimony, sickened by it.

On September 6, President McKinley awoke early as was his custom. At 7:15 A.M., fully dressed for the day in his habitual black frock coat and black silk hat, he eluded the small Secret Service entourage that surrounded the Milburn house and took a solitary walk dow Deleware Avenue. Later that morning, accompanied by a host of city and exposition officials, the McKinleys boarded a train for Niagara Falls. They visited the falls, walked along the gorge, and toured the Niagara Falls Power Project, which the President referred to as "the marvel of the Electrical Age." After lunch the presidential party returned to Buffalo. Mrs. McKinley went to the Milburn house to rest, and the president to the exposition, where he was scheduled to meet the thousands of people who, in spite of the oppressive heat, were waiting at the Temple of Music, a large, vaguely Byzantine structure on the north side of the fairgrounds.

No one had waited longer than "Giant" Jim Parker, a six-foot six-inch Negro waiter from Atlanta who had been standing outside the temple since mid-morning. Finally, at 4:00 P.M. the doors of the Temple of Music opened and hundreds of people made an orderly, single-file procession to the front of the auditorium where President McKinley, flanked by John Milburn and his personal secretary, George Cortelyou, stood waiting. It was extremely hot in the room—over ninety degrees—and everybody was carrying handkerchiefs, either wiping their brows or waving them at the president. Leon Czolgosz, however, used his handkerchief to conceal a tiny handgun, and as the fast-moving line brought him directly in front of the president, Czolgosz shot him two times in the stomach. Parker, who was standing directly behind the assassin, smashed him to the floor. While Czolgosz was pounced on and beaten by the attending soldiers and guards, McKinley, amid the screeching pandemonium in the room, was carried out and several minutes later was being rushed in an electrical ambulance to the exposition hospital.

John Milburn took command immediately. When he learned that Roswell Park, the medical director of the exposition, was in Niagara Falls performing a lymphoma operation that Presly Richey, McKinley's personal physician, was touring the exposition grounds, Milburn pointed to Dr. Matthew Mann, one of the several physicians who had gathered at the hospital, and told him to take charge of the case. Mann examined the president and determined that unless his wounds were immediately sutured they would prove fatal. Thus, at 5:30 P.M. Dr. Mann, the city's leading gynecologist, but a man with limited experience in abdominal surgery, began to operate on the president of the United States. Meanwhile, Dr. Park, who had been brought back to Buffalo on a special train, entered the hospital after the operation had begun but soon enough to notice that Mann was working under the most difficult of conditions.

Like all the buildings at the exposition, the hospital was a temporary structure, ill-equipped and able to handle only the most routine medical emergencies. Most serious of all was that the lighting was totally inadequate. Indeed, there were no electric lights at all in the operating room and one of the attending physicians was forced to improvise by using a looking glass to reflect the rays of the setting sun. Only toward the end of the operation did they succeed in rigging up an electric light.

The operation itself was fairly simple. When Dr. Mann could not find the second bullet (the first one had merely grazed the skin and had caused no damage), he assumed that it was safely lodged in the lumbar muscles. Noting that it had caused no damage to the intestine or to other abdominal organs, all that remained for him to do was to close the wounds in the front and back walls of the president's stomach. This done, the operation was completed.

Meanwhile, crowds were forming everywhere. As the news spread throughout the fairgrounds that Czolgosz was being held in one of the rooms in the Temple of Music, hundreds of people tried to break through the cordon of guards surrounding the building. When this failed they tore up the rope and stanchions that supported it. Crowds blocked the electrical paddy wagon that transported Czolgosz from the Temple of Music to police headquarters downtown and the crowd that waited for him there was so large that the wagon was forced to wait while mounted policemen broke it up. As the crowds downtown grew throughout the evening, two National Guard regiments were called out to prevent the anticipated storming of headquarters. Crowds had also formed outside of the exposition hospital and along the route that the electrical ambulance took as it brought President McKinley to the Milburn house following his operation. This crowd, however, was quiet and stunned. Roswell Park wrote about it in his diary: "The passage through the crowd and down Delaware Avenue was one of the most dramatic incidents I have ever witnessed. The fair grounds were crowded that day and it seemed as though the entire crowd had gathered to witness this event. Every man's hat was in his hand and there were handkerchiefs at many eyes. I never saw so large a crowd so quiet."

The Milburn house, so recently renovated, was now converted into a virtual military camp. On the outside it was surrounded by armed guards. Inside special telegraph machines had been installed as the house became the center of an international communications network. Across the street press tents were set up for the more than 250 newsmen covering the story, the most that had ever covered a public event. All of them rejoiced when Dr. Mann issued the first of many medical bulletins. The doctors were "gratified," Mann reported, by the president's condition. "The results," he said, cannot yet be foretold [but] hopes for recovery are justified."

As the president and the people of Buffalo settled in for what appeared to be a long period of recuperation (John Milburn engaged rooms for his family at a downtown hotel), the rest of the world reacted to the news. Europeans, recently shocked by the murder of King Umberto of Italy and the attempted assassination of Kaiser Wilhelm, were particularly concerned. Czar Nicholas II and the Russian royal family, cruising off the Danish coast on their yacht, arranged to meet with Kaiser Wilhelm on his royal yacht, *The Hohenzollern*, in the North Sea. There they agreed to double their security measures and to avoid, at least for a while, all public appearances.

In New York City people were more concerned about the whereabouts of J. P. Morgan than they were with the medical bulletins emanating from the Milburn house in Buffalo. The shooting of the president had triggered dire predictions of a stock market collapse and many people, by now accustomed to the fiscal heroics of Morgan, wondered desparately where he was. Some reports had him closeted with advisors on his private yacht, *The Corsair*. Others said that he was in conference in his private room at Delmonico's. Still others said that he was busy on the telephone in the library of his Murray Hill mansion. As people throughout the country wondered if, how, and when the great financier would come to their rescue, Morgan, who in fact had never left his office, hired three private detectives to protect himself.

Meanwhile, in a basement room of police headquarters, Leon Czolgosz made a confession. "Not until Tuesday did the resolution to shoot the President take hold of me. It was in my heart—there

11

was no escape for me. I could not have conquered it had my life depended on it." The deed, he swore, was his own doing. He had no accomplice and no connection with the notorious anarchist cell in Paterson, New Jersey which had nurtured Gaetano Bresci, the murderer of King Umberto. Over and over he swore that he had no confidants, that he was absolutely alone. But nobody—not the police, or the press, or the politicians all over the country clamoring for anti-anarchist laws—wanted to believe him and they sought desperately for any clue that hinted at conspiracy. Unwittingly, Czolgosz gave them the lead they were looking for. To the police he confessed: "I am an Anarchist—a disciple of Emma Goldman. Her words set me on fire."

The word went out from Buffalo and immediately a national dragnet tightened around the anarchist leader. When a dozen of her colleagues in Chicago were arrested for complicity in the shooting of McKinley, Goldman secretly set out from St. Louis to join them. In spite of her best efforts to disguise herself, she was arrested in Chicago the next day at the request of the Buffalo police.

Convinced that the tentacles of the anarchist conspiracy reached Buffalo, the police began a relentless scouring of the East Side for suspects. Anyone who had had any contact with Czolgosz was arrested: Nowak, whose hotel he had stayed in; Pasczek, whose tavern he had drunk in; and Paul Redlinski, a barber who had cut Czolgosz's hair a week earlier. On a tip from two Polish priests on the East Side, the police arrested Helen Petrowski, a twenty-five-year-old school teacher. The priests said that she had been teaching anarchism and free love. Her dead husband, they said, had also been an anarchist— a man who died because his "constant brooding on the subject of the ideal social fabric fatally affected his brain." Along with Mrs. Petrowski, the police arrested "a dark curly-headed man with a decidedly Polish appearance" and a Russian Jewish physician who in 1894 had led a march of the poor on Buffalo's City Hall.

But the press and the police were far more intrigued with the Goldman connection. Everything, it seemed, pointed in her direction. Not only had Czolgosz mentioned her as a source of inspiration, but also the police said he had talked about her in his sleep several times. Czolgosz's ruminations were given further substance when a local psychiatrist told the police that certain details of the assassination attempt—particularly Czolgosz's use of a white handkerchief—suggested a feminine touch.

The district attorney in Buffalo immediately initiated extradition proceedings, but the Chicago police stalled. Under intensive questioning, Goldman, whose family lived in Rochester, admitted to having visited Buffalo and the Pan American Exposition twice during the summer, but denied ever having met with Czolgosz. She was, she said, opposed to the use of violence and even volunteered to nurse the wounded president back to health (She had studied midwifery and nursing in Vienna). Although they were convinced of her innocence and refused to comply with the district attorney's extradition request, the Chicago police detained Goldman for fifteen days, long after Mrs. Petrowski, Nowak, Pasczek, and the others had been released for lack of evidence. When finally allowed to go, she was denied the right to lecture in Chicago and her magazine *Free Society* was denied the use of the mails. Her family suffered, too. Her father was excommunicated from his synagogue in Rochester and his furniture store was boycotted for months.

Meanwhile, the optimistic medical bulletins about President McKinley continued, and as they did the shock of the assassination attempt wore off and the city began to enjoy the attention it was getting as the accidental capital of the nation. The comings and goings of the nation's political celebrities who had convened in Buffalo following the shooting were discussed in minute detail. Vice-President Roosevelt was dining at the home of Ansley Wilcox, about a half a mile south of the Milburn house on Delaware Avenue. Attorney General Philander Knox and Secretary of State John Hay were staying at the Buffalo Club, the prestigious men's club founded by Millard Fillmore, and Secretary of War, Elihu Root was addressing the Buffalo branch of the Grand Army of the Republic on how the government was coping with the emergency.

Continued progress in the president's condition was reported. On September 9, the press was told that "if the President continued to improve we may safely say that he is convalescent." Senator Mark Hanna, a close personal friend of the president, said that "any day now he will be smoking cigars again." On September 10, following a conference with the president's physicians, Roosevelt summarized the situation. "I am absolutely certain," he said, "that everything is coming out all right." Two days later, in spite of reports that McKinley had spent a restless night, Roosevelt, brimming with confidence, announced that he was leaving for his home in Oyster Bay, Long Island. That same day, William Buchanan, the director of the Pan American, announced plans for "President McKinley Day" at the exposition, a special day to celebrate the recovery of the president. The celebration was necessary, Buchanan said, to dissipate any possible odium that might have been cast upon the exposition, "to raise it from a landmark of doom to a symbol of happiness."

At 6:00 P.M. on September 12, McKinley's physicians reported that the president was "not so good." McKinley had just taken his first oral meal since the shooting (he had previously been fed intravenously) and was not able to digest his food. However, he was given calomel and oils and by midnight had moved his bowels, and the trouble was reported to have passed. However, by 2:00 A.M. on September 13, it became clear that the president was suffering something far more serious than indigestion. His pulse, which had been abnormally high ever since his operation, quickened still more and his heart weakened considerably. Dr. Park arrived at the Milburn house at 3:00 A.M. and at 6:00 A.M. Senator Hanna, who had just gone back home to Cleveland, once again set out for Buffalo on a special train. Stunned by the sudden activity at the Milburn house, crowds began to congregate along Delaware Avenue in front of the house. Fearing the worst, Chief of Police William Bull activated three hundred police reserves, as a threatening crowd of close to two thousand people marched down Main Street in the direction of police headquarters, where Czolgosz was being held.

However, nothing that had happened—not the summoning of McKinley's friends, family, and cabinet members; not the desperate effort to contact the vice-president, who was mountain climbing in the Adirondacks; not even the increasingly pessimistic report of the medical team—could convince some people that the end was near. Congressman Alexander of Buffalo told a crowd of still gullible reporters that "It is not true that the physicians are without hope or that those gathered in the house are despondent. Everybody about the house is hopeful. The two men who know him best, Cortelyou and Hanna, are cheerful and confident."

But Alexander could not wish away the truth, and McKinley weakened steadily throughout the day. At 4:00 P.M. on September 13, his pulsations increased again and at 5:00 P.M. he suffered a heart attack. Aware himself of the futility of further efforts to save him, at 8:00 that night McKinley asked to have a last word with his wife. At 9:00 he lost consciousness, and at 2:10 the following morning he died. That morning the Pan American Exposition was closed for the first time and Theodore Roosevelt became the twenty-sixth president of the United States at a hasty swearing-in ceremony in Wilcox's house on Delaware Avenue.

What was most upsetting about the president's death was that it was so totally unexpected. Coming after days of nothing but optimistic reports about the his health, the news of McKinley's death confused and angered the public more than it saddened them. For it soon became apparent that from the beginning there had been little grounds for optimism, and while nobody was accusing the medical team of lying outright, there was no question but that the public had not been told the truth. In the hours following McKinley's death, some of the truth began to emerge. Dr. Park said that once he bullet had penetrated the abdomen, the president became a doomed man. He was, he said, amazed that McKinley had lived as long as he had. Another said that there was no case record of a person the age of the president surviving a serious stomach wound. Citing the recent case of the Princeton quarterback who had been shot in the stomach by a Negro spectator, another doctor said that regardless of age or physicial condition, a stomach wound was fatal more often than not.

Most schocking of all was the fact that ever since Tuesday, September 12, the president's physicians had been aware that gangrene had set in, and while they believed that they had removed the poisoned areas, there was every reason to suspect that the disease would spread. Cortelyou had urged that the doctors again search for the bullet and even had Thomas Alva Edison send his most sophisticated x-ray machine to Buffalo for that purpose. But, satisfied that the bullet could cause no harm, the doctors refused to reexamine the wound. The autopsy confirmed Cortelyou's suspicions and what the doctors must certainly have guessed on Tuesday: that the spread of gangrene along the path of the unfound bullet into the stomach, kidney, and pancreas had killed the president.

Two days after McKinley died, a grand jury, meeting for the first and only time, indicted Leon Czolgosz for murder. His trial proceeded expeditiously. It opened on September 23, and by the end of the first day, a jury had been selected. On the second day both prosecution and defense attorneys completed their cases, the judge charged the jury, and in less than half an hour a guilty verdict was returned. The case was closed twenty-four hours after it opened.

Czolgosz's trial was a sham from the very beginning—a kangaroo court. Most disturbing was the conduct of the defense. Czolgosz was defended by two court-appointed lawyers, Loran L. Lewis and Robert G. Titus, aging former judges who had not argued in court in years. On the opening day of the trial, Lewis requested of the judge that the court be in session only four hours a day: "Neither Judge Titus nor myself is a young man and neither of us is in perfect health. We have had little opportunity to consult with each other. We believe that the trial will not be injured by having short hours. We have concluded to ask Your Honor during this trial to sit from ten to noon in the morning and from 2 to 4 in the afternoon. I mention four P.M. because my home—my summer home—is in Lewiston and the train leaves at 4:40."

Their laziness extended into the courtroom, too. Titus and Lewis made only the most perfunctory challenges of the jury. The result was a shocking miscarriage of justice. All of the jurors admitted that they were inclined to find Czolgosz guilty and that they would consider acquittal only if presented with reasonable evidence to the contrary. Czolgosz's lawyers made no effort to communicate with their client, called no defense witnesses, and constantly apologized to the court for their client's "dastardly act," while through it all tearfully referring to the greatness of "our martyred President." But their most serious shortcoming was their failure to raise the issue of Czolgosz' sanity. While they did instruct the jury that Czolgosz must be considered sane before he could be found guilty, the lawyers made no attempt to offer any testimony or evidence dealing with their client's mental state at the time of the shooting.

There was nothing to prevent Titus and Lewis from raising the question. Indeed, the presiding judge had already done it. In his charge to the jury, Judge Truman White had said that if Czolgosz was "laboring under a defect of reasoning" at the time of the crime, he should be acquitted. The Erie County Bar Association, too, had been concerned about the sanity question; in order to be absolutely certain that they would be able to bring Czolgosz to trial, the bar had at least gone through the motions of deliberating the defendant's mental condition. On September 8, two days after the shooting, Czolgosz was examined by a team of local psychiatrists and an expert in forensics from Bellevue Hospital in New York. Their decision was that Czolgosz was indeed sane and thereby fit to stand trial. They enumerated their findings. He was, they said, not a victim of paranoia because "he has not systematized delusions reverting to self and because he is in exceptionally good condition and has an unbroken record of good health." Nor was he a "degenerate." The phrenologically oriented physicians stated that their examinations revealed none of the stigmata of degeneration: "His skull is symmetrical; his ears do not protrude, nor are they of abnormal size and his palate is not arched." Dr. MacDonald from Bellevue concurred in a separate report. "Czolgosz is," he said, "the product of anarchism. He is sane and responsible."

Yet these hastily written reports could not still the many questions that began to surface in the months after Czolgosz's execution. A growing number of psychiatrists were becoming convinced that a closer scrutiny of Czolgosz's personal history—the death of his mother when he was twelve, his father's subsequent remarriage to a woman he detested, his constant brooding and dreamy behavior—combined with an attempt on the part of his attorneys to introduce testimony dealing with the question of his sanity, would have raised serious doubts in the minds of the jury about the defendant's sanity at the time of the crime. But these were questions that the legal fraternity in a city desperately bent on revenge were unwilling to ask. Had McKinley lived, Czolgosz would have received a maximum of only ten years' imprisonment. But the president had died, and the law entitled the people to their revenge.

Ever since he had shot the president on September 9, Czolgosz had been hounded by crowds. First the bloodthirsty mob at the Temple of Music. Then the mass of people who had waited, not certain for what, for days outside his jail in police headquarters in Buffalo. And now, on September 26, as he arrived at Auburn Prison, a mob of over three thousand converged at the Auburn railroad station in an effort to get their hands on the man who had assassinated the president. Under heavy guard, Czolgosz walked amidst the screaming, clawing crowd, making his way slowly into the prison. Once inside, he succumbed to the stress, becoming hysterical, falling to the ground, and shrieking and writhing on the floor. He was immediately strapped into a chair and given a hypodermic. Again, as at the trial, little time was wasted in dispatching the jury's verdict of execution by electricity. Afraid that Czolgosz, like Gaetano Bresci before him, would kill himself in his cell, the execution was scheduled a month hence. On October 29, 1901, Leon Czolgosz died in the electric chair. Local newspapers reported the details:

Warden Mead of Auburn raised his hands and at 7:12:30, electrician Davis turned the switch that threw twenty-seven hundred volts of electricity into the living body. The rush of immense current threw the body so hard against the straps that they creaked perceptibly. The hands clinched up suddenly and the whole attitude was one of extreme tenseness. For forty-five seconds the full current was kept on and then slowly the electrician threw the switch back reducing the current volt by volt until it was cut off entirely. Then, just as it had reached that point, he threw the lever back again for a brief two or three seconds. The body, which had collapsed as the current reduced, stiffened up again against the straps. When it was turned off again, Dr. McCauley stepped up to the chair and put his hand over the heart. He said he felt no pulsation but suggested that the current be turned on for a few seconds again. At 7:18 the current was turned off for a third and final time. At 7:20 the warden announced: 'Gentlemen, the prisoner is dead.

Cornell University had already been promised Czolgosz' skull and Syracuse University his body.

Meanwhile William Buchanan was trying to rescue the Pan American Exposition from the wreck of McKinley's assassination. All during the summer, every nation in the hemisphere and every state in the Union had been honored with a "Day" at the exposition. But after the shooting of the president, the country had lost its taste for the exposition and as the weather turned colder, the tourists stopped coming. Director Buchanan, declaring that November 1 was "Buffalo Day," had no choice but to turn to the city in a last desperate effort to at least making closing day a success. However, it didn't work. Mayor Diehl would not even consider proclaiming another civic holiday, and all but a few businessmen ignored the request of the exposition's board of directors to grant half-day holidays to their employees. Even President Ely of the International Street Railroad Company, a director of the exposition, refused to lower streetcar fares for the day.

Buffalo Day began in failure and ended in mayhem. That night the exposition was completely wrecked. People could not believe what had happened. The newspapers were aghast:

"People went mad. They were seized with the desire to destroy. Depradation and destruction were carried on in the boldest manner all along the Midway. Electric light bulbs were jerked from their posts and thousands of them were smashed on the ground. Some of the Midway restaurants were crushed into fragments under the pressure of the mob as if they were so much pasteboard. Windows were shattered and doors were kicked down. Policemen were pushed aside as if they were stuffed ornaments. The National Glass Exhibit was completely destroyed. Pabst's Cafe was demolished and Cleopatra's needle was torn to the ground."

Frank C. Bostock, "The Animal King," reported trouble, too. Earlier in the summer, Regal, one of his largest African lions, had died of heat prostration. Now, on the last day of the exposition, Jumbo the elephant, his star attraction, became unmanageable. For several days Jumbo had refused to eat. Then, on the morning of Buffalo Day, he attacked Bostock. That afternoon he knocked his keeper unconscious. Bostock decided to destroy his prized animal. He told the press that he was going to hold a public execution at the stadium on the exposition grounds. Tickets, at fifty cents a person, would be available at the gate. He said: "It is likely that Jumbo will be hanged, or choked to death with chains, in which case other elephants will be used."

There was immediate opposition. Mayor Diehl, John Milburn, and William Buchanan issued a joint statement condemning Bostock's plan. The method of execution, they said, was simply not in accord with the ideals of the Pan American and therefore must not be permitted to occur on the fairground. They had, however, no objection to electrocution.

On Saturday afternoon, November 3, over seven thousand people filled the Pan American stadium to witness the electrocution of Jumbo. The mammoth elephant was chained to two large wooden blocks in the center of the stadium. Long electric wires connected him to a transformer several hundred yards away. Bostock stood in front of him and made a short speech. He told the crowd about Jumbo's military career. He recalled the long voyage from the kingdoms of Africa to the Niagara Frontier and how hard it had been for Jumbo to adjust to life along the Midway. These events, Bostock said, had completely altered Jumbo's sanity. He had become a killer and death by electrocution was the only solution. With no further delay, Bostock gave a signal and Lewis Mills, the electrician, pulled a lever and eleven thousand volts of electricity were shot into the elephant.

Yet nothing happened. The electricity didn't work and Jumbo was still alive. The crowd, almost spontaneously, started to laugh and Bostock, himself incredulous, promised over the din of the laughter that he would refund the tickets. Only later did he realize that Jumbo's hide had the effect of rubber and was impossible to penetrate. Jumbo's execution was stayed.

A week later John Milburn announced that the exposition had lost over $6 million and that the Company would have to default on over $3.5 million in bonds. Milburn told the board of directors that he was going to Washington, where he would meet with New York's congressional delegation in an effort to convince Congress to pass a Pan American relief bill. He hoped, also to meet with President Roosevelt, who was reportedly sympathetic.

Yet Milburn's spirit was unbroken. He denied that the money lost on the exposition was "a foolish expenditure," as some had charged. The Pan American was, he said, a "masterpiece," and the city its "chosen showcase." Milburn asked the board to think of the millions of dollars that had poured into the city and to believe that the exposition had made Buffalo known all over the world, a city destined to rank with New York and Chicago.

Yet somehow Milburn wasn't convincing. His words didn't ring true. Nothing had turned out as Milburn had hoped it would. The exposition for which he had worked so devotedly had ended in a nightmare of violence and destruction. Once again Milburn looked ahead and, not liking what he saw, left. He was going to New York, where he had accepted a partnership in a law firm.

Jim Lee, who owned and operated a Chinese restaurant on the East Side, left Buffalo earlier, immediately after the exposition closed. Buffalo, he said, had been good to him. He was proud that his restaurant was one of the only establishments on the East Side that was frequented by the finest Delaware Avenue families. But he could no longer tolerate the rumors circulating about him. Lee was accused in the press of being the leader of a smuggling ring. From Vancouver to Buffalo, via Winnipeg, Toronto, and a midnight passage across the Niagara River, Lee, it was charged, was smuggling hundreds of Chinese into the country. Lee vehemently denied the allegations, maintaining that since his arrival in Buffalo in 1891 he had made his money honestly, and that he had never done anything illegal in his life. But now, he said, he was forced to leave and on November 2, 1901, Jim Lee left Buffalo for his brother's farm south of Canton in China.

In early December, 1901, it was reported that the exposition buildings had been sold to the Harris Wrecking Company of Chicago. A local committee was formed to buy and preserve the Electric Tower as a lasting monument to the exposition, but failed to raise the necessary funds. On January 20, 1902, the statue of the Goddess of Light was sold to the Humphrey Popcorn Company of Cleveland and the tower was finally torn down. That same day eighteen canal boats were withdrawn from services on the Erie Canal. They had been sold to the Philippines Islands where, the newspapers felt, greater opportunities for profit existed.

The Pan American Exposition and the assassination of William McKinley are best understood as a metaphor for the rise and decline of Buffalo, New York. And while it may be obvious what caused the failure of the Exposition, the causes of the cataclysm in the contemporary city are less well understood. In order to come to terms with the historical forces that led first to the rise and then to the decline of Buffalo it is necessary to go back to the beginning.

CHAPTER 2

Ups and Downs During the Early Years of the Nineteenth Century

Eight months after it was incorporated in April 1813, the village of Buffalo was burned and completely destroyed by two hundred British soldiers. Crossing the Niagara River several miles north of Buffalo, the British made their way systematically down the banks of the river routing and burning whatever settlements they found on the way. As news of the British invasion spread, the five-hundred-odd people who lived in the village of Buffalo left.

It is surprising that there was such little resistance. Buffalo was no mere frontier camp, a collapsible outpost in the wilderness, but rather a substantial community. It had newspapers, taverns, a hotel, a jail, two physicians, and two druggists, as well as a relatively thriving mercantile trade. The village was also, considering its newness (people had only been living there since the early years of the century), highly organized. There was a medical society and a Mechanics Society and the Ecclesiastical Society of Buffalo. It was, then, a village of considerable legitimacy.

The villagers too were substantial, serious, and hard-working people, not the fly-by-night transients who well might abandon rather than defend an assaulted community. While there were certainly many who did pass through Buffalo, temporary travelers who stayed on for a while before moving someplace else, there was by 1813 a group of cohesive families whose ties to the community were considerable. Most of them were young and most had come with their families. And, perhaps most important for most of these people, the decision to move to Buffalo was difficult, serious, and highly conscious. The trip alone was such that only the most committed and purposeful people let alone whole families, would even bother to make it. People arriving from the East made the journey partially on foot, partially on wagons, and partially on inland waterways. When William Hodge, for example, came to Buffalo in 1805 with his wife and two children, he went first by wagon from eastern New York to Utica. There he joined twenty other people, also families, and rode a flatboat up the Mohawk River, through Oneida Lake, and onto the Oswego River. This they rode, with many interruptions for portages around the rapids, until they arrived at Lake Ontario. Transferring here to a lake boat, the trip to the lower part of the Niagara River at Lewiston was relatively easy until they came to the entrance of the river and the looming presence of Niagara Falls. At the falls the Hodge's boat was taken out of the water and carried by oxteams around the falls. Then, by rowing, poling, and towing, the Hodge party made it through the Niagara River to Buffalo Creek and the village of Buffalo.

Another family, that of Samuel Fletcher Pratt, had three generations living in Buffalo by 1825. A veteran of the American Revolution, Captain Pratt made the overland trip to Buffalo with eight children in 1805. One year later, apparently pleased with his new home, he returned to Vermont to bring his aging parents to Buffalo.

While the journey, then, required devotion, commitment, and desire, village life required extraordinary adaptability, ingenuity, and hard work. For many of the settlers, it was impossible to do in Buffalo what they had done earlier in other communities. Ebenezer Johnson had been trained as a physician in New England. When he came to Buffalo with his wife and child in 1810, the existing village physician refused to allow Johnson to practice. The established pharmacist, meanwhile, denied him the right to open a pharmacy. Johnson, however, did not leave town, as well he might have, but chose to stay in what must have appeared to him to be, despite its frontierlike appearance, a rather closed community. Johnson survived by abandoning his chosen profession and entering instead the real estate business.

Juba Storrs came to Buffalo from Connecticut in 1808 eager to practice law. When opportunities proved limited in his chosen profession, he too began to buy and sell land. Granted that the lure of real estate development was very strong on the urban frontier, its popularity was due also to the fact that it was often difficult and sometimes impossible to do the work in the village for which one was prepared and trained.

In most cases, it seems, these kinds of work changes were profitable. William Hodge had been a farmer in eastern New York. But, given the difficulty of getting produce to market in the isolated village of Buffalo, Hodge, awed by the seemingly inexhaustible quantity of trees in the area, took up carpentry. In 1813 alone he made over three hundred coffins for the American and British soldiers killed in action along the Niagara Frontier.

And yet despite their tenacity and their will to build a community in the wilderness, the village's settlers chose not to defend the fruits of their energies and, when the British came, they simply left.

Not only the citizenry had deserted Buffalo. The United States Army too (in this case the New York State Militia) had left their posts at the first indication of a British assault on the village in late December 1813. At least half of the fighting force abandoned Buffalo before the British even arrived, while the rest deserted shortly after the first exchange of fire. Several efforts to rally the militia men failed, and despite some chronicles that hint otherwise, there is no record of any serious fighting effort to defend Buffalo.

It was, perhaps, in an effort to purge themselves of feelings of guilt over their passivity in the face of attack that the citizens of Buffalo in June 1814, after having returned to their torched community, staged the execution of five solders for desertion. The details of this execution, like so many in Buffalo's history, were carefully recorded:

> The unfortunate victims of martial law are made to kneel upon the ground their eyes bandaged and each with his coffin in front and an open grave behind him. Twenty paces in front of them a platoon of men were drawn up as executioners. The entire army was then formed on three sides of a hollow square to witness the execution. The artillery stood by their guns with lighted matches, to suppress any possible opposing demonstration. . . . When the firing squad had poured the contents of their muskets upon the victims, four of the five men fell beside their coffins, while one, a young man of twenty-one, sprang to his feet, wrenched the cords from his arms and then tore the bandage from his eyes.

Four apparently, were a sufficient offering, and this lone survivor was strangely spared.

By the spring and summer of 1814 many of the former residents had begun to drift back to Buffalo. This time, however, the army was there and, while their protection may no longer have been necessary since the scene of the fighting had shifted away from the village, their presence stimulated the revival of the town. The soldiers had to be housed, clothed, and fed for as long as the war continued. It was no wonder then that, like General Jackson at New Orleans, the people of Buffalo chose not to hear about the signing in December 1814 of the peace treaty with Britain. Indeed, it was not until late January 1815 that, with mixed feelings, the villagers of Buffalo greeted the peace and the news that the several hundred soldiers stationed there would soon be leaving. Their ambivalence is understandable, for despite the buoyant return after the burning of the village, signs of revival in the years following the end of the war were few and far between. The village did acquire a government structure; in addition, a bank was formed, self-help societies and organizations became active, and local citizens vociferously supported those advocates in the state legislature of the long-discussed proposal to build a canal from the Hudson River at Albany to the Great Lakes at Buffalo. But, as one contemporary diarist put it, in writing about a scene of Buffalo in 1817, "insolvency ensued more distressing, if possible, than even after the destruction of the village."

What was most distressing to the inhabitants of Buffalo was the extent to which they were so utterly dependent on national political decisions and economic events over which they had no control. When the army was disbanded and the troops were sent home, the villagers had hoped that the federal government would compensate them—at least in part—for the damages they had suffered during the war. Despite the intense efforts of more influential local citizens, however, this never happened, and the community suffered desperately from a lack of cash. Creditors even advertised that they would cancel debts in exchange for produce. The Holland Land Company took wheat, and a printer took pine. And while local citizens were able to organize a bank in 1816, it was quickly wiped out when Congress a year later required the resumption of specie payments.

While the community had grown some since the end of the war (there were approximately two thousand people in 1820, compared with fifteen hundred people ten years earlier), Buffalo suffered because of its isolation. Contact with the outside remained extremely complex and difficult. At late as 1820 there was but twice-weekly mail service. With few settlers in the West and no direct connection with the East, trade was minimal. Only the Erie Canal, debated for years and finally a legislative reality in 1817, could save the village. The citizens knew this, and they waited.

While construction of the canal proceeded throughout the late teens and early twenties, it was not yet clear whether the western terminus of the canal would be located in Buffalo or in Black Rock, a town of similar size several miles down the Niagara River. While the water was calmer and less rapid in Buffalo, the village lacked a harbor.

The entrance to Buffalo Creek was simply too shallow to permit the passage of any boat of significant size. It was clear that unless the creek was dredged and a harbor constructed, Buffalo would be bypassed as the canal's terminal point. Realizing the calamitous impact this possibility would have, the villagers themselves, in an incredible and inspirational burst of energy and creativity, undertook to dredge their own harbor and build a pier.

The effort was organized by one Samuel Wilkeson, a successful merchant who had made a small fortune in lumber, real estate, and general merchandise. Now, with the help of a handful of other established frontier entrepreneurs, he raised the money, invented the machinery (Wilkeson developed a pile-driving system by converting a cast-iron mortar remaindered from the War of 1812 into a hammer strong enough to drive wooden piles into the Niagara River), and organized the work force in order to insure Buffalo's selection as the western terminus.

As a result of his efforts Wilkeson, like Denver's Lattimore and Chicago's Ogden, became a hero to late nineteenth and early twentieth century chroniclers of local history, writers whose works abound with idealized and mythic descriptions of Wilkeson organizing work crews, overcoming hazardous weather conditions, negotiating with recalcitrant legislators, raising money, and all the time placing the good of the community over and above his own self-interest. Albert Bigelow, writing in 1893, referred to the "labors of Judge Wilkeson [why were so many urban pioneers judges?] . . . with head and hands—nay, with his whole body and all his remarkable powers and how he would be waist deep in the water directing and urging on the work." Working against insurmountable odds, H. W. Hill wrote in 1921, "with the help of a kindly Providence [Wilkeson] having abandoned his own private business, called his men out to work—without suitable tools, without boats, teams or scows. Neither the plan of the work nor its precise location was settled. But the work was commenced." Two years later, in 1821, the creek had in fact been dredged; the pier, eighty-four feet long and eighteen feet wide, whose function was to prevent the accumulation of sands in the mouth of the creek, was built; and Buffalo had been selected as the western terminus of the Erie Canal.

The rivalry with Black Rock had been intense and formidable, inspiring an incredible outpouring of individual and community effort that became legendary to later generations of Buffalonians. Indeed, if there is one thing that virtually every contemporary resident of the city of Buffalo knows about the city's history, it is that at some

25

time—exactly when not everybody is certain—Buffalo and Black Rock were bitter rivals, each desperately eager to be selected as the site of the western terminus of the Erie Canal.

If the accounts of the later-day chroniclers are correct, it is understandable that this achievement, which occurred so early in the history of the city, captured the attention and the imagination of later generations. For the rivalry with Black Rock not only produced heroic feats of individual skill and initiative (traits so highly admired in Victorian America), but also, it seems, fostered a broadly based community effort that marshalled the energies of a settlement whose heterogeneity had already begun to create far more conflict than consensus. The parade that marched in October 1825 to celebrate the opening of what was called "The Grand Canal" indicated a diverse yet, on this occasion at least, united community:

> At its head rode the Grand Marshal and his aides. Next in line was the Buffalo Village Band, supported by Captain Rathbun's rifle company. Then followed in the order named: canal diggers with shovels, ax men with axes, stone cutters, masons, ships carpenters, sailors, captains of vessels with their officers, blacksmiths, carpenters, joiners, wheelwrights, cabinetmakers, chairmakers, shoemakers, tailors, silversmiths, gunsmiths, coppersmiths, bakers, brewers, painters, citizens, military officers in uniform, professional men, civil officers, strangers of distinction, orators, clergy and DeWitt Clinton, the governor of New York.

The opening of the canal, while cheered by many, had an adverse effect on some people too. William Hodge owned a tavern and inn on the main east-west road into and out of Buffalo, about three miles east of the heart of the village. Since the early years of the century Hodge's tavern had been the resting place for the large five-, six-, and seven-horse wagons with their six-inch-wide wheels that were used to transport goods between Albany and Buffalo. Hodge knew that the opening of the canal doomed his business. Another event of that year, however, gave Hodge more business than he knew what to do with, for only three months earlier, over twenty-five thousand people, according to contemporary accounts, came from miles around to witness a "hanging bee": the execution of the Thayer Brothers— Nelson, Isaac and Israel—for the hacking murder of John Love:

> It was a most impressive scene. When each brother had been placed by the sheriff so as to stand under the beam and on the fatal drop (which was made to swing back) and directly under the hook to which the rope was attached, their white caps were drawn down

over their faces. Then the awful silence was broken by the terrible wailing of the three brothers, which grew more loud and intense each moment until the sharp sword of the sheriff severed the rope that held the scaffold. The noise did not cease or lessen even then until their heels had left the platform and they had dropped to the length of their ropes. The screams of the Thayer Brothers were echoed a thousand fold by a simultaneous and involuntary exclamation from the thousands of spectators who till then had stood as if almost breathless and silently gazing on the awful scene.

The Seneca Indians also had little to gain from the Erie Canal. Although their home, the Buffalo Creek Indian Reservation, was located just a few blocks from the village harbor, none of the two thousand Senecas was present at the opening ceremonies in October 1825. Confined to the ever-shrinking reservation that had been their home since the late 1790s, and surrounded by a rapidly expanding white population, the Senecas lived on the outskirts of Buffalo in a state of fear and poverty.

The Senecas had been on the defensive since the Revolution when, as allies of the British, they were slaughtered and banished from their ancestral home in the Genesee Valley by the brutality of General Sullivan's scorched-earth tactics. Seeking refuge from the Revolutionary War armies, the Senecas moved westward to the safety of the British forts along the Niagara River. By the conclusion of the war, approximately two thousand Senecas had migrated westward to Fort Niagara on Lake Ontario, and then southward through what would become the city of Buffalo, to their final resting place along the banks of Buffalo Creek. It was not until 1794, however, that this was to become a reservation and, like so many developments in Indian history, this one occurred without the participation of the Senecas, as a result of land-grabbing white settlers.

In 1791 Robert Morris, fresh from his widely heralded triumphs as the finance commissioner of the revolutionary government, bought four million acres of land lying between the Genesee and Niagara Rivers in Western New York from the state of Massachusetts. Immediately thereafter, he sold the land to a private Dutch syndicate known as the Holland Land Company. Because this was a foreign company not permitted to own land in the state, a dummy holding corporation was created until 1798, when the state of New York changed the law to accommodate the Dutch land speculators. But because there were extensive Indian claims on the land, the Holland Land Company refused to turn over a large percentage of the $4 million purchase price until Morris cancelled Indian claims on the land. Despite Morris's eagerness to resolve this issue (Morris was facing critical financial difficulties as a result of land deals in the new District of Columbia and indeed later was confined to debtors' prison in Philadelphia between 1798 and 1801), the Senecas, under the leadership of their *sachem* Red Jacket, were in no rush (the Senecas were led by a number of civilian leaders called sachems and military leaders called chiefs). Finally, in 1797 Thomas Morris, representing his father, succeeded in convening a council at Geneseo, New York in an effort to convince the Senecas to sell him their land. (Remember that the deal with the Holland Company was contingent upon the Seneca sale to Morris. Had the Senecas known about Morris' desperate financial circumstances, they may well have held out for a better arrangement.) At any rate, Red Jacket led the resistance to the treaty, and after fourteen days of fruitless discussions, the council broke down and Red Jacket, in the richly metaphoric language of the Seneca, "covered up the council fire." Morris was desperate.

Realizing the seriousness of his father's precarious financial situation, Thomas Morris, with the aid of several Seneca chiefs opposed to Red Jacket's tactics, tried a new strategy. Morris was told by one of the disgruntled chiefs that while the sachems had the power as civil magistrates to negotiate treaties, in matters referring to the sale of land, Seneca women and warriors could impose themselves over and above the sachems. Thus informed, Morris began caucusing with the Seneca women, bribing them with promises of beads, silver brooches, and clothes if and when the treaty was concluded. The chiefs, already angered by sachem rule, did not need to be bribed and within a few days the council reopened. In the interim Red Jacket had withdrawn and Cornplanter, the principal war chief opened the proceedings. The bargain was struck, Indian titles on the Holland purchase were extinguished and the Senecas were left with $10,000 and three reservations on the Niagara Frontier. A local chronicler wrote in disbelief in 1923:

> It seems incredible that Morris should have been able to get such relinquishment of valuable land at less than a third of a cent an ▸acre, especially in view of the fact that the completion of the transaction meant that the Indians could no longer live by the chase, having no hunting grounds and must thereafter be dependent upon the white man's benevolence.

While clearly difficult to comprehend, the reasons for this pathetic giveaway should be understandable. Not only did Morris effectively exploit divisiveness within the tribe, but also it is clear that the Seneca's had little understanding of the value of money. Indeed, their experience with treaties in general was very limited. With the exception of a treaty in 1784, the Senecas had never made a land agreement. But most compelling of all was the clear sense of the futility of resistance. Despite this, Red Jacket had opposed the treaty, as he continued to oppose all future agreements with the growing number of white settlers who made their way onto the Niagara Frontier following the conclusion of the Holland purchase. The reservation that the Senecas were confined to at the beginning of the nineteenth century was large (approximately 130 square miles) but, despite their receipt of annual annuities from the federal government, poor. Writing to his superiors in the War Department in 1817, Buffalo Indian Agent Erastus Granger reported:

> The situation of the Indians is truly deplorable. They have exerted themselves for the year past in trying to raise crops but have failed in their expectations. Their prospects have failed. Their hunting grounds are gone. They have availed themselves of their money arising from their public funds but they fall short. They are in fact in a state of starvation.

As wards of the Federal government, unable to hunt, unable to grow crops, and confined to the reservation by fear and prejudice, they spent their pitiable federal funds on liquor.

Meanwhile, the Senecas had become the target of missionary activity. While Quaker missionaries had been only intermittent on the Reservation in the mid-1790's, the Baptist mission established in 1800 lasted with but one interruption until 1836. Its presence on the reservation provoked bitter division within the Seneca community. From the very beginning the tribe was split between Christian and pagan factions. opposed equally as much to Christianity as he was to questionable land deals with the whites, Red Jacket, in his mid-fifties during the War of 1812, was the leader of the pagan faction throughout the first three decades of the century. In countless speeches throughout this period, the Seneca sachem railed against the "Black Coats" who, he said, were simply advance agents for the land speculators. He despised Christianity and any attempt to convert his people. By the end of the teens he had, in the words of a late nineteenth century biographer, "become utterly averse to any further intercourse or association with the whites, having arrived at the conclusion that the only means of preserving his race . . . was by creating a wall of separation, strong and high between them."

Red Jacket opposed not only Christianity but also the establishment and extension onto the reservation of white-run schools and of the laws of the white man. In 1821 a Seneca woman was found guilty of sorcery and, in conformity with Seneca tradition, was sentenced to death. When the chosen executioner hesitated in his duty, a young Seneca named Tommy Jemmy seized a knife and killed the sorcerer. Jemmy was seized by white authorities, indicted, and tried for murder. Jemmy, with Red Jacket as his counsel, argued that the Senecas constituted a separate community and therefore were subject to their own laws. In a witty, sarcastic speech, Red Jacket pleaded the cause of Tommy Jemmy:

> Do you denounce us as fools and bigots because we still believe that which you yourselves believed two centuries ago? Your black coats thundered this doctrine from the pulpit, your judges denounced it from the bench, and sanctioned it with the formalities of law; and you would not punish our unfortunate brother for adhering to the faith of his fathers and of yours? Go to Salem! Look at the records of your own government and you will find that hundreds have been executed for the very crime which has called forth the sentence of condemnation against this woman and drawn upon her the arm of vengeance. What have our brothers done more than the rules of your people have done?

Although Jemmy was vindicated by a higher court, Red Jacket's vehement opposition to the white man's ways did not end. Indeed, his feelings had grown so strong that in 1820 or 1821 he petitioned Governor Clinton for the removal of white missionaries and teachers from the Buffalo Creek reservation:

> The Governor must not think hard of me for speaking thus of the preachers. I have observed their progress and when I look back to see what has taken place of old, I perceive that whenever they came among the Indians, they were the forerunners of their dispersion; that they always excited enmities and quarrels among them; that they introduced the white people on their lands, by whom they are robbed and plundered of their property; and that the Indians were sure to dwindle and decrease and be driven back, in proportion to the number of preachers that came among them. Each nation has its own customs and its own religion. The Indians have theirs— given to them by the Great Spirit—under which they were happy. It was not intended that they should embrace the religion of the whites and be destroyed by the attempt to make them think differently on that subject from their fathers.

Governor Clinton, whose pet project, the Erie Canal, did more to increase the size of the white population on the Niagara Frontier than any other development, was sympathetic. At his urging the state legislature passed a law which forced the removal of "all persons other than Indians" from the Seneca lands. The Seneca mission closed and the missionaries and teachers retired to Buffalo.

This was only a temporary victory, however, for the pressure of the land dealers and the expanding white population in Buffalo was too much for the Seneca reservation to resist. Ever since the end of the War of 1812 a land company called the Ogden Company had had its eyes on the Buffalo Creek reservation. In fact, as recently as 1819 Ogden land agents had come close to negotiating a deal with the Senecas that would have exchanged all of their lands in New York State for some cash and a new home in Green Bay in the Wisconsin Territory. This treaty, negotiated by Christian factions among the Senecas who were disposed to accommodating the land developers, was vetoed by the last-minute intervention of Red Jacket. Lest Red Jacket assume far too heroic proportions, it is best if the records speak for him. Indian Agent Granger, representing the government at the council, wrote:

> At the meeting Red Jacket, on behalf of the Senecas, rejected the proposition to remove or contract the limits or dispose of any part of their lands. The rejection was so unqualified and so preemptory as to forbid all reasonable expectation that any good purpose would be effected by continuing the council.

Although defeated in 1819, the Ogden Company persisted. During the early 1820s they continued their overtures to the more pliable elements among the Senecas and by 1826 felt confident enough to call another council in an effort to purchase for once and for always the lands on the Buffalo Creek reservation. This time, notwithstanding the continuing efforts of Red Jacket, Ogden was successful and the Senecas agreed to sell eighty-one thousand acres of land including all of the Tonawanda, Allegheny and Buffalo Creek reservations. In exchange they received fifty-three cents per acre and a promise from the federal government that land in the Green Bay area of Wisconsin would be theirs in perpetuity.

Unable to convince his own people, Red Jacket tried to persuade President John Quincy Adams to delay the treaty. Although Adams had originally approved it, Red Jacket's request forced him to seek further explanations. With the deal now held up, the Ogden Company, frustrated twice by the same Red Jacket, began to organize the Christian faction among the Senecas in an effort to depose their aging sachem. Accusing him of defaming the president of the United States (why such a charge would carry so much weight among the Senecas is an interesting question), of disturbing and dividing the Seneca councils, and of opposing education, the Christians among the Seneca were able to strip Red Jacket once again of his power.

Red Jacket was soon vindicated, however. Several months later, in the spring of 1828, President Adams, stating that the deal with the Ogden Company was fraudulent and did not represent Seneca opinion, negated it. Now Red Jacket was reinstated.

Although pleased with the victory in this last battle, Red Jacket was a tired and deeply disappointed man. For years he had fought against the white man and argued among his own people for the right of the Seneca to their own land and their own way of life. On both fronts he had been badly defeated. What hurt him most, however, was the defection of his own family members. In 1821 Red Jacket's oldest son, to the sachem's great dismay, was married in the first Christian wedding ceremony ever held on the reservation. Three years later, Red Jacket's wife of over thirty years converted. His pride was stronger than his pain, and Jacket immediately stopped living with her.

Red Jacket, who died in 1832, did not live to see the unhappy resolution of the Ogden land deal. In 1838, for the third time in twenty years, the company again cast their eyes on Seneca land and consummated the same deal that President Adams had cancelled eleven years earlier. This time the president, Martin Van Buren, approved it and when ratified by the Senate, the deal became law. Despite much protest from the Senecas and an elaborate campaign organized by the Philadelphia Friends, the deal, amidst well-publicized and substantiated charges of bribery and double-dealing, went unchallenged. Times had changed. After eight years of merciless Indian removal under Andrew Jackson and under the pressure of a rapidly growing population in the city of Buffalo, there was little sympathy for the few thousand Senecas still living along the Niagara Frontier. And while advocates of the Senecas were able to negotiate a compromise which left the Indians some of their land on the Allegheny and Tonawanda reservations, by 1850 Red Jacket's Buffalo Creek reservation was abandoned and cleared for development. The Indian presence, so strong throughout the first twenty-five years of the century, had been completely eliminated. It is little wonder that it was following his visit to Buffalo in 1831 that Alexis de Tocqueville wrote:

In the heart of this society, so policed, so prudish, so sententiously moral and virtuous, one encounters a complete insensibility, a sort of cold and implacable egoism when it's a question of the American Indians. The inhabitants of the United States do not hunt the Indians with the hue and cry as did the Spaniards in Mexico. But it's the same pitiless instinct which animates the European race here as everywhere else.

However gone, the Senecas were not forgotten. Particularly Red Jacket. Indeed, by the turn of the century Red Jacket had become Buffalo's favorite Indian. Streets, awards, memorials, and contests were named after him and his portrait, which depicted him wearing a gold medal given to him by George Washington, was hung prominently in the halls of the Buffalo Historical Society. As part of this community-wide effort to expiate the guilt of the past, the directors of the historical society in 1884 announced that they would exhume the body of Red Jacket, buried in the old Indian cemetery on the other side of the Buffalo Creek, and move it to Forest Lawn Cemetery in the city where it would be placed, along with the bodies of other Seneca chiefs, under a massive stone monument topped with a larger-than-life statue of Red Jacket himself. Incredibly, in the dedicatory speeches commemorating the event no attempt was made to hide the fact that all of this was being done in direct contradiction to Red Jacket's specific wishes that no white man dig his grave and that no white man bury him. At the reburial of Red Jacket, one of the directors of the historical society said:

The God put it into the hearts of these good men of the Buffalo Historical Society to take charge of his remains, give him a decent burial in a white man's graveyard and over his grave erect a monument which should tell his story to all future generations.

Five years later another director of the society, in writing about the Senecas as he remembered them in Buffalo, wrote:

Why attempt to civilize the Indians, or ameliorate their supposed conditon? Only teach them with the strong hand of power to fear our superior race and let them alone in their rapid decay, until like the bison of the western prairies they are obliterated from the earth, as one of the ancient, traditional races of men.

The completion of the Erie Canal was seen by contemporaries as a new beginning after a series of false starts. Now a census was taken, the first engraving of the city was made, and a special brochure

33

called *Buffalo in 1825* was printed to commemorate the great event. From the description of S. Ball, the author of the pamphlet, it was clear that the completion of the canal had finally ended Buffalo's isolation. The village had become a growing and increasingly diversified community. Among its population of 2,412 were a wide variety of skilled laborers, or mechanics, as they were then called. There were two bookbinders, four goldsmiths, three tin- and copper-smiths, seven blacksmiths, two cabinetmakers, three wheelwrights and coach builders, two chairmakers, one cooper, three hatters, two tanners and curriers, five boot- and shoe-makers, two painters, four tailors, fifty-one carpenters and joiners, nineteen masons and stonecutters, three butchers, and one brush maker.

By listing the number of business establishments, Ball also indicated that there was a substantial property-owning class. Within it were three print shops (which gave employment to ten people), twenty-six dry goods stores, thirty-six groceries, three hat stores, seven clothing stores, four pharmacies, one hardware store, six shoe stores, three jewelry stores, two bookstores and binderies, eleven "houses of public entertainment," one rope walk, three canneries, one brewery, one livery stable, and eight storehouses. Ball says nothing about the substantial number of laborers, the people who did odd jobs in the above-mentioned establishments and who worked in the rapidly growing construction industry.

The waterfront was the fastest growing section of the town. All of the streets in the village sloped down to the waterfront, where by 1830 several dozen stores, warehouses, offices, and sail makers crowded each other for space at this critical junction of the canal and Lake Erie. It was here that most of the unskilled day laborers sought work in the late 1820s and early 1830s.

But there was far more concern in Buffalo with the state of the economy in general than with any one particular group of workers, for the opening of the canal, while ending the village's isolation, created a new set of problems.

One of these was that with the opening of the canal the local market was suddenly flooded with goods manufactured in New York City. Afraid that the dominance of "the Emporium," as it was called in the local press, could easily undermine the shaky hopes of the village, a handful of local businessmen tried desperately to channel some of Buffalo's commercial vigor into manufacturing. The Buffalo *Emporium*, a paper that represented the business elements in the town, warned that "if the citizens of this Village intend to thrive and prosper they must encourage manufactures." Mr. Ball sounded a similar note. Pointing out the absence of a grist mill in the village, Ball asserted that "there can be no hazard in saying that surplus capital could not be better invested than in a steam grist mill." Going beyond the call for a grist mill, Ball said that "the establishment of any other factory would be of advantage to the community."

The message seemed to have been effectively delivered, for in 1827 a corporation was formed whose purpose was to create waterpower for manufacturing in the village of Buffalo. From an elevation of about two and one-half miles above the Buffalo Creek, the site of the terminus of the Erie Canal, another canal—or rather a large conduit—was built which funneled water over a falls at a place named the Hydraulics, thereby creating enough power for small-scale manufacturing. It worked, and one year later a sawmill, a grist mill, a woolen factory, a hat body factory, a brewery, and an iron foundry were all located in this area. The foundry was capable of quite sophisticated iron work. In a newspaper advertisement, the owners proudly claimed that

the iron works are now in full operation and are erected on an extensive scale, being particularly calculated for casting and finishing all kinds of works for steam engines, flouring mills, saw mills and machinery of every description. We have on hand an extensive assortment of patterns combining many important improvements in the application of cast iron. Millwrights and others about to erect flour mills or machinery of any kind, will find every article in their line of the finest quality.

Consciously then, with planning and with purpose, the citizens of Buffalo were altering the economy of their village.

The size and character of the village population changed too. Virtually overnight Buffalo had become an open city, with a growing number of transients, several hundred foreigners and close to a hundred free blacks. The changes were abrupt and dramatic, the reactions often wrought with fear, anxiety, and paranoia, and many sensed that things were not right. The community seemed easily threatened by the unknown. These feelings were manifest throughout Western New York during the late 1820s and early 1830s and moral, religious, and political revivals were the order of the day. Whether the threat was real or imagined, in 1828 the Buffalo *Emporium*, whose name suggests a concern for markets not morality, demanded public action to deal with what they felt was a considerable increase in "vice and immorality." The newspaper called for a "union and concentration of effort among the friends of morality and religion." Indeed, the

Emporium went so far as to call for the formation of a new political party that would make the crusade against vice its solitary platform. Responding to these and other pressures, the legislature in Erie County in 1828 empanelled a special grand jury to investigate organized vice. Several months later the panel in fact reported widespread "dissipation, habitual drunkeness, gambling and houses of ill fame where so many of the rising generation are stripped of their property and character." Apparently accepting these conditions as a fact of life on the urban frontier, the panel suggested no remedial actions. Philosophically, they simply concluded that these vices "are the sorest evils which burden our community."

Another fact of life in the village was that despite the existence of a deep, however vague, religious faith (bordering at times on moral righteousness), the people of Buffalo were simply not churchgoers. Indeed, with well over three thousand people in the community in 1828, there were only five churches. And yet belief in God was very strong: particularly when it had to do with the weather. With almost paganistic faith, the villagers of Buffalo thanked God for a benign winter, an early spring, ice-free lakes, calm waters, and gentle winds. A rainstorm in February 1828 brought this response from a local newspaper: "The ways of Providence are inscrutable. That being who suffers not a sparrow to fall to the ground without his notice, tempers the blast, thunders at his pleasure and scatters the lightening around. We behold the glory and adore."

But beyond a deeply held faith in the divine order of the universe, religion itself seemed to hold little interest for the people of the village. When in 1831 Charles G. Finney, the phenomenally successful revivalist who had single-handedly created the religious fervor west of the Genesee River (particularly in Rochester) that has led that area to be called the "Burned-Over District," came to Buffalo the reactions were mixed. On the one hand, his fervent, crusading, emotional brand of evangelical Protestantism provoked much criticism. One newspaper indignantly wrote that "such scenes of turmoil, confusion and tumult have no place in an assemblage of religious people." Indeed, the Buffalo *Workingman's Bulletin*, among whose political beliefs must certainly have been the right to public assembly, recommended, in its capacity as "a friend of good order," that Finney be prosecuted "under the act to prevent tumultuous gatherings." Nevertheless, Finney had a dramatic impact on Buffalo. For two weeks he packed the First Presbyterian Church, a bastion of Protestant respectability, and was personally responsible for the 119 people who received an "original confession of faith" (versus the 15 people who had done so the year before and the 10 the year after). Finney's influence was greatest among the most prestigious and powerful men in the village: among those who were born again during the Finney revival were Reuben Heacock, a banker; Samuel Wilkeson, of Erie Canal fame; and John Chase Lord, a prominent lawyer who, following Finney's visit, gave up the law and entered the Presbyterian Theological Seminary in Auburn, New York.

Mordecai Noah, a Tammany politician from New York City, launched a different kind of religious crusade in 1825, the year the canal opened. Dismissed from a diplomatic post in Tunis for what he was convinced was anti-Semitism, Noah became a Jewish nationalist, obsessed with the notion of creating a Jewish homeland on Grand Island, a large island in the Niagara River several miles north of Buffalo. Bought by New York State from the Indians in 1813, by 1819 Grand Island was overrun with squatters and poachers who were stripping the island of its enormous supply of virgin wood. Under pressure from local real estate developers, the New York State Militia forcibly removed these outlaws and in 1820 Grand Island, ideally located midway between the shores of Canada and of the United States, was subdivided into building lots. In 1825 Noah, with the help of a fellow Tammanyite, bought 2,555 acres and began to lay his plans for the formation there of a Jewish state.

While unable to convince the state legislature to support his plan, Noah had better luck in Buffalo where, despite his Jewishness, he impressed his Gentile acquaintances. One of them wrote, "Although a native of the U.S., the lineaments of his race are impressed upon his features. He was a Jew, thorough and accomplished." Noah's word alone, it seemed, was enough to generate considerable excitement in the long-isolated village. Hearing that dedication ceremonies for Noah's would-be state were to be held on the island, hundreds of locals, fully expecting a modern-day Moses with hordes of Jews in tow, lined the shores of the Niagara River in September 1825 in hopes of getting a glimpse of the group's entry into the Promised Land. One commentator noted that the local speculators brought with them a "supply of cakes and ale, pastries and pies and cold meats to give the Jews a good stomach for their undertaking."

Bad weather, however, forced a cancellation of the ceremonies, which were moved instead to St. Paul's Episcopal Church in Buffalo. While Noah himself was not troubled by the anomaly of the situation, others were. The "strange and remarkable ceremony" opened with a "Masonic and military" procession, followed by a mixture of Christian and Jewish rites and closed with a speech by Noah in which

he outlined his plan for the establishment of a Jewish state in Grand
Island on the Niagara River. Deeming it "expedient to reorganize
the nation of Israel under the direction of the Judges," Noah annointed
himself a judge of Israel. He proposed, he said, to levy a tax of three
shekels on each Jew throughout the world for the purpose of financing
the Jewish state. Then, in addition to urging all Jews of the world
to join him on Grand Island, he also invited the Karaites, Samaritans,
Falashas, and even the American Indians, whom he was convinced
were the ten lost tribes of Israel.

Upon completion of this ceremony, a large celebration was held
at a local tavern where a "grand salute of twenty-four guns climaxed
the affair while a band played a medley of patriotic airs."

Noah received far more support in Buffalo than he did in any
Jewish community, Ridiculed, denounced, but mostly ignored by Jews
in New York City and in Europe, Noah soon forgot about his Jewish
state on Grand Island. Before the winter of 1825 he had already
moved back to New York.

Crusades in Buffalo in the 1820s were political as well as religious.
Anti-Masonry was particularly potent. Fomented by the murder in
Batavia (a small canal town midway between Buffalo and Rochester)
in 1826 of one William Morgan who, it was alleged, was murdered
by Masonic vigilantes following his threat to reveal the ancient secrets
of the Masonic Order, anti-Masonry quickly became a political force
that for several years terrorized Western New York. An anti-Masonic
smear campaign spread throughout Western New York (in the same
"Burned-Over District" that was being scorched by the Finney revival).
Fear and panic spread as serious discussions about boycotting Masons
and even forcing them out of the village were aired in the local press.
A local physician and long-time Mason was beaten up in front of his
home, charged with practicing "odd and deviant medical experiments."
A local judge, a Mason, was ridiculed as charges in the press were
made about his "secret and arcane" judicial proceedings. Teachers,
lawyers, and ministers were drummed out of their positions and of
the more than 125 Masons in the village in 1828 many left and
many more renounced their allegiance to the secret society, while still
others stayed, hoping to weather the storm. The anti-Masonic purge,
the Finney religious revival, and the nascent workingman's movement
all added up to the same conclusion. Frustration, discontent, disillusion,
and disappointment were rife along the Niagara Frontier.

In addition to the religious rivalism and the anti-Masonry, Buffalo's
establishment was rocked by the creation in the village in the late
1820s of a workingman's movement. Everybody knew and even

expected that the poorest people in the village, the primarily Irish laborers who worked the canal, for example, were unhappy and discontented. Barely an eyebrow was raised when a riot among the Irish occurred along the canal, "a usual occurrence in those days." It was more confusing and upsetting however to find dissatisfaction and even anger among the established workingmen of Buffalo. Yet by the late 1820s the Workingman's party and its newspaper, the *Workingman's Bulletin*, were among the most active local branches of what was becoming a political phenomenon throughout the urban Northeast.

While the party loosely defined a workingman as any person who "worked" (thus, store owners and even small-scale manufacturers like Abraham Daggart, a munitions manufacturer, were members), the party was characterized by a strong bias against large landowners, real estate speculators, and people who, however hard to define, were not members of "the laboring classes." (It is interesting how important land—both urban, in the case of real estate developers, and rural, in the case of large landholders—figured as a grievance of reformers during this time period.) Thus, because they were often unclear as to who their constituency really was, the party resorted to vague and inflammatory rhetoric: "The aristocracy has swelled in the wildest excess of luxury while the workingman has strained every nerve to his utmost to support this extravagance." What particular extravagance the *Workingman's Bulletin* was referring to was never made clear. The point, however, is. Some people, the party believed, were getting something that they were not entitled to, and the party didn't like it.

The perception of the workingman as different, and of the community as divided among class lines (however circumspectly defined), was reinforced by the village establishment which, upon learning of the increased political activity of the local Workingman's party, chided them as "untried strangers" who should best "stay out" of village politics. The anger that this suggestion provoked became still more bitter when the party was refused permission to hold a celebration at the Presbyterian Meeting House. (The Baptists gave them space at their church.) Although no official explanation was recorded, the Workingman's press drew their own inferences. Responding to what they sensed as increasing hostility, the *Workingman's Bulletin* wrote: "That we appear like 'strangers' to those who have been in the habit of looking upon us only as tools, is no wonder; and that we are untried in some respects is correct, for it is too true that we have had little to do with political affairs." Not content with accepting

39

this situation for long, the newspaper continued: "The conditions of our country strongly suggest this. Had the laboring classes of people been less supine and more attentive to their duty, we apprehend that the institutions of our villages would have presented a more flattering appearance than they do now."

What most concerned the editors of the *Bulletin* was not that the poor be treated specially but rather that they be treated the same as everybody else. Thus, they demanded a militia system that affected everybody equally, the abolishment of imprisonment for debt, and for the indigent a program of public works rather than placement in the county poorhouse. They also were strong advocates of a public school system.

Even on the urban frontier, education had always been tainted with class prejudice. Writing about schools in the village of Buffalo in 1825, S. Ball noted that there was one "Young Ladies Academy," the "Young Gentlemen's Academy," and four "common schools." Unlike the host of fly-by-night private schools that proliferated in the village—for example, Dr. Catlin's Academy or Palmer's Academy— these two schools were not private business ventures but rather an effort by like-minded people to create special schools for the children of their class. There were even special uniforms which distinguished private students from students in the common schools. Samuel Welch, a chronicler writing in the 1890s, recalling these schools of the 1830s wrote that the students "paraded in blue jackets and trousers, the jackets or roundabouts covered profusely with bright silvered globular buttons." As for the common schools, Oliver Steele, who became the city's first superintendent of schools in 1837, wrote that "few people took any interest in [them] and few children, except those of the poorer classes attended them."

Commenting further on status and social class, Welch remembered that there was "no exclusiveness nor holding aloof from each other on the supposition of better family antecedents, connection, breeding, education or the magnitude of wealth." Similarly, he wrote that there was at that time little residential separation by social class: "The hightoned 'upper ten,' the well-to-do and the well-known people, were scattered broadcast over the city and its suburbs. There was no so-called 'West End' or assumed aristocratic quarter." In fact, he wrote that on only one street—Eagle Street— did "all nice people" live.

To a certain extent, Welch was accurate. There were no special residential sections for the wealthy, and rich and poor did tend to live in very close proximity to each other. After all, the community was very small and there was only a limited number of places where anybody could live. Thus, for example, at the Hydraulics, the site of the city's first manufacturing district and home to Buffalo's first generation of Irish immigrants, lived the banker Reuben B. Heacock, "in a fine large stone mansion."

The affluent had, however, begun to stake out land for themselves in the areas surrounding the city from which, by virtue of private transportation, they were within commuting distance of the center of the city. Overlooking the Niagara River north of the city, and on farms to the south, east, and north, a growing number of wealthy Buffalonians had begun to erect large, private homes on abundant, landscaped lots. The best known belonged to Ebenezer Johnson, the physician turned entrepreneur and politician. In the early 1830s Johnson purchased close to one hundred acres north of the settled area of the city on Delaware Avenue and, with great ostentation, erected a magnificent home that suggests that life styles on the urban frontier were far from egalitarian. The home fronted on Delaware Avenue, which according to Welch was "a broad country road, green with native trees." The house was near the front, alone in its glory, with extensive grounds, mostly surrounded by high picket fences. A part of the grounds were given up to a special park, through the fences of which could plainly be seen the glancing antlers of a herd of deer. In the rear was a beautiful grove of handsome trees, and beneath these a pond fed by springs and stocked with fish. Swans floated on the pond, and there was a boat house. The walks, nooks, and dells were cultivated in rustic semi-wild conditon. The picketed front fences were relieved by high arched gateposts, with the most southerly gate leading down a long lane or driveway to the rear grounds, and the others around by a drive to the front of the mansion, where on the broad steps several carriages could discharge their guests at the same time. Welch notes that during the construction of this impressive private residence, the townsfolk would make weekly pilgrimages to the site, "inspecting its progress." Perhaps, like the Erie Canal several years earlier, Dr. Johnson's mansion had become a new and different symbol of the community's progress that too was in some way shared by everybody.

Welch's recollections of a peaceable, egalitarian community thus are often contradicted by his own evidence. While insisting that there were no distinctions based on class, he does report that "there were a few families who, by right of education, accomplishment, condition and influence were entitled to a certain precedence which was quietly acknowledged by those of lesser mental and financial acquirements." Whether these deferential feelings were limited to Welch or applied to the rest of the community is difficult to say, but it is clear that Welch had in mind a significant number of people, far more than the "few families" mentioned above, who were deserving of such respect. They included, according to his own memoirs, the families of twelve judges, three generals, one commodore, five colonels, five doctors, twelve lawyers, and about fifty of a group who Welch calls "Merchants, Bankers and others."

Unaware of its implications, Welch pointed out yet another indication which perhaps better than others symbolized the growing gap between the social classes in the small city. Until the middle of the 1830s, Welch offers, the steamboats that plied the lakes linking Buffalo with Erie, Cleveland, Detroit, and other lake ports, were all of one class. Everybody slept in the same dormitory and ate in a common dining room aboard ship. With the introduction of upper cabins in the mid-1830s, however, this suddenly changed. For the first time, the more affluent could reserve private staterooms in the upper cabins, leaving the dormitories for the others.

It was perhaps an awareness of the increased gap between the affluent and the rest of the community that led to a growing militance among the "laboring classes," as they were known, during the 1830s. What little evidence there is on the subject suggests that there was considerable trade union activity in the middle of the 1830s. The decision by the chief justice of the Supreme Court of the State of New York in an 1835 case involving striking shoemakers in Geneva, New York triggered concern and action among Buffalo workingmen. Incensed at Justice Savage's ruling in the case of *People v. Fischer* that "the right does not exist either to enhance the price of an article or the wages of a mechanic by any forced or artificial means," a local supporter of trade union activity suggested that the "mechanics of Buffalo" should, despite the Judge's ruling, follow the example of their brethren in England and form trade unions. Arguing that there the "trades unions will soon compel the aristocracy to disgorge some of their ill-gotten wealth," the anonymous writer of this letter to the editor of the eminently Whiggish journal, the *Commercial Advertiser*, urged the formation of a mechanics' society in Buffalo. Such a group, it was said, could fight not only for the advancement of learning among this class but also for a two-dollar minimum daily wage.

The formation of the Mechanics Association in 1836 represented a major change in local thinking about ways to remedy the problems facing the laboring class. For while the *Workingman's Bulletin* was willing to take positions on such issues as the militia, imprisonment for debt, and public schools, its point of view was so steeped in laissez-faire liberalism that it could not support united action on behalf of the workingman. It was, for example, bitterly critical of any tendencies that smacked of monopoly. The newspaper was as adamant in its criticism of the practice of licensing physicians as it was critical of the charter to the Bank of the United States. "We would," the *Bulletin* wrote, "allow any man to practice physics and surgery who pleases and let each depend on the skill he may be able to manifest." Similarly, the newspaper maintained, a man's business was his own affair and if he chose not to hire a person because that person was Catholic, there was nothing anybody could or should do about it. To make matters worse, their market-oriented economic thinking was steeped in Christian moralism. While, for example, the *Bulletin* did call for county-funded public works projects for the chronically unemployed in the village, they insisted that only those who pledged abstinence and sobriety were to be eligible. It is not likely that the publishers of this newspaper would have taken kindly to the union activities that began to spread in the 1830s. No longer suited to the changing mood of Buffalo's working people, the *Bulletin* discontinued publication in 1832.

Despite its hostility to the burgeoning trade union movement, the *Commerical Advertiser* was the most widely read local paper and the one used by workers' groups to advertise their activities. Thus, what often appeared in the paper was a somewhat clipped version of the announcement that a particular trade's group wished to make. The *Commercial Advertiser* did not try to hide its censorship, and indeed boasted of it as a form of public service. Thus, following the notice in their pages in November 1835 announcing the formation of the Stone Cutters and Stone Mason's Protective Society, the editor wrote that since so much of that particular announcement was "objectionable," they had printed only what was "important to know." Similarly, when the paper received a letter from "A Worky" which announced the formation of the Operative Builder's Society, they chose not to print it because "some of the assertions, if really true, show that evils of an oppressive character exist in this city."

While the newspaper did not deny the seriousness of the workers' problem, it did try to talk them out of their grievances. Speaking for respectable opinion in the city, the editors of the *Commercial Advertiser* appealed to the workers' sense of citizenship and concern for the community. Suggesting that "it would be far more creditable to the city to abate these evils, if possible [were they suggesting that it might not be possible to abate them?] by amicable arrangement than to increase these alleged [were they suggesting that they did not exist?] difficulties by trumpeting them to the world," the press urged conciliation and moderation. Perhaps somewhat surprised at the increasingly hostile turn that labor relations had taken, the *Commercial Advertiser* urged that "in a community such as ours" disputes between workers and employers "always regulate themselves." The traditional, paternalistic, and more benign approach to dealing with one's employees was apparently breaking down, and despite the newspaper's warning that "a liberal and equitable regard should be taken by employers to the price of labor and that it should be enhanced under fair competition in a corresponding degree," the workers—at least the skilled workers— were ready to take matters into their own hands. In 1836, less than a year after Justice Savage's ruling in *People v. Fischer*, the Mechanics Association of Buffalo was organized.

Despite the efforts of the local press (dominated by conservative Whig opinion until the advent of several Democratic newspapers in the late 1830s and early 1840s) to characterize the Mechanics Association as a potentially threatening class-conscious group of laborers, the Mechanics (consisting of a cabinetmaker, a shipbuilder, several shoemakers, masons, joiners, tailors, a boiler maker, a locksmith, a machinist, a millwright, a painter, a coppersmith, a moulder, a founder, a gunsmith, and a carriage maker) were far more concerned with the education of their members and with the dignity of their work, leaving the more controversial issues of wages and hours to the various trade unions. Thus, for example, they were strenuously opposed to the use of prison labor in the making of such items as furniture, tools, hardware, and carpeting not because prison labor cheapened the costs of these items, but because it compromised the dignity of their labor. Arguing that disrespect for labor was one of the principal causes of crime, and pointing to an increasing trend in the country to equate labor with criminality, they wrote:

> The custom of our courts in passing sentence on convicts and calling labor punishment has a direct tendency to make labor disreputable. The punishment part should be something beside labor and the labor part a privilege which they are permitted to enjoy, particularly if they are taught mechanic arts, which, like the other sciences, are, or ought to be, attractive and a pleasure.

Anticipating the impact that increased technological changes would have on the skilled trades within the next few decades, the Mechanics insisted that the use of labor as a punishment was "an act of injustice toward us which we consider not second to our pecuniary interests."

The Mechanics were also concerned with the education of the city's skilled workers. Again citing the example of the English laboring classes, the Mechanics allocated funds for the establishment of a library and a lecture program. Meanwhile, they worked to improve public education in Buffalo. Unable to afford the private academies and unhappy with the state-funded "district" or "common" schools, the Mechanics made a bold suggestion that they establish their own schools throughout the city "for the purpose of collecting and teaching the children of all classes of mechanics." Perhaps convinced that the authorities would never establish decent public education, and perhaps feeling the need to band together to teach their children a separate set of values, the Mechanics argued for but never established a school system of their own.

Thus, despite the seemingly nonthreatening position of the association, this proposal for a separate school system, run by and for mechanics and their children, suggests that the Mechanics Association saw their city, notwithstanding the benign, nostalgic recollections of Samuel Welch, as one split clearly along class lines.

There was discontent in the surrounding rural community too, as farmers were becoming increasingly unhappy with what they sensed were the autocratic ways of the Holland Land Company. The Holland Land Company was a large multi-million-dollar Dutch real estate consortium headquartered in Amsterdam. Its board of directors—Stadnitski, Vollenhoven, Schimmelpenninckm, Van Staphorts, and Willink—represented six Dutch banking houses which had pooled their money in 1792 to form the company. It function was to buy large undeveloped tracts of land west of the Genesee River, survey it, and then sell it to settlers. As the company's resident agent in Western New York between 1800 and 1820, surveyor Joseph Ellicott was the single most powerful person in the area for the first two decades of the century. For twenty years Ellicott presided unchallenged over the three million acres of land that constituted the Holland Land Company purchase. He did what he liked on such matters as land sales, the terms of those sales, tenant relations, politics, and finances, and reported only by mail to the Dutch company's representative Paul Busti, an Italian who lived in Philadelphia. It was Ellicott who decided whether the company's land would be sold in large or small lots (by opting for the latter, over the objections of the company's board, who wanted to unload the land quickly, Ellicott guaranteed that the purchase would be sold to families and not to large manorial landlords like those who had developed the Hudson River Valley); where and when roads and bridges would be build; and when and

45

how banks would be established. He also supervised the company's myriad political negotiations with the state legislature. It was Ellicott, for example, who negotiated a deal with the legislature whereby the company was exempted from all school or road taxes (they did pay extensive real estate taxes, however). Similarly, it was Ellicott who determined the location of new counties, county seats, towns, and villages. And it was Ellicott who, as company surveyor, planned the village of Buffalo.

Drawing on his experience as an assistant to Pierre L'Enfant, the French landscape architect who had laid out Washington, D.C., Ellicott conceived in 1804 a grandiose, baroque town plan for Buffalo. Consisting of public squares, radiating boulevards (each named for a director of the Holland Land Company), and a large chunk of land reserved for his own personal use, Ellicott's plan, drawing on the lay-outs of both the Versailles Gardens and Washington, D.C., seemed hardly appropriate for this tiny frontier village.

The farmers on the Holland purchase, however, were far more concerned with the debts they owed the company than with Ellicott's town plan. Their problem was that most of them had bought their land at inflated prices and high rates of interest and now, in the middle and late 1820s, were not able to make good on their loans. Many had fallen far behind on their payments. Trouble began when the company began, in 1827, to press for payment, foreclosing and ejecting those unable to pay. Under this threat, a large group of Erie County farmers, allegedly led by Whig politicians in Buffalo eager to make political hay by provoking the ever unpopular land company, convened the Agrarian Convention of the Holland Land Purchase in Buffalo in 1827. The convention demanded that the company help the farmers by absorbing some of the back debt themselves. While some compromise was effected, the situation worsened in 1833 when New York State began to demand that now the company make good on back taxes owed the state. Left with what they felt was no choice, the company squeezed their debtors still harder.

Many, rather than pay, rioted. Such was true of the farmers in Mayville, a farm community south of Buffalo. Here farmers, urged on by the *Commercial Advertiser*, which insisted that unlike rioting city laborers the farmers be taken seriously, sacked the land company's offices:

> The people engaged in this transaction are not the floating, profligate population of our large cities who, driven by their needs and ungovernable instincts, are liable to be urged into excesses of the

46

wildest kind; but they are those to whom we have proudly pointed as the peculiar boast of our land, in whose intelligence, sobriety and obedience to the laws we behold a sure guarantee of the perpetuation of our liberties.

Unlike his urban counterpart, it seemed, a rioting farmer could do no wrong.

Joseph Ellicott, meanwhile, had long left the company, eased out by the American director in Philadelphia, who was unhappy with Ellicott's autocratic ways and had demanded his resignation in 1820. Ellicott moved to New York City where, according to contemporaries and acquaintances, he became increasingly hostile, moody, and withdrawn. In 1825 he was admitted to Bloomingdale mental asylum. He committed suicide in 1826. In 1843, Ellicott Street in Buffalo was named after him.

Increasingly concerned about the violence and social upheaval within the village and in the surrounding rural areas, certain members of Welch's "leading, older and influential" families petitioned the state legislature in 1832 for permission for the village of Buffalo to become a city. Eager to impose a sense of legal order on a situation that appeared increasingly volatile, a committee, consisting of eighteen men, all of whom appear on Welch's list of judges, generals, lawyers, businessmen, and bankers, met in December 1831 to create a charter for the city of Buffalo. With few disputes or controversies, these men very quickly dispatched of their work. Within two months they had written the document and submitted it to the legislature. In April 1832, a bare four months since the first conclave, Buffalo became a city.

The view of the city of Buffalo that is conveyed in the city charter is of a highly structured, well-organized, and tightly regulated community. Containing the rules and regulations that governed the city, the charter left little to the imagination. Virtually every aspect of daily life in the city was closely supervised by the common council (the mayor was appointed by the council and had powers similar to a village justice of the peace), including the management and control of finances and of all property, real and personal. The council also passed legislation regulating streets, roads, and waterways; punishing "every kind of fraudulent device and practice;" abolishing gambling; punishing the sale of liquor to minors, servants, and Indians; regulating and prohibiting the "exhibition of shows of every kind or the exhibition of any natural or artificial curiosities . . . or theatrical performances;" and suppressing prostitution, "houses of ill-fame and billiard tables."

While sobriety and morality, it was hoped, would govern behavior, the demands of business and commerce would dictate how streets were to be used in the city. The city's "streets, side-walks, lanes and alleys" were off limits not only to carriages, sleds, carts, and sleighs, but to recreation as well. The "rolling of hoops, playing at ball, flying of kites or any other amusement or practise" was strictly prohibited. The streets were intended for business, not play. The council was also greatly concerned with the control and regulation of noxious odors, and had the power to regulate the location of soap factories, tanneries, stables, privies, slaughterhouses, markets, and gunpower storehouses.

The council's greatest concern was with fire hazards, and here their regulations were virtually Talmudic in scope and detail. There were ordinances dealing with the construction and location of stoves, stovepipes and chimneys; the placement of hay and straw; the use of candles; the storing and disposal of combustible materials; the work-places of carpenters and joiners; and the construction of fire escapes. In addition, the council created and administered an elaborate code dealing with the proper methods of fire extinction; the role of fire wardens; the function of fire companies; the work of hook, ladder, and axe men; and the duties and responsibilities of citizens in the event of fire.

The council also passed detailed regulations regarding the manu-facture and sale of bread, and elaborate controls for the sale of meat. Butchers' dress was controlled:

> No butcher or any other person in his employ shall appear at his stall for the purpose of cutting, handling or vending meat unless he shall be neatly and cleanly dressed with a white shirt, and white apron tied before and with oversleeve extending above the elbows.

So too were the details of their trade: "No mutton or lamb shall be brought into the market and sold, unless previous to the sale and delivery that part of the leg directly below the joint of the knee be taken from such mutton." Similarly, butchers were prohibited from bringing into the market any "untried fat, commonly called 'gut-fat.'"

It is perhaps understandable that these well-to-do Protestant des-cendents of the New England village chose to create a city charter that governed so extensively the daily affairs of the people of Buffalo. Suggesting a view of mankind and of human behavior far darker and more pessimistic than that usually associated with Jacksonian America, the city charter of Buffalo created a government whose function was to maintain and provide for public order in a severe and austere manner. That there was in reality far less order than the local founding fathers would have hoped for is perhaps not as significant as the fact that this charter gave these like-minded men of affluence the impression, and permitted them to believe, that city affairs were controlled, predictable, and nonthreatening. The facts of the matter revealed otherwise. For not only were the social relations between the city's economic classes increasingly unpredictable, but even natural events seemed to threaten the stability of the community. In 1832, two months into its incorporation, Buffalo was overrun by cholera.

Contemporary accounts indicate that the cholera plague caught the community completely off-guard.When asked to explain its cause, city spokesmen (among them the physician and first mayor of Buffalo, Dr. Ebenezer Johnson) propounded an elaborate theory that revealed as much about their world view as about their knowledge of epidemiology. It was caused, they said, by Irish immigrants in Quebec who had brought the dread disease with them from the old country. From Quebec, they reasoned the disease was carried down the St. Lawrence into Lake Ontario, thence through the Welland Canal into Lake Erie, and thus to Buffalo.

Whatever its source, the cholera paralyzed the community. A four-man council was given plenary power conferred by the city council to do "whatever it saw fit." (Did the citizens of Buffalo have so little faith in their new government that they abandoned it at the first sign of crisis?) The council's first action was to quarantine the city. All traffic—lake and canal boats, stages and coaches—was stopped immediately. A makeshift hospital was opened, staffed by volunteers, but there was little they could do about the baffling disease. One contemporary observer wrote:

> Buffalo was severely afflicted by this visitation. . . . The treatment of the disease was mostly experimental, its nature not being understood; indeed the epidemic at times seemed to have full sway, without check. . . . A man might be in apparent good health in the morning and in his grave the same night. Often people were taken away for burial in the night of the day of their death . . . The death carts patrolled the streets, and when there was an indication of a death in a house, the driver would shout: 'Bring out your dead.' Bodies were not permitted to remain unburied over an hour or two, if it were possible to obtain carriers, or a sexton to bury them.

The plague spared no one. While "the more destitute, heedless and imprudent [contemporary words for the poor] suffered greatly," the

disease also "burst into the dwellings of the careful and more cir-
cumspect. . . . It was not the poor only who suffered. The upper
and brighter walks of life yielded also." By July 1832 over 120 people
had died.

What seemed to bother the people of Buffalo more than the loss
of life, however, was the realization of their continued vulnerability.
Hardly twenty years after it was burned by the British, Buffalo was
struck again. And again there was little that the citizens could do.
As "the disease darted like a forked lightning at right angles, at
obtuse angles, at oblique angles up one street, down another alley
and into almost every quarter of the little city," the people watched
and prayed. Six months later they were visited by yet another cataclysm:
In November 1832 a fire destroyed sixty buildings in the heart of
the city. The expectations of the city fathers had been seriously
damaged. At the end of the year, the Buffalo Lyceum sponsored a
well-attended debate on "Whether the progress of civilization has
advanced the tide of human happiness." Many people in Buffalo had
their doubts.

Despite the completion of the Erie Canal, and not withstanding
the increase in the city's population from 2,412 in 1825 to 19,715
ten years later, the economic conditions of the city were unstable,
and built to a large degree, it seemed, on dreams and fantasy. Nobody
was more of a fantast and a dreamer than Benjamin Rathbun. Despite
his outgoing even flamboyant, entrepreneurial activities, Rathbun was
a shy, retreating man who had acquired an air of substantial mystery.
Although it was known that his family had first settled in Connecticut
in the 1670s and had made their way to Western New York after
the War of 1812, nobody knew for certain where or when Benjamin
Rathbun was born. Some thought in Connecticut, others in Albany,
still others in Cazenovia. The mystery surroundig his birth (in a
small city like Buffalo everybody knew almost everything about
everybody else) was augmented by the fact that Rathbun was always
dressed in black. He was invariably compared to Napoleon. Welch
recalled: "Rathbun was almost precisely the build and height as
Bonaparte. His square face, firm lower jaw; his appearance and manner,
together with his immobility and his reticence completed the comparison." Like Napoleon, Rathbun, it was said, was never seen to
smile.

He was, however, an extraordinarily deft businessman, and by the
late 1820s owned and operated the Eagle Tavern, the largest and
best-known hotel west of the Genesee River; a line of stagecoaches
linking Buffalo and Albany; and a line of horse-drawn omnibuses

which ran from the waterfront to the edge of the city at Goodrich
Hill. Welch recollects that these last "were handsomely fitted out
and richly upholstered, with seats for fourteen to eighteen passengers;
drawn by four horses, with young men of sixteen to twenty in uniform
for conductors." Each omnibus bore a name: *Experiment, Encouragement, Enterprise, Expectation, Eclipse* and *Pilot*.

But Rathbun's deepest interest was building. Virtually alone he
built the city's first business district along Main Street. By 1835 he
had built a fourteen-story stone warehouse; thirteen two-story frame
buildings; and eighty-nine brick buildings, including fifty-one stores
from three to five stories high, one four-story warehouse, the Eagle
Street Theatre, and thirty-one private homes between two and four
stories high and ranging in cost from $400 to $10,000. Rathbun was
proudest of the American Hotel, a five-story, cut gray-stone building,
topped with a columnar complex. Two of the rear stories equalled
the height of three of the front stories as a result of an elevated first
floor. The hotel contained a large dining room, and a grand ballroom
and concert hall with double staircases and topped with a domed
ceiling "so constructed as to be almost perfect in acoustic qualities."
By the end of 1835, guided by a vision not unlike Hamilton's for
Paterson, New Jersey, Benjamin Rathbun had begun to survey the
entire Niagara Frontier in search of a site for the development of
manufacturing.

To carry out his vast building projects, Rathbun opened a stone
quarry and two brickyards. He built an entire street—Mechanic
Street—near the Erie Canal, where were located Rathbun-owned
machine shops. At the foot of the street he built the largest warehouse
in Buffalo.

His labor force of over two thousand people was intricately organized. Each branch of work was supervised by a separate foreman.
Thus, there were foremen for the carpenters, the joiners, the masons,
the stone masons, the brick masons, the house painters and glazers,
the roofers, and the coppersmiths, and a supervisor of the machine
shop. In addition, he employed two architects, an agent for the purchase
of lumber and for the supervision of the lumberyard, a superintendent
of the canal and river boats that delivered his supplies, a warehouse
clerk, an overseer of the teaming department, an overseer of the
brickyards, and three foremen of the day laborers. In early 1836
Rathbun's daily disbursements were over $10,000 and the value of
his buildings under construction was over $500,000. To help meet
these costs he opened his own bank which, in a day when banks
were spawned almost daily, was considered sufficiently reliable that

the notes it issued, bearing only the dollar amount and the signature of "B. Rathbun," were accepted as currency by all the other banks in the city.

By the middle of 1836, however, Rathbun found himself caught in the midst of a national credit squeeze. As a result of President Jackson's tight money policies, credit throughout the whole country became intensely scarce, and soon Rathbun's creditors began to call in their loans. The effect was immediate and disastrous. Describing the impact, a local historian wrote that "panic pervaded the city and we tumbled from the zenith to the nadir." Unable to continue his building and unable to pay his creditors, Rathbun's operations caved in and with them the business of many people in Western New York. In a desperate effort to stave off the inevitable, Rathbun began to issue forged bank notes. The ruse soon became apparent, and now hounded by both creditors and the law, Rathbun was arrested in August 1836.

Rathbun's collapse was a source of great disappointment: Now he would not be able to build the Buffalo Exchange, a dream that he had nurtured for years. Over the years Rathbun had himself made many sketches, and eventually actually a completed design, for a massive building that would serve as both a personal monument and a focal point of the city's business life. A monumental square-block, four-story brick building, the Exchange was to have a limestone facade lined with ten pilasters and four free-standing columns. Designed to be the primary business building in Buffalo, it was to be topped with a cupola at least as high as the building itself. The Buffalo Exchange would have stood 222 feet tall.

The economic crisis created in the city by Rathbun's collapse was more severe. The city's banks, all wrapped up with Rathbun in one way or another, went under, and the two thousand-odd workers who had been employed on Rathbun's projects were now out of work. Private schools closed as even the privileged suffered. Hotels were empty, the harbor languished, and the city sank deeper and deeper into a depression that was national in scope.

Yet despite Rathbun's forgery, despite the fact that his free-wheeling real estate schemes crumbled, bringing down with them the city's long-hoped-for dreams of prosperity, the people of Buffalo never blamed Rathbun. Treated as a benevolent patron, a hero to all of those people who harbored similar dreams of success, Rathbun remained on bail while the state tried in vain to convict him. His first trial ended in a hung jury, and it was not until the trial was moved to Batavia in September 1838 that he was found guilty and sentenced to five years' hard labor at Auburn. While the model prison at Auburn permitted no contact with the outside, the people of Buffalo thought often about their erstwhile Napoleon. He was a fantast and a dreamer, and the people of Buffalo loved him.

Rathbun's collapse locally, combined with a national depression brought on by a burse speculative bubble and an end to easy credit (President Jackson's reversal on currenty—first by his highly inflationary veto of the Bank of the United States, followed shortly after by an order requiring that all currency by backed by specie—brought havoc to an economy already racked with speculative growing pains), had destroyed Buffalo's economy. Referring to the late 1830s, Samuel Welch recalled that these were "very hard times amongst all classes of people. The auctioneer's hammer was heard from door to door. All building enterprises had ceased; laborers, mechanics and other citizens were idle and daily becoming poorer." Given the atmosphere of gloom and panic, the Patriot War of 1837 was a crisis ready-made for the anxiety-ridden community.

The war started in early 1837 when William Lyon McKenzie, seeking independence for the province of Ontario, launched a rebellion against the Canadian government. While quickly routed by Canadian and British authorities, McKenzie and his handful of troops took refuge on Navy Island, a British possession down the Niagara River from Buffalo, midway between the United States and Canada. McKenzie's middle name, and his rhetoric of freedom and independence, struck a responsive chord along the depression-plagued Niagara Frontier and, sensing sympathy in an area already badly scarred by the British, McKenzie came to Buffalo in search of volunteers for his would-be war of independence. Despite the efforts of the local press to discredit McKenzie and its warnings to the local citizenry to stay out of the affair, McKenzie enjoyed a fair amount of success in Buffalo, and by the summer and fall of 1837 was joined at Navy Island by several hundred volunteers who, according to Samuel Welch's end-of-the-century recollection, consisted of an "unemployed, idle, nonproducing lot of tramps."

Welch's characterization of McKenzie's Buffalo volunteers accurately reflects the division in local opinion regarding the Patriot War. Unlike the unemployed workers and the stragglers who joined McKenzie, the property-owners, newspaper owners, and merchants—Welch's "high-toned upper ten"—were desperately afraid that American involvement in the rebellion could well lead to another war with Great Britain. It was the memory of the burning of Buffalo, still vivid in the minds of the older, more established residents, rather than lack of sympathy for McKenzie's cause, that led them to criticize McKenzie's rebellion. They were, however, quite concerned about the presence, so close to Buffalo, of an army of the unemployed. The *Commercial Advertiser* wrote that "this parading set of ragamuffin volunteers should have an end put to it at once. The exhibition is disgraceful and to allow these fellows to be swaggering through the streets day and night with arms in their hands is annoying to every quiet citizen." Sympathy for McKenzie's rebellion was one thing; it was quite another, however, when demonstrated by an armed group of the unemployed. Increasingly dismayed by the drift of events— merchants and bankers had just received word that Rochester banks had refused to redeem notes drawn on Buffalo banks—respectable people were frightened for the future.

Soon, however, the division within the community was healed, following the British attack on the *Caroline*, a privately owned steamer in the Niagara River. Under the impression that the *Caroline* was bound for Navy Island with volunteers for McKenzie, the British boarded and burned the ship and then ignominiously let it drift down the river, eventually crashing over Niagara Falls. Immediately local opinion jelled. The newspapers, now filled with exaggerated reports about the number of Americans killed in the *Caroline* incident, urged instant and harsh retaliation. When it was found that but one person— a man named Amos Durfee—was in fact killed in the affair, there was an outpouring of anger and grief in Buffalo. Over two thousand demonstrating, sloganizing citizens attended Durfee's funeral, demanding immediate American action against the British. Announcing that now, unlike before the attack on the *Caroline*, anger "pervades all classes in the community," the *Commercial Advertiser* called for the formation of the militia and demanded an apology from the British. The former request was filled immediately. Indeed a new regiment, drawn, Welch tells us, from "the elite and chivalric men of Buffalo" and called the City Guards, was formed.

Despite the "military ardor and excitement" in Buffalo, President Van Buren moved cautiously. Eager to placate irate local opinion, the president dispatched to Buffalo General Winfield Scott, who, although an aging and retired general, was a local hero because of his role in the War of 1812. Unbeknownst to Buffalonians, who believed that Scott's presence was intended to bolster American military strength along the Niagara Frontier, his main duty was to disband McKenzie's army on Navy Island. Meanwhile, McKenzie, who had brought his wife to the American Hotel in Buffalo, was arrested, and amidst a large, spontaneous demonstration, was taken into federal custody.

Although anger, bitterness, and resentment against Great Britain lingered for years (Britain did not officially apologize for the sacking of the *Caroline* until 1842), the jingoism that had pervaded the city in late 1837 and early 1838 quickly vanished. President Van Buren had, it was thought, taken seriously the grievances of the people of Buffalo. After all, he had sent a strong note of protest to the offending British government. He did dispatch troops to Buffalo. And, given the atmosphere of disappointment, failure, and depression that then existed in Buffalo, these events at least gave the people of Buffalo something to be thankful for.

CHAPTER 3

The Impact of Commerce and Manufacturing on Mid-Nineteenth Century Buffalo

From the moment that the Erie Canal was completed in 1825, Buffalo was seen as a way station, a conduit whose primary function was the movement of goods and people from east to west and vice versa. Writing in 1825, before the canal had officially opened, S. Ball, the local chronicler, wrote that "the future prosperity and opulence of this village depends upon the extent and profits of the commerce on the Western Lakes." Thus not a destination in and of itself, Buffalo was conceived as a city in between, a temporary stopping place for people and things presumably on the way to some better place, a cog in a much larger national and even international system of markets. For this reason then, Buffalo, unlike the larger manufacturing centers that developed later in the century—Chicago, St. Louis, and Pittsburgh—did not see itself as competing with other cities. The people of Buffalo knew that the prosperity of their city was closely linked with the fortunes of other cities in that system. In 1836 the editor of the *City Directory* wrote:

> Buffalo has no rival. It can have none. For it is the medium through which all others, both the East and West, must draw their wealth and resources. And so, far from feeling distrust or jealousy at the prosperity of our neighboring cities, we look upon them as auxiliaries to our own. . . . The abundance of all the riches of the hinterland flowing through their thousand channels, pass through our hands on its way to the ocean—while the luxuries of the old world center here, thus rendering the city of Buffalo that which it may ever claim to be—the Great National Exchange.

Buffalo's growth as a major port of transshipment, then, was dependent on a set of other developments over which the city had little control. The fact of the matter is that until the late 1830s and early 1840s the "Bread Basket of America" lay east of the city in the Genesee River Valley in the vicinity of Rochester. As long as the people in New York City ate bread and drank beer from grain grown there, and as long as the citizens of London, England relied on domestically produced grain, there was no movement of agricultural produce through Buffalo.

The completion of the Erie Canal, however, did more to facilitate the development of the American West than any single act since Jefferson's purchase of the Louisiana Territory. It was now just a question of time before the territories and states in the American Midwest—Ohio, Indiana, Illinois, Wisconsin—suddenly now enjoying enormous population gains, would begin to ship agricultural produce eastward. When that happened Buffalo would become the great port of transshipment that its publicists predicted. Meanwhile, as hundreds of thousands of people abandoned the East Coast for the Midwest, they invariably passed through Buffalo.

By the end of the 1830s Ball's prediction had begun to come true. In 1836, the first year that Ohio's grain crop surpassed New York's, 1.2 million bushels of it were unloaded in Buffalo. Four years later 4 million bushels were unloaded in Buffalo's increasingly cramped harbor.

All of it was unloaded by hand. The grain was packed for shipment in barrels and stored in the holds of lake vessels. Upon arriving in Buffalo these barrels were raised from the holds by block and tackle, weighed, and then either swung across the dock to a waiting canal boat or carried into warehouses on the backs of stevedores. If the grain was shipped in bulk it had to be shovelled into barrels and then raised from the ship's hold and poured into the canal boats. If it was to be stored it had to be shovelled into sacks or baskets and carried up long ladders into the warehouse, where the contents were emptied into storage bins. At most, on a good day, when there were no strikes or delays caused by weather or mechanical breakdowns, the stevedores could unload about two thousand bushels, about one boat full of grain. The workers found it even more difficult during peak season. Within one twenty-four hour period in September 1842, for example, forty such boats carrying over one hundred thousand bushels of western wheat arrived in Buffalo harbor. The task was immense.

Joseph Dart, a local merchant and tinkerer, had been thinking about this problem for some time. He knew of course that a steam-powered elevator had been invented and developed by Oliver Evans in England in the 1790s but that it had never been used for the unloading and storage of grain. In 1841 Dart tried it. It was, he said, "a simple apparatus consisting mainly of a series of buckets attached to a leather canvas belt which revolved on pulleys." With capital raised by a small group of local investors, Dart built his own elevator in the fall of 1842. During its first hour of operation it unloaded one thousand bushels of grain. Dart quickly discovered that by putting the buckets closer together along the leather belt he would double its capacity. That first winter Dart's brand new wooden elevator, standing tall and alone in the Buffalo harbor, stored over fifty-five thousand bushels of wheat. All of it had been loaded mechanically.

Dart's elevator quickly became the pride of the community, the object of pilgrimages by fascinated tourists from all over Western New York. One of them described it: "The huge elevator, by the use of steam, runs its trunk into the holds of vessels, swallows up the grain without stopping to take a breath and discharges it in one continuous process through its conductors and spouts it into large storage bins or canal boats without effort except trifling puffs of steam." Writing about his trip to Buffalo, almost thirty years later Anthony Trollope wrote:

> I went down to the granaries and climbed into the elevator and saw the wheat running in rivers from one vessel into another. . . . I saw corn measured by the forty bushel measure with as much ease as we measure an ounce of cheese and with greater rapidity. I ascertained that the work went on weekday and Sunday, night and day; rivers of wheat and maize ever running. I saw the men bathed in corn as they disturbed it on its flow. I saw bins by the score laden with wheat. . . . I breathed the flour, drank the flour and let myself be enveloped in a world of breadstuff. . . . I began to know what it was for a country to overflow with milk and honey, to burst with its own fruits and be smothered with its own riches.

Along with the Erie Canal, Dart's steam-powered grain elevator was critical to the city's commercial development. For there was now no limit to the amount of western grain that could be handled in the city's port. As a result, Buffalo quickly developed intimate and intricate trade relations with other ports on the Great Lakes. What happened in Milwaukee, which shipped most all of its grain directly to Buffalo, or in Chicago, fifty percent of whose total grain production also came to Buffalo, was suddenly critical to the fortunes of the city. Thus, details of weather conditions (heavy winds in Milwaukee or Detroit, ports clogged with ice), marine disasters 209 sailors lost their lives in 1850, as twenty lake vessels sank in the Great Lakes), labor strife, price increases, and political developments, were all monitored extremely closely with the clear understanding that the slightest alteration of either natural or man-made events might upset the extremely delicate trade balance that was the life blood of Buffalo and the other cities along the lakes.

Most of Buffalo's grain, transshipped from lake to canal boats, passed right through the city, bound for Rochester, Syracuse, Albany, and New York City, where it was processed into flour. By the middle of the 1840s, however, international events were such that an ever-increasing amount of the grain transshipped through Buffalo was going to continental Europe and England. In 1846, in a legislated effort to create a manufacturing economy, England abolished the Corn Laws, which ended the system of tariffs that had for so long protected English farmers from foreign competition. Overnight, the vast English and European market opened up, and while Russia continued to be a major supplier, an increasing amount of American wheat now made its way to Europe. Continental wars also disrupted the traditional channels of the European grain trade, to the immeasurable benefit of the American farmer and those cities which, like Buffalo, shipped their cargo. Indeed, during the Crimean War, fought between England and Russia during the middle 1850s, the movement of grain into and out of Buffalo reaches its peak to date.

Despite the tremendous growth in the grain trade and the beginnings of grain-related manufacturing, this was a complex, precarious, and unstable business. Most of Buffalo's grain merchants were commission merchants who bought their product in bulk, sight unseen, from midwestern producers and then sold it either in Buffalo or still further down the line in cities in the East. Even with the constant increase in the size and speed of the lake steamers it still took upwards of two weeks from the time a grain shipment was loaded in the Midwest to when it was unloaded in Buffalo. Price fluctuations were often precipitous, with chances greater than not that the Buffalo dealer would not be able to get his desired price. It was not until the full development of railroads and the telegraph that the local dealer, now much more closely in touch with the shifting trends in the grain market, would be able to make more accurate judgments about price.

The grain business was also highly competitive. Ten years after the creation of Dart's elevator there were more than ten steam-powered elevators in the city. The total number of bushels of grain had increased from 5.5 million to over 22 million per year, and while the demand was great and growing, it still could not keep up with the supply. The result was constant price wars in the Buffalo grain industry, with resulting unstable working conditions and consistently low pay. In the mid-1850s the average mill worker worked six days a week and earned $1.50 per day. While strikes—work stoppages more than strikes—actually were frequent, they rarely resulted in more than layoffs; and while wages for dock workers, mill hands, and others in the grain trade did improve throughout the last half of the nineteenth-century, it was not until the 1890s and the early twentieth-century that any real employment stability was achieved.

Buffalo's merchants were far more successful in bringing stability to their end of the business than were the workers. Given the intricate and delicate nature of the grain trade, merchants were constantly seeking ways to make business more controlled and predictable. One businessman, W. G. Fargo, sought to bring order to his trading business by creating a system of inter-urban partnerships. Fargo's first job was as a runner for Pomeroy and Company, an express company that worked the canal and the overland routes between Buffalo and Albany in the 1840s. A year after Dart's elevator was erected, Fargo, realizing that the future now lay in western and not eastern commerce, left Pomeroy and formed a partnership with Henry Wells, a Cleveland-based express man. Several years later, still relying strictly on lake and overland freight routes, Fargo and Wells extended their territory to include the lake ports of Chicago and Milwaukee, as well as Cincinnati and Galena, Illinois. In 1846 Fargo formed yet another partnership, this time with a Cincinnati express agent named William Livingston. Under the terms of their agreement Fargo moved to Cincinnati, and Livingston settled in Buffalo. Apparently unhappy about travelling at a time when there were few railroads in this part of the country, Livingston and Fargo swapped residences in 1848. Working once again out of Buffalo, with active connections throughout the Greak Lakes and the Mississippi and Missouri rivers, Fargo took his business operations one step further. In 1850, two years before the integration of five small and independent railroad lines into the New York Central Railroad, Fargo merged his companies into the American Express Company. The next year Fargo's Buffalo-based concern had made contact with San Francisco. Buffalo's line of trade had become still longer and thus more complicated, tenuous, and delicate.

Buffalo merchants also worked together in an effort to conquer the inherent instabilities of national lake-borne commerce. When in the 1850s, for example, shallow waters at the St. Clair Flats in Minnesota caused a serious slow-down in lake traffic emanating from there, the recently formed Buffalo Board of Trade raised funds to contribute to the United States Topographical Engineers to help defray the cost of dredging. For years the city's merchants had, through their support of the Whig party, worked to convince federal and state authorities to improve the city's harbor. (It is no accident that before his conversion to Known-Nothingism, Millard Fillmore, the city's leading politician, was a staunch Whig.) And in most cases they were successful. For throughout the middle of the nineteeth-century the federal government funded a wide variety of harbor improvement projects, including the repair and maintenance of the canal's entrance, piers, and breakwalls, and other physical improvements vital to the city's commerce. As a result of federal generosity, harbor space had quadrupled by 1855, and a new ship canal and numerous new ships and basins had been constructed.

From the beginning, the maintenance and improvement of the Erie Canal was supposed to come from canal tolls. But because these were insufficient and because merchants in the towns along the canal route felt the tolls would only benefit the railroads, they were neither adequate nor popular sources of funding for the constantly called for improvement (particularly the widening and deepening) of the canal. Anyway, following the depression of the 1830s, the state had little money for internal improvements. Indeed, throughout most of the 1840s the state carried an annual debt of close to $20 million. Under pressure from merchants and politicians in Buffalo and other canal towns, the legislature did finally (in 1851) come up with an elaborate scheme for the issuance of $9 million of "canal revenue certificates," which permitted the state to issue bonds in anticipation of tolls and other revenues to be collected in the future. The excitement that this generated in Buffalo was short lived, however, for in 1852 the New York State Court of Appeals found the act unconstitutional.

Added to the confused and ambiguous atmosphere surrounding the future of canal improvements were the beginnings of doubts about the future of the canal itself. For gradually throughout the 1850s it was becoming clear that the railroad was successfully challenging the canal as the primary means of transportation for both people and produce.

There was no denying the increasing importance of the railroad to Buffalo. By the end of the 1840s, rails had begun to compete for right-of-way space along the waterfront, in an effort to distract some of the less bulky produce like flour, lumber, and livestock from the canal boats. By 1855, three years after the incorporation of the New York Central Railroad, an annual review of trade in Buffalo reported that:

> Its [the railroad's] facilities for the transportation of freight, always immense, have been lately increased by the erection of the largest depot in the world, on the creek . . . occupying the whole space between Ohio Street and the dock, and enabling the road to receive freight directly from vessels lying at the wharf. Connections are also made with two of our largest grain elevators, so that nothing is wanting to complete the perfectness of its arrangements for the transportation of property. The road has been crowded with freight during the past season and at times for several weeks together, unable to accommodate the pressure of its business.

While the rise of large, increasingly national railroad systems that now linked Buffalo with New York, Philadelphia, Erie, and Cleveland did do irreparable damage to the Erie Canal, they in fact posed no threat at all to the city's commercial position as a port of transshipment—the largest inland port, in fact, in the United States. However, because the canal had become so inextricably intertwined, symbolically if not actually, with the image of the city, the Buffalo merchants, politicians, and editorialists, unable to distinguish between damage to the canal and to the city's economy, reacted with shock and horror as the fortunes and the revenue of the Erie Canal began a steady plunge.

Although Buffalo's location at the end of the Great Lakes guaranteed its importance as a port of transshipment, regardless of other transportation developments (that is, until the advent of trucking in the 1920s), the city's leaders could not quite grasp this fact, and lived in fear and anxiety that the railroads would somehow deny them the prosperity that lake trade was bringing to them. The annual reports of the board of trade and newspaper editorials throughout the 1850s were filled with speculation: Would the completion of the Welland Canal between Lakes Erie and Ontario distract trade away from Buffalo to Oswego? How would the consolidation of eight separate railroads—the Mohawk and Hudson, the Utica and Schenectady, the Syracuse and Utica, the Auburn and Syracuse, the Auburn and Rochester, the Tonawanda, the Attica and Buffalo, and the Buffalo and Niagara—into the New York Central damage the city? Would the completion of the Erie Railroad between New York City and Dunkirk, New York (on the eastern shores on Lake Erie), turn that small town into a major grain entrepôt? Would the rising railroad lobby exert undue influence in Albany and thus defeat efforts to improve the canal? Would the high tolls on the canal (thirty-five cents per barrel of flour as opposed to eight cents per barrel on the Welland Canal) seriously hurt Buffalo's trade position?

Despite these fear-filled questions, the fact of the matter was that the development of railroads—particularly those feederlines west of the city, like the Illinois Central that connected Chicago with an ever-growing agricultural hinterland—only tended to increase the flow of raw materials eastward on the Great Lakes system to Buffalo. That a growing percentage of these goods were transshipped onto railcars rather than on canal boats may have damaged other cities along the canal but did nothing to damage Buffalo's standing as the preeminent inland port in the United States. Thus, despite the anxieties of the city's commercial establishment, whose understanding of what was good for Buffalo was often clouded by a sentimental attachment to the Erie Canal, the railroad had no adverse affect on the city's economy. In fact, it had a dynamic impact on the city's nascent manufacturing economy.

While grain products—oats, barley, corn, wheat, rye, and soybeans—were the city's primary imports from the Midwest, a huge variety of other products were shipped to Buffalo via the Great Lakes. These included pork and bacon, beef, whiskey, lumber, tobacco, lead, oil, hemp, feathers, beeswax, furs, sugar, potatoes, iron (over two thousand tons in 1846), leather, ashes, lard, butter, cheese, cotton, wools, beans, fish tallow, copper, and cranberries. The result of this busy and diverse commerce was the creation of an incredibly rich manufacturing economy based on the processing of these products. By the middle of the 1840s the foundations of a highly diversified manufacturing economy were in place. There were a few small breweries, leather works, construction materials, manufactories, clothiers, furniture and piano makers, saddlers, and boat builders, and a handful of iron foundries that produced agricultural equipment, boiler engines, screws and nails, and stoves. By the 1850s this fledgling manufacturing economy, most of which had been cottage-based, began to develop into a sophisticated, technically ingenious, increasingly automated factory system. This is most clearly seen in the iron industry.

Raw iron found its way into Buffalo soon after the completion of the Erie Canal. Desperately eager to get their hands on the stuff, early foundry operators like George Tift, whose first business venture in Buffalo was a grain elevator, and Sherman Jewett, a merchant, arranged to have iron brought to Buffalo by complicated and circuitous routes. Some came directly along the canal route from the Syracuse vicinity. More came from St. Lawrence County in the northwestern part of the state, via Lake Ontario and the Welland Canal. To be smelted, iron required coal. But until the early 1850s there was no rail connection between Buffalo and the coal fields in northwestern Pennsylvania and southern New York. Some small amount came overland in the 1840s, but coal is far too bulky and the amount required for smelting far too great for this method of transportation to be economical. In 1851, however, the first direct rail line, owned and operated by the Delaware, Lackawanna and Western Railroad Company, linked Buffalo with the coal fields of the southern tier in the neighborhood of Binghampton. Three years later the completion of the Buffalo and Pittsburgh Railroad put Buffalo in still more direct contact with the bituminous coal fields of western Pennsylvania. The iron trade prospered.

By the middle of the 1850s many of the materials and artifacts of everyday life were made out of iron, and virtually all of them were made in Buffalo. There were house trimmings and "household hardware," shovels, hoes, iron bench screws (which their maker, Pratt and Company, reminded consumers were "fast taking the place of wood screws"), iron balconies and verandas, bells, locks, and refrigerators and heaters for homes, offices, hotels and public rooms. For banks there were fireproof vaults and doors. For hotels there was Jewett and Roots' "New Hotel Stove" with two ovens, one for meat and the other for pastry, and each separate from the other "so that meats and pastry can be baked at the same time without interfering." For all kinds of wells there were chain pumps with decorative covers which the manufacturer assured the customer "combined ornament with utility." For the lifting and repairing of locomotives and other heavy machinery there were jackscrews made by Pratt and Company with "particular attention being paid to evenness of thread and exactness of fitting of the different parts to prevent cramping or friction." For the manufacture of "heavy forgings and hammered shapes—such as car axles, steamboat and propeller shafts and cranks, connecting rods, piston rods, [and] locomotive frames," Pratt recommended its steam hammer. Four feet tall and weighing five thousand pounds, the steam hammer was strong enough to manufacture these items. For farmers there was a huge agricultural equipment market, dominated by John A. Pitts, who sold more than $100,000 worth of agricultural machinery yearly. His most popular product was a machine that threshed and cleaned grain in one operation. He made twenty-five of these every year. Pratt and Company also manufactured the "Eagle Feed Cutter, a machine combining strength and simplicity in so great degree that it must commend itself to every man at a glance."

Among the largest of Buffalo's iron factories was Jewett and Root's Stove Factory, which in the 1850s made 90 different kinds of stoves, employed over two hundred men, and used one thousand tons of anthracite, five hundred tons of bituminous, and four thousand tons of iron annually. Their square-block factory in the First Ward, adjacent to the terminus of the Erie Canal, covered five acres with a specially designed loading dock on the Ohio basin, a small feeder canal for the Erie. The factory complex included two moulding rooms, each 200 feet by 150 feet; a four-story building for nickel plating; a warehouse; and a separate five-story administration building. Jewett and Root produced a variety of stoves for homes, offices and public facilities. One called the President was the most elaborate.

Hart, Ball and Hart, manufacturers of heating and ventilating equipment, made a wide range of cast-iron furnaces that burned coal and wood. They made wood heaters for railroad cars, ventilating stoves for school rooms, and a cooking range called the Cosmopolitan. Hart, Ball and Hart, who had developed and patented it, were particularly proud of the Cosmopolitan:

> The fire chamber is materially different in form from that of any other range in use and is so constructed as to equalize the heat under all the boiler openings. The oven is of extra size, with its flues so arranged as to secure, in the highest possible degrees, an equal heat on all sides. Under the oven is a capacious hot closet, where is continuously found a mild and gentle heat, rendering valuable service for warming dishes and food. The water back is large and powerful, furnishing at all times, without an extra fire, an abundant supply of hot water for baths, laundry and other purposes. Provision is also made for the attachment of hot-air fixtures by which, in addition to its culinary department, it serves an important purpose for warming a dining room or parlor, either above or adjacent to the apartment in which it is placed.

Still more iron products were manufactured by the Buffalo Architectural Iron Works. In response to the rapid increase in iron as a building material, this company produced brackets, stairs, wrought iron and cast-iron fences, bank doors, sills and guards, iron columns, and "the only perfectly fireproof rolling shutters for store fronts and public buildings."

The largest iron factory in Buffalo was the Buffalo Iron and Nail Works. Located in the northwest section of the city along one of the many creeks that emptied into the Niagara River, Buffalo Iron and Nail was a highly mechanized, ordered, tightly supervised manufacturing establishment. There is no question but that for the two-hundred-odd men who worked in the Buffalo Iron and Nail Works, the industrial age had arrived.

The Buffalo Iron and Nail Works consisted of four semi-attached brick buildings. In the front of the largest building, the scrap-iron house, was a railroad feeder line. To the side of the building was the pig iron yard. It was in this yard, surrounded by high fences to prevent "surreptitious appropriation by outsiders," that the company stored vast piles of Pennsylvania pig iron. From the yard the iron was moved into the scrap house, where it was stored in bins containing thousands of tons of scraps, from car wheels to bits of wire. In the scrap house, larger sheets of iron were broken down into smaller pieces by a pair of gigantic steam-powered shears. Behind this building, between it and the main mill, was the coal yard, where over six thousand tons of coal were stored. Here also were huge piles of sand from Lake Oneida, "almost pure silex," used for the bottoms of the scrap furnaces. Next to the coal yard in this very coherently arranged industrial unit was the main mill. Here, in this building 176 feet long and 140 feet wide, on a floor that was entirely paved, were the six puddling furnaces and six scrapping and heating furnaces that performed the blending process in the making of iron products.

Puddling is the process whereby carbon is removed from pig iron, in order to strengthen the iron and make it less brittle. It was done by hand in the following way: First, five to six hundred pounds of pig iron were put into the brick furnace. Then heat was applied to melt it down. As it was melting in the brick furnace, the puddler stirred it with an iron rod through a hole in the furnace. Through contact with the air, impurities in the pig iron rose to the top of the furnace. As the iron began to solidify, the puddler stirred it into three balls. Then he opened the furnace door and lifted the balls, each "about the size of a bushel basket" with iron tongs and put them into the "squeezer," where the remaining slag was squeezed out and shaped into a bar three to four feet long. (According to the *Commercial Advertiser* this process made "a series of concussions resembling a running fire of artillery.") This whole process took about two hours, and the average worker, working twelve-hour shifts, did this a total of six times. Writing in 1910 that "there have been few essential changes in puddling furnaces within fifty years, Historian John Fitch said that "puddling is very hard, hot work and few positions are more taxing physically."

From here the iron plates were passed into the nail factory and cut into a variety of sizes, "from the smallest nail to the largest spike." In 1859 the company owned twenty-six nail machines capable of producing 15,000 pounds, or 100 kegs, of nails per day. These, "as fast as cut," were conveyed in hoppers to a room below where they were packed and shipped.

The whole plant was powered by two steam engines, one of 125 horsepower for the main works and another of 30 horsepower for the nail factory. The steam for these engines was produced by three boilers. Concerned with loss of energy, the owners took care that the waste heat from these boilers was used to heat another boiler which supplied the cylinders.

Not only was the physical plant carefully organized, but the labor force too was highly regulated. The *Commercial Advertiser*, proud of what was apparently a new organization of work, described it approvingly: "The office of the mill manager is so situated that he commands a view of the entire mill." Management had a very effective supervisory system within the plant: "The internal regulations of the works are admirably arranged, the result of a system which tenders the mill force far more effective than under other circumstances."

As is made clear in the description of the iron-moulding process, mechanization was well advanced in mid-nineteenth century Buffalo. This was true in other industries, too. The *Commercial Advertiser*, a journal which never failed to demonstrate its pride in the city's industrial progress, described the machine shops of Pitts' agricultural works: "All the floors are devoted to wood work of the machines and contain the usual, besides other apparatus, such as buzz saws, lathes, spoke machines, jointing machines, etc., *ad infinitum*." Noting the superiority of these machines (they "accomplish more work in a better manner than could be done by hand"), the *Commercial Advertiser* concluded excitedly: "All this forms a scene very exciting and pleasant. The din of machinery and the clash of hammers, the ingress of materials and the egress of manufactured parts, all combine to render the scene stirring and interesting." Work then, in these mid-nineteenth century industrial establishments, was mechanized, organized and regulated. And while there are no available accounts of work within these factories of the 1850s, it is clear from these descriptions that it was certainly dangerous and difficult.

One of the earliest and largest machine shops in Buffalo was created when a local inventor named Ketchum formed a partnership with a local capitalist named Howard for the purpose of manufacturing Ketchum's Mowing Machine, claimed by Mr. Ketchum to be the first mechanical grass-cutter ever invented. It was, according to contemporary accounts, "of easy draft, simple in construction, durable, and possessing a feature unique to the Ketchum machine to prevent clogging." While the machine was at first made in pieces in a series of different shops throughout the city, a factory was soon erected, again in the First Ward. Order and organization prevailed in this branch of the iron industry too. Referred to as "the most comprehensive works in the U.S. in this class of manufacturing," a handbook guide to the city's manufacturers described the plant in terms that well might suit an assembly line: "In this works every department is complete and systematically arranged for the rapid construction of these machines." The Ketchum Reaper was apparently well-made too. It won first prize at state fairs in New York, Pennsylvania, Ohio, Michigan, Delaware, and Maryland.

There were many industries in mid-nineteenth century Buffalo that had nothing to do with iron. The largest of these was tanning. Unlike iron, the leather industry, with over two hundred employees, was organized along the cottage system of production, with separate pieces of the whole product produced in the homes of different workers. Describing Forbush and Brown's Shoe and Boot Manufactory, the city's largest, the *Commercial Advertiser* wrote: "Aside from the cutting out and finishing up of the manufacture of boots and shoes, most of the labor is performed outside of the premises."

While iron, with approximately sixteen hundred workers; tanning, with five hundred; and shipbuilding and agricultural machinery, with about two hundred workers each, were the dominant industries, there was a staggering degree of variety and diversity in the manufacturing sector of Buffalo's economy.

Most of these factories were small, employing between six and twenty workers, who earned an average of between $25 and $30 per month. There seems to have been little rationale for these wages, with iron workers in one shop earning $25 while workers in another earned $30. Rarely did men receive less than $20 per month, while the highest recorded salary in 1855 was the $45 per month earned by the six male employees who worked for J. Benson's Confectionery. Women, whose numbers appeared to have been few in local industry, and children, of whom there were quite a few, earned considerably less than their adult male counterparts.

Work conditions were difficult and controlled in the iron industry. Noyes' mill-equipment factory, also located in the increasingly industrialized First Ward, was characteristic of the increasingly industrialized work environment. The *Commercial Advertiser* described the Piranesi-like environment: "We must proceed to state what we saw within the dusky walls of the great factory. Diving down to the level of the canal wharf we find the engine, of the power of fifty horses . . . its might throbs, turning illimitable wheels, shafts and cranks scattered throughout the structure."

The work process—what people did, how much they earned, the environment of work—received hardly any notice in contemporary records and accounts. What local reporters and publicists were far more interested in was the technical inventiveness and genius of the first generation of Buffalo industrialists and entrepreneurs. There was Mr. A. B. Nimbs, who invented a floating grain and coal elevator and William A. Kirby, inventor of the Kirby mower. The city also had thirty-seven breweries which brewed 109,000 barrels of ale and beer per year; clothing, jewelry, and furniture-making shops; several boat building facilities; a handful of printers of lithographers; paper mills; a factory for the production of mirror and picture frames; an optical equipment shop; several piano and organ makers; a patent medicine plant; and a pressure vacuum gauge shop.

All of these operations required skill and ingenuity. The furnace and heating system at the Fletcher Furnace is typical of the sophisticated technology in use at the time. Designed by a Buffalo engineer named Harvey Fuller under contract to the Pratt company, it was described in wondrous terms by a guidebook to the city's manufacturers:

> The wind from the wind cylinder passes horizontally from the engine room near the ground to a wind receiver seven feet in diameter and thirty feet high; and from the top of this cylinder, horizontally, about one hundred feet, into the heating oven which is on the opposite side of the stack from the engine house, over the cast house at the top of the furnace; and from the heating oven the hot blast passes through six tweyers, each three-and-one-half inches in diameter, upon the mass of material to be smelted.

Using Fuller's furnace, the Pratt company could produce twenty-five tons of pig iron daily.

Job printing was another industry that was using advanced and complicated machinery. Employing a locally patented "striker" which "does the work of four hands," it produced "chromotypic print" which permitted color printing. Buffalo was a significant printing center which produced large quantities of school books, "pocket books," diaries, printed office papers and forms, and newspapers.

George J. Hill developed a machine that printed, numbered, and counted railroad tickets at the same time; and E. B. Holmes owned and operated a barrel factory and invented new machinery for making barrel stave jointing and stave dressing machines. George Prince developed a new and patented method for the making of melodeons, George Hayes for the improvement of vulcanizing machines, and George Sangster for the making of iron lanterns. Doctor J. Fermenich developed an improved faucet with "gutta percha" tubing. Bernard Dascomb invented a new and improved method for the manufacture of starch which shortened the fermentation process from ten days to thirty-six hours. James McNamera invented a machine for hoisting brick and mortar in the construction of buildings which, according to contemporary accounts, did the work of twenty men. In mid-nineteenth century Buffalo, the inventors were "as valuable a class of citizens as the manufacturers themselves."

By 1855 far more than the foundations of an industrial economy were securely in place in Buffalo. With the ranks of the labor force growing daily, an increasingly national transportation network based on the Erie Canal, the Great Lakes, and a rapidly expanding system of railroads with power in the form of steam (coal did not become a major energy source until after the Civil War), all that the city's manufacturers really lacked was a greater and more consistent infusion of investment capital for the development and expansion of manufacturing. This problem was accentuated during the financial panic of 1857 when the overheated national economy, plagued by rampant speculation in railroads, expansion of a non-specie-backed paper currency, and unprecedented inflation, suddenly collapsed. While the impact locally was not as shattering as the panic of 1837–38, it did lead to the widespread closing of local banks. The result was a critical credit squeeze. To local capitalists and would-be manufacturers, the panic of 1857 was a hard, yet valuable lesson whose severity they thought might well have been avoided, or at least cushioned, had the city's economy been more diversified and less dependent on commerce.

For many years the manufacturing interests of Buffalo had complained about the banks of the city, whose vision of the economy, they believed, was narrowly limited to trade. Indeed, banks did favor

merchants over manufacturers. Commercial loans were short-term—
often as short as one to fifteen days. Manufacturers, with their
expensive investments in durable machinery, required longer term
loans. These most bankers were unwilling to provide. Describing the
situation thirty years after the panic, a historian of the city's industry
wrote about the discriminatory loan policies suffered by the city's
small but growing manufacturing community:

> The brains and manhood of Buffalo were then to be found on her
> docks . . . and those public institutions, by a strange misnomer
> called banks, were mostly engaged in buying and shipping grain.
> The struggling manufacturer who approached a bank cashier in
> those days to obtain what was facetiously called an "accommoda-
> tion," would probably be told to call some other day. His business
> paper, given for honest labor and materials, would be promptly
> rejected if it was drawn for a period longer than thirty days. . . .
> Economy and savings were impossible given such conditions and it
> brought inevitable disaster.

In an effort to remedy this situation, two manufacturers—Pascal
Pratt, the city's leading iron maker, and Brownson Rumsey, owner
of the largest tannery—founded the Manufacturers and Traders Bank
in 1856 for the specific purpose of making credit available to Buffalo's
manufacturing community. That same year Pratt, Rumsey, and several
others formed the Association for the Encouragement of Manufacturers.
In an economy overwhelmingly oriented towards commerce, the manufacturing interests, although growing, were in a distinct minority.
Conditions were changing quickly however, particularly after the
second panic within twenty years threatened to undercut the local
economy. Now not only the manufacturers, but others too, realized
the increasing significance of diversifying the city's economic base.
The *Commercial Advertiser* wrote in 1857:

> A city to have stability and permanence must have a great and
> growing manufacturing interest. Commerce alone will not affect
> this. . . . With commerce and industries combined, who could place
> the limit of our city boundaries in half a century from now?

Despite the increased importance of manufacturing in the economic
life of the city and the gradual recognition of its significance by
bankers and editorialists, it was not until the years after the Civil
War that Buffalo's economy shifted irrevocably toward industry.

CHAPTER 4

Ethnics: Germans, Irish, and Blacks

The shift from a commercial economy to one rooted primarily in manufacturing was noticeable, yet gradual. Far more rapid and dramatic were the alterations in the composition of Buffalo's population. The growth of the city's population in the middle of the nineteenth century was truly spectacular, more than doubling between 1845 and 1855. While a fair number of these people were native-born Americans migrating to the city from New England and rural New York, the greatest percentage were foreigners. By 1855 over sixty percent of the 74,214 people who lived in Buffalo were foreign-born. Almost half (31,000) were Germans and a fifth (18,000) were Irish. Although the massive waves of immigration that had brought these people to Buffalo during the late 1840s and early 1850s had finally begun to recede, by 1855 these foreigners, most of whom were Catholic, were overwhelming the native-born citizens of Buffalo, a phenomenon of dramatic circumstance for everyone.

Although representing a majority of the population, these two huge foreign groups lived in their own separate ethnic enclaves, largely isolated from the rest of the city. In 1854 a local journal, describing the Germans on the city's East Side, said that "their customs and habits are as unknown to us as those of the Tartars." They were, "as far as social intercourse is concerned, completely isolated." And unlike the increasingly xenophobic views of other journals in mid-nineteenth century Buffalo, this one, called *Democracy*, expressed a desire to "break through the barriers which surround [the Germans]."

These barriers were largely self-imposed. This foreign, primarily Catholic, and young (the average age of Buffalo's Germans in 1855 was twenty-two, of the Irish, twenty; while the average native-born citizen was almost equally young at twenty-three), immigrant group could create a solid, secure, and predictable community, free from the suspicious and often hostile presence of the increasingly defensive Protestant native-born citizenry. In a novel written in 1949, Roger Dooley, himself a product of the city's Irish First Ward, describes a nineteenth-century woman's view of what she called "Heinietown." Although set in the late nineteenth century, her view is even more appropriate to the 1850s:

> When Rose was little, the long street-car ride had seemed like a trip to a different country—a strange country where all the grown-ups talked in a sing-song, up-and-down twang and even the children could often speak Geman better than English and the stores and bakeries all had funny names printed on the windows in fancy German lettering.

And while she made no particular ethnic references, Mabel Dodge, writing about her childhood on posh Delaware Avenue on the city's West Side, said that it was "over there" on the East Side where lived "the hard-faced men unknown to us all. Our instinctive feeling towards the East Side was one of contempt."

Unlike the highly commercial, increasingly industrialized First Ward—the south side of the city, near the terminus of the Erie Canal and the city's growing railroad nework, where the Irish lived—the Fifth, Sixth and Seventh Wards east of Main Street were predominantly residential. In small frame homes, with an average value of less than one thousand dollars, Buffalo's Germans lived in quiet, tree-shaded, somewhat suburbanlike residential streets. While there were a few places of employment—a few small cigar factories, and several small breweries—scattered here and there, the East Side was primarily a stable, quiet, young, family-oriented community. In addition it was, more often than not, economically secure and rather comfortable. Many of the German immigrants living in the city came to Buffalo with skills already acquired, and in the middle of the nineteenth century most of the skilled workers in Buffalo—shoemakers, masons, tailors, musicians, blacksmiths, boilermakers, butchers, upholsterers, painters, tinsmiths, stonecutters, clockmakers, bakers, cigar-makers— were German-born. Not only were few of them unskilled laborers— work more usually performed by the Irish—but also many of them were quite well educated. *Democracy* wrote in 1851 that "there are found among the German people a large number of cultivated, in-tellectual minds, scientific and philosophical geniuses." Thus the

Germans, it seems, came to the United States and to Buffalo extremely well prepared for life in their new home.

For many, however, the adjustment must surely have been difficult. One German, contemplating emigration, wrote a cousin about his forthcoming journey: "I can tell you that it is very hard on us. Nothing to sell and nothing to earn. . . . I have decided to emigrate too." He wanted to be well-prepared, and told his cousin: "When I come I shall bring all kinds of seeds with me and wish I would know the necessary house tools that one needs in America." It was clear, however, that he really knew little about his future home: "Is the cattle in Buffalo like in Gemany? How much does a cow cost?" Towards the end of his letter, he begged for reassurance and asked his cousin to write and tell him "if you think I would not be unhappier than in Bluderhausen." He wanted to come though and, as if trying to convince himself as much as his cousin in Buffalo, wrote: "I like hard work and love freedom." In the end, however, his concerns were far more mundane and he concluded this poignant letter with a question: "Does food grow enough and is there healthy enough water?"

Many immigrants decided not to stay in Buffalo. Indeed, in September 1854 the *Daily Courier* noted that "the total number of people daily leaving Buffalo for the West by steamboat and railway cannot be less than three thousand." Among these may well have been one George Klatz who, having left Buffalo for Indianapolis, where he owned a dry goods store, wrote back in 1860: "Business is pretty good here. . . . I feel astonished that not more of the Eastern people come to Indianapolis to settle down. In fact, a poor man that wishes to work can do better here than in Bufffalo."

Despite the well-developed urban survival skills that many of them possessed, Buffalo's Germans were isolated. While they left their neighborhood to go to work throughout the city in the mornings, evenings found them coming back home to a community that by the middle of the 1850s had a flourishing and very well developed local structure and support network that consisted of several German-language newspapers and churches; a variety of cultural groups, including an increasingly well known singing society; innumerable social organizations; and even their own militia company, called the Steuben Guard.

Although separate and highly ethnocentric, and indeed often silent and seemingly invisible to the outside world, when it came to parrying threats to their native culture or to pursuing measures to strengthen their cohesiveness, Buffalo's Germans were able and eager to express themselves to the larger community. In fact, as early as 1836, when the German population was minimal, leaders of the German community made the first of what would be several unsuccessful requests for the establishment of a publicly funded German-language school. When this failed, this young, extremely new community formed their own German school board and in 1837, with money raised within their own neighborhood, opened a bilingual school of their own.

The desire to perpetuate the German language was a critical element in the cultural cohesiveness of the German community. In both Catholic and Protestant German churches, sermons were delivered and scriptures were read in the native tongue. German was also the language used in the five German Catholic schools that existed in Buffalo in 1850. Indeed, many Germans insisted that their language achieve official status, demanding that Buffalo should become officially bilingual, with all laws and ordinances printed in both languages. Other groups, such as the German Young Men's Association, a cultural nationalist group founded in Buffalo in 1841, were dedicated to the perpetuation and preservation of the German language and culture.

The community's struggle for public recognition of the German language and German culture continued throughout the next decade as German leaders made persistent and periodic requests for the appointment of German teachers in schools in German neighborhoods. It was not until 1866, perhaps as a kind of guilt-ridden recognition of the role that Buffalo's German population had played in the war effort, that the common council finally relented and did appoint several German teachers to teach German in four schools on Buffalo's East Side.

Again, despite their obvious eagerness to remain separated physically and culturally from the rest of the city, the approximately thirty thousand Germans who lived on the East Side in 1850 showed little shyness when it came to political activism. Perhaps as a result of their vociferousness on behalf of the German language, Germans became politically active soon after their initial arrival in the city. In 1838, one Fredrich Dellenbach, a physician, became the first German to run for and win a seat on the common council. However, it was not until 1854, when the population of the German settlement had reached over thirty thousand, that a German ran for and was elected to a citywide office—comptroller. Perhaps it was a result of ethnic stereotyping, which depicted the Germans as frugal people, that this position remained a German political monopoly for the remainder of the century.

German political participation took a more activist turn following the arrival in the United States of German political refugees from the failed revolution of 1848—"the '48ers." Buffalo's German community was involved with and sympathetic to the political upheavals in Germany and Poland from the very beginning. Throughout the spring and summer of 1848 there were rallies, parades, and demonstrations on the East Side celebrating, and demonstrating solidarity with, revolutionary upheavals occurring not only in the fatherland but in France and Hungary as well. During that volatile spring of 1848 the German Revolutionary Society was formed on the East Side, and soon political refugees from Germany and eastern Europe began to make their way to Buffalo. Soon Buffalo, along with New York, Milwaukee, and Cincinnati, became a stopping point in the constant fund-raising efforts of European political refugees in search of money and support. None attracted more attention than Louis Kossuth, who delivered several speeches in the German community in 1852.

Even before Kossuth's visit, however, the revolutionary spirit of central Europe had penetrated to the heart of Buffalo's German community. Throughout 1849 and 1850 there was a flurry of community activity that for the first time had a distinct class and political orientation instead of the strictly cultural and ethnocentric activities that had previously characterized the community. The summer of 1849 saw the formation of the German-American Workingman's Union. Although organized in the German community, it hoped to attract support among like-minded native-born Buffalonians to abolish the system of payment for work known as "store pay," an arrangement that gave credit for merchandise as a large part of a workingman's salary. Although this system was prevalent and customary among the unskilled Irish day laborers, it must surely have offended the highly skilled German tailors, whose talent and labor could not possibly be fairly recompensed by credit at the local grocery. Thus, in 1850 two hundred German tailors, joined now by shoemakers who had recently formed their own trade union, again went on strike demanding abolition of the hated store pay system. The sight of these two groups of skilled workmen demonstrating in the streets of Buffalo gave further encouragement to other tradesmen in the community and by the end of 1850, carpenters, blacksmiths, and wheelwrights had joined the apparently blossoming union movement by adding unions of their own. In addition, the end of 1850 saw the formation of the German Workingman's Sick Benefit Society and two cooperatives for the sale of furniture and shoes and boots.

The failure of the 1848 revolutions in Germany and other countries in central Europe had an important, and as yet unexamined, impact on the developing German communities throughout urban America. Had those revolutions been successful, many of the still highly nationalistic and ethnically conscious German immigrants throughout the United States might have considered returning to their beloved fatherland. The failure of the revolutions, however, shattered any lingering hopes that Buffalo's Germans may still have entertained for returning. Now more than ever they were a part of America. It was this realization, more than any abstract revolutionary notions that filtered across the Atlantic, that inspired the new-found militancy of the German community. It was the '48ers, for example, who formed the Turn Verein in 1853 (several years after Turn Vereins had been organized in New York, Milwaukee, Chicago, and Cincinnati). The Turners, unlike the strictly ethnocentric groups that had previously emerged within the German community, were not dedicated primarily to the strengthening of German national and cultural ties, but rather were more concerned that the German immigrants "become energetic, patriotic citizens of the American Republic" who would use their intelligence and ingenuity not in the exclusive pursuit of their own national and ethnic concerns but rather to "represent and protect the common good of all people by word and deed." For example, unlike the more parochial views of the established German newspaper, *Der Weltburger*, the Turners were strong advocates of abolitionism and of equal rights for women.

The failure of the German revolution in 1848, and the dashing of hopes for reform that accompanied it, coincided with the economic success of the first generation of Buffalo's German population. For now, during the late 1840s and early 1850s, there began to surface, on what had always been perceived as the stolid, uniformly working-class German East Side, a group of merchants who in a rather short period of time had managed to become quite wealthy. These were men who had emigrated here in the late 1830s and early 1840s and who, following a few years of menial work, had suddenly become successful, not only within the context of their own community but within the city at large. What is most interesting about this first generation of German businessmen—people like Solomon Scheu and Albert Ziegler, both brewers; Jacob Schoelkopff, a tanner; and Stephen Becker, a wholesale grocer—was that they had stayed in their homeland until after they had acquired an education and a trade. Scheu, for example, had been trained as a baker before he arrived in this country in 1840 at the age of sixteen. Schoelkopff, who by the end of the 1850s owned one of the largest tanneries in Buffalo, had been trained as a tanner during his youth in Germany. Albert Ziegler, whose brewery made over forty thousand barrels of beer per year and was the biggest in Buffalo, had worked as a brewer as a teenager in Wurtenburg. Thus, within ten or so years after their arrival in Buffalo (usually after a short stay in New York City), these men had become eminently successful businessmen, the object of envy and admiration not only within their own community but throughout the whole city. The success of these men, coinciding with the failure to achieve political change in Germany, had a significant impact on Buffalo's Germans. For these years were a critical time of transition for them, a time during which the German immigrants began to see themselves increasingly as Americans rather than as Germans. This rather sudden change in the way Buffalo's Germans perceived themselves would have implications not only within their own community but within the city at large.

For still other reasons, the year 1848 marked a period of dramatic importance in the life of the city's immigrant population. For just one year earlier Pope Pius IX had created the diocese of Western New York and had appointed John Timon of Pennsylvania as the first bishop of Buffalo.

Proud of his Irish ancestry (he boasted that he was "born in Pennsylvania, conceived in Ireland"), he "accepted with joy", he said, his mission of "planting the flag of the faith in the very center of infidelity and Protestantism, and in spite of the opposition of the anti-Catholic bigots." It was only natural that the new bishop, boastful of his Irish ancestry, flaunting an Irish lilt in his voice, and eager to speak Gaelic to anyone who would listen, was enthusiastically received by the city's beleaguered Irish population. Here on Bufflo's south side, in an area known as the Old First Ward, where the great majority of the 6,300 Irish people in the city lived—along the docks, near the railroad terminal and the city's rapidly expanding factories—Timon was a hero from the moment of his arrival. Isolated in the First Ward as much by choice as by prejudice, Buffalo's Irish—very much like the Senecas earlier in the century—were separate and, as far as the rest of the city was concerned, largely invisible. While there were Irish families scattered in other parts of Buffalo, once they settled in the First Ward, few left. Many moved around within the ward (since a large number of people rented their flats and homes there was constant movement within the ward), but hardly any ever moved out. The tightly knit, ethnocentric bonds of Irish nationality and Catholicism provided a supportive and comforting environment for this highly vulnerable immigrant community.

Who were Timon's Irish? Somewhat younger than either the Germans or the native-born Americans, the Irish of Buffalo lived in large, extended families in small one-and-a-half- and two-story frame houses in the narrow, wind-swept streets just off Lake Erie in the south side of the city. Unlike in the purely residential German East Side, land use in South Buffalo was alternatingly residential and industrial. Schools, churches, and homes shared the limited land area with breweries, grain elevators, railroad yards, and market places. Hemmed-in between the lake in the west, the small yet clearly defined central business district in the north, the railroad tracks in the east, and the Buffalo Creek in the south, Irish South Buffalo—Timon's Buffalo—was densely packed. Irish people (particularly the men who lived in the several large boardinghouses in the neighborhood) were everywhere: on the streets, in the taverns, working hard at unskilled jobs along the docks and in the factories.

While the Irish had been in Buffalo for over twenty years prior to the arrival of Bishop Timon in 1847, it was not until he came that the rest of the people of Buffalo became daily and seriously aware of them. Strikes by Irish workers along the canal had been regular but easy dealt with occurrences. The Irish churches and religious societies were highly ethnocentric and invisible, and the periodic Irish newspapers had no circulation beyond the confines of the First Ward. Timon's arrival changed all of this. Now, for the first time, Buffalo's Irish working-class population had a brash and bold spokesman who rallied and inspired the Irish and in the process frightened the older German and WASP community. Timon's immediate problems, however, were not with the increasingly anti-Catholic and anti-foreign native-born Protestant residents of Buffalo, but rather within the Catholic community, which was already sharply divided along ethnic lines.

Particularly bitter was the long-standing bickering and hostility that characterized relations between Germans and Irish Catholics. Until the formation of one bishopric in 1848, relations between these two groups were not particularly contentious. East Side German Catholic churches had their own German priests and, while prior to the arrival of Timon there was no special Irish parish even in the predominantly Irish First Ward, there were several Irish priests in the First Ward who conducted services in the homes of the Irish Catholic immigrants. It was the attempt by Timon to institutionalize and centralize the Catholic community under his jurisdiction that caused serious rifts within the Catholic community, while frightening the dominant native-born Protestant community, pushing it to the bigotry that characterized much of the relations between Protestants and Catholics during the 1850s.

Bishop Timon was brash and he acted quickly, almost by instinct. In the process he offended first the German Catholics and then the city's Protestants. Within weeks after his arrival in 1847, for example, Timon moved the bishop's see from St. Louis Church in Buffalo to a ramschackle wooden-frame Irish church on the fringes of the city's Irish working-class neighborhood in the south part of the city. This in itself was a considerable insult to Buffalo's German Catholics, who had come to dominate St. Louis and to make it the most significant and impressive Catholic congregation and edifice in the city.

St. Louis's history prior to the arrival of Bishop Timon had been stormy and rent with the incredibly divisive factionalism that already had come to characterise the city's ethnic community. It was founded in 1829 by a French Catholic who donated the land for the construction of a church meant, according to the donor, for all Catholics "without distinction of nationality." But the Germans quickly came to dominate church activities, and by 1837 the Irish, with no church of their own to retreat to, left, forming their own church two years later. While the French and German Catholics were able to bury their differences, their coexistence was also short-lived, and in 1846 a large group of the former withdrew to form yet another ethnic church. Thus, by process of elimination, St. Louis had become a completely German church. Such had been the history of the congregation at the time of Timon's arrival in 1848. The German parishioners of St. Louis, among them the prosperous and highly respected businessmen mentioned earlier, although somewhat offended by Timon's abrupt departure to St. Patrick's, were probably not sorry to see him go. Like the rest of the Irish working class, he too, they felt, belonged in the First Ward. Thus, by the early 1850s, Bishop Timon had become completely identified with the working-class Irish neighborhood of South Buffalo.

The rift between Timon, with his largely Irish following, and Buffalo's German Catholics became greater still when the brazen bishop challenged the lay leaders of St. Louis over their claim that the church's landholdings belonged not to the bishop but rather to themselves.

Since the establishment of St. Louis in 1829, control of the church's property had belonged to a lay board of trustees. Whether motivated by contempt for the prosperous Germans who dominated the church (all of the board members were German), by his own ethnic insecurity, or by a genuine obligation to strengthen the hand of his new office, Bishop Timon wasted no time in challenging the board of St. Louis. Insisting that all church property was owned directly by the bishop, Timon ordered the board of St. Louis to turn over to him the deed to their property. When they refused, Timon in 1850 issued a ban of interdict on the church. The ban lasted for over two years, during which time the strong-willed, increasingly ethnocentric bishop refused to allow any priest to officiate at services at St. Louis. It is perhaps somewhat ironic that in defense against what they charged was Timon's "theocracy," the German trustees of St. Louis turned to the Protestant legal community and hired as their attorney one James Putnam, a scion of one of Buffalo's esteemed New England families and, with Millard Fillmore, an early member of the city's Know-Nothing party.

Not only were the German Catholics alienated by the behavior and the policies of John Timon, but now even the distant, often imperious WASP establishment began to worry about the bishop. For Timon's action in the St. Louis case was a challenge not only to the German hierarchy but more importantly to the laws of New York State, according to which the trustees of St. Louis were correct: Trustees chosen by the congregation did in fact control all church property. Thus what was on the surface a strictly parochial power struggle between German Catholics and the Irish bishop was in fact a strong and strenuous challenge to the secular authority of the whole community.

Timon expressed little timidity in still further challenging the generally agreed-upon notion of secular dominance in general and the city's proud and historical Protestant establishment in particular. His first target was the city's schools.

Buffalo's public schools, where children read the King James version of the Bible, sang Protestant hymns, and read nativistic textbooks, were overtly anti-Catholic. They were, according to Timon, "proselytizing institutions" at which Catholic children "must assist at Protestant religious exercises, or be flouted or punished." Similarly, Catholic children were excluded from the Buffalo Orphan Asylum; Catholic women were not permitted at the Home for Indigent Women; and the Catholic mass could not be said at the Erie County Poor House, despite the overwhelming number of Catholic inmates. (When Timon personally asked the superintendent of the poor for permission to say mass, he was denied on the grounds that for the inmates to "mingle together" would be dangerous. And besides, the superintendent

81

said, "the comfort and solace of religion" would only weaken the inmates' desire to reform and thus to leave.) While he gave lip service to fighting the Protestant establishment's control of the city's public institutions, Timon clearly wanted to establish his own parochial network of institutions. Thus, soon after his arrival in Buffalo, John Timon had turned his back on the Protestant community and had created a completely separate religious, educational and welfare system of his own.

Schools were his first priority. Objecting bitterly to Catholics having to pay taxes to a system that supported Protestant-controlled public schools, Timon demanded that the state come to the aid of Buffalo's Catholic schools. When this failed to happen, Timon embarked on an ambitious program of school building that made it possible for Catholic parents throughout Buffalo to take their children out of the public school system and place them in Timon's growing parochial network instead. In addition to opening schools in the churches (St. Boniface and St. Mary's on the German East Side, St. Patrick's and St. Bridget's on the Irish South Side), Timon brought teaching orders of nuns and priests from Europe (Oblates, Christian Brothers, Sisters of the Sacred Heart, Grey Nuns, Jesuits, and Sisters of Charity) to open several teaching academies and high schools for the city's Catholic children. Under the auspices of these orders, hospitals like the Sisters of Charity, Catholic foundling homes, homes for the Catholic aged, and a Catholic orphanage were all instituted within several years of Timon's arrival in Buffalo. By thus importing not only foreigners but Catholics as well to teach the city's Catholic youth, Bishop Timon shocked, surprised, and frightened the city's long-dominant Protestant leadership.

Timon's parochial community building was early put to the test. Despite the rapid expansion in commerce and industry that charac-terized the city's economy during the early 1850s, Buffalo was highly susceptible to downturns in the business cycle and, as we have seen, was even more vulnerable now than it had been during the national panic of 1837. For now, in addition to the traditional extension of credit and land speculation, there had been an enormously risky overexpansion of credit to newly-developing railroads. When this particular bubble burst, credit dried up throughout the country and placed an inordinate squeeze on rapidly growing communities like Buffalo. The three years prior to the Civil War was a time of unprecedented economic hardship in Buffalo, a time during which everybody was vulnerable, but none more so than those at the bottom of the economic scale—the Irish Catholics.

The depression of the late 1850s put a great deal of stress on the already marginal community-based organizations that existed in South Buffalo. The Catholic orphanage, which opened during the cholera epidemic of 1849, now desperately needed money. The *Catholic Sentinel*, a newspaper published throughout the 1850s that reflected the concerns of the city's Irish population, wrote in 1857: "The almost unprecedented severity of the times has thrown upon our hands a large number of destitute children whom widowed mothers are no longer able to provide with the common necessities of life and who must perish if we do not come to their relief." In a concluding plea for ethnic solidarity, the *Sentinel* implored: "No one will sympathize with them unless it be those of our nation or faith." In an effort to spur private contributions, Bishop Timon announced that Pope Pius IX would grant "spiritual privileges and indulgences" to all who sent gifts to the orphanage.

Timon and the editors of the *Sentinel* soon realized, however, that community-based charity could not possibly support and sustain the needy in the area. In what must have been a difficult decision, the bishop, recognizing the limits of community self-help, now turned to the state. Citing the English Poor Law of 1854, he called for a program of public works and for a system of poor relief that would be funded out of the property tax. Pointing to the need for a new custom house, several new bridges over the Buffalo Creek, and the dredging of Buffalo Harbor, the *Catholic Sentinel* saw no reason why the unemployed of the city could not be hired to build these improvements. Barring this and the adoption of a poor relief fund supported out of city taxes, the *Sentinel* warned about possible violence: "Our citizens are remarkable for their love of law and order but 'necessity knows no law' and an empty stomach often drives reason out."

It was not only the immigrant press that demanded these changes. The staunchly Whiggish and Protestant paper, the *Commercial Advertiser*, was also concerned about economic conditions in 1857: "If the coming winter should prove as hard as we have reason to fear it shall be, what shall be done with these poor creatures?" Unable to avoid the opportunity to make snide, prejudiced statements about the city's immigrants, the *Advertiser* concluded their plea somewhat perversely: "Their [the immigrants'] reasoning and moral faculties are limited and thus riots may well ensue." The *Express* was less concerned, though equally as insulting, and suggested that if Catholics had only spent less money on building their churches they would have had enough to care for their poor. Since they did not, the *Express* felt that the municipality had no choice but to help out.

No changes were forthcoming, however, and the Irish poor, like the poor in other communities of the city, had to rely on themselves and their own parochial institutions. These, in response to the hard times, were growing. The fall of 1857 saw the formation in the First Ward of two workingmen's unions which resolved that "as the Workingmen of Buffalo compose the bone and sinew of the community it is their duty to meet together for the purpose of discussing all subjects that have a bearing on our interests." One of these groups, the Buffalo Workingmen's Cooperative Association, was frankly communistic. At the heart of their argument was that not only was "the tyranny of irresponsible capital" unfair and exploitative but that it also led to the production of inferior goods:

> One of the principal causes of badly renumerated labor in this country is the production of such an amount of inferior manufactures, that if the workmen had the capital in his own hands and could afford to spend the same amount of time in producing a less quantity of good manufactures as is spent upon worthless articles a greater demand would be created for home productions and labor would be plentiful and better paid. It is a great mistake to suppose that the workman loves to produce inferior goods—on the contrary, where he can produce without the interference of the seller whose desire is to get large profits, he will invariably produce a better article.

While there is no record of the impact of these fascinating, cooperative working-class organizations, it is clear that if the city refused to do anything and if the charitable organizations were strapped for funds of their own, the working people in the immigrant communities would at least try to do something for themselves.

The immigrants, but the people of Buffalo in general, had, it seemed, little control over the most important aspects of their daily lives. Not only were they vulnerable to national economic cycles, but they were equally terrorized by the increasingly regular visitations of cholera. The first epidemic had occurred in 1831, a cruel and tragic way to celebrate the official designation of the village as the city of Buffalo. The summer of 1849 brought yet another epidemic. That of 1854, however, was the worst to date.

In some ways the people of mid-nineteenth century Buffalo had become used to death. Indeed, death had become something of a public event. Not only were the names of the deceased routinely listed in the daily newspapers, but at the end of every week, the papers listed the total number of weeky deaths and the causes of death. Thus in September 1854, when the cholera had begun to recede, the *Commercial Advertiser* noted that during the past week one person was murdered, one had died in an accident, three of "congestion of the brain," eight of consumption, three of convulsions, four of "debility," seven of diarrhea, two of delirium tremens, two of "diseases of the uterus," two of dropsy of the brain, nine of dysentary, one of typhoid fever, two of "inflammation of the brain," one of old age, one of premature birth, and thirty-seven from cholera.

But cholera, unlike the other diseases, raged through whole communities, terrorizing cities all over the world and wasting whole families in the process. Journals kept by the Buffalo Medical Society during the epidemic of 1854 reveal the damage caused by this dread disease. "Mr. McGraw's daughter, aged sixteen, had died one hour previous to his death." Writing about Elizabeth Eichert, who died one morning, the attending doctor noted that "her husband died yesterday or last night in an immigrant tavern." And of Mr. and Mrs. Michael Ried, both of whom died on August 9, 1854, in the Sisters of Charity Hospital, it was recorded that they "were recently arrived immigrants who were very poor. Both had had diarrhea for several days and their bodily strength had much exhausted." Sometimes the doctors made particular notes about their patients. Heinrich Notta, age twenty-eight, was "found sick in the streets and sent to the hospital." Jacob Eggert, age fifty-eight, was "one of a large number of immigrants just arrived on the Niagara Falls cars. I visited him as soon as the case was reported by the railroad company but he was already dead."

What was particularly upsetting about cholera was that nobody knew quite what to do about it. Other than to urge people to eat their vegetables and to take "every effort to promote cleanliness in the streets and in private premises," the city's considerable medical profession was baffled and confused by the disease. Despite intense efforts to understand it and to treat it, the city's doctors were helpless. They confessed as much in the *Buffalo Medical Journal*, a scholarly and scientific monthly journal that had first appeared in the late 1840s: "We cannot learn that anything new has been elicited in the treatment of cholera." They listed a series of different treatments, including bloodletting, purgatives, mercury, and astringents. Opium, "in moderately large doses," was believed to be the most effective remedy.

If they failed to find a cure, it was not because they did not try. Indeed, the pages of the medical journal are filled with long and scholarly articles dealing with possible explanations and treatments, records of experimentation in other cities, and testimony of international experts on the subject. And despite the growing rift that existed between the immigrant Catholic population and the city's Protestant elite, the city's medical profession, Protestant to a man, labored intensely in desperate efforts to cure their predominantly foreign-born patients. About a patient who recovered, Dr. C. C. Gay wrote:

> Patient was attacked in the morning. I saw her at 4 PM. Ordered three doses of calomel repeated every hour. Vomitted soon after taken. Seven o'clock PM prescribed calomel with chloride sodium and calomel every hour. Ten o'clock PM colomel retained until now. Vomitting again. Prescribed calomel with chloride sodium followed with double doses of calomel every half hour till five doses were taken. No more vomitting or purging. She will recover.

Despite their best efforts, the impact of the disease was dramatic and devastating. At the end of one week in July during which Dr. Gay and his colleagues saw several hundred patients, one anonymous physician noted in the medical journal that "260 people died here this week. The panic is indescribable."

It is interesting to speculate about the influence of cholera on the patterns of community development in the immigrant world, particularly among the Irish, who were affected so overwhelmingly by these epidemics. Did the disease, because of the strange way it seemed to focus so overwhelmingly upon the Irish community, strengthen the already deep religious feelings of that group of people? Did it perhaps lead them to a still sharper perception of themselves as separated, distant and apart from the rest of the city? One thing that is certain is that in the months following the cholera plague of 1854 the Buffalo *Catholic Sentinel* published more news from Ireland than it ever had or would. There were weekly items of the most routine interest: "Mr. Spurgeon [as if he were so well known among Buffalo's Irish that his first name need not be even mentioned] has undertaken the editorship of the *Belfast Magazine*, the first number of which has just been issued." "Christopher O'C. Fitzsimmon of Glencullen has been appointed High Sheriff of Wicklow." "On the morning of the 2nd of June, 1854 James Donegan, the person who murdered a man named Cassidy in Dale Street, Liverpool, was arrested in a house in Cornwallis Street in that city." Occasionally the news items reflected less mundane concerns. One spoke of "destitution of the severest kind

which continued to prevail in Drogheda." Another item announced
that "by the direction of Col. Greville, M.P., one hundred pairs of
warm blankets have been distributed among the most necessitous poor
of the parish of Millingas."

While the cholera epidemic and the economic decline that followed
it in the late 1850s certainly rocked the immigrant communities in
general and the Irish community in particular, and surely strengthened
the religious and introspective tendencies of the people, the end of
the decade produced an oddly bourgeois and strangely passive feeling
on the part of a fair segment of the city's Irish population. There
was a growing number of elaborate day-long cruises on lake steamers,
church bazaars, and other forms of amusement and recreation which,
although in many cases organized primarily for the purpose of raising
funds for community activities, leave a clear impression of leisure for
its own sake. In many ways, it seemed, the spokesmen for the Irish
community were able to forget and even accept the difficulties that
the decade of the 1850s had brought. In an editorial at the end of
the decade, the *Catholic Sentinel* wrote:

> For some days we have had rain, snow storms, high winds, real
> old fashioned [Are the editors identifying with a past that was not
> even theirs?] March weather and are today visited with rain and
> snow. Business along the docks looks spring-like: the ice is out of
> the Creek and is fast disappearing from the lake. Ship carpenters
> and caulkers are busy generally at fair wages and most mechanics
> are employed. In fact, the appearance is rather favorable for good
> business. True there are many persons idle and looking for work,
> but this is always the case in large cities.

Thus, despite the years of sickness and economic hardship that had
afflicted them, and despite Bishop Timon's successful efforts at building
a community that was brashly and self-consciously ethnic, working-
class, and Catholic (In his sermon dedicating St. Joseph's Cathedral,
Timon clearly articulated his view of his flock: "Our children will
tell their children that we were very poor when we built this church.
. . . But yet each of us would have been happy to give his blood,
if human blood was necessary to cement the stones of this cathedral."),
the majority of Buffalo's Irish immigrants were not bitter. Indeed,
they even seemed optimistic.

Cramped together on several streets of the city's East Side, and
sandwiched in among a rapidly expanding German population, was
a small but well-organized community of blacks. Some had come to

Buffalo via Canada and others, born free in older eastern urban centers, had migrated to Buffalo following the completion of the Erie Canal. By mid-century the seven hundred–odd black people living in Buffalo had two churches and a separate, segregated school for their children. And while many black men worked as common laborers and most black women as domestics, there ws a considerable large number of skilled workmen in the city's East Side black community. Indeed, the job descriptions of many of them that were noted in the censuses of the mid-nineteenth century read like a handbook of trades. There were barbers, carpenters, hack drivers, masons, chefs, hotel keepers, and musicians. Two of the barbers—one named D. Paul Brown, the other named James Whitfield—achieved considerable local success as authors. Brown's play about slavery was performed in the Eagle Street Theatre in 1845 (black audiences sat upstairs), and James Whitfield's anti-slavery poems, with such rhetorical titles as "How long O Gracious God, how long shall power lord it over Right?" were privately published.

Free, creative, and nationalistic—Buffalo's blacks celebrated the emancipation of the British West Indies in 1843 with a parade, speeches, and toasts denouncing slavery and championing Garrisonian abolitionism—the community had by the 1840s begun to attract national attention. The city's reputation as a critical junction on the underground railroad began to spread and soon blacks—some former slaves, others born free—were coming to Buffalo. One of them was William Wells Brown, a runaway slave from Missouri who had moved to Buffalo from Cleveland in 1836.

Brown quickly became active in the city's Anti-Slave Society as a lecturer and organizer. One of Brown's special gambits was to station members of the society in the vicinity of the American falls at Niagara Falls, and when wealthy southern tourists came to view the falls with their slaves in tow, Brown and his men would secretly lure them from their masters and inform them that according to the law of New York State their journey in this free state had made them free men. (This, of course, was to be undone by the Dred Scott ruling in 1854.) Brown dedicated his life to reform. Sometimes it was temperance, other times women's suffrage and prison reform. But always he fought for the abolition of slavery. While living in Buffalo during the late 1830s and early 1840s, Brown took jobs that specifically placed him in close contact with slaves. Once he worked as a cook on a lake steamer that travelled between Buffalo and Cleveland, secretly concealing fugitive slaves bound for the Canadian border. Brown personally led them into the hands of another abolitionist agent who in turn smuggled them across the Niagara River to freedom in Canada. During the spring, summer, and fall of 1842—the months when the lake and the river were passable—Brown smuggled over seventy fugitives to Canada.

Buffalo's reputation as a center of anti-slave activity grew, and in August 1843 the city hosted two national abolitionist conventions. One was the National Convention of Colored Men. The other was the National Convention of the Liberty Party. One of the delegates who journeyed to Buffalo for both conventions (and a journey it was, for in the 1840s Buffalo had no railroad connections) was Frederick Douglass, who only five years earlier had escaped from slavery in Maryland. Although more likely than not he exaggerated his popular acceptance, Douglass reported that he had an extraordinarily successful week in Buffalo:

> For nearly a week I spoke every day in this old post office to audiences constantly increasing in numbers and respectability [perhaps he was becoming a curiosity who attracted the attention of the wealthy] til the Baptist church was thrown open to me. When this became too small I went on Sunday into the open park and addressed an assembly of 4,000 persons.

Both conventions meeting within a few days of each other, took an uncompromising abolitionist position. But local abolutionist William Brown was bitterly critical of the Liberty Party, a white-dominated group that had nominated two former slave holders to national office. He accused them of capitalizing on the long and hard work of the black abolitionists, primarily his own:

> Who was it that came to Buffalo and tore the veil of prejudice from the eyes of the whites of this city? Who was it who came here when the doors of the churches were barred, and with their might voices caused them to open them to the friend of the slave. Who are we indebted to for the great change in public sentiment in this city?

Brown, unfortunately, was hopelessly optimistic. For the sad fact of the matter was that there had been no change. If anything, "the veil of prejudice" in the city had become thicker and more difficult to penetrate as the years passed. Brown may have tried to fool the delegates of the Liberty party, but he couldn't fool himself. In 1844, after a speech in the town of Attica (thirty-five miles east of Buffalo), Brown was refused accommodation in that hamlet. Following this incident he left Buffalo forever. Later in the year the Liberty party could muster no more than 410 votes in the city that had hosted their national convention.

Thus, simply that Buffalo had been a center of abolitionist and then of Free Soil political activity in no way suggests a more liberal attitude toward blacks. Indeed, there was little actual abolitionist sentiment in the city. The growing number of Irish and German immigrants, most of whom were Roman Catholics and Democrats, had little taste for it, while the rest of the white population was far more interested in federal harbor and canal improvements than in the rhetoric of black liberation. Like most Americans in the middle of the nineteenth century, Buffalonians were distinctly racist, and while many may well have abhorred slavery (no working man in his right mind would want to compete with slave labor), the overwhelming majority had no desire whatsoever to live among blacks. This was true of the reform-minded WASP community who supported the colonization of America's blacks in Africa as well as for the German and Irish immigrant community who for racial as welll as economic reasons wasted little love on the black race. *Der Weltburger*, the Democratic German-language newspaper that so enthusiastically supported Kossuth's battles for freedom in eastern Europe, wrote during the Kansas-Nebraska debate: "We want no Negroes in the northern states because we anticipate nothing good from the mixing of the black and white races. We want the region of Kansas to be reserved for honest white workers."

For most people in the city, blacks were viewed as oddities, a strange and exotic segment of the population. Witness the description of Samual Ward, a delegate to the Negro convention from Cortland, New York:

This S. R. Ward is one of the finest specimens, intellectually and physically, of the African race that we have ever seen. Intensely black, tall, erect and muscular and moving with the easy grace of a panther, he has the manner and cultivation of a polished man of the world and would command respect and attention in any assemblage.

But Ward however was a rarity. For the most generous hopes that the majority of whites entertained for black Buffalonians was colonization in Africa. Indeed, some of the city's most influential people—among them Congressman Millard Fillmore and Judge Samuel Wilkeson, creator of the Buffalo harbor—were active members of the

American Colonization Society. Wilkeson, in fact, had been the director of the society for two years. As such Wilkeson had a plan that would not only rid the country of its black population but at the same time would strengthen the nation's manufacturing economy. It was an ingenious scheme: Congress would create a protective tariff, the proceeds of which would create a fund for the reimbursement of slave owners for every slave freed. Thus, according to Wilkeson, everybody, including the plantation South which had for so long opposed it, would benefit from the protective tariff. While this particular program was never enacted, colonization did, according to contemporary accounts, have the support of a broad cross section of local opinion. As one newspaper noted, "the candid-minded in every section of our community indulge the hope that the day will yet come when the descendants of Ham will be gathered together in the land of their ancestors."

While awaiting their supposed colonization, the blacks of Buffalo (about seven hundred in the mid-1850s), although mixed residentially with the Germans on the near East Side of the city, lived in a strictly segregated society. There were two separate black churches, special suffrage demands required that blacks be property owners in order to vote, and blacks were forced to attend a special "African School." Despite the clear-cut color lines, the white community was able to rationalize much of this segregation. The separate school was maintained, the superintendent of education claimed, not because of racial prejudice but rather because of the alleged inferiority of the black children. He wrote in 1843:

> They require greater patience on the part of the teacher, longer training and severer discipline than are called into exercise in the other schools, and generations must elapse before they will possess the vigor of intellect, the power of memory and judgement that are so early developed in the Anglo-Saxon Race. Hence, the importance of a distinct and separate organization of the African School.

Yet, ironically, in the segregated Eagle Street Theatre, Negro humor—minstrel shows and Negro impersonators—was the most popular entertainment. Throughout the 1840s and early 1850s, Tom Rice, billed as "The Father of American Minstrelsy," and creator of the character Jim Crow, played to packed houses. And in 1842, Ned Christy founded the Christy Minstrels in Buffalo. With Billy Birch on the tambourine and Christy on the "bones," Christy's minstrel show was all the rage. Christy sang:

Now darkies sing and play and makes a little fun.
We'll dance upon the green and beat the Congo drum.
We're a happy set of darkies and we're assembled here to play.
So strike the bones and tambourine and drive dull cares away.

Blacks and whites did meet, however—particularly on the city's waterfront, where black and Irish day laborers worked together. More often, however, they met at strikes, where blacks were often used as strikebreakers. Indeed, by the middle of the 1850s racial riots between Irish and black waterfront laborers had become so common that the rest of the community had come to accept these occurrences as a result of "the mutual jealousy and dislike subsisting between the Celtish and the African races." The newspapers were unwilling to recognize that antagonism between the races was caused not so much by natural dislike as by the fact that virtually every one of the fairly regular work stoppages of Irish dock workers was broken by black strikebreakers. Race relations in the city, severely damaged by this historic ploy, were further poisoned during the Civil War years by the imposition of a federal draft in the summer of 1862, in the aftermath of the Battle of Gettysburg.

Buffalo's immigrant population had never been enthusiastic about the war. Not only were they predominantly Democratic, and thus hostile to the war goals of the Republican administration in Washington, but they deeply resented what they deemed to be the inordinate amount of concern and attention that some of the city's Protestant establishment (particularly the Unitarians) lavished on the cause of slavery. This resentment became still more bitter when it became clear that the burden of fighting in the Union army fell with tragic unfairness on the city's immigrant population, particularly the Irish.

According to the law, a draft was imposed on a community only in the event that a predetermined quota was not filled by area volunteers. In order to fill their quotas, as much a matter of community pride as a question of self-preservation, the city's political and economic leadership orchestrated an elaborate campaign calculated to induce people other than themselves to enlist. First a series of private funds, endowed by widely appreciated and applauded businessmen, were created for the families of any men who offered their services to the Union cause. Then, following the creation of the draft, the stakes suddenly became higher. Now, compelled to fill an annual quota of 3,808 for the county, prominent Buffalonians became concerned that they too might be called upon to restore the Union. Thus, in a frenzied and last-ditch effort to hire the needy to volunteer, the common council, at the intense urging of Mayor Fargo, created a special city bounty fund of $180,000. The Erie County Board of Supervisors did the same with a special fund of $150,000. When supplemented by yet another bounty fund created by the board of trade, the fund became large enough. With still more private funds, the average bounty increased from $150 to $500. While even this generous bounty fund did not prevent the imposition of a draft in Erie County, it did enable most of the wealthier and more influential citizens to escape it. Among them was Grover Cleveland, a young and politically ambitious lawyer who, by paying $500 to one George Breiske, a recently arrived Polish immigrant, was able to pass the war in the comfort and prosperity of his blossoming legal practice. No wonder Dr. Brunck, editor of the German-language newspaper *Der Demokrat*, was led to suggest that when it came to the Civil War, "the Yankee rich men are in league against the foreign poor man."

The draft and the bounty system provoked intense reactions among the city's immigrants, particularly among the unskilled laborers, who were most vulnerable to the system. When combined with labor grievances, these reactions sometimes became violent and cruel. In late July and early August 1863, in protest against low wages, somewhere near one hundred dockworkers and stevedores, primarily Irish, went out on strike. When their employers responded by hiring black laborers as strikebreakers, violence erupted. Coming within months of the Emancipation Proclamation, the strikebreaking by black scabs took on an ominous and complex meaning for the Irish waterfront workers. Were the Irish people really expected to offer their lives to free people who offered thanks by breaking their strikes? Blacks, then, were the most obvious objects of the Irish anger and confusion, and in early August 1863, large numbers of Irish dockworkers struck out violently against the injustices of their predicament.

Afraid that the disruption of the waterfront would seriously interrupt the booming war-time traffic, the city authorities responded quickly and forcefully. The Sixty-Fifth and Seventy-Fourth militia regiments, just returned from riot duty in New York City, were activated, and together with local police and a citizen posse of several thousand, were marshalled to contain the violence. These measures, along with a special plea for calm from Bishop Timon, failed to halt the angry dock workers who, striking out at Buffalo's blacks as the most obvious enemy, stampeded away from the waterfront, across the Main Street business section, and into the small, black residential section in the eastern part of the city. Finally, after several hours of uncertainty, the rioters were dispersed. Citing one black fatality, newspapers were generally pleased that, compared to those in New York City, anyway, the draft riots of Buffalo were "tame."

The intense frustration that the war caused among the city's immigrant community, particularly among the Irish, lasted throughout the war. (Indeed, the city of Buffalo supported General McClellan's presidential candidacy in 1864 and his support for reconciliation with the South.) Never resolved, it came to play a critical role in the rise of Irish nationalism that occurred in Buffalo immediately after the war was over, in the form of the Fenian movement.

Fenianism, an Irish nationalist movement whose primary goal was to capture Canada and hole it hostage until England surrendered Ireland, was an outgrowth of the Irish experience in the ghettos of American cities as much as it was a result of homespun, indigenous Irish nationalism. For the Irish, festering in the frustrating difficulties of adjusting to their new surroundings, nationalism, as much as Catholicism, provided an outlet, a means to forget about America and concentrate instead on a homeland that was no longer theirs. Fenianism, however, like the petty announcements about home that appeared regularly in the *Catholic Sentinel*, kept alive faith in the idea that Ireland was still the home to which the Irish of America would someday return. Unlike the hundreds of local Irish who celebrated St. Patrick's Day by praying for Irish freedom and by singing the Soldier's Song, the Fenians were willing to die for their cause. To invade Canada and fight the British on that alien shore was to them an act of heroism, not stupidity.

Although it began in Ireland in the late 1840s, Fenianism gathered strength and became a movement to reckon with only as a result of the phenomenal response to it by Irish city dwellers. By the early 1850s there were Fenian circles in all of the large cities along the eastern seaboard, complete with Fenian sisterhoods and Fenian sanitary commissions, which made bandages for the invading army of Irish raiders. Although Fenianism originally fed on the frustration, disappointment, and anger of America's urben Irish, it was exacerbated by their perennial hatred of the British, which in America was directed at the Protestant urban elite. A common belief within Buffalo's Irish community was that the British—and therefore by extension the city's Protestants—had used, if not caused, the potato famine of the 1840s as a way of reducing the population of Ireland through starvation. To this was added the belief that the British had made the hunger worse by permitting the export of Irish meat and grain at a time when the Irish peasants were themselves starving to death. Accusing Britain of tyranny and murder, and believing that local Protestants would not hesitate to do the same, Irish hatred of Britain and Protestant America boiled over into the militant Irish nationalism of Fenianism.

To this was added the bitterness and frustration of the war experience. Not only had the Irish served in disproportionate numbers, but they had done so in an effort whose most tangible result, that of emancipation, offered Irish-Americans nothing but the promise of competition from cheaper labor. To most of America's urban Irish, first abolitionism and then the war on slavery were part of a hypocritical plot by the wealthy against the immigrant workers. In reporting the meager settlements that a New Hampshire shoe manufacturer had made with his workers several years prior to the war, the *Catholic Sentinel* wryly commented: "Great country where the last cent is ground out of poor workmen in order that Eastern aristocrats may move in wealth." What irked this Irish Catholic paper still more was the belief that these "aristocrats will supply Abolitionists and fanatical preachers with money to carry on the war against slavery. Out with the hypocrisy of New England that would rob honest industry to lavish thousands upon anti-slavery humbugs."

Thus, when thousands upon thousands of Irish-American men were mustered out of the Union army with no work, no prospects, and nothing to show for their years of thankless sacrifice, the Fenian movement at least offered them an opportunity to use their newly-acquired soldiering skills, while providing a focus of cathartic expression for both their disappointments and their primal love of their mother country. These sentiments are clearly apparent in one of the more popular Fenian songs:

We are the Fenian Brotherhood skilled in the art of war
And we're going to fight for Ireland, the land that we adore.
Many battles we have won along with the boys in blue
And we'll go and capture Canada, for we've nothing else to do.

Thus, the stage was set for the Fenian invasion of Canada.

Because of its location, as well as the strength of the local Fenian brotherhood, Buffalo was chosen as the launching place for the invasion of Canada. For several weeks prior to the secretly planned invasion of June 2, 1866, hundreds of Fenian brethren, including contingents from virtually every city in the northern United States, descended on

Buffalo. By the end of June over one thousand of them were billeted in homes, taverns, and boarding houses in Irish South Buffalo. Rumors spread of hidden arms supplies secretly cached under taverns, stores, and homes. Even St. Bridget's Church, it was said, was being used as a hiding place for ammunition. While this caused some concern for the local establishment—the newspapers were filled with items referring to the fact that "the groggeries and rum shops were thronged" in South Buffalo, and that "throughout the worst quarters of the city the presence of a new element is unmistakable"—the public stood benignly by. They were even slightly amused, as well as pleased, by the adventure (anti-British sentiments in Buffalo were still strong almost thirty years after the *Caroline* affair), as over one thousand Fenian soldiers pushed off in boats across the narrow Niagara River into Canada. Although a United States Army vessel patrolled the river, threatening to blockade the invasion, no action was taken and the Fenian soldiers were permitted to land in Canada. After several days of early victories, however, the tattered Fenian Army was quickly trounced by Canadian volunteers. The affair was over as quickly as it had begun. And although the local newspapers closely followed the trial of the Fenian soldiers in Canada, Fenianism was quickly forgotten. While Irish nationalism, reinforced by the intense nature of urban Catholicism, remained always strong, it lost its militant fervor in the years after the Fenian invasion.

With Bishop Timon as their leader, ethnic and religious solidarity remained the primary, molding characteristic of Buffalo's Irish community long after the Fenian debacle. Indeed, in many critical ways Timon embodied the essence of Irishness in the city. At times parochial and paranoid, Timon concentrated on the solidification of his own Irish, working-class community. At other times brazen and self-confident, he fearlessly challenged the haughty supremacy of the city's Protestant elite. Nothing embodied this latter quality more than Timon's long and secretly nurtured plan to build a cathedral in Buffalo.

Timon began to plan his cathedral shortly after his arrival in Buffalo. His ideas, however, remained a secret. While he made no secrets of his extensive travels—in 1850–51 Timon travelled throughout Europe and Mexico—they did not know that the primary purpose of his travels was to raise funds for the construction of a cathedral. Word eventually did leak out, corroborating people's suspicions, but then it remained unknown as to where Timon would locate his church. Given his prior predilections, it was generally felt that he would build in the First Ward.

Timon, however, had other ideas. Unbeknownst to all but a handful of advisors, Timon had in fact selected a site nowhere near either the First Ward or the German East Side. Instead he had chosen the most visible and centrally located piece of real estate in the city, on Church Street right between the two oldest Protestant churches in Buffalo. Over a two-year period, Timon had secretly assembled plots of land in this most prominent and prestigous section of downtown with the specific yet unstated ambition of erecting thereon a massive Roman Catholic cathedral.

When in 1852 Timon's real estate activities became known, there was a last-minute effort within the Protestant community to buy back the land. It was too late, however, and in 1852 the cornerstone of St. Joseph's Cathedral was laid. Two years later the cathedral was completed.

At highly publicized and dramatic opening celebrations, which drew Catholic prelates from all over the country to Buffalo, Bishop Timon congratulated himself and his flock for their success in America. In a sermon filled with religious homily, Timon proudlly told his parishioners that "you are no longer strangers and foreigners in this land but fellow citizens [not, notice, with the rest of Buffalo but rather] with the saints."

The WASP community had different ideas, for in this very year, when the cathedral, whose enormous facade and tall steeple dominated the cityscape, was completed, WASP reaction to Catholicism was reaching its militant zenith.

CHAPTER 5

Buffalo's WASPs Respond to Change

Despite their rapidly increasing numbers and the vociferousness with which Bishop Timon called attention to them, Buffalo's Catholics remained largely isolated from and ignored by the city's Protestant establishment. Separated by their religion, ethnicity, social class, and even geography, the Germans (both Catholic & Protestant) and Irish posed very little actual threat to the continued white Anglo-Saxon Protestant domination of all aspects of life in mid-nineteenth century Buffalo.

Protestants were everywhere. There were Protestant laborers, skilled workers, tradesmen, artists, artisans, architects, businessmen, policemen, and firemen. They dominated the city's economic life, monopolized the legal and medical professions, controlled the city's public school system, and ran the city's government.

Buffalo's medical profession was restricted to all but a few highly educated, relatively affluent young men. While highly exclusive, the city's class of physicians prided itself on its commitment not only to good works but also to excellence in medical research. Since the first days of its settlement, there had been physicians in Buffalo. The first generation of them however, all educated in the East, found the appeal of money-making on the urban frontier far more alluring than the practice of medicine. The city's first physicians, it seems, were particularly attracted to real estate and finance. Ebenezer Johnson, M.D., was senior partner in the banking firm of Johnson and Hodge at the time that he became Buffalo's first mayor. Josiah Trowbridge was another eastern-trained physician who found his fortune in real estate rather than medicine and, like Johnson before him, went on to become one of the city's early mayors. For these men medicine was far more an avocation than a vocation.

Not all of the city's physicians were good in business. Yet so tempting was the expansionist climate of investment that many people— even those with no feel for speculation—got involved. One of these was Dr. Bryant Burwell. Like so many people in Buffalo, Burwell's real estate investments were wiped out during the debacle of the late 1830s. The income from his medical practice (Burwell specialized in obstetrics) was barely enough for him to support his widower's existence. He was, he felt, able to identify with the rest of the city's poor. Confiding to his diary, he wrote in early 1841: "People are getting very poor here . . . many are suffering for fuel and food. I wish I was rich so that I might find them employment." Later in the year, upon hearing of the death of his brother, a farmer, Burwell wrote: "I believe that he has at least left his children some property so that they will not be beggars as my children would were I to die now." In his last diary entry in December 1841, Dr. Burwell noted ruefully: "Last winter at this time we had fifteen banks in operation in Buffalo. The best of the lot failed about four weeks ago. What will be the result I know not. . . . One thing will necessarily follow: The banks are gone and therefore money will be difficult to obtain. Some of our merchants will fail. But perhaps [he concluded philosophically] all will be better for it. I observe that affliction generally improves human character."

As a result of economic circumstances, then, Buffalo's physicians were forced to concentrate more on medicine than on real estate, and by the middle of the 1840s there began to emerge a regular and well-organized medical profession. There was now a medical college (affiliated, ironically, with Timon's Sisters of Charity Hospital, a fact that irked several of the city's Protestant ministers), a county medical society, and even a medical journal.

Buffalo's physicians were concerned primarily with their own private practices. While patients would sometimes visit the doctor in his office, it was far more customary for the physician to make house calls. Dr. Burwell spent the better part of his working day either walking or riding on horseback, making the rounds of his patients: "This has been a very busy day with me. I have visited many patients in Buffalo and some in Black Rock [a neighboring community north of the city] and I have been to see Mrs. John Ketchum of Hamshill, fourteen miles from here." Burwell took pride and satisfaction in his work, and when the day was done he was able to write: "I have been useful to all, injurious to none and am weary—yet cheerful."

In addition to their own practices, Buffalo's physicians rotated working for the city in the six health districts and in the penitentiary, the orphanage, the almshouse, and the county poor house. And, if the pages of the *Medical Journal* are an adequate guide to the concerns and issues of the contemporary physician, Buffalo doctors had to keep abreast of a wide range of medical developments. The *Medical Journal* contained reviews of books and long articles on a wide variety of medical research, much of it written by members of the local medical establishment. There were articles on epilepsy, croup, fetal circulation, veneral diseases, and pleurisy, plus a great deal of literature on such epidemiological phenomena as typhoid and, most particularly, cholera.

Cholera, as we have already seen, was a brutal and frightening affliction in the mid-nineteenth century city, and the citizenry in general and the medical profession in particular lavished a great deal of time and energy in trying, if not to cure it, at least to understand it. There were monthly articles on the disease, learned discussions and letters on the latest and best techniques for dealing with it, comparative studies of the cholera in other cities, and extensive data on the havoc that the disease wrought throughout the world. In an effort to better deal with it, the city's medical profession became experts on epidemiology, studying the content of the lead in the city's water pipes, urging a system of registration for the sick, advocating more effective treatment and disposal of the city's waste products, and constantly urging the citizenry to be more hygienic in its personal care. Behind their understanding of the cholera was a frankly admitted, nonapologetic recognition that cholera affected the poor far more cruelly than it did the better off. An article in the *Medical Journal* in September 1855, after the cholera season had finally begun to pass, pointed out that:

> Our city presents the anomaly of being, at once, the healthiest and the most sickly of any American town. [This was an exaggeration. Buffalo, with its relatively cool summertime climate, was not nearly as affected by cholera as cities with hotter, more humid summers.] The larger mass—nearly the whole of the American population— live in a security as to life and health which can hardly find a parallel in any other place of its size. But let anyone turn to the dirty, unpaved and crooked streets in which our foreign population dwell and he will wonder that so many survive. A calculation of the number of deaths upon the unpaved streets would show how much dryness and dampness have to do with health.

The medical professionals' concern for public health led them to investigate conditions in the Erie County Poor House in 1855. In a report that was printed in both the Buffalo *Medical Journal* and the *Commercial Advertiser*, the delegation of physicians warned their readers that "however incredible our story may appear, it is but too truthful." Much to their shock and amazement (had they really no idea beforehand?), they reported that there were "more than three hundred paupers kept in a foul, ill-ventilated building, on a diet which will just keep the wheels of life in motion." According to their report, more people died in the poor house from cholera that year than in the entire city of Buffalo.

The diet, they charged, was tragically insufficient:

> During three or four months of winter and spring no vegetables were given out. This was owing to the high price of potatoes, but no substitutes such as beets, carrots or turnips were provided. Since the appearance of cholera, there have been no vegetables of any kind. As a consequence of this . . . there has been one death from scurvy, a disease hardly ever known except in ships on long voyages.

Deeply offended and outraged that such horrifying conditions existed— worse, they said, than "anything which Dickens ever described in Botheboy's Hall"—this delegation of visiting physicians demanded that the management of the county poor house be changed immediately.

In addition to their concerns with public health, the medical community of Buffalo did their best to keep current with the state of medical science. They were quite interested in psychosomatic causes of illnes, particularly the relationship of anxiety to stomach disorders, headaches, and circulatory problems. They reported extensively on European investigations of hysteria, an affliction they believed affected women far more than men. Because of the former's "greater docility, yielding and impressible character, traits which are more apt to produce mental disturbances," hysteria was to them a female disease.

This was one of the reasons the faculty of the College of Medicine offered for their refusal to admit women into their program. Their position reveals a great deal about the established and accepted view of women in contemporary Buffalo life. They couched their position in standard views of male superiority, particularly popular notions concerning female weaknesses that would, these male physicians believed, prevent them from functioning as physicians. Dr. Hamilton, a faculty member of the medical college, wrote that

> This movement involves some considerations of deep interest, not only to the profession, but to the great world of humanity; and at

the risk of speaking some disagreeable truths, we shall inquire into their meaning and bearing. The idea of inequality in the sexes, and of positive superiority in the male, is written in every part of God's works, and words. This condition is distinctly and frequently expressed in Holy Writ; and is as plainly enunciated in the physical conformation, and the recorded history of the two sexes.

Added to this were the inherent physical and emotional characteristics that made it unthinkable that women should become physicians:

The cool head, the steady nerve, the sinewy muscle, the facile hand, the power of endurance under great fatigue and loss of sleep without becoming nervous, are the *physical* peculiarities in which woman is lacking. Calmness in danger, with readiness to act boldly and quickly in emergencies, the power to reason rapidly and correctly under distracting influences, the will and mental courage to assume responsibilities unpleasant and injurious to the reputation, are *mental* qualities which she also needs; while the faculty of perception which she possesses in great perfection, will but place before her in the most vivid light the dangers that beset her patient, without the power to analyze, and reason order out of the chaos of perceptions, which crowd and confuse her brain.

What pseudoscientific notions of the physical and emotional differences between men and women did for sexism, phrenology did for racism. As a result of extensive measurements of the crania of different racial groups in Buffalo, a writer for the Buffalo *Medical Journal* reported that the "Teutonic races" had the highest "cranial capacity," with ninety-two cubic inches. Second were the Celts with eighty-seven; then came the American Indians with eighty-four. The smallest brain size was reported to be the Negro's with a cranial size of eighty-three cubic inches. The *Journal* maintained that while "the cranial capacity of the Negro is only nine inches less than the Teuton and therefore does not especially mark him for servitude, the automatic facts of difference should have some influence in modifying our support of the race." While this writer stopped short of recommending the perpetual enslavement of blacks, it was clear that he drew considerable comfort from, and probably a fair amount of support for, his notion that modern science justified and fairly reinforced the discriminatory practices of the age. Concluding his report on his local phrenological investigations, this physician confidently noted that "it is impossible for eighty-three inches of Negroid cerebral matter to compete with ninety-two of Teutonic brain."

Thus concerned with public health and with scientific research (however specious this research sometimes was), the medical profession of mid-nineteenth century Buffalo, dominated by a New England-educated WASP elite, regarded itself as a special and different and somehow chosen group of men, with a unique responsibility to guard the health and the general medical welfare of the whole community, and set apart from the more humdrum, routine pursuits of business which occupied the greater proportion of men of their social set. In countless homiletic articles and graduation addresses and messages to the medical students, many of them delivered by the city's leading Protestant divines as well as by the medical faculty, the young physicians of Buffalo were reminded of their special and unique role in the city. "If you desire the gaudy trappings of wealth, if you sigh for the day when you shall possess lands and houses; if you long to look upon large chests of precious gold," Fredrick Hamilton, dean of the medical school, told the graduates in 1854, "well then turn back. Tear up those useless parchments and with brave heart begin again." In an address to the following year's graduating class, the city's leading Presbyterian divine, John Church Lord, struck a similar chord. His speech, entitled "On Medical Science and Materialism," urged the young doctors to "wait for success in the paths of honor and probity; for this success [unlike what other he did not say] will be enduring and accompanied by a good conscience toward God and man."

Also WASPs, and also playing a critical role in the affairs of Buffalo, were the city's lawyers. In the mid-1850s there were over 120 lawyers in Buffalo, by far the single largest professional group in the city. Yet despite their numbers and the social esteem that they clearly enjoyed, lawyers were not the preeminent urban power brokers that they came to be later in the century. Most of their work involved small transactions: suits for personal damages; libels; commercial and contract cases; and real estate infractions involving easements, abutments, and mortgages. The more critical legal matters, those cases involving railroad business, incorporations, mergers, and other high-priced, high-stakes economic dealings, were handled far more regularly by the legal fraternities in New York City and Albany. Lawyers did not even dominate local politics in mid-nineteenth century Buffalo. While three of the four people who served the city as mayor during the 1850s were lawyers (the fourth was a physician), most of the ward-based politicians in Buffalo were not professional people at all, but rather small-scale neighborhood businessmen.

Nor did the bankers form a dominant elite in pre–Civil War Buffalo. Indeed, banking was an extremely unstable, unpredictable business during these years, offering the bankers little power, position, or security. The entire, albeit shaky, financial underpinnings of the city were destroyed by the panic of 1837. As a result, it was quite some time before banks and banking were reestablished. In 1840 three new banks were formed, only to be "suspended" two years later. In 1844 six new banks were formed. These banking houses, bearing such names as Oliver Lee's Bank, White's Bank, and Hollister's Bank, were small, private banks with limited capital available. And while the 1850s did see the formation of several substantial banks with far greater capitalization, another crisis, the panic of 1857, followed by the financially unstable years of the Civil War, did much to retard the development of more financially sophisticated and politically powerful banking institutions.

While Buffalo's WASP physicians, presumably motivated by nobler callings, professed to turn their backs on material rewards, another group of men consciously and purposefully engaged in the pursuit of wealth. In the process they became extremely successful businessmen, dominating the economic life of the city. The members of the business elite of mid-nineteenth century Buffalo had much in common. Most had been born in either rural New England or central New York in the late eighteenth or early nineteenth centuries. Raised in the country, they had come to Buffalo in the 1820s and 1830s, either because they had family connections here or simply because Buffalo was a much touted, rapidly growing frontier community. The most successful businessmen also had in common the fact that although they started modestly, in one branch of trade, each quickly expanded his operations so as to dominate a wide range of activities connected with that particular trade. Sheldon Thompson, for example, started in the forwarding business, acting as a middleman, receiving produce from the Midwest and shipping to dealers in the East. It was simply a question of time before his concerns with delivery and shipments led him to acquire and to operate a fleet of steam-powered lake boats and canal boats. Then, as a result of his activities in the midwestern grain states, Thompson had become, by the end of the 1840s, one of the largest holders of undeveloped land in Ohio, Wisconsin, and Indiana.

George Tift, a descendent not of old stock New Englanders, but rather of Protestant immigrants from Alsace-Lorraine, started life on a farm in Rhode Island. When his older brother inherited it, however, Tift moved to Orleans County in New York, where he worked on, and gradually acquired, a farm which he turned into grain fields. The grain business led him to Indiana in 1841, where he began to make extensive contacts with Buffalo grain merchants. More intrigued with processing than with growing, Tift moved to Buffalo in 1842 and went into the milling business. Within a year he had bought out a lake and canal boat transportation company that plied the water route between New York City and Michigan.

Tift, like the other businessmen, was restless, turning over his enterprises almost immediately upon developing them. By 1844 he had sold his boat company, and with the receipts formed a commission business. By the end of that year he had also sold this business, and with three partners acquired four grain mills. In the meantime, Tift had lent considerable sums of money to Buffalo speculators eager to develop the coal fields of western Pennsylvania. When these men defaulted during the panic of 1857, Tift took possession of these lands himself. While there had been some discussion about the possibility of using Pennsylvania coal to smelt Lake Superior iron, the project had never been undertaken until Tift built two blast furnaces in Pennsylvania and bought a fleet of lake steamers to bring in the iron from the shores of Lake Superior. By 1860, as a result of these activities, Tift had become president of the Southern Tier Railroad, the first rail link between Buffalo and the coal fields of Pennsylvania, and of the Buffalo Engine Works which, with its several hundred employees, had overnight become one of the largest foundries in the country. Tift, Thompson, and all of the other successful businessmen-merchants of the middle nineteenth century dominated the local banking scene as bank presidents or as bank directors. The hands of a few successful businessmen were coming to exert substantial power and control.

Some men, like Merwin S. Hawley, chose to drop out of business altogether. Although he became enormously successful in Buffalo as a grain merchant, Merwin Hawley never liked the city. He had come reluctantly in 1840—via Rochester, and before that rural Western New York—without his pregnant wife, who chose to stay in Rochester until he called for her. While Merwin was able to make several trips back home during his first year in Buffalo, he missed his wife terribly, writing her long, plaintive love letters, urging her to join him, but understanding her reluctance to do so. Meanwhile, he wrote to her of Buffalo in tones that indicate that while pleased with his growing business success, Hawley felt lost and unhappy in the city itself. His letters are filled with critical stories of back-biting society—he mockingly told his wife that one "Harry Millard got married here to a public servant and was so scoffed at he was glad to leave." He despaired of the weather: "We have had much slippery walking. L.F. Tiffany slipped down the last of December and broke his thigh bone.

He was getting along very well but died very suddenly about two weeks ago. Our neighbor, Mr. Kingsley, also slipped down and broke his thigh bone some little time ago." Another letter included this entry: "The coldest night we have had occurred last Friday night. Spaulding Exchange [a large business block] burned down and Erie Hall and all down to Hibbard's Clothing store. Lloyd Street to Commercial Street all burned to ashes."

In 1842 the Hawleys' infant daughter died. Hawley was deeply affected by this tragedy and wrote movingly about it over thirty years later in a handwritten autobiography:

> How well do I remember and would never forget, while having her in my arms and expecting the departure of her innocent spirit, watching if possible to see some manifestation of the passing of a soul so pure and tender [Hawley had crossed out "gentle"] from its earthly tenement to its eternal paradise. But she ceased to breathe so gently that the precise moment could not be distinguished.

This experience tragically changed Hawley's life. Later that year, at a Presbyterian revival in Rochester (Hawley never joined a Buffalo church), he "accepted Jesus and rejoiced in his pardoning love." Silently, he and his wife vowed not to have another child.

Following the death of their daughter, Mrs. Hawley (had she thought Buffalo not a good place to raise her child?) moved to Buffalo. Even then, however, Hawley, unlike the others of his class, did not buy a home, but chose rather to live in rented rooms. He became increasingly involved in his grain business. He added a grain elevator to his forwarding and commission trade and, following the panic of 1857, agreed (according to his diary, he was under considerable pressure) to assume the presidency of the failing International Bank. Yet, despite his active and apparently successful business career, Hawley remained distinctly removed from the community life of Buffalo. His name appears nowhere as one of the citizens involved in the wide range of community activities—the growing number of clubs, associations, charities, and libraries—that characterized the increasingly organized community life of the city. Indeed, in dozens of letters and in over seventy pages of his handwritten autobiography, there are virtually no references to his life in the city of Buffalo. While he did write extensively about his business, he mentioned no friends and, with the exception of his support for the Buffalo Historical Society (Hawley became increasingly concerned with genealogy during the Civil War years), he made no references to social or community activities. When he did, it was in mocking tones. Hawley went out of his way to criticize local social customs. In his autobiography he wrote: "We had not a relish for the fashionable gayeties and dissipations which to a great extent had supplanted the free and friendly social intercourse that had once been a distinguishing feature of good society." He added a rhyme of his own:

While the busy crowd,
the vain, the parvenue, the proud,
Their jollity prolong;
Though singularity and pride
Be called our choice, we'd here abide
Nor join the giddy throng.

Although Hawley resigned himself to living in Buffalo (he accepted with sadness and great disappointment a failed opportunity to establish a flour business in New York City in the early 1850s), it was with little enthusiasm. He chose consciously, it seems, to remain an outsider in his adopted city. Indeed, he left Buffalo at every available opportunity, travelling extensively throughout the forties and fifties.

Although involved with and highly successful in his grain businesses, Hawley was not a compulsive entrepreneur, and by the end of the 1850s he had begun to consider and even plan for his retirement. Despite the intense pressures of shepherding a bank through the cyclical turns of the post-panic years and the tumult created by Civil War fiscal policy, Hawley and his wife began to take longer and longer vacations, travelling ever further from Buffalo. He enjoyed these vacations immensely, writing: "The variety of the exercise of rambling, travelling and amusement, with the freedom from anxiety and care which I enjoyed produced such favorable effects upon my nervous system [Hawley had complained increasingly about migraine headaches] that I began to consider seriously permanent retirement from my business affairs." Finally, in 1863, in the middle of the enormous wartime economic boom, Hawley sold his grain businesses and resigned his directorship of the bank. From then on he devoted all of his time to travels away from Buffalo and to genealogical research on the origins of the Hawley family.

The Hawleys loved to travel, and in exquisitely written, precise and detailed diary entries, Merwin recorded his observations of the cities, towns, coastline, and rural hinterlands of the northeastern United States and Canada.

Travelling by coach and by railroad, the Hawleys were serious and energetic tourists. Sometimes visiting friends, at other times on their own in hotels, they toured all of the major cities on the East Coast. Their favorite was New York City and they returned there several times during the fifties and sixties, staying at the luxurious Madison Square Hotel or with their friends, the Johnsons, who lived in Brooklyn. On one visit there, the Johnsons took their guests by coach to Coney Island to go swimming. Hawley described the event with humor and excitement: "The drive was delightful and without delay the grotesque garb was donned by us all, when Mrs. Johnson gallantly led Mrs. Hawley into the gently sloping surf at intervals rolled over their heads and gave her an introduction to His Majesty, Old Neptune." After their swim, Hawley informs us, "the Johnsons' hospitality was further manifested by hosting us to that rare and unique feast, a clambake, after which, on the edge of the evening, with musical hearts, we drove to our lodgings in the city." From here they went by train to New England, stopping at Nantucket on the way to Mt. Mansfield, Vermont. The Hawleys, it can be gathered, loved the shore and Merwin here, as in other passages in his autobiography, described it affectionately: "The pleasant sands from the native trees in that quiet old city and the gentle but delicious breezes from the Sea were so attractive that we remained over the day and over Sunday, enjoying that magnificent Sea shore." It was early autumn, a time of year when they liked to travel to New England, particularly Vermont: "The trees now wore their most gorgeous and most variegated colors and the fields their richest green; the apple trees were overloaded with choicest fruit; pears, plums and grapes were super abundant and the chestnut trees were prolific beyond all former examples. The hills and valleys of Vermont were never more beautiful than in the soft autumnal atmosphere." On the way back to Buffalo they stopped at Cooperstown, New York: "In this rural town of refinement and wealth, we sojourned ten days, enjoying the health-inspiring atmosphere from the hills, made classic by Cooper's romantic pen, and from the fine country surroundings and the unsurpassed drives and rambles."

Thus, willing to travel despite what others may well have considered the press of business, and to retire well before being forced to by the misfortunes of health or the economy, Merwin Hawley was something of an anomaly at a time when unremitting enterprise had become a cardinal principle of American urban life. And yet despite this somewhat singular behavior, Merwin Hawley remained unabashedly conventional in the ideals that he passed on to his children. One niece in Iowa wrote to him often, requesting his permission to leave the farm where she worked as a piano teacher in order to come to Buffalo. "I am anxious to go east and see something of the world," she wrote. "I am shut up here where there is no chance to improve my manners except what common sense teaches me. Would that I could see more of good society." But Hawley, while indulgent of his own discontent, offered nothing but homilies to his sad and lonely niece. He constantly reminded her of her duties and responsibilities and her obligation to stay where she was. "It is gratifying to me," he sermonized, "to know that you are fulfilling your obligations and performing your duties to your father. You must stay until you are no longer needed there. I am pleased especially that your kind and genial disposition and correct ladylike deportment ensure you the affectionate regards of many friends." Hawley's own ability to transcend the expectations for men of his social position in no way made him more tolerant of these same traits when exhibited by other members of his family.

This somewhat hypocritical intolerance also marked the thinking of Bryant Burwell, another individualistic, vaguely iconoclastic member of Buffalo's mid-century WASP gentry. Like most of the city's WASP population, Burwell was born in central New York and moved to Buffalo as a young man in the years following the War of 1812. After going east for a medical education, Burwell returned to Buffalo in the early thirties, where he opened his own practice.

In 1838 his wife died, and Dr. Burwell fell into a period of sadness and depression that lasted for at least six years. These experiences, however, increased the subtlety and precision of his world views and gave his diaries a perceptive, jaded, and critical quality. His vision both of his personal life and of the life of his community is pervaded with darkness and depression.

Burwell's perennial sadness was heightened by the seemingly endless procession of deaths in his family. Even at a time of high mortality rates, the tragedies of the Burwell family seem unusual. Within a five year period, Burwell witnessed the deaths of his wife, his son, a brother, and two sisters. Burwell wondered when it would end: "Will any brighter day ever dawn on the darkness which continues to enshroud me?" Later on, in 1844, with macabre merriment he wrote: "Heigh ho. Whether or not I shall ever come back to life again is extremely doubtful . . ." He was always depressed and personally unfulfilled. In January 1842 he wrote: "I am in a cramped and confined position in life—not one of quiet but of torpor. I feel that I am not what I should be nor indeed what I might be." He was very conscious of time and purposefully marked its passage. In January 1843 he wrote: "One month of the present year is now gone. Thus time is ever rolling on. I thought I could appreciate more

fully than I do the immense importance of each moment as it flies."
A year later the sentiment was similar: "And with this night ends
the first month of the year. How fast our moments fly. How soon
our days will end. . . . As usual I am groping my way through life."

Burwell tried to purge himself of his unhappiness by working very
long hours, both in his office and travelling throughout the city and
surrounding countryside treating his patients. On a Sunday night in
June 1844 he wrote: "Since five o'clock this morning I have been
continuously engaged among the sick. All are doing well." Often he
was thankful merely to keep his patients alive: "Besides the old man,
none of my patients have died during the past month." Burwell drew
strength and satisfaction from his work and clearly saw it as an
alternative to his otherwise miserable and depressing existence. "I am
doing much for others and my own happiness is greatly augmented
by adding to the happiness and usefulness of all around me. I live
no longer for pleasure. Rather I ask not the question of how much
I am enjoying life but rather how much can I bestow on others?"
Despite his own sadness, he was not mean-spirited and seemed to
wish well on the rest of his community. At the end of a particularly
long and arduous day he wrote in his diary: "The day has been hot,
dry and sultry. The night is still: not a breath of wind in motion.
The sky is almost starless. Silence is over the city. Thousands are
enjoying their sleep. May their dreams be happy and their sleep
refreshing."

Even the marriage of his youngest daughter Julia failed to cheer
him. Rather, it seemed to add to his sense of loss. "Death and
matrimony, almost alike, distance my family and separate me from
them. The world is cheerful and happy—at least so it seems to a
casual observer."

Then, in early 1844, Burwell met Mary Cleary, and for the first
time since his wife's death his mood began to improve. He was a
generous and sensitive suitor, pleased "to see all the little things
scattered around her rooms that I have given her," and hurt and
proud when she went without him on a six-week trip to New York
City. He persisted, gently and carefully, cajoling this reluctant widow
to accept his marriage proposal. Appealing to her on practical grounds,
he urged her to consider the benefits of marriage: "In your present
position in life and society, you are fully aware, Mrs. Cleary [does
his use of her surname imply a more threatening tone?] you cannot
act with that freedom and independence you could if shielded by the
love and protection of a husband." He proceeded to point out to her
that as a woman in contemporary society "every act of yours will

be severely scrutinized and the criticism of the world is not always just and generous." Finally, after almost nine months of intermittent courtship, Burwell did in fact convince her, and in February 1845 they were married.

Burwell now quickly shed his mantle of sadness, becoming suddenly extroverted, very social, and involved in the affairs of the day. His diary, no longer wallowing in melancholy, now contained references to city elections, the Oregon issue, lectures and concerts, and other public events. With a far more active social life, Burwell began to withdraw from his medical practice, bringing in his recently graduated son to continue where he was leaving off. Also, following his marriage, Bryant Burwell became suddenly pontificating, stuffy, self-righteous, and eminently bourgeois. In a letter to his bachelor son George, he wrote in terms that had never before appeared in his diary or his letters: "Matrimony is the great upholder of society. It is the chief protection against almost every temptation to err; it is the only true foundation and security for our happiness. Without it society would go into chaos and religion would be banished from the earth." To his youngest daughter Anna, who since her mother's death was being raised by her sister Esther in Rochester, Burwell wrote these stultifying homilies:

> How do you get along with your music? Do you practise it, faithfully, patiently and improvingly? I hope so. Do not neglect your work. Do everything neat and nice. Keep your room, your clothes and your hands clean. Be attentive to all things. Help everyone. Take care of your Grandma—do not plague your Grandpa. Never let a cross or saucy word escape from your lips. Be careful of fires. Do not go out and take cold. Read all your lessons, do all your work, practise your music and dancing. Go to bed early and rise early. I hope I shall get a good account of your conduct when I return. Everything good or bad that you do or say must be told to me. If you behave well I shall be happy. If not, I shall be unhappy indeed. It is late. I cannot write more. Good night—one kiss—there—good night. Every your affectionate father, Bryant Burwell.

While Burwell may well have been able to dominate the behaviour of his daughter, and while other members of the Protestant establishment may well have done the same with the city's banks, its legal and medical professions, and its public and charitable institutions, they were somehow not as comfortable and secure as their positions of power and influence would indicate. For increasingly throughout the 1850s a feeling was emerging that things were in fact getting out of control. Writing home after a long period of absence, a former resident of the city wrote to his wife in Albany: "Yesterday forenoon I went down Main Street and did not see a person I knew except an old beggar who used to bother me twenty years ago. I came back feeling sad that so few years had made me such a stranger."

The 1840s and 1850s were times of "riots and mobs and crimes which," according to the *Commercial Advertiser*, "give fearful foreboding." The increase of crime, drunkenness, and poverty that was suddenly creeping out from the city's ethnic ghettoes, and the sudden demand for women's rights ("a plot that will strike a blow at the peace and virtue of society by unfitting women for the sphere for which she was made"), were extremely unsettling and threatening phenomena that would have been easier to cope with and understand had the solutions been simple.

Behavior too, or at least the WASP establishment's view of it, was changing. Despite the twenty-five Protestant churches which the *Commercial Advertiser* noted confidently "stand as beacon lights to warn of the fearful danger to which men are exposed" (they mentioned no Catholic churches), a subsequent issue of the same newspaper indicated that beneath the air of apparent self-satisfaction lay a deeper sense that things were somehow not right. Citing the increase in crime in Buffalo, particularly murder, the *Commercial Advertiser* wrote: "Life is cheaper than it was a quarter of a century since." But it was more than crime that worried them. They felt that "the sad laxity of morals in business, politics and society in general is such that it needs a storm of thunder and lightening—whirlwinds sweeping as a tornado in the tropics—to purify the air and lighten the face of the sky." These changes were sometimes blamed on the instability of the economy—the newspaper noted that the greatest number of arrests were made in December, when the canal was closed, and the fewest in July, the peak season of commerce—and sometimes on the corrupting influence of urban life in general. One Protestant minister wrote in 1854 that "I sometimes fear that the tendency of city life is to weakness of body and soul."

Also, while the rapid increase of German and Irish Catholic population had not jeopardized their actual control of the fortunes of the city, the rise of immigration in general and of Catholicism in particular did pose a serious threat to the WASP notion of good behavior and citizenship. Convinced that they knew what was best for the people at large ("the masses," as the aristocratic *Commercial Advertiser* referred to the citizenry); motivated by a desire to control, order, and direct the development of their community; and eager to set a good example, Buffalo's WASP elite, like their peers in cities throughout the northeastern United States, sought to solidify and expand their influence in the city. The creation of a public school system was one means that the city's WASP leaders used to perpetuate their values as much as their control.

Increasingly concerned that the system of district schools that had been in existence since the late 1830s was spawning a parochial and fragmented citizenry, the superintendent of schools and the members of the school board—Protestants all—created a central high school in 1854. While there was some discussion about the nature of the programs and curriculum—the school board was particularly concerned that "that miserable apology for books called novels" not be permitted in the central school—the board was far more interested in the broader, ideological social goals of the school. For them the function of the school was clear, and its mandate obvious: "To the central school falls the great work of reducing the great mass of rough and shapeless blocks congregated from every strata of society to a beautiful, symmetrical and systematic structure." Hoping that the central school would be an egalitarian educational melting pot for children from all classes and segments of the community, the superintendent was proud of the school's diversity, and in period reports to the board he noted that among the school's students were the children of attorneys, physicians, "gentlemen," public officials, merchants, ministers, and mechanics.

Temperance was another form of social control. While temperance had been an issue in Buffalo since the early 1830s, by the mid-1850s the Temperance movement had become extremely popular and vociferous. There was a temperance hotel; several temperance groups, including the Temperance Society of the Bar of Erie County and the Sailors and Mechanics Temperance Society; and a monthly temperance newspaper which delighted particularly in printing stories of drink-related accidents and deaths: "Robert Burns, aged eighteen, and his father went to the same bed drunk. The old man lay upon the neck of the young man and strangled him to death." Thus, if opposition to women's rights seemed like a natural way to deal with the problem of domestic upheaval, Prohibition, which according to its supporters would "weed out the hot beds of crime and the sources of woe and poverty," was a facile way of denying the complex and volatile changes that were in fact occurring in mid-nineteenth century Buffalo.

Although not aimed directly at them, it would have been difficult for the city's Irish and German communities not to have interpreted the Temperance movement as a deliberate attack on them. After all, the beer business, with its vast array of malt houses, breweries, and

113

taverns that dotted the East Side, had become a major avenue of social mobility for the city's Germans. And while the city's Irish had little economic stake in the alcohol business, drink certainly played a significant role in the community life of the city's Irish population. Indeed, hardly a St. Patrick's Day passed when Bishop Timon did not urge his parishioners to avoid drink, and not "to be riotous and intemperate" but rather to "act as our forefathers did when Ireland was the Island of the Saints."

When all other explanations for the presumed decline of the community's spiritual and moral life were found wanting, the WASP establishment turned to the more tangible and visible cause of their discontent. And during the 1850s the city's problems were blamed increasingly on the rapidly growing number of Catholic immigrants.

Few of Buffalo's Protestants questioned the 1835 ruling of the Protestant General Assembly, a national Protestant group, that the Roman Catholic church was apostate and therefore not really Christian. These beliefs were echoed by Buffalo's preeminent Protestant divine, John Church Lord: "The pretended miracles and lying wonders of Paganism and Popery have not a single feature in common with the miracles of Christ as revealed in the Bible." These ideas, however, were far more than the subject of harmless theological disputations. Indeed, by the time that John Timon arrived in Buffalo as the archbishop of Western New York, these notions—be they interpreted as anti-Catholicism or Protestant chauvinism—had come to provide the rationale for the creation of a deeply divided society in which religion, more than ethnicity, had become the determining factor.

Not only had Protestantism (or, depending on one's point of view, anti-Catholicism) become engrained in the city's social and educational structure, but much of the intellectual current of the time was deeply imbued with a hatred and fear of the Catholic religion. For had not their ancestors fled England in order to escape an Anglican church increasingly corrupted by the poisons of popery? Was Buffalo, for so long a frontier bastion of New England Protestantism, now suddenly on the edge of that same precipice? Reverend Lord spoke to the converted when he warned: "It is high time for the Protestant minister to blow the trumpet of alarm. Let the citizens of the Republic see to it that the swarm of locusts are stayed in their course; for if once in possession of power, they will shadow at noon day the sun of our liberties with clouds of thick darkness."

Anti-Catholicism, then, was ideologically rooted as much as it was based on xenophobia and ethnic prejudice. For a man like the Reverend Dr. John Church Lord, who with John Winthrop and Jonathan

Edwards shared a vision of America as a "Redeemer Nation," Catholicism was an ideological anathema. With its rigid and mysterious doctrines, its arcane and authoritarian priesthood, and its ritualistic practices, Catholicism represented a threat not only to Protestantism but, more importantly, to Americanism. Reverend Lord, in an open letter to the city's Catholics, wrote, telling them that Catholic priests "seek to isolate you in the community as a separate class, to keep you in ignorance. . . . They treat you like slaves rather than as freemen and hope God will give you wisdom, grace and courage to cast off this yoke." It was this passionate belief that the promise of America depended on the free, unfettered development of the mind that, as much as ethnic and religious bigotry, motivated this influential minister.

Anti-Catholicism also characterized the Sabbatarian movement, which became significant in Buffalo only after the arrival and settlement of the Germans. It was not until it became apparent that Sunday picnics were an intrinsic aspect of German urban culture that the Sabbatarian movement to gather strength among the city's Protestant establishment. Indeed, throughout the 1850s, no German picnic was ever enjoyed without, as the German-language newspaper *Der Weltburger* put it, "the fear that a gang of American rowdies would disturb the feast."

While there is no record of an attack ever having taken place, and while no churches or convents were ever burned or similarly desecrated in Buffalo, there was an undeniable increase in anti-Catholic and anti-foreign activity during the 1850s that made it difficult for the city's Germans and Irish to feel particularly safe, stable, and secure. This was still more true following the rise in the late 1840s and early 1850s of the Know-Nothing party.

Several delegates from Buffalo had attended the first National Convention of the Native American Party in Philadelphia in 1845. By the end of the decade the proposals of that party—such as severe restrictions on immigrtion and a twenty-one-year waiting period prior to becoming a citizen, during which time aliens could not vote or bear arms—had become popular and widely discussed in Buffalo. Indeed, in 1849 there was organized in the city a local chapter of a New York City–based organization known as the Order of the Star Spangled Banner. This society, shrouded in ritualistic clothing, hand-shakes, and symbols, required of its members that their parents and at least one set of their grandparents be native-born, that they worship the American flag, and that they revere George Washington, and met secretly to parade in full-dress revolutionary clothing, marching to the music of a bugle, fife, and drum corps.

Gradually, however, the American party, now increasingly known as the Know-Nothing party, began to have a national significance over and beyond its reactionary views regarding immigration. Increasingly concerned that the two dominant political parties in the nation reflected strictly sectional constituents—the Democrats in the slaveholding South and the newly-emergent Republicans in the anti-slave North—the Know-Nothings, under the leadership of Millard Fillmore, tried to steer a middle course that would avoid conflict by promoting compromise. Locally, however, the party remained primarily a vehicle for anti-foreign sentiment. In Buffalo, their political campaign of 1856 was marked by constant references to a "Pure American common school system," "hostility to all Papal influence in whatever form," "Protection of Protestant Interests," and "Eternal Enmity to all who attempt to carry out the principles of the foreign church."

Even the *Commercial Advertiser,* which tended to avoid the strident xenophobia of the Know-Nothings, consistently resorted to the worst kind of racial and religious pandering. Sometimes this was cloaked in sophisticated terms, and once they quoted Alexander Hamilton to the effect that "hardly anything contributed more to the downfall of Rome than her precipitate communication of the privileges of citizenship to the inhabitants of Italy at large." At other times, for example, when they described the different sections of the city, they made no attempt to hide their venomous bigotry. The First Ward, overwhelmingly Irish, was characterized as composed of the

> verrest tag-rag and bot-tail who ever got drunk at a wake, men who infallibly chose a location in a swamp, and live in a shanty with pigs under the bed and chickens roosting on the headboard. . . . these fellows are hewers of wood and drawers of water . . . simply because they are drunken wretches, without the ambition or the brains to better their conditions.

The Second Ward, predominantly native-born, it characterized as having

> considerable wealth among its citizens, and a world of intelligence and strength of character. It contains the elements which make a city prosperous and powerful, the manufacturers and the skilled workmen, whose brains are too fertile in resources to permit of poverty. In the wards where Americans live, where the skillful inventive mechanic, the tradesman, the professional man, or the wealthy citizen who, beginning in poverty, has built up an estate around him by simple force of intellect—where these men live the people's ticket was successful.

The Fourth, Sixth and Seventh wards it characterized as being

> as little American as the duchy of Hesse Cassel; their population
> speaks a foreign language, reads foreign papers, isolates itself from
> the American element, and, steeped in ignorance of American politics,
> it clings to the bald name of democracy, and claims the right to
> subject the sons of the soil to the despotism of the brute force of
> numbers.

The prejudicial tone of much of the city's Whig and Republican press, plus the selection of Buffalo's own Millard Fillmore as the presidential candidate of the Know-Nothing party in 1856 (oddly, Fillmore was notified of his selection while in Europe, shortly after a private audience with Pope Pius IX), created a great deal of anxiety within Buffalo's immigrant community.

Both on the German East Side and in Irish South Buffalo, large, regional meetings were held to discuss the eventuality of a Fillmore victory. At a convention of Irish-Americans in the First Ward at which Bishop Timon celebrated mass, the delegates, many of whom had come from New York City, Cleveland, and Detroit for the event, seriously and intensely debated a possible mass emigration to Canada in the event of a Fillmore victory. Meanwhile, a group of German Pietists who several years earlier had founded the Ebenezer Community south of Buffalo, decided that this was the time to leave, and in 1857 they moved to Iowa.

Fillmore was a poor choice to head a national ticket. After all, his presidency (Fillmore had succeeded to the presidency when Tyler died in 1850) had been lackluster and undistinguished. To Southerners he was suspect because of his Northern and Whig background, while Northerners distrusted him because of his vacuous position on slavery and his stand on the Fugitive Slave Law. Fillmore had always hated abolitionism and abolitionists. As the unsuccessful candidate for governor of New York State in 1844, he blamed his defeat on "the Abolitionists and the Foreign Catholics in this state." Then as president, he had signed the Fugitive Slave Law of 1850, which said that slaves were no longer freed even when they escaped to the North. While most liberals in the North regarded this legislation as anathema, a blow to the hopes of escaped slaves, there were many Northerners who supported the law. One of them was Reverend Lord. In a sermon in which he urged Fillmore to sign the bill, Lord argued that slavery had divine sanction and should therefore not be interfered with. "The existence of domestic slavery was expressly allowed, sanctioned and regulated by the Supreme Law Giver in that divine economy which God gave the Hebrew State [when in doubt, he blamed the Jews]. Abolitionists," he concluded, "must not assume that we are wiser and better men than the Saviour and the Apostles and that the government of God and the Gospels need revision." Fillmore, apparently convinced by the argument, signed the bill. As a result, many members of his own church, the Unitarian Society of Buffalo, demanded his resignation from the congregation.

The failure of the Know-Nothing party nationally (it received twenty-five percent of the popular vote, and the electoral votes of only Maryland) and locally (Fillmore received only twenty-seven percent of the votes in his home town), indicates not so much a lessening of anti-immigrant and Catholic feeling but rather the fact that the slavery issue now dominated national politics. It was Fillmore's inability to take a persuasive position on that issue rather than his party's strident xenophobia that doomed his chances in the presidential election.

Fillmore's campaign had the ironic effect of strengthening the ethnic and religious consciousness of Buffalo's Irish and German Catholics. Indeed, the bitter attacks on the Irish and the Germans in the mid-1850s were such that Fillmore and the Know-Nothing party had made it impossible for Buffalo's Catholic immigrants to forget who they were and where they came from. Forced to explain themselves, their behavior, and their customs to the outside Protestant world, they became far more aware of their ethnic and religious identity. Mostly it was the Irish who were the target of this campaign of hate. Less often was it the Germans. But always it was the Catholics. It was the *Catholics* who filled the prisons, *Catholics* who were rowdy and drank too much, *Catholics* who corrupted American politics, and *Catholics* who desecrated the Protestant Sabbath. Constantly complaining that "there is scarcely a crime that is not laid at the door of a Catholic," the Catholic press (the *Catholic Sentinel* and the German-language *Der Weltburger*) was constantly on the defensive, parrying these relentless and malicious charges. Indeed, so scurrilous had become the charges of Catholic criminality that the editor of the *Catholic Sentinel* requested, and received, permission to investigate the county prison in an effort to disprove the commonly-held notion that Irish Catholics constituted the majority of the inmates. Following his visit, the editor presented his findings: natives, 496; natives of Ireland, 227; natives of Germany 136. He concluded: "We do not offer these figures for the purpose of insidious comparison, but as an act of justice to a class of citizens assailed with all the venom of

Know-Nothing bigotry and fanaticism. . . . It is deeply to be regretted that so much crime of both native and adopted citizens exists, but we know of no good reason why one class of citizens is pointed out as especially dangerous to life and property when the facts prove that others are more guilty."

The xenophobic attacks of the Sabbatarians produced a similarly healthy and intelligent reaction from within the immigrant community. Like the Temperance movement, Sabbatarianism was rife with anti-Catholicism. One letter to the *Commercial Advertiser* in 1855 mused: "Can you inform me why it is that Catholics love to show themselves in the streets on the Sabbath with bands of music?" The response took the form of an anti-Sabbatarian movement fueled principally by the leaders of the German community. Citing Luther, Calvin, Justin Martyr, and others, Buffalo's anti-Sabbatarians insisted that "Christians should have nothing to do with a superstitious observance of days." Seeking out a religious position that was both Christian and modern, the anti-Sabbatarians, in opposition to the increasing fundamentalism of the city's mid-century Protestant divines, rejected the "Puritanic barbarism" of the Sabbatarians and insisted that that group's concern was not for the physical rest of the "poor laborer," but rather "to make a public show of piety in order to withdraw attention from their own shortcomings." The anti-Sabbatarians, led by the German-born editor of *The Democrat*, Dr. F. C. Brunck, as well as other prominent German citizens, insisted on the right to observe the Sabbath in ways that would both "amuse and instruct."

While thus forging the presumably opposing forces of modernism and ethnic identity, the endless attacks on the city's Catholic immigrants began to create the stirrings of a class consciousness that defied ethnic and religious divisions. Dr. Brunck, one of the most progressive-thinking people in mid-eighteenth-century Buffalo, periodically expressed these views. To him the professed views of the local Know-Nothings masked the true feelings of its proponents. Behind their restrictive immigration policies, Brunck believed, was not so much hatred of foreigners per se, but rather a desire to control the working class. In a bold effort to reach out to the Protestant laborers, Brunck said: "We adopted citizens shall be the first sacrifices to aristocracy. They hate us . . . because we belong to the working classes. But you native born workers they love as little."

Despite Brunck's efforts, it is clear that xenophobia and anti-Catholic prejudice pervaded not only the upper classes, the self-appointed guardians of the Puritan tradition, but also the poorer working classes who, if not as a religious menace then surely as an economic threat, were poised to distrust the Catholic immigrants. Thus, with the approach of civil war the lines separating the different religious, class, and ethnic groups in Buffalo were wide and sharp. As we have already seen, the tensions of war only exacerbated them.

To the Protestant elite, the demands of German and Irish Catholics appeared threatening and aggressive. Their hatred of the King James Bible appeared, and indeed, in Bishop Timon's stentorian tones, sounded, like opposition to the Bible itself. And when a group of liberal Germans attended a convention of the National Central Union of Free Germans which called for the abolition not only of slavery, but of that very Bible as well, many Buffalo Protestants began to seriously wonder about the "delusive nature of Catholic toleration."

Perhaps underlying WASP fear and hatred of Buffalo's Catholic immigrants were their own feelings of inferiority. Behind all the delusionary efforts to convince themselves of their own superiority, there is the hint of a still deeper-rooted feeling of doubt and uncertainty. For among the articulate analysts of mid-nineteenth-century Buffalo society, there was the sense of malaise, of decay and failure, of things somehow gone wrong. In sermons advocating a return to hard work, in editorials admiring the German attachment to "The Fatherland," in an odd Paean to "The Irish Girl" ("Health abounds in her veins. There is strength and power in her muscles. For they have been developed by harder exercise than thumbing the harp and fingering the pianoforte") and in the plaintive journals of Dr. Bryant Burwell and the sad denouement of his story, there is a distinct and unavoidable sense of failure.

Although Burwell's melancholy was temporarily relieved by his marriage to Mrs. Cleary, the depression that had afflicted him for years following the death of his first wife soon returned. By the middle of the 1850s, his family began to notice critical and frightening changes in him. His memory had been gradually declining for years and, according to a letter written by a niece, his speech had begun to slip, to the point where he could only whisper and then only with great difficulty. But what was most disturbing about Burwell's never clearly defined ailment was "the great depression that borders on suicide." As his affliction dragged on, Burwell, who had been practicing as a physician in Buffalo for close to forty years, suddenly began to daydream about becoming a farmer. The more sickly he became, the more his thoughts turned to the past, to another time and place—his childhood on the farm. His niece wrote: "One thing he wants badly is a farm. We were obliged to interfere last October to prevent him from buying an old worn-out farm. He is determined to buy it and go in it to live. . . . Slowly the powers of his life are gradually failing by a sort of general decay." In December 1861 he died.

Bryant Burwell died during the Civil War, an event that traumatized the city of Buffalo. Despite its devastating effect, both contemporary and latter-nineteenth-century accounts of the war sentimentalized and glamorized it, depicting it as one of the great and glorious moments in the history of the city. Behind these misleading descriptions was more than the understandable attempt to ennoble the death and sacrifice that ocurred. For seeping through all of the purple prose that the war generated, all of which was written by members of Burwell's social set, is a desperate cry for redemption.

From what? More than any others, the WASP elite benefitted from the Civil War. Not only were they able to avoid service in the military (some of the WASP elite did, however, choose to serve as officers in local militia companies), but they profited enormously as a result. Buffalo grew and prospered greatly during the war. The population continued its rapid increase—from 81,029 in 1860 to 94,210 five years later—and its lake-oriented economy boomed, as other commercial arteries and outlets like the Mississippi River and New Orleans were closed to raw materials from the Midwest. By the end of the war, Buffalo's position as the leading inland port in the United States was more firmly fixed than ever.

With their new and unprecedentedly large profits, the city's merchant capitalists, like their peer in other northeastern cities, purchased millions of dollars of Union government bonds, thereby underwriting the Union war effort. Most of these bonds had been purchased with paper dollars called "greenbacks." As the war progressed and more greenbacks were printed, they quickly began to lose their value. Thus, investors who had bought their bonds with depreciating currency desperately hoped that at the war's end the government would redeem their bonds at their face value and in specie, not paper. It was this issue, and not the question of civil rights for the freed slaves, that created a strong and loyal Republican following in the moneyed urban centers of the Northeast like Buffalo. Afraid that if returned to power the Democrats would repudiate the federal debt incurred during the war, the city's investors, regardless of their political affiliations, supported the Republican policy of the face value redemption of war bonds.

They were less than unanimous, however, in their support of Republican war policies. Many of the city's most prominent leaders, among them Millard Fillmore, argued constantly for compromise and a return to the *status quo ante* as a means of ending the war.

Fillmore's lack of enthusiasm had more to do with his general sympathy for the Southern cause. He detested President Lincoln. Early in the war, the former president, desperate to return to the fray, tried to convince first federal and then state authorities of the imminence of a British invasion of Western New York. Citing the area's vulnerability and thus its strategic importance, Fillmore requested that large sections of the Niagara Frontier be fortified and placed under his command. When the plan was rejected, Fillmore blamed Lincoln and continued throughout the war to undermine Union efforts to win.

Lack of enthusiasm for the Union effort, particularly following the announcement of the Emancipation Proclamation in the fall of 1862, extended well beyond Fillmore. Indeed, in 1863 the city elected a host of Democrats to local offices, and in the presidential election in 1864 threw its support to the candidate of compromise, General McClellan.

Community guilt is hard to define and easy to hide. Certainly, the good fortune that the city's elite enjoyed—avoidance of the draft, the accumulation of enormous amounts of capital, unprecedented commercial prosperity—had somehow to be redeemed. It was perhaps to purge itself through good works that the WASP elite organized an elaborate and energetic home-front campaign to support those who did have to go and fight. WASP women presided over the Ladies General Aid Society, which claimed to have made 30,000 shirts, 16,688 pairs of drawers, 9,300 pairs of socks, and 5,588 pounds of bandages for the Union army. These same ladies administered the Soldier's Rest Home and several Christian benevolent groups catered to the spiritual needs of wounded local soldiers. While the female members of the gentry engaged in these and kindred activities, the men, piously and sanctimoniously, donated some of their new-found wealth for the foundation of the Buffalo Historical Society, the Fine Arts Academy, and the Natural Science Society.

While far more attention was given to these energetic and magnanimous home-front activities than to the actual trauma of the war itself, there is no hiding the heavy toll that the war must have taken in Buffalo. The local casualties—over five thousand of the close to fifteen thousand men from Erie County who served in the Union army were killed in action—the violent draft riots, the political divisions, and the imposition of a federal draft all weighed heavily on the city, plaguing and tormenting it for the duration of the war. Perhaps a still more difficult burden to bear, a load that even the most energetic and assiduous wartime work on the home front could not mitigate, was guilt, a guilt that was shared by the more affluent members of the community who, with several hundred dollars, had been able to purchase their safety at the risk of other people's lives.

CHAPTER 6

The Coming of Industry

Merwin Hawley must have sensed something when he quit the grain business in 1860. Perhaps he, like a growing number of merchants, had begun to realize that as long as Buffalo was so desperately dependent on commerce, so inextricably a part of a national commercial network, its economy would be weak and vulnerable. With such haphazard and tenuous links, the whole international chain of commerce of which Buffalo was a part was easily broken. A long winter on the lakes; a dock strike in Chicago, Cleveland, or Detroit; or a wreck on the Sault Ste. Marie Canal, could at any time disrupt and damage the city's economy. The effects of national depression were even more serious, and the impact of the panic of 1857 on Buffalo had been staggering, wrecking the economy for several years. Having been so quickly absorbed into the national economy, Buffalo, it had begun to appear, had little security.

Even the Civil War had done little to alter the commercial orientation of Buffalo's economy. Unlike New York City, where textile factories blossomed under the impetus of federal contracts for blue Union uniforms, or Springfield, where federal defense dollars bought the rifles that subsidized that city's industrial economy, Buffalo had enjoyed few such boosts as a result of the war. Despite the iron foundries and other scattered manufacturing enterprises that existed in 1860, Buffalo, as compared even to places like Rochester and Syracuse, was, as far as manufacturing was concerned, backward and undeveloped. (In Buffalo less than five percent of the work force worked in manufacturing in 1860, versus close to ten percent for the other cities.) Those industries that did exist at the end of the war— iron foundries, ship builders, clothing manufacturers—produced strictly for the local market. The products of Buffalo's factories simply did not make it into the national economy.

Even the grain trade was fickle and offered little stability. For years grain had been the foundation of Buffalo's economy, the product which, more than any other, had fueled tremendous growth and expansion in the city's economy during the 1840s and 1850s. However, the shift of the grain trade from the northern to the southern parts of Ohio, Illinois, and Indiana during and after the Civil War posed serious problems for the city's economy. Suddenly, Buffalo's preeminence as an inland port, a break-point in the movement of goods from the farms and forests of the Midwest to the cities of the East, was seriously threatened. For as the grain belt moved further away from the lakes, it became cheaper and easier to ship eastward not on lake boats bound for Buffalo but rather on railroads that directly connected the farms of the Midwest with the cities of the East.

While this had serious implications for the city's economy, the development of railroads between Buffalo and New York City had a traumatic impact on the city's morale. The Erie Canal had always epitomized Buffalo. For years it had served as the symbol of the city's birth, its link with the past, and the source of its prosperity and reputation. Yet as early as the 1860s, the canal was rapidly becoming obsolete, unable to compete with the railroads, which had been in business in the area less than a decade. Too slow, too expensive, and frozen-over several months of the year, the canal was simply too inefficient to serve as the major conduit of both goods and people between New York City and Buffalo. In 1869 the Board of Trade, a group of merchants representing what was commonly referred to as "the Canal interests," dismally reported that "some classes of freight have almost altogether left the canal. From Buffalo the movement of flour by canal during the five years ending with 1869 was more than seventy-five percent less than in the five years ending in 1864." Indeed, in 1869, for the first time ever, the two rail lines which linked Buffalo and the East—the New York Central and the Erie—carried more grain than did the canal. Writing in a book called *The Manufacturing Interests of Buffalo, 1865*, a local newspaper owner said: "Our position is not as invincible as it seemed before the advent of the locomotive. Twenty-five years ago we held the key to the exchanges of the East and the West. . . . But the great lines of railroad began to be built, ignoring the beaten tracks of traffic— defying and overcoming natural obstacles." It was quickly becoming clear that national economic patterns were changing. The city's economy had to change too, or else face disaster.

Some people in the city were aware of what was happening. They realized the importance of shifting the emphasis of the economy, and believed that it was possible to do so—that it could, in fact, be somehow willed. Writing in 1862, the editor of the city directory bemoaned the fact that "Buffalo flourished from year to year dependent mostly on its commerce and the manufactures which commerce coerced into existence." He insisted that "self preservation dictates that wealth be turned toward manufactures." He was not alone in this view; during the 1860s there were several groups dedicated to the creation of a diversified manufacturing economy in the city of Buffalo. One, founded in 1860 by a Scots builder of iron lake boats named John Bell, was called the Association for the Encouragement of Manufactures. Arguing that the "limits of commerce to the support of the town have been reached," and blaming the "old fogeys" who had refused to invest in manufacturing, Bell urged that Buffalo "seek safety in manufacture." Later in the decade, Bell, now as president of another group dedicated to the same purpose—the Mechanics Association—was the driving force behind the first annual Industrial Exposition, held in Buffalo in 1869.

The primary purpose of the Mechanics Association was "to bring machinery to the nearest possible state of perfection." The purpose of the exposition was to do nothing less than alter the city's economy, or at least to change the way people in Buffalo thought about machines, mechanization, and industry. Inviting people from all over the Northeast to submit industrial machinery to the exhibition, the Mechanics Association hoped to bring the power, significance, artistry, and value of machinery to the attention of the people of Buffalo.

Although they had originally hoped to lease whole sections of the waterfront for a permanent display area, the association had to settle for the use of a large indoor skating rink, that often doubled as a convention center, for their exhibition.

For the Mechanics Association, industry meant invention and inventiveness more than it did mechanization and production. The graphic symbol of the exhibition was a lithograph that depicted an anvil, a printing press, a locomotive, a lake steamer, a gigantic cog wheel, and some agricultural equipment. Rising above the hallowed head of the "Goddess of Liberty" was a balloon, "symbol of the possibilities of the future." With no worker and no factories, this was a pristine vision with little to do with the realities of late nineteenth century industry.

The association thus tended to view industry as a craft rather than as a form of production. This notion was further apparent in the seven departments into which the association divided the articles on exhibition: fine arts and education, the dwelling, dress and handicraft, chemistry and minerology, engines and machinery, intercommunication, and agriculture and horticulture. Each department had seven sub-categories, and displayed a broad range of equipment, materials, and machinery. The department of fine arts and education included, in addition to paintings and sculpture, musical instruments, bookbindings, stationery, maps, charts, "philosophical instruments" [among which were mathematical and measuring devices], chronometers, watches and clocks, telescopes, microscopes, lenses, cameras and other optical instruments. The department of the dwelling included stoves, heating and cooling devices, all kinds of kitchen equipment and household furniture, and an extensive selection of construction and building accessories. In the department of dress and handicraft were clothing, jewelry, sporting equipment, toys, trunks, razors, pocket pens and pencils, and "specimens of dentistry, artificial limbs, wigs and hair-works, surgical apparatus and surgical instruments." Presented in the department of chemistry and minerology were soaps, toilet preparations, waxes, acids, alkalies, mineral waters, wine, leather, tobacco, paints and dyes, samples of baking and pastry cooking, sugars, preserved fruit, vegetables and meats, and "beverages and stimulants, excluding so-called Patent Medicines."

But the department of intercommunication and the department of engines and machinery were the largest, most extensive, and most popular sections of the exhibition. The former displayed all manner of railroad engines and cars, carriages, wagons and sleighs, models of vessels "for navigating the ocean, rivers, lakes and canals," electric telegraphs, and "army apparatus used in movements or in camp." The latter exhibited "stationary engines driven by steam, heated air and other gases," machinery for working metals (lathes, drills, screw cutters, and steam hammers), machinery for working in wood, machinery used in the manufacture of leather goods, and "gearing, millwork and elements of machinery for varying speed or power." Finally, the exhibition had the department of agriculture and horti-culture, where were shown, in addition to machinery and equipment, "all specimen of food prepared on the farm, including butter, cheese, fruits, vegetables, cereals, roots and seeds."

While Bell and the Mechanics Association were trying to create a climate and a consciousness conducive to the development of industry, individual entrepreneurs were doing their best to exploit the locational advantages of Buffalo. Bell, a manufacturer of iron lake ships, realized the importance of location and had talked often about the city's "proximity to the coal regions of Pennsylvania, the facilities for obtaining ore from the Lake Superior iron regions and our importance as a shipping point and distribution center." During the 1870s and 1880s, Buffalo businessmen began to reach out to bring these critical raw materials into the city in ever-increasing amounts. One of these men was Frank H. Goodyear.

Born on a farm near Cortland, New York and raised in the small town of Holland, near Buffalo, Frank H. Goodyear, the son of a physician, came to Buffalo in 1872 at the age of twenty-three. With the help of local investors (Buffalo's capitalists were eager, it seems, to supply seed money to enterprising young men who sought their fortunes in the city), Goodyear established a retail coal and lumber business. By the early 1880s he had acquired large timber tracts and several lumber mills in the rich timber country of western Pennsylvania. Without access to a national market, however, Goodyear's timber was worthless. At that time timber was floated to the sawmills on local streams and Goodyear, seeking other routes, began to dream of building a railroad between his forests in Pennsylvania and the port in Buffalo. But there were difficult obstacles to overcome. For one thing, the grades in the forests were extremely steep; for another, there was no mechanical means to pick up the huge logs and load them on the flatcars. Working with a local steam shovel company, Goodyear developed the Barnhart Log Loader, which operated something like a steam shovel at a construction site. Having solved the problem of loading and unloading, Goodyear proceeded, despite the steep grade, to build his railroad. The first link—the Sinnemahoning Valley Railroad—was built in 1885–86. Goodyear and his brother Charles (a lawyer, Charles joined Frank after the latter had suffered what would today be called a nervous breakdown) gradually expanded the railroad until, by the mid-1890s, it, now known as the Buffalo and Susquehanna, came to within ninety miles of Buffalo.

Meanwhile, as they rapidly stripped bare their timber lands, the Goodyear brothers had been buying up huge tracts of coal fields in neighboring sections of Pennsylvania. One thing led to another. Lured like others by the discovery of iron ore in the Messabi range, Frank and Charles began to acquire ore fields there. With coal in Pennsylvania and iron in Minnesota, it was only natural, the brothers thought, to complete the connection of the Buffalo and Susquehanna Railroad to Buffalo. The capital requirements of this venture were enormous, but with the help of a New York brokerage firm the Goodyears, going public for the first time, raised $17 million for the completion of their railroad. Not convinced that an adequate market existed yet for their coal, the Goodyears, expanding almost inexorably, now felt compelled to create an iron company. Between 1900 and 1901 they bought large tracts of undeveloped property in South Buffalo, formed the Buffalo and Susquehanna Iron Company, and built three large blast furnaces.

Iron ore had been discovered on the shores of Lake Superior as early as the 1840s, but it was not until the 1870s and 1880s that its exploitation began in earnest. The enlargement of the Sault Ste. Marie Canal, and the construction of gigantic lake freighters like the Buffalo and Susquehanna's *Frank H. Goodyear*, led to an enormous increase in the amount of iron ore received in Buffalo. By the end of the 1880s Buffalo was ready to challenge Pittsburgh as the iron and steel capital of the country. Because Buffalo could now receive ore directly from Lake Superior without breaking bulk at Cleveland, Erie, or other lake ports, it was far cheaper to ship ore directly there than to Pittsburgh. The Buffalo *Express* gleefully took note of this development in 1891: "When a project is on hand for the building of a blast furnace, nobody will think for a minute of Pittsburgh. That place has had its day. Making iron is a matter of geography." Other areas were badly hurt by this sectional realignment that was occurring. Complaining about the effect of the accelerated production of Lake Superior iron ore, Abram Hewitt, the illustrious New Jersey iron master, commented bitterly: "The great Lehigh region is ruined and our own plan in New Jersey is now useless."

Although still heavily dependent on lake commerce, the city's economy was becoming increasingly linked with the railroads. In 1900 Buffalo was, after Chicago, the leading railroad terminus in the United States. There were seven direct lines connecting Buffalo with six different East Coast cities; six direct lines to Chicago, Kansas City, Omaha, and St. Louis; and two direct lines between Buffalo and Pittsburgh. The New York Central was so big that it had its own police force (some officials of the Pennsylvania Railroad complained that they should also have one). The railroad companies had created a new industry in the city. They owned 3,600 acres of city land and had laid 660 miles of track within the city limits. They directly employed twenty thousand men and indirectly gave work to thousands more in the car wheel shops, palace car shops, locomotive and freight car shops, and in the largest bridge company in the world, all of which were located in the city. And while the people of Buffalo were extremely proud of their railroad network (not a brochure was written, or a boosterish editorial composed, that did not minutely describe the city's railroad connections), the rails had begun to create serious problems. As a result of the railroads, the Erie Canal had by 1900 become virtually obsolete. As if this development was not sufficiently threatening to lake commerce, by the turn of the century almost every lake steamship company had been bought out by the railroads. The Pennsylvania owned the Erie and Western Transportation Company; the New York Central owned the Western Transit Company; the New York Central, the Pennsylvania, and the Erie together owned the Mutual Transit Company; and the Erie Railroad owned the Union Steamboat Company. Thus, by either controlling the freight rates on their railroads or by dictating lake freight policy, the railroads had come to exert a controlling influence over the city's commercial economy. While some may well have discerned the potentially hazardous control exercised by the railroads, most people in turn-of-the-century Buffalo were willing to overlook it. For without the railroads, they knew, there could be no industrial economy.

In addition to adequate means of transportation, industry required labor and energy. Both were plentiful and cheap in Buffalo. The first was provided by the thousands of eastern European immigrants willing to work for almost nothing under practically any conditions. The supply of electrical power from nearby Niagara Falls was equally cheap and virtually unlimited. At the turn of the century a growing number of corporations gave this as a primary reason for their decisions to relocate and build new facilities in Buffalo. In 1899 the American Malting Company, known as "The Malt Trust," announced that it was shutting down its operations in Cleveland and Erie and would build a new plant along the banks of the Buffalo Creek in South Buffalo. The president of the company explained the advantage of Buffalo's cheap electrical power. "You can shut it off when you don't need it," he said. "You can't switch steam off and on like that." American Radiator, a Chicago-based manufacturer of boilers, chose Buffalo in 1901 for the same reason: "Even though we are making boilers, there won't be a particle of steam in our Buffalo plant. That's rather odd, isn't it? We are building boilers for other people but haven't any use for them outselves. . . . You see the entire plant will be powered by electricity from Niagara Falls."

Added to this meld of capital, labor, energy, and transportation were the continued efforts of publicists and city boosters to create a climate of opinion conducive to the development of industry. Beginning with the Industrial Exposition of 1869, these efforts culminated with the Pan American Exposition of 1901. Viewed by local boosters as an international, image-building extravaganza, the Pan American became an unprecedented opportunity to trumpet the virtues of Buffalo as an emergent center of American industry. During and immediately after the exposition there were countless pep-talk articles and uplifting editorials urging the citizenry to seize the time and capitalize on the publicity that Buffalo had received during the Pan American: "Now is not the time to rest. We must redouble our efforts and hold what we have gained." And if people failed to realize the advantages of Buffalo as an industrial center, they said, Buffalonians should not stop talking about the city: "The way to insure the prosperity of Buffalo is to talk Buffalo all the time."

But more than talk was involved in this communitywide effort to create a warm and welcome climate for industry. Throughout the early years of the twentieth century there was little debate about the general desirability of attracting industry to the city. What people did argue about, however, was how to do this. Some favored bounties in the form of tax abatements; others, the suspension of laws regarding smoke nuisances. "Smoke," one alderman argued in 1901, "shows people where business is being done. It is a sign that men are at work and are earning money and contributing to the prosperity of the city." Others, also concerned with the city's image, argued in favor of smoke control ordinances because "smoke is evidence that a city is behind the times."

Everybody, it seemed, agreed with the notion that "appearances count" and that "a good appearance is a good investment in the city's future." Similarly, there was little argument when it came to defining the city's relationship to its new industrial ventures. Time after time during the late nineteenth and early twentieth centuries, the city did what it could to ease the capital burden of corporations building in Buffalo. For the Goodyear's railroad and iron foundries, the board of aldermen dredged a canal. For the Urban Flour Mill they improved the harbor front, and for the Lackawanna Steel Company they built a new sewer line. And to the close to twenty railroad lines that made their way into Buffalo in 1901, the city had granted the right of way to over six hundred miles of the city's streets and waterfront. Few people in power questioned these policies (although neighborhood leaders, as we will see, did come to fight the railroads over the grade crossing issue), and few offered alternatives. A consensus prevailed. Nothing, it seemed, would be tolerated that interfered with the coming of industry to the city of Buffalo.

The newspapers were particularly eager to cultivate an atmosphere sympathetic to industrialization. The press covered every aspect of almost every economic development that occurred. From the time the first rumors of construction or expansion were heard, through to the completion of a project, virtually all of the city's newspapers covered in close and exacting detail all aspects of each company's development: stock options, intricate financing schemes, the wining and dining of out-of-town corporate executives, pictures of the officers and their families, magnificent and dramatic panoramic photographs of the construction of the facility, and the machinery and equipment being used and built. Accompanying these compelling images were long, detailed accounts of how products were made and how the machinery worked. The *News* glowingly described the Goodyears' largely automated blast furnaces in 1903: "The iron ore and limestone are taken out of the lake boats by automatic machinery, carried by overhead bridge to the storage yards, there picked up by buckets and deposited in bins by means of electric trolley cars, dropped into scoops which in turn automatically drop the coal into the furnaces." People were fascinated and intrigued by what was happening, mesmerized by the sounds and appearances of industry, uncertain, yet hopeful, that the changes were for the good.

Whether beneficial or not, these changes certainly were occurring quickly. In a newspaper article written in 1905 under the headline "Recent Acquisitions," The Buffalo *Times* reported that since 1890 there had been 412 new factories built in the city, 300 of which were new concerns. The amount of capital, they reported, that was invested in industrial production was $137 million, an increase, according to the *Times*, of over forty percent. The value of manufactured products similarly was up forty percent. While these figures may well have been somewhat inflated, there can be no question but that the increase in the local industrial economy was enormous, overwhelming, and unprecedented. Among the new companies that located in Buffalo at the turn of the century were the Buffalo and Susquehanna Iron Company with one thousand employees, the Urban Flour Mill with two hundred employees, the Snow Steam Pump Works with eight hundred employees, the Buffalo Foundry Company with three hundred employees, and the Buffalo Structural Steel Company with four hundred employees. And while there were among these companies some flour mills; cereal makers; and shoe, soap, and furniture factories, the overwhelming number of the new factories involved iron and steel.

Of all the changes and developments that were occurring in the city's economy, nothing better illustrates the dramatic impact of turn-of-the-century industrialization than the coming to Buffalo of Lackawanna Steel.

During the Fourth of July weekend of 1899 John Milburn, a local lawyer, entertained Walter Scranton, the President of the Lackawanna Iron and Steel Company of Scranton, Pennsylvania, in the style customary among American robber barons. Milburn, who had come to Buffalo from England in 1874 at the age of twenty-three, had a special magnetism in the city. He was a highly sophisticated person, a man, it was said, whose "deliberate and cultured speech, rich with smile and gesture . . . made all succumb. He loved his wine, his cigar and he understood them." He also understood modern industry and was particularly interested in electrical power. By the middle of the 1890s his law firm did the legal work for three men intimately involved in the development and generation of electrical power in Buffalo: John J. Albright, the president of the Ontario Power Company; George Urban, Jr., president of the Buffalo and Niagara Falls Electric Light and Power Company; and W. C. Ely, president of the International Railroad Company. Milburn was with these men at midnight on August 15, 1896, when the first electric current was transmitted from Niagara Falls to Buffalo. He recorded his reactions at the time: "Niagara Falls is an inexhaustible mine of wealth from which electricity will flow into Buffalo and act like warm blood running through the human body." He was right. Later that year Ely's IRC became the first streetcar system in a large city to be electrified, while one year later Urban's Flour Mills was the first major industry to be so powered.

Perhaps because, like the Scotsman Bell, his foreign upbringing gave him a broader view of the local scene, John Milburn was acutely aware of the terrible impact the decline of the lake trade would have on the economy of the city. He also realized that circumstances existed at the turn of the century which offered Buffalo a unique opportunity to develop along new and different lines. Sensing that time was running out on the old commercial economy, Milburn, along with several of his more foresightful colleagues, consciously went about the business of creating a new economic order.

As attorney for the Goodyear brothers, who had extensive interests in Pennsylvania, Milburn had come to acquire a large amount of stock in the Lackawanna Steel Company of Scranton, Pennsylvania. Scranton was a town with a dwindling coal supply and a growing steelworkers' union, and Milburn knew that Walter Scranton, president of Lackawanna Steel, was looking for a new location for his operations. Milburn led him to Buffalo.

At that Fourth of July dinner attended by the Goodyear brothers; John Albright; W. C. Ely; George Urban; Jacob Schoellkopf, president of the Niagara Falls Hydraulic Power Company; and William B. Hoyt, attorney for the New York Central Railroad, Scranton was wined and dined like visiting royalty. Following the nine-course meal, Milburn euphorically described how recent developments greatly enhanced Buffalo's desirability as an industrial center. It was, Milburn said, close to the largest and cheapest power source in the world—Niagara Falls. Its extensive railroad and shipping lines put the city in direct contact with the newly discovered iron mines at Messabi, Minnesota as well as with steel markets all over the country. And, unlike the rapidly unionizing workers in Scranton, Milburn pointed out, Buffalo's labor force, in the form of over fifty thousand east European immigrants who were pouring into the city in desperate search of work, was large and docile. Most important of all, Scranton would be able to build his plant south of the municipal boundaries of Buffalo, beyond the jurisdiction of the city. Scranton, in short, was given a town of his own.

When the announcement was made in April 1899 that the Lackawanna Iron and Steel Company was relocating in Buffalo, the news came as a shock and a surprise to the people of the city. While there had long been talk of activity along the waterfront south of the city—there had been periodic reports first that the Rockefellers, and then later that a mysterious British steel magnate, were planning to build a steel plant there—these had been nothing but rumors. The fact was that for several years local iron interests had been secretly at work putting together the pieces of an intricate and gigantic deal that would single-handedly remake the city's economy. From the beginning Scranton had secretly insisted on two conditions: one, that he be given the requisite lakefront property and two, that local investors participate. Both conditions were met. Quietly at work assembling the land, John J. Albright, the largest iron maker in Buffalo, had by early 1900 bought over one thousand acres of lake front property. The city of Buffalo gave the company twenty-five more acres that had previously been developed as a waterfront park. (New York State participated in the deal too. In 1900 it gave Lackawanna Steel three hundred acres which the company wanted to build on. Commenting on the hearing that certified this decision, John Milburn said that it was "merely a question of forms.") Added to this generous gift of land was a financing plan that pleased Scranton and his board of directors. Looking for local participation without local domination, Scranton insisted that at least five percent, but no more than ten percent, of the total $40 million capital worth of the company be provided by local investors. Drawing on the enthusiastic support of local iron and railroading interests, Milburn and Albright had brokered the financial aspects of the deal even more easily than they had the real estate, and by early 1900 the package was complete. While nine Buffalo investors were needed to raise the necessary $4 million, the Vanderbilts alone invested $1 million in the venture as a precautionary measure in order "to conserve the interests of the N.Y.C. Railroad."

Although at first shocked that such a momentous event could have been unfolding not only without their participation but, even more significantly, without their knowledge (one paper commented somewhat angrily that "the queries have been so numerous and so varied that Buffalonians have been at a loss"), the press tried to rationalize the furtive deal. The *Express*, trying hard to hide its hurt, wrote about the people behind the deal: "They had the money—real, hard cash and their money talked for them far more eloquentlly than columns of newspaper space could have done." Indeed far from letting their hurt show at missing this, the greatest scoop in the economic life of the city, the local press quickly became the staunch and virtually unquestioning supporters of the steel company. Indeed, between 1900, when the news first broke, and 1904, when the plant finally began to produce steel, the newspapers, as they followed the daily progress of the construction of the plant, the offices, and the worker housing, were so ostentatious and lavish in their praise of the company and the developments that were occurring that their coverage soon smacked of propaganda. Oftentimes using rhetoric worthy of fantasy and make-believe, the press talked about "the marvelous story of a city that is rising as if by magic." Another paper wrote similarly: "As if the site of this hive of activity had been touched by the magic wand of a queen fairy, this wonderful plant is rising in our midst, stupendous, massive." To local publicists, the construction of the steel plant was more than a significant event in the life of the city. It had become, to some anyway, "a monument to the industrial activity of the American capitalist, evidence of the splendid executive ability of the men who manage its affairs."

The public was equally fascinated by the erection of this massive lakefront facility. By 1902 streetcar lines had begun to run Sunday tours to and from the plant. There, with the help of specially trained guides, hundreds of people were shown the work in progress. The Buffalo *Times* advised that "a man should make more than one or two trips out to the steel plant to get a true idea of its magnitude. It will take you almost twenty minutes to walk from one end of the plant to the other and that's without stopping on the way. If you stopped and looked at everything it would take you about a month to make an inspection of the place."

By 1904, as construction neared completion and the company began to actually produce the steel, the adulatory rhetoric accelerated. The size, sounds, and smells of the plant brought unanimous praise from the city's newspapers:

> On entering the gates the visitor is first impressed with the immensity of the plant before him. As far as his eye can reach he can see the signs of industry, see the hugh furnaces belching out their molten contents, the cupolas spouting fire, smoke and cinders like the dragons of song and story. From the great brick structures housing the huge machines come the roaring and pounding of the big wheels driven by thousands of pounds of pressure. Across the yards come the shrieking donkey engines pulling their weighty loads to and from the mills and everywhere there is a nerve-racking roar of sound and a bewildering rush of men and machines.

Work too was described in graphic detail, but invariably in terms of machines, not men. The newspapers wrote lyrically and in endless detail about the "wondrous workings of an immense crane that acts as if endowed with a brain and a nervous system [with] a series of chains and pulleys that magnetically lift iron and steel." They also described "gret blowing machines," a "wonderful system of gas engines," and the "magical process of making steel balls. . . . From the fire belching soaking pit ingot is taken white hot and sent racing along in a steel car to the rollers where it is to be transformed into a steel rail." Later in the process, the rhapsodic journalists wrote, "Like a tortured soul in the infernal regions, the ingot is allowed no rest. It is buffetted and whirled about first through this roll, then that and ever watchful of its progress are the careful workmen, standing about like demons silhouetted in the very varying light."

Accustomed as we have recently become to analyzing the departure and arrival of industry in terms of the number of jobs lost or gained, it is surprising that the steel plant was never discussed in terms of the number of jobs it was creating. This is particularly striking given the recent depression of the mid-1890s. The fact of the matter is that, despite the more than six thousand men that the company did employ once it actually began to produce steel in 1904, the people of Buffalo were largely disappointed by the number of jobs that were actually made available to the local work force.

The labor situation at the Lackawanna plant was complicated. First, approximately fifteen hundred laborers were hired to clear the land and build the plant. As the facility neared completion and the company prepared for the production of steel, however, these laborers (primarily European immigrants) were laid off. At this point the company began to hire a new, industrial work force. It was clearly an employers' market, as thousands of people journeyed to the plant from all parts of the Northeast looking for work. Indeed, ever since plans first became public, the site had been a regional mecca for the unemployed. Given preference, however, were the more than two thousand who followed the company from Scranton to Buffalo. (When asked about the impact of his relocation decision on his home town, Walter Scranton replied: "It's tough on Scranton.") Indeed, by 1904 seventy percent of the total work force had come from Scranton. The result was that there simply were not that many jobs available. With apparently few illusions about the impact of the plant on the local labor force, the *Express*, like the other papers, unquestioningly accepted this, reporting it routinely and as a simple matter of fact. "The steel plant people get hundreds of applications for work every day, but the company is not able to give employment to everyone that asks and many go away disappointed." Somewhat later in the year the *Courier* came to similar conclusions in describing the hiring process at the plant:

When it comes to the hiring of ignorant foreign laborers who literally besiege the office day after day the task is a harder one (than hiring English speaking laborers). All nationalities, all creeds, all classes and characters of men are represented in this motley throng which applies every day for work. There are Italians, Austrians, Croatians, Slavs, Austrian Poles, Hungarians, and Russian Poles, a few Scandinavians, French and a few negroes and representatives of several other nationalities.

With a detachment that indicates that somehow the problems of the labor force, unlike those of the plant itself, were of no concern, the *Courier* concluded blandly and acceptingly:

An interesting study it is, to watch a swarm of those rough, uncouth fellows crowd about the doors of the office and clamor in a half-dozen tongues for work. They line up along the sidewalk and often the line reaches a quarter of a mile down the road. All eyes are on the door of the office and all are awaiting the welcome words, that help is needed. All are eager and expectant, but many are doomed to disappointment.

Even the large managerial force was not drawn primarily from the local labor market. Indeed, most of these positions seem to have been filled by an emerging class of highly mobile professional business administrators and executives. Walter Scranton had been the president of the company throughout the late nineteenth century and it had been his decision to relocate the company and to build at Buffalo. Scranton, however, soon became bored with the project. His rare visits to the construction site and his growing disinterest in the affairs of his company soon began to irritate his board of directors and they, complaining that he did not devote enough of his time to the interests and well being of the company, in 1903 cut his salary from $50,000 to $35,000 per year. Within the year he was replaced by Edward A. Clarke. Unlike Scranton, who had succeeded to the presidency of the company by virtue of his family ties, Clarke was a professional manager only forty years old. A Harvard graduate, Clarke had served as the general manager of Illinois Steel and then as chief executive officer of International Harvester.

Professionalization also characterized lower management positions. Thomas Mathias had been brought to Lackawanna Steel as supervisor of the rolling mill from U.S. Steel's Homestead plant. Robert Wainright, an executive in charge of personnel, had, prior to his arrival in Buffalo, served similar capacities in Boston, Philadelphia, and Pittsburgh. These people moved out of Buffalo as quickly and easily as they moved to it. J. P. Shadduck came to the Lackawanna plant from Carnegie in 1903, but in 1904 took a job as production supervisor with the Tube Works Company of Lorrain, Ohio. Walter Dexter, a senior accounts clerk with the firm, brought in from New York City in 1904, moved to Cleveland two years later. He explained to the press: "I am leaving Buffalo because the moist atmosphere from the lake does not agree with me." In any case, what Dexter's and the others' careers demonstrated was that the management of the steel company was a highly mobile and transient work force with no real ties to either the company or the community.

The industrial work force enjoyed no such freedom. Indeed, their work and their working days were extremely regulated and controlled. The *Courier* was careful to report that the company kept strict records of all people who worked at the plant, "so that not a man can loaf or beat his time a minute without the heads of the different departments being cognizant of this act and his wages cut accordingly." And when the plant managers requested that the United States Army relocate the federal army post from Fort Porter along the Niagara River to a site adjacent to the plant, the Buffalo *Times* applauded the request: "In case of any serious trouble in the plant a force of soldiers could be sent in at once." Although their request was denied, it had become clear that by the time the Lackawanna Steel plant opened for business in 1904 it was widely regarded as little more than an engine of production.

The company tried to control not only the work environment but the surrounding community as well. One of the attractions that had lured Walter Scranton to the site in the first place was that the area—known as Stony Point—was in a state of municipal limbo. Scranton was particularly pleased that the company's site was legally a part of West Seneca, and not of Buffalo. For in the former (a small, hardly developed, exurban community south of Buffalo), property taxes were virtually nonexistent. The company wanted to keep it that way.

The people of West Seneca had different ideas. Unwilling to assume the added burden of building the roads, sewers, schools, and other improvements that the expansion of the steel mill required, they demanded that a new municipality incorporating the plant be created. The problems (West Seneca politicians referred to them as "steel germs") were mounting and had to be dealt with. One of these was typhoid fever, which by 1903 had reached epidemic proportions in the residential areas surrounding the mill. Company spokesmen, however, desperate to remain a part of West Seneca, minimized the impact of the disease. "These cases," one of them said, "are among a lot of Italians living in shacks. They would have had the disease even had sewers been installed." Although unable to convince the people of West Seneca, they had better luck in the state legislature, where intense lobbying efforts by Lackawanna Steel to prevent the incorporation of a new town paid off for at least several more years. By 1909, however, West Seneca had had enough. The depression of the past two years had caused extremely serious problems for the town, and its desperately strained budget required relief. With thousands of steel workers suddenly unemployed, it was the fear of a threatened increase in crime and violence that finally led the company to support the town's demand for the creation of a new community. Realizing that the town's small volunteer police force simply could not do the job, the Lackawanna Steel Company relented and supported the bill creating the city of Lackawanna. Convinced that "the steel plant people will look after their new town's future themselves," Buffalo's industrial interests, relieved that the burden would not be theirs, supported the legislation.

Like other large companies of the time—Cadbury in England, Pullman in Chicago, U.S. Steel in Gary, Indiana—Lackawanna Steel tried to control the home environment of its workers. It was an age of corporate paternalism, when local companies like Pratt and Letch-worth, American Radiator, and others sold noontime soup and bread to their workers at cost, and when a variety of company-sponsored recreational activities—bands, bowling tournaments, picnics, softball games—had become normal and popular aspects of industrial employment. Lackawanna Steel, however, went still further, and in 1901 began the construction of two "villages," each consisting of approximatelly five hundred attached brick houses. Some were for rent; others for purchase. Writing about the company housing in 1910 in the *Survey*, a progressive journal, John Fitch found it to be basically good. Comparing it favorably to similarly priced housing in Buffalo, Fitch noted that unlike the latter, the Lackawanna company's homes all had inside toilets. The Buffalo *Times*, writing in 1904, had a less sanguine view. A correspondent, whose objective tone did not mask his disapproval, wrote: "The houses are built in long rows and they stretch over a mile. There is no space at all between the houses. Each adjoins the other. They are very plain in appearance. . . . The streets have been cut but they are not yet paved." He concluded: "When all the houses are completed the company will derive a nice revenue from them." He was wrong. Despite a population in the community of close to fifteen thousand and the existence of a critical housing shortage, most of these company homes were empty in 1910. Although more modern and cheaper than equivalent worker housing, these homes were undesirable. With no stores, no taverns, and no public meeting places, there was, as Fitch reported, "no opportunity here for social pleasure." Workers in the plant much preferred to commute from homes in the older neighborhoods of Buffalo.

Lackawanna Steel was constructing an enormous facility, and it took several years to complete. By 1904 the company had already built six open-hearth furnaces; different mills for the production of light rails, steel plate, and steel slabs; and a "merchant mill" for a variety of smaller, diversified items. In addition, they had dredged a ship canal for receiving Mesabi iron ore (by 1905 eighty percent of all Mesabi iron was sent to lower Great Lakes ports, primarily Buffalo) and had constructed miles of railroad tracks, some of which linked the plant directly to the coal regions of western Pennsylvania, others which served their own steel distribution needs. They had taken millions of dollars of orders by 1904. While their primary customers were American railroads, the Lackawanna company also sold steel rails to the Philippines, Australia, and Japan. In June 1906, Lieutenant Commander Shiegetoshi Takehuchi of the Imperial Japanese Navy visited the plant and placed a multi-million dollar order for armor plating. By the end of the year Lackawanna had similar orders from Russia, Germany, and England.

In 1906, the first year that the company was in full operation, Lackawanna shipped over one million tons of steel while their net earnings reached $5 million. Within one year, however, the company was in deep financial difficulty. As the rest of the industrial economy, particularly the railroad industry, was devastated by the depression in 1907, Buffalo's nascent steel industry was overwhelmed. Production dropped by over forty percent, and by the end of 1907 over four thousand of Lackawanna's six thousand steel workers were unemployed.

In early 1908, the salary of office workers was cut by ten percent and mill hands, who normally earned between 12¢ and 17¢ per hour, now got a flat hourly rate of 12¢. Despite losses of $1.3 million in 1908, President Clarke was optimistic and predicted an early return to prosperity and full employment. But the newspapers, at least, did not believe him. Writing in early 1909, the usually bullish *Commercial Advertiser* wrote: "There is no warrant for published statements intimating that the steel business is picking up again . . . "

As the steel mill floundered, the attitude of the press, which to date had been boosterish beyond belief, began to change noticeably. Now, for the first time, the press began to pay close and often gruesome detail to the accidents that occurred within the plant: "While Julius Kolas was at work on a pile of ore, one of the pieces became dislodged and fell on him. He was taken to the Emergency Hospital where it was found that both his hips were smashed, his right arm fractured and that he also had internal injuries. He died on the operating table." Late in 1908, the *Times* reported that "August Pohl, a young man employed on the rolling mills at the Lackawanna plant, was severely and perhaps fatally burned while taking away the red-hot iron from the rolls. Pohl was standing in front of the rolls which, curling up like a snake, wound itself around both of Pohl's legs. He is resting at home as easily as can be expected and it is thought that he will be able to return to work. His legs will be useless." (Despite the increasing reports of accidents, the New York State Factory Investigating Commission, which visited the plant in 1912, for some reason made no reference to conditions in the Lackawanna mills.)

The newspapers began to take a far more concerned, critical, somewhat investigatorial approach not only to industrial accidents but also to the conditions in the company housing. Whereas prior to the depression of 1907 the papers had reported fairly objectively on the progress and nature of the company-built homes, they now began to complain about the lack of sewers, the unpaved streets and poor sanitation, and the potential for fires. In the summer of 1908, the *Express* even hinted that waste discharged from the plant was contaminating Buffalo's drinking water. The public's notion of who was responsible was also changing. The *Times* noted in 1909 that "the working class is not responsible for existing conditions." Obliquely, they continued that "it is not our intention to state who is. There are conditions which could easily be changed by the steel concern itself. Others by the township authorities." The increasingly pervasive feeling was that the community had somehow been had.

The press had become bitter and disillusioned. The promise of the steel company, which they had done so much to promote and exaggerate, was simply not being realized, and Buffalo's newspapers, the champions of growth and industrial development, felt betrayed. Naively unaware that the fortunes of the new industrial order were no longer in the hands of the local community, the press demanded accountability. Why, they wondered, had no dividends been paid on company stocks? Why had four thousand of the six thousand man work force been so abruptly dismissed? Why had not local stockholders, who provided so large a percentage of the company's capital, been granted more power in the company? And why, finally, had the president of the company, Edward Clarke, still not moved his home from New York City to Buffalo?

An article written in the *Boston Transcript* in 1909 and clipped and pasted by a local history buff in an early twentieth century scrapbook on Buffalo's economy, suggested that perhaps the people of Buffalo had begun to have doubts about rapid growth of industry there. The author ended his article by comparing Buffalo with Cleveland and Detroit. These latter, he wrote, became great cities through the "combination of great natural resources and advantages along with the dynamic energy of their people." With Buffalo, however, there was a marked absence of the latter. Without elaboration or further explanation, the author concluded somewhat mysteriously, yet given the disillusion of 1907–1909 suggestively: "In fact many would be willing to assert that it was in spite of and not because of the efforts of Buffalonians themselves." Perhaps the people of Buffalo already had had enough.

No more insulated now than before from the cyclical vagaries of the national economy, Buffalo's new industrial order had, in the minds of some, at least, begun to do more harm than good. It was too late to change, however. The die had been cast.

CHAPTER 7

The Response to Industrialization: Life and Labor, Values and Beliefs

Industry boomed in the early years of the twentieth century, particularly the iron and steel industries. In 1910 over ten thousand people worked in the more than 150 iron and steel factories in the city (six thousand worked at Lackawanna). But still, despite their dominance, iron and steel represented only ten percent of Buffalo's industrial output. By 1910 other industries had come to play an increasingly important role. Over 3,600 people now worked in the automobile industry, 3,400 in the manufacture and repair of railroad cars, and 1,800 in the manufacture of copper.

Meanwhile, Buffalo's commercial orientation, rooted in the city's traditional function as a clearinghouse for the raw products of the Midwest, remained strong and diversified. On one September day in 1910 thrity-one ships arrived in the harbor carrying lumber, livestock, pig iron, corn, flour, barley, rye, and over one million tons of grain. The next day thirty-three boats docked, despite warnings of high winds off of Detroit and the threat of a tugboat workers' strike in Green Bay and Chicago.

In 1910 Buffalo was still the greatest grain port in the world, and showed every sign of so remaining. The dozen or so gigantic steel elevators that lined the lakefront handled two million bushels of grain daily. Their storage capacity was over twenty million bushels. Because of its superb shipping and storage facilities, Buffalo had become second only to Minneapolis as a milling center. In 1894 George Pillsbury, the Minneapolis flour magnate, built a huge steel grain elevator in Buffalo. The following year the H–O Cereal Company of New York moved its plant to Buffalo. H–O, the manufacturer of Korn Kinks, "the world's most nutritious breakfast food," employed nine hundred workers in 1905. But the largest milling company in turn-of-the-century Buffalo was the Urban Company. The first in the United States to be powered by electricity, the Urban mills were capable of producing 1,200 barrels of flour daily. George Urban, Jr., the president of the company, was particularly proud of a manufacturing process that was capable of making uniform particles of flour. Urban explained that the advantage of this breakthrough was that the amount of water required to make dough would be constant, and thus all of the flour particles would become dough at the same time.

The grain trade led naturally and logically to the development of a brewing industry. Ever since the city was founded, beer had been brewed in Buffalo. In 1901, there were nineteen independently owned breweries in the city producing over 750,000 barrels a year. (Barrel-making was a big business in Buffalo, too.) The largest, the Gerhard Lang Company, produced 300,000 barrels a year. Like so many of the city's German-owned companies, the Lang brewery was a second generation business owned by Jacob Gerhart Lang, a graduate of Doctor Wyatt's School of Technical Brewing in New York City. Lang's beer, like that brewed locally by Philip Schaefer, William Simon, Magnus Beck, and others, was known throughout the Northeast and Midwest.

While trade in grain led to the manufacture of flour, cereal, and beer, the passage of lumber through the port of Buffalo made the city one of the great lumber centers in the country. In the early days following the completion of the Erie Canal, Buffalo merchants had handled the shipment of lumber and were involved in all aspects of the lumber trade. Some, like Frank and Charles Goodyear, by buying up millions of acres of Pennsylvania timber land, had come to control the initial stages of lumber production. In 1905 the Goodyear brothers bought half a million more acres of timber lands on the Bogue Lusa Creek in Washington Parish, Louisiana. Their company—the Southern Lumber Company—built several saw mills and a railroad, and planned a town, "complete with its own colored quarters." Chronicling the history of his family, a scion of the Goodyears wrote: "On May 13, 1907 Frank H. Goodyear died of Bright's disease, worn out with ceaseless activity and worry. Although only five feet eight inches in height, he weighed two hundred and twenty pounds and overeating was undoubtedly a cause of his early death." His appetite had obviously been enormous, but while it killed him, it helped to reshape the economy of the city of Buffalo.

Irvine J. Kittinger reached forward into the more advanced stages of lumber manufacturing. In 1901, Kittinger took control of his father-in-law's slumping furniture business. Within two decades Kittinger was internationally known as the maker of the finest quality furniture.

The excellence of Buffalo's shipping facilities made the city second only to Chicago as the most important livestock center in the world. Arriving from Canada and the West on lake boats and railroads, over a million cattle, sheep, and hogs were processed yearly in enormous livestock yards. There was a special bank which catered strictly to the needs of the countless livestock dealers, commission merchants, wholesale butchers, and meatpackers which made up the extensive industry. Livestock contributed to the diversity of the city's manufacturing base. Jacob Dold, president in the early years of the twentieth century of the largest packing house in Buffalo, wrote:

> There is no part of the animal which is not used. Certain glands, membranes, tissues, and bone oils are sources of valuable medicinal preparations. Some of the bones of better quality are converted into knife handles, buttons, etc.; other bones, after yeilding their contents of fats, oils and glue stock are used for poultry foods, and fertilizers. The intestines are converted into sausage and other containers, strings for musical instruments. Hoofs and horns are converted into combs and other novelties. Hair bristles are used in the manufacture of brushes and upholstery. The blood is used in certain meat food products.

No livestock by-product was more successful than soap, and by the early twentieth century the Larkin Soap Company had become the largest in the world. John Larkin, the son of a prosperous iron merchant and a graduate of Buffalo's Bryant and Stratton Business College, was a creative entrepreneur, equally as concerned with marketing strategy as with production, and was constantly experimenting with innovations in merchandising. His first step was to rely on catalogues rather than salesmen, and like other mail-order houses of that time, Larkin concerntrated on advertising gimmicks. In charge of Larkin's advertising was Elbert Hubbard, who became vice-president of the firm following his marriage to Larkin's sister.

Hubbard's first campaign was a promotion that offered a box of "Sweet Home Soap: laundry soap, toilet soap, a washing compound and a bottle of perfume—all for $6.00." His next ploy was a "guess-what premium." Featuring such items as collar buttons, pictures of American presidents, lockets and other doodads, Hubbard placed one in each box of soap. His most talked about strategy was a club plan by which a Larkin customer could order soap in wholesale quantities, sell it to friends and neighbors, and thereby earn himself a premium of a silk-shaded Chautauqua lamp, a Chautauqua oil heater, or a Chautauqua desk.

John Larkin conceived of his company as one big and happy family. (Indeed, two brothers-in-law were executive officers), and prided himself on the benevolent and paternalistic treatment of his employees. Larkin organized employee associations, glee clubs, service organizations, sports clubs, and a company newspaper, *Ourselves*. And yet, in spite of this corporate communalism, Larkin was quick to recognize individual success, like that of Darwin W. Martin.

Like so many people who settled in Buffalo during the nineteenth century, Martin hailed from a rural county in the central part of the state. He came to the city in 1879 at the age of fourteen and immediately went to work for John Larkin. Unlike Hubbard, his more restless superior who had quit the company to found an arts and crafts colony called the Roycrofters, Martin was a loyal employee. He became secretary of the company in 1893, a position he held until his retirement in 1925.

But beneath his devoted and hard-working corporate exterior, Martin was a man of great imagination and creativity. He was an obsessive tinkerer, fascinated by the new office technology that was beginning to emerge during the 1830s. In 1896, after several years of experimentation, Martin patented a mechanized card ledger system that soon became standard equipment in offices all over the country. Martin was also an innovative and creative manager, constantly experimenting with new and improved office techniques. In order to process the thousands of mail orders entering the office from every state in the country, Martin grouped the company's sales department by state, with each separate group handling orders from a different state. Letters to his customers were dictated into wax cylinders. The contents of letters were transmitted from the cylinders through a tube into a typist's earphones.

Martin was also a passionate devotee of Frank Lloyd Wright, who by 1901 had already achieved international notoriety as a radically different kind of architect, a designer of suburban homes in Oak Park, Illinois who had rejected totally the notions of home building that had guided genertions of American architects. One of the Wright-designed homes in Oak Park belonged to Martin's brother, and when Martin saw it during a Christmas visit there in 1900, he became an immediate disciple of that intemperate genius. In 1901, he convinced

Larkin to commission Wright to design a new office building for the company.

Wright hated all cities; it therefore came as no surprise to Larkin and Martin that he also hated Buffalo. He hated Larkin's posh Victorian mansion, where he stayed in 1901. He hated Delaware Avenue, the city's most fashionable street, with its imperious and stylized mansions: the several ersatz-Renaissance homes designed by Stanford White, the Italianate prive clubs, and the Byzantine synagogue which stood along the tree-lined boulevard. And yet, as much as he loathed the city, Wright welcomed the opportunity to work on a major office building (to date he had designed only private homes). He was also glad to be in the city where Louis Sullivan, his revered "meister," had created the first modern skyscraper in 1896, the Guaranty Building.

When it was completed in 1904, the Larkin Building, like the Guggenheim Museum built over fifty years later, was constructed around an open interior space skylighted from above and surrounded by repeating tiers of balconies. The building adhered strictly to the functionalist credo that Sullivan and Wright believed in so deeply. Elevators, in plain view of everybody, brought office workers from the main floor, where they all worked in one open space, up to the offices on the balconies above. Four corner towers, each ninety feet high, contained the staircases, while all plumbing was contained in special stacks built into the walls. One of the building's most novel features was that it was hermetically sealed against the dirt of the surrounding industrial area. With the absence of windows, air was circulated by the first commerical air conditioning system ever devised.

The problem was that neither Larkin nor his employees liked the building. They hated the straight and uncomfortable office furniture that Wright had designed for it. They hated the company restaurant where they were encouraged to eat, and the company orchestra that played during lunch. But most of all they disliked the fact that the building's open spaces ended the privacy and freedom from the scrutiny of their superiors that small, separate, and compartmentalized offices had always afforded them. But no one hated the building more than Larkin himself, and, to the utter disgust of Wright, Larkin installed a huge pipe organ and offered noontime recitals for the "spiritual uplife" of his workers. Darwin Martin's enthusiasm for the eccentric architect, however, was not diminished by what was generally regarded as the fiasco of the Larkin Building, and in 1905 he commissioned Wright to design a home for him in one of the newer residential sections of the city. The Martin house, completed in 1906, fast became a showcase of modernism in a city whose architecture was wallowing in clichéd Victorianisms.

Buffalo was proud of Larkin (if not of his building) and the fantastic success of his soap company, and in 1900 one of the city streets bordering on the company's office and factory complex was renamed after the founder of the company. Larkin expressed his gratitude in 1901 when he contributed a pavilion to the Pan American Exposition. Housing a display demonstrating the different steps in the manufacturing of soap, Larkin called it the "Wash-ington Monument."

Buffalo had other industries which had nothing to do with either heavy industry or commerce. One of these was the production of chemicals. Dispatched by his father in Germany to learn chemistry in 1899, Jacob F. Schoellkopf, Jr. returned to Buffalo several years later. He and his brother Alfred then formed the Schoellkopf Aniline and Chemical Works, manufacturing aniline dyes and sulphuric and muriatic acids, and making millions through the sale of explosives during World War I. National Aniline, as it was later called, was the first of many area chemical companies.

Another operation which owed nothing to industry or to the location of the city was the Buffalo and Honduras Company, which opened a banana and rubber plantation in Honduras in 1901. Stimulated by America's expansionistic foreign policy, and the spirit of the Pan American Exposition, the secretary of the company offered a good reason for the interest of Buffalo capitalists in the venture: "You, know, there has been some talk that laziness on the part of the natives might hurt us. But we have not found that to be true. We've had no trouble in getting natives who are willing to work hard. The goods are there and so is the labor. It's a fine investment."

Also growing rapidly, and quickly capturing the imagination of the people of Buffalo, was the automobile business. In 1899 a man named Truman Martin, the manager of the New York Electrical Vehicle Transportation Company (a Whitney subsidiary), opened an electrical automobile dealership in Buffalo. A year later George N. Pierce, a world-renowned bicycle manufacturer, had hesitantly begun the manufacturing of a gasoline-powered automobile. In 1901 the Pierce "motorette," a two and three-quarters horsepower automobile with a maximum speed of fifteen miles per hour, finished first in a Fourth of July race between Buffalo and New York. In 1903 Pierce offered three automobiles: a five-horsepower run-about, the six and one-half horsepower Stanhope, and the sixteen and one-half horsepower Arrow. Pierce reported that in all three models, "the noise of the exhaust has been almost entirely eliminated, owing to a new system adopted in construction." Prices for Pierce's automobiles ranged from $1,000 to $2,500.

The Conrad Motor Carriage Company began production of steam-powered vehicles in 1900. A year later they switched to gasoline and began the manufacturer of a light run-about and a twelve horsepower touring car. The founder of the company, F. P. Conrad, had studied in France, and used the French system of automobile construction that had been developed by the French inventor Panhard. Conrad's hope was to manufacture an automobile that anybody could drive and "would not require an engineer to operate." In 1902 there were five hundred automobiles in Buffalo, and a chapter of the Automobile Club of America was actively lobbying on behalf of the city's motorists.

Throughout the city were small and large manufacturing operations producing an incredible variety of items: pianos, jewelry, watches, organs, wallpaper, photographs, print, furniture, statuary, flatware, crockery, paint, wire, caskets, candy, tea, coffee, ice cream, cigars, wine, pharmaceutical equipment and drugs, shoes, rubber, clothing, millinery, umbrellas, eye glasses, sewing machines, typewritters, plumbing equipment, cement, bottles, cans, fur, rubber products, flags, and banners. The Buffalo Pie Baker, claiming that they "save the modern housewife the heat and worry, the care and the time which mothers give to their work," made several hundred pies daily. Making similar claims for the effect of merchanization and inventiveness in his industry, the president of the Queen City Company, a maker of artificial limbs, boasted: "The empty sleeves and the crude wooden leg have given way to the delicately and artistically constructed arm and leg."

Although increasingly oriented toward factory work, Buffalo's work force was not yet dominated by unskilled laborers. Indeed, out of a total work force of 181,000 in 1910, less than 10,000, including the workers in the Lackawanna Steel mills, were unskilled industrial workers. The far greater number were semi-skilled workers in the city's breweries, piano factories, and foundries. Even the automobile workers were numbered among the more skilled workers. Pierce Arrow was proud that there were no "all around mechanics" at their plant. Also counted among the skilled work force were the 6,781 machinists and mill wrights; 5,369 carpenters; 942 compositors and linotypers; 1,225 brick and stone masons; 2,141 iron moulders; and 1,888 painters, glaziers, and varnishers.

With few exceptions these industrial laborers worked in small factories. While Pierce Arrow employed well over a thousand men in the early twentieth century, the other automobile factories were small, employing under a hundred men each. Breweries, slaughtering houses, and clothing factories were smaller still, employing averages of 51, 48, and 28 workers per factory respectively.

Offices too were small. But their numbers were growing rapidly at the turn of the century, and business management and administration were among the fastest growing job categories. In 1910 there were 1,032 manufacturing superintendents and 1,852 manufacturing officials. Bookkeepers, cashiers, and accountants were also a growing group of workers with over six thousand people, more than half of whom were women. There were over 30,000 women in the work force in 1910. While the greatest number of them (7,127) were domestic servants, 6,000 women worked in clerical occupations, 3,412 did home work as dressmakers and seamstresses, 2,583 were in retail, 2,285 were teachers, and 725 were trained nurses. A small number worked in factories, primarily laundries (which were included in that category).

Service trades claimed a growing number of both male and female workers in the economy of early twentieth century Buffalo. Indeed, second only to general labor, the largest category of work listed in the 1910 census was that of retail dealers. In that year over seven thousand people, seven hundred of whom were women, owned their own stores. Six thousand more people worked in these stores. Another significant sector of the service economy was composed of Buffalo's 1,037 saloon keepers, 659 waiters, 627 waitresses. Added to the ranks of these skilled and service sector workers was the growing class of people in the professional services. In 1910 there were 754 physicians and surgeons, 714 lawyers and judges, 410 draftsmen, and 367 clergymen. None of these were women.

Also significant is that while the American-born children of foreign parents and the foreign-born themselves did unquestionably make up the great bulk of unskilled laborers and domestics, this group was well represented within the skilled trades too. With the exception of such professions as law, medicine, and drafting, there was no occupatin that was dominated by second-generation Americans. In the semi-skilled trades—brewing and automobile manufacturing, for example—there were far more foreigners and first-generation Americans than there were second-generation American workers. Similarly, there were three times as many foreign-born retail store owners than those born in this country, more foreign-born policemen, and more foreign-born musicians and teachers of music. Despite the existence of a largely foreign-born industrial proletariat, the foreign-born and the children of the foreign-born were well on the way to achieving parity with the second-generation American work force.

This was not true, of course, for blacks. There were 698 blacks in the work force in Buffalo in 1900, and while they included one lawyer, one physician, several clergymen, one undertaker, thirteen actors, thirteen restaurant owners, twenty-one musicians, twenty-one barbers, and three female nurses, the great majority (574) worked in domestic service. Three hundred twenty-six were waiters, and eighty-three black males worked as general unspecified workers. With the exception of a small black work force in the factories of Lackawanna Steel, blacks worked in industry only as strikebreakers. For these people, anyway, the economic boom of the early twentieth century had little meaning.

But most people accepted this. Certainly few permitted it to compromise their heady expectations and their buoyant predictions of continued growth. Convinced that their diversified manufacturing base guaranteed them continued prosperity and a cushion against downturns in the national business cycle, few people were aware of the increasingly apparent weaknesses that haunted Buffalo's economy. For, despite what they may have thought about the advantages of a diversified economy, like it or not the fortunes of the city had become increasingly intertwined with the railroad industry, and with the national economy as a whole.

Despite their important role in the industrial life of the city, Buffalo had always been ambivalent about the railroads. In the middle of the nineteenth century, people's anxiety was based on the perennial fear that the railroads would undermine the Erie Canal. Despite desperate and annual efforts to maintain the competitiveness of the canal—tolls were first lowered, then eliminated altogether—the worst fears of the canal interests were realized with the rapid development of the railroad after the Civil War. By the end of the 1860s the canal was doomed and the board of trade mournfully reported in 1869 that "some classes of freight have almost altogether left the Canal. From Buffalo the movement of flour by canal during the five years ending with 1869 was more than 70% less than in the five years ending in 1864." Indeed, the year 1869 was the first that the combined movement of freight on the Erie and the New York Central railroads exceeded that shipped on the Erie Canal. These trends continued through the remainder of the century. Even the $60 million improvement program launched with vote approval in 1903 to enlarge the canal, a development which made it possible for the canal to handle 1,000-ton boats instead of 250-ton freighters that it normally carried, failed to restore the canal's competitive capacity.

The city's prosperity, however, was no longer tied to the canal, and as long as Buffalo continued to function as a port of transshipment, even if it was from lake boats to railroads rather than to canal boats, the city's economy thrived. As long, in other words, as the produce of the West and Midwest continued to move eastward by lake boat to Buffalo, regardless of how it left Buffalo, the economy could easily survive the obsolescence of the canal. But what had become increasingly apparent by the late nineteenth century was that a growing number of western producers had in fact begun to shift away from lake steamers to railroads. This phenomenon was a deadly serious threat to the health of Buffalo's diversified economy. A journalist writing in 1893 described the predicament of the 1880s: "She looked eastward and she saw the railroads speeding their trains eastward and westward by her very gates—yet not knocking for admission."

Because there is always more profit in the long rather than the short freight haul, railroad interest preferred and encouraged producers to ship directly from the Midwest. As a result, during the early twentieth century, eastern port cities like Baltimore and Philadelphia, and southern and western ports like New Orleans and Galveston, began to make considerable inroads into trade normally bound for Buffalo. Not only did shippers want to avoid the time-consuming and expensive break-of-bulk that occurred in Buffalo, but the railroad interests wanted to avoid the less profitable short haul between Buffalo and New York City. Because they had come to own and control most of the lake shipping firms, the railroad interests, by refusing to improve their yards and facilities in Buffalo, and by intentionally channelling trade from lake streamers to rails on the long-haul line, effectively undermined and weakened the health and diversity that still characterized the city's economy in 1910.

Meanwhile, consolidation and absentee-ownership, trends that when fully developed would wreak havoc in the economy later in the century, were barely, yet clearly, apparent by 1910. In 1883 the Solar Oil Works, one of several local companies that piped in oil from Pennsylvania, was bought by the Tidewater Pipe Line Company. Ten years later Tidewater was bought by Standard Oil. In 1863 Buffalo had thrity-five breweries that produced 152,000 barrels a year. In 1896 nineteen breweries produced over a half million barrels. By 1906, only thirteen produced close to a million. In 1901 the Urban Mills, the largest in Buffalo, was bought out by Standard Mills of Minneapolis. Three years later the newly opened mills of the Washburn

Company, also of Minneapolis, replaced Standard as the largest flour company in Buffalo. That same year the Buffalo Cereal Company, manufacturer of the popular breakfast cereal "Force," was acquired by Quaker Oats. In 1905 Hengerer's and J. N. Adams, the city's largest department stores, were bought out by Associated Merchants of New York City. In 1898 the three largest independent and locally owned streetcar companies were bought out by a Morgan-controlled investment group and were consolidated into the International Railway Company. In 1902 the International Railway Company was in turn bought out by the International Traction Company of Philadelphia. The trends were ominous.

Despite the incresing nationalization of Buffalo's economy, factories were small, and relations between employers and their workers informal and fairly intimate. In many cases there was little social distance between one and the other. Oftentimes they came from the same environment. E. S. Miller, the president of the Gerhard Lang brewery, lived right around the corner from his factory. E. M. Hager, the owner of the Hager Furniture Company, lived on Oak Street, in the heart of the German neighborhood where many of his employees also lived, attended church, and participated in community groups and activities.

Desite their relative closeness, conflicts between capital and labor were nevertheless a regular and predictable aspect of life in late nineteenth century Buffalo. Few of these conflicts, however, lasted for long; none involved large groups of workers; and none, with the exception of the perennial battles between striking Irish dockworkers and black scabs, resulted in violence. These patterns, accepted and expected by the community at large, continued largely unchanged until well into the latter part of the century. Then too, most of the labor conflicts were isolated confrontations involving small groups of skilled workers who demanded recognition of their unions, a shorter work day, and occasionally a pay increase. While worker's grievances were no doubt heartfelt and sincere, they were, because of the relationship between employer and employee, much like conflicts within a large, extended family, and were generally resolved in a peaceful and informal manner.

Organized labor in Buffalo, as in other cities in late nineteenth century America, was far more fractionalized than it was united. Consisting of trade unions of skilled workmen, the organized labor movement was Catholic; conservative; and concerned primarily with the recognition of their unions, a shorter work day, and what was referred to as a "fair return for labor."

While there had been trade unions in Buffalo since the late 1820s, it was not until 1884 that they federated in the Central Labor Union. Reconstituted in the wake of the depression of the early 1890s as the United Trades and Labor Council (UTLC) this central union was a very loosely knit federation consisting of six sharply defined and clearly delineated sections: building trades, printing trades, German trades (where all locals conduct their affairs in German), the railroad section, and the miscellaneous section. Within each of these separate categories were a whole host of separate trade union locals. The building trades was the largest section, and included the Amalgamated Sheet Metal Workers; the Society of Carpenters and Joiners; the Bricklayers and Stone Masons; the Tinsmiths; the Electrical Workers, the Plasterers, Painters and Decorators; and the Steamfitters. Each of these locals had a life and organization of its own, separate and apart from the central union. The same was true of the other sections. The iron trades consisted of separate locals of coremakers, machinists, German machinists, machinery moulders, iron moulders, and pattern makers. The printing trades had lithographic artists and engravers, printing pressmen, and typographical workers. The miscellaneous section consisted of separate locals of beer barrel coopers, beer driver's helpers and stablemen, boot and shoe workers, cigar makers, bicycle frame makers, screw makers, retail clerks, and licensed hucksters (who, differentiating themselves from the "scalper hucksters" insisted on their "God given rights of having the privilege to peddle our produce all day"). Added to these many different layers of skilled trade unions was the German section, which mirrored all of the above for those workers who preferred to have their affairs conducted in German.

The leaders of these unions of skilled workers were not firebrands. Rather they were serious, hard-working, highly skilled laborers who had spent many years at their particular trades. Charles Sheel, the president of the Sheet Metal Workers, was born in Buffalo in 1857 and began working as a cornice maker at the age of seventeen. Joseph Connor, another officer in the Sheet Metal Workers union, had been working as a tin-roofer since 1875, when as a boy of eighteen he began practicing his father's trade. John Jones, the president of the Carpenters and Joiners, was born in the British Isles in 1850. When he came to Buffalo he had already learned his trade and quickly became active in local union affairs. Frank Lettes learned the carpenter's trade as a boy on a farm in Montgomery County. He too continued his childhood-learned skills following his settlement in

Buffalo in the early seventies. Commitment to a trade and to a body of skilled workers characterized local trade union leaders, who were not likely to jeopardize the integrity of their work or to disrupt the existing relations between worker and employer through the use or threat of violence.

It was this diversified collection of trade unions, and not the radical Knights of Labor (which had alienated the city's Catholic labor establishment), that was the central and most influential labor organization in Buffalo. The UTLC left bargaining and dispute settlement to each individual local and chose instead to define general policy for the skilled labor movement as a whole. It worked out an agreement with the city in 1897, for example, whereby the city promised not to do business with employers who worked their employees more than eight hours a day. Similarly, it lobbied successfully for the passage of local legislation that barred the use of convict labor in the printing and binding of government books and records. Similarly, the UTLC protested when the city insisted on using cheap Polish and Italian labor to work on such public projects as street and railroad construction. Despite their largely Irish and German membership, the UTLC, because of its sensitivity to cheap labor, was extremely hostile to immigrants and immigration. Few Italians or Poles belonged to the trade unions that comprised the UTLC, and the one Italian union on the West Side in the 1890s—the Italian Freight Handler's Union—was not affiliated with the UTLC. The UTLC was similarly hostile to the Chinese. By the turn of the century the Laundry Workers had become increasingly concerned about the proliferation of Chinese hand laundries. In a publication called *Clean Clothes: An Illustrated Magazine Devoted to Cleanliness, Sanitation and Sound Textiles*, they urged their readers to boycott the Chinese laundries, saying not only that they exploited their workers, but also that they had "unclean premises, using destructive washing materials. They offer the customer no protection against contagious diseases, the germs of which can be carried home in a bundle of clothes."

Because of the variety and scale of manufacturing in late nineteenth century Buffalo, ownership of factories was diversified and the scale was small. The largest brewery—Gerhard Lang—employed fewer than two hundred workers, while the more than dozen others averaged between thirty and thirty-five. The same was true for the building trades. There were any number of building contractors in Buffalo. The "leading builders," according to the UTLC, were eight men who employed no more than thirty workers each. Like the brewers, all of the rest were small-scale businessmen, often from the same ethnic group and neighborhood community as their skilled employees, who for some reason had been able to muster the capital necessary to become businessmen. It was within this kind of environment, then, that most of the strikes in late nineteenth and early twentieth century Buffalo occurred. These were different kinds of conflicts, generating different kinds of responses and reactions, than the large, industrywide conflicts. When German brewery workers struck against the Lang, the Germania, and the Royal Lion breweries, as they did periodically during the 1880s, they were striking against members of their own community who, as a result of the nature of the work environment and of the structure of the community itself, they knew personally and sometimes intimately.

While this may well have produced great stress and tension within these communities, it also created a degree of recognition that helps to explain the success that these skilled workers had in dealing with their employers. By the late 1880s most skilled workmen had achieved employer recognition of their unions, enjoyed an eight-hour day, and were working at wages that they at least regarded as acceptable. These trade unions had earned a degree of prosperity and acceptability. All of them paid modest death and accident benefits, and almost all of them worked in closed shops. By the 1890s the skilled workmen had become a clearly identified part of the Buffalo establishment. And they knew it too. A UTLC publication in 1897 contains a long section on the history of Buffalo that might well have been written by a bank, a newspaper, or the chamber of commerce. Like other boosterish and buoyant accounts of the city's history so popular at that time, this workingman's understanding of Buffalo's past contains no evidence of conflict. To them, it seemed, Buffalo was a unified, cohesive community.

The railraod strikes of 1877 and 1892, however, had a far more damaging impact, altering the way people in Buffalo thought about the relations between capital and labor. Virtually every city and small town in the industrial Northeast was affected by the railroad uprisings of 1877, when thousands of railroad workers struck protesting ten percent wage reduction on all of the railroads throughout the region. Violence occurred everywhere—in small towns in West Virginia, New York, and Pennsylvania; and in Pittsburgh, Baltimore, Chicago, and Buffalo. In Buffalo, where disputes between capital and labor had traditionally been limited to small, isolated confrontations between skilled workers and small-scale businessmen, the railroad strike of 1877 came as an incredible shock, creating panic, uncertainty and terror in the city. In early July 1877, on the East Side and in South

Buffalo where railroad lines and yards were so prevalent, strikers concentrated on disrupting the movement of passenger and freight cars. They pulled out switch lights, greased the tracks, took possession of the locomotives, uncoupled trains, and successfully threatened strikebreakers. Then, storming factories throughout the East Side, armies of strikebreakers tried, largely without success, to induce other industrial workers to join their cause. An account of the strike, written in 1893, reported:

> Among the establishments visited were the planing mills of Boller & Rectenwalt and Joseph Churchyard, which were closed temporarily. The manufactory of Jewett & Root and other factories received attention, but with no success. Stone yards, coal yards, the Hamburg canal (state work), and other places where men were employed were called upon, and wherever intimidation could be made effective, the men were driven from their work. About three o'clock the depredators paid their respects to the establishment of John T. Noye & Son, and unceremoniously broke in one of the doors and took possession. The district telegraph box, communicating with No. 1 station, was pulled, and almost immediately Police Superintendent Byrne, with thirty patrolmen, was on the scene. The officers were drawn up in a double line across the street, facing down Washington Street, and made a charge, wheeling rapidly into Scott street. The clubs were brought freely into use, but without any intention of inflicting serious injuries, and the mob fled, panic stricken and with aching bones. This virtually put an end to interference with the manufacturing establishments.

Justifiably frightened by the occurrences in the streets of their city, the local press panicked, and by wildly exaggerating the situation in Pittsburgh and Baltimore, implied that real anarchy would result in Buffalo, unless the authorities responded quickly and harshly. They did. At first the mayor, a German-born grocery merchant named Becker, issued a call for volunteers, "special patrolmen without pay," to supplement the police. Three hundred, among them thirty-five railroad engineers and firemen, responded. Then on July 23, one day after the strike had begun, the mayor requested that the governor dispatch 1,600 state militiamen. The 300 volunteers, plus the 1,600 state militiamen, plus 1,800 Civil War veterans, plus the regular police force, were marshalled to deal with the emergency. In street clashes, eight soldiers were wounded and eight strikers killed.

The strikers got little local support and were quickly demoralized. No other group of workers joined them, no newspaper endorsed their efforts, and within a week their resistance was broken. By the end of July railroad workers in Buffalo accepted the wage reduction and returned to work.

If the reaction and the impact of the strike in Buffalo was indicative, the railroad rebellion of July 1877 seemed to have made little impact on the conflicts between capital and labor. The strikers never received the support of other industrial workers and there appears to have been little worker solidarity created as a result of the strike. Indeed, it was not until August 1892 that another industrywide strike occurred. And then it was again a strike of railroad workers. This time it was the switchmen who, when denied their demands for a ten-hour day, and a wage increase from 21¢ per hour for night work and 19¢ to 23¢ for day work, went out on strike. Again, the authorities wasted no time.

The railroads had decided to break the strike with scabs, and as hundreds were being brought in from Pennsylvania it was decided by the mayor and the city's moneyed men that troops were needed to deal with the violence that would predictably result. Eight thousand state militiamen were activated and charged with protecting the property of the railroad and the strikebreaker's right to work.

Sensing that the source of the worker's strength was in their communities, the authorities struck as close to home as they could. They mayor requested special emergency legislation enabling him to shut down saloons. When this failed, the troops actually chased striking railroad workers through the streets of their communities and on several occasions broke up and dispersed meetings being held in local taverns.

Again, the severity and the swiftness of the official response, plus the apparent indifference of not only other railraod workers but of the industrial work force in general, put a quick end to the switchmen's strike. Within ten days it was over, and the strikers returned to work with nothing to show for their efforts.

While difficult to quantify, it is easy to speculate that the conflicts that these two strikes produced must surely have been extraordinarily upsetting in the life of the community. For, far more than being an abstract conflict between capital and labor, these strikes pitted residents of the same city against each other, not only in disagreement but in violent conflict. Eight thousand state militiamen, a fair portion of whom were from Buffalo, were enlisted to bear arms against people who lived not even as far away, sometimes, as the other side of town. The lines were not clearly drawn between workers and employers or even between ethnic and non-ethnic groups. Indeed, the striking switchmen were pursued and confronted by troops who more likely than not were Irish, German, and even Polish and Italian. How does a city repair the damages caused by conflicts like this whose effects locally must have been even more divisive than the war between the states was nationally?

The grain scoopers' strike of 1899 revealed still different patterns. Like the other labor conflicts involving skilled and semi-skilled labor, the strike of the grain scoopers indicated that more was at work in turn-of-the-century strikes than simple conflicts between capital and labor, employers and employees. The strike of the grain scoopers in 1899 was not against the owners of the grain elevators, but rather against the local saloon owners who, acting as labor contractors (an Irish version of the Italian *padrone* system), had come to control labor on Buffalo's waterfront. The strike of scoopers against the domination of the saloon keeper–labor contractors, like those within the German breweries, often had the overtones of an intra-ethnic and even intra-class conflict.

No contracts on formal work arrangements existed on the docks. Whenever a freighter loaded with grain arrived in Buffalo's harbor, hundreds of men, primarily Irish and Italian, flocked to the docks hoping to be picked by the boat captain to unload the grain. Most of the time was spent waiting, first for the boat and then to be picked. While they waited, the men congregated in the dozens of local saloons that clustered around the dock area. Taking advantage of this large labor pool, several saloon keepers became intermediaries between the workers and the ships' captains, on the take from both, as the former sought jobs and the latter workers. The longshoremen and the grain scoopers were virtually indentured to the saloon keepers, who not only found them jobs, but insisted on paying them in the saloon itself, thereby encouraging them to spend their earnings in the saloon. It is not surprising that, given his extensive control, the waterfront saloon keeper emerged as a dominant political and economic force in late nineteenth century Buffalo.

The most powerful was William Connors, a former sailor and longshoreman, and a tavern owner in South Buffalo. By 1895, "Fingy" Connors, so named because he had lost two fingers on his left hand in a waterfront accident, owned his own brewery and was the publisher of two Buffalo newspapers. His long-time control of the work force on the waterfront was jeopardized, however, when in 1899 the grain scoopers, joined subsequently by the longshoremen, struck.

Connors didn't have a chance. For now, unlike during the railroad strikes, the strikers had the support of a wide variety of interest groups. Grain elevator operators and railroad companies were eager to resume the shipment of grain, and after several months began to bring extensive pressure to bear on Buffalo interests to settle the strike. Connors was the perfect scapegoat, the man everybody loved to hate. Temperance groups, both Catholic and Protestant, viewing the strike as an opportunity to attack the saloon, rallied to the cause. Ministers from every faith and denomination in the city lent support. Political reformers jumped at the chance to chasten one of Buffalo's strongest ward politicians. Aristocratic reformers were eager to side with such a respectable working class movement. The pressure was overwhelming, and in May 1899, after a month-long strike during which Buffalo's harbor had come to a complete close (wheat was backed up for three weeks in Duluth, Minnesota), Connors gave in. The grain scoopers had won: Connors and the other saloon labor contractors recognized the Longshoremen's Association as the bargaining unit for the scoopers and longshoremen. As important, the strike ended the use of the saloon as a hiring hall and garnered a guarantee that wages would be paid in an office and not in the saloon. While the scoopers and longshoremen drew strength and satisfaction from the victory, most people construed the strike as the defeat of Connors and what he represented—the saloon, the ward, the lurking power of Irish immigrant vitality—rather than as a workers' victory. Connors didn't need the victory anyway. By the time the strike was settled he had already lost interest in the docks. In the future he would devote himself to his newspapers and to politics.

Unlike the railroad strike of 1877 and 1892, there was little violence during the grain scoopers' strike of 1899. There had been similarly little violence during the depression that had begun in 1893. Throughout 1893 and 1894 there were several large meetings and demonstrations demanding that the city government provide work and food to the desperately needy work force. In the summer of 1893 over five thousand Polish men and women held such a rally on the East Side. Later in the summer, close to a thousand of them marched to City Hall. Other groups—trade unionists, laborers, ethnic organizations—made similar protests and demands, and while the press tended to respond cautiously and anxiously, never quite certain what might result, violence never did take place. Indeed, the absence of violence and the general calm that prevailed in the city during the mid-1890s suggest a certain consensus, a feeling that everybody was going through the hard times together.

Of course they weren't. Indeed, the wealthy were reacting to the upheavals of the 1890s in different, sometimes strange and sometimes predictable ways. Ansley Wilcox was one of them. Above all, Wilcox believed in accountability. Nobody, he maintained, was "entitled" to anything. Certainly nobody got anything for nothing. As director of the Charity Organization Society (COS), the private citywide fund whose charge was caring for Buffalo's poor, Wilcox was in a position of great influence and power over the needy. Born in Augusta, Georgia and educated at Yale, Wilcox moved to Buffalo in 1878. He soon married into one of Buffalo's oldest and wealthiest families, was admitted into the bar and, by the end of the 1880s, was a partner in a leading corporate law firm.

Wilcox had very definite ideas about poverty, its causes, and its remedies, and had been active in the COS since his first years in Buffalo. In 1892 he became the chairman of the board of the organization.

For years Wilcox had supported his mother, an aging widow in Augusta. Sending her weekly checks for over fifteen years, Wilcox insisted that she provide detailed accounts of how she spent his money. In her weekly thank-you note to him she documented her expenses: three dollars to repair the stove, thirty-six dollars to paint the roof, eight dollars for the dentist, two-fifty for books, and three dollars per day for food, "including milk." In one note, thinking that she had skipped a week, she wrote: "I believe I have failed to thank you for the check you mailed last week. I will try to use the money with discretion but there is always some most unexpected demand coming up. I am moderate in my outlays, yet the summing up is so big."

Wilcox, believing that in his mother's case, at least, poverty was "honest, industrious, independent, self-respecting [and] entirely worthy of respect," continued to support her. What he despised, however, was pauperism and as head of the COS he refused to condone it. To Wilcox, "pauperism was poverty when it has become dependent, dishonest; when it has lost its ambition and abandoned hope."

The problem for Wilcox and other late nineteenth century reformers was to somehow separate what they considered the deserving from the nondeserving poor, and to create a system of charity and relief that encouraged initiative and independence. Wilcox was most critical of the contemporary practice of providing relief to the poor in their homes, known as "outdoor relief." Insisting on the same degree of accountability he exacted from his mother, Wilcox opposed what he called the "give and ask no questions" principle of charity. Home relief, the simple giving of cash to those considered needy, was thought to encourage pauperism. Wilcox, for example, was convinced that the Polish recipients of these cash benefits used the money to buy passage for their friends and relatives from Poland. This kind of a "no strings attached" system of poor relief would lead the Poles to become "dissolute, depraved and degraded, cursed with a plague spot that will widen and increase." Unless "alms be accompanied with curative measures," Wilcox argued before the society, charity was simply "supplying pablum to the vices of the vicious and stimulant to the vicious tendencies of the weak; poison to those who are not yet depraved." The poor, Wilcox maintained somewhat confusingly, should be treated like children and like the way he treated his mother: with "kindness, patience, sympathy and with a firmness which verges on sterness." Always thinking that they were treading the line between charity and indulgence, Wilcox and the other directors of the COS were never sure whether they were alleviating the problem or making it worse. Sometimes the pressure of circumstances forced them to adopt policies that they soon regretted. Their doubts often paralyzed them. During the winter of 1893, as unemployment and uncertainty mounted, the COS spent weeks debating whether or not to open a soup kitchen. Finally, arguments suggesting that such a program would "make more paupers in one winter than years of organized charity could ever cure," prevailed. The poor would have to sacrifice still more in order to be deserving of aid. The kitchen idea was abandoned.

Hoping to assuage their own consciences as well as to aid the truly needy, Wilcox and the COS, following the heed of similar organizations in New York City, developed a labor test in 1894. Convinced that "not more than one tenth of all applicants for aid are worthy," Wilcox believed that the "stone breaking labor test" would distinguish once and for all those willing to work from the slackers. The labor test asked that all able-bodied men who were applying to the COS for support break six cubic yards of stone at a wage of seventy-five cents per yard. Wilcox noted contentedly, finally persuaded that the lazy and nondeserving would be discovered and ferreted out, that "those who stand this test, with the cold and exposure involved, are considered to have demonstrated sufficiently their willingness to work," and would therefore be deemed deserving of support. As unemployment grew during the middle years of the 1890s, so too did the conviction that relief could not be had without work. Wilcox's speeches and COS reports throughout this period constantly argued the necessity of "refraining from indiscriminate alms giving," and reminded people that "intelligent giving and intelligent withholding are like true charity."

While Wilcox and the other affluent members of the board of the COS despised those undeserving who fraudulently misrepresented themselves as needy, they were benign and patronizing towards those whom they had determined were deserving. Indeed, they refused to blame these people for their poverty. If housing conditions were unsanitary and in need of improvement, it was not up to the poor, but rather to the privileged, to remedy them. For, in the eyes of Wilcox, "these people, we must remember, are not capable of appreciating their surroundings even when free to choose their homes." Indeed, when conditions worsened during 1894, Wilcox did not become resentful of his childlike, deserving charges, but rather blamed himself, suggesting that somehow the COS itself had failed in the "thoroughness of its work." He urged the social workers in the organization to take a more active interest in their cases, to make more home visits, to seek out the children of the families in need, and to treat the poor as they would a friend.

To the end Wilcox and his fellow philanthropists insisted that the causes of poverty and the means to remedy it were personal and individual, a matter of behavior and attitude, not a question of economics. Nowhere in the hundreds of pages of COS reports during the late nineteenth and early twentieth centuries is there any indication that poverty and unemployment were in any way connected to the regular swings in the city's economy.

Still believing that they controlled the economic destiny of the city, despite growing evidence to the contrary, Wilcox and his fellow affluent do-gooders expected the poor to do the same. Persistence, hard work, diligence, application, and strength of character could raise a man from poverty and ignorance. But if that failed, Wilcox said in one of his speeches as director of the Charity Organization Society, there was always kindness: "Whenever a family has fallen so low as to need relief, send them at least one friend—a patient, true sympathizing firm friend—to do for them all that a friend can do to discover and remove the cause of their dependence and to help them up into independent self-support and self-respect."

If poverty was both caused and relieved by the conduct and behavior of individuals, the COS was willing to take some steps that would soften the blows and alleviate some of the hardship of being poor. The COS lobbied for tenement laws, for the construction in neighborhoods throughout the city of municipal baths, for night schools and vocational schools, and for including parish churches in poor relief programs. Similarly, the COS supported the host of settlement houses and other outreach activities sponsored by the city's wealthier congregations during the depression years of the mid-1890s. Although not a temperance group, the COS played an active role in the Anti-

Saloon League. Convinced that the neighborhood tavern was a primary cause of "deviance, drunkenness, misbehavior and dependence," the COS urged vigilant enforcement of Sunday closing laws and other measures designed to control the taverns. Arguing also that it was a demoralizing site for the poor, Wilcox argued unsuccessfully for a city ordinance that would ban the presence in Buffalo of street musicians and organ grinders.

Efforts to control the community life of the city's poor and foreign population did not stop with these measures. Indeed, the desire to control and to mold the recipients of public aid motivated virtually all of the free services offered in late nineteenth and early twentieth century Buffalo. This was particularly true of public education. Here, as in the dispensing of relief, nothing was given for free: Everything served a purpose. Homework was beneficial because it "furnished the opportunity for the practical application of the most important principles of behavior while cultivating the habits of neatness and orderly arrangement while giving pupils a knowledge that will bring substantial financial reward in business life." "Cookery and domestic science" was taught to girls because, as the director of manual training bafflingly observed, "good housekeeping is one of the most powerful forces we can employ in dealing with the great social problems which are becoming so acute in our large cities." To boys, it was important to teach science, because through it "the child is brought to know truth, to feel the benign influence of beauty in natural form; to respect life in any form—his life—because in his study of plant and animal life he has gained a glimpse of the divine laws of which even the humblest structures are made." Public school educators went beyond concern for the curriculum in their efforts to mold good citizens. Steeped in reverence for the ways of New England, and displeased with the bastardization of spoken English that was occurring in the polyglot city, the supervisor of German for the public schools became obsessed during the 1890s with elocution and with the accents of his pupils. Convinced that "pleasant voices, correct pronunciation and good enunciation are distinctive marks of education, culture and [note the emphasis] breeding," he urged all grammar school teachers to pay particular attention to the "well known fact that in Buffalo the sounds of 'a' in words like half, aunt, ask, dance, grass, etc.; of 'o' in on, dog, gone, etc., of 'u' in tube, Tuesday, etc. are very commonly mispronounced." Believing that "such habits are not easily corrected," he insisted that his teachers devote extra time to this task.

There were other notions of how to prepare the city's youth for a life of success. A local professor of dance tried to convince the board of education to develop a program whereby local newsboys would be taught dance and etiquette. Convinced that "some of our most intelligent and wealthiest men of today started life as newsboys," he asserted that if given a chance "the newsboys of today would make their mark as businessmen." For this to happen, the professor maintained, "he must cultivate himself beginning with the art of dancing, deportment and etiquette."

It was in order to exert greater control over the government of the city that political reformers—among whom were not only Wilcox, but virtually all of the wealthy, influential and powerful members of Buffalo's business and social establishment—attempted throughout the late nineteenth and early twentieth centuries to strengthen the governmental structure of Buffalo by centralizing it.

In Buffalo, in the middle of the nineteenth century, real political power lay with the aldermen. The city was divided into thirteen separate wards and each one, regardless of size, elected two aldermen. In addition to the mayor and the aldermen, the people chose a whole range of elected officials: the commissioners of police, fire, health, and public works, as well as the superintendent of schools. By the 1870s the downtown establishment—the business leaders, the bar, the newspapers—had begun to realize that this political arrangement was not in their best interest. For one thing, the aldermanic system was riddled with corruption. For another and still more important reason, it gave far too much power to the working-class and increasingly ethnic enclaves of the city. What the downtowners wanted instead was a political system that reflected their vision of the good city, a city united behind the political and economic interests of the central business district. In 1880 these groups, committed to a major change in the political structure of the city, rallied behind the candidacy of Grover Cleveland and elected him mayor of Buffalo.

Cleveland had been a popular man around town, a bachelor well known in both legal and social circles. He loved beer (he was the attorney for the Brewers Association) and enjoyed eating at the city's many restaurants and taverns. Buffalo was proud of its food, particularly its German cooking, and Cleveland ate out most every night: sometimes at Schneckenburger's, famous for its sausages and sauerkraut, and sometimes at Charley Diebold's, which specialized in "the best pig's knuckles in the Queen City."

Cleveland's popularity grew, and in 1871 he was elected sheriff of Erie County, the best paying and most difficult job in local government. As the chief law enforcement officer in the county, Cleveland presided over one of the most crime-infested cities in the country. Allan Nevins,

Cleveland's principal biographer, has written that Buffalo was "one of the roughest and most dangerous towns in America. It was sown with saloons. Along the waterfront were solid rows of dives of the worst order—barrel houses, dens selling Monongahela whiskey at four cents a glass, brothels and gambling joints. Cutting affrays were a daily affair. There were streets where the police walked at mid-day and only in pairs, for an officer who came along might shortly be found floating face down in the Canal. The Irish longshoremen loved nothing more than a fight and the prostitutes numbered in the hundreds." And the Erie County jail received more convicts than any jail in the state.

Cleveland plunged into the job, working harder than any sheriff in memory. He refused to shirk any of his assigned duties, even those that custom had long relegated to subordinates. One of these was the hanging of condemned criminals. During the summer of 1872, Sheriff Cleveland, upon receipt of a sworn statement from county physician Conrad Diehl that they were mentally sound, personally sprung the trap on two convicted murderers.

Cleveland was a Democrat in a predominantly Republican town. But because Buffalo was governed by an arrangement between the well-oiled political machines of both parties, electoral majorities were not necessarily the determining factors in the outcome of elections. The office of mayor, for example, alternated between Republicans and Democrats with predictable regularity. The mayor was hand-picked by the political machine and his office and power were not taken seriously. Terms lasted for only two years and once elected, a man rarely served again. The mayors of the late 1870s—be they the likeable Democrat and Bavarian, brewer Solomon Scheu, or the wealthy Republican brick manufacturer, Alexander Bush, who succeeded him— had no inclination to disrupt the rule of those who really ran the city: the aldermen.

But Cleveland was different. First as mayor of Buffalo, and then as governor of New York, Cleveland revealed the distinctly anti-Democratic bias of much of the late nineteenth century "progressive" reform movement. Like other reformers, Cleveland had far more faith in a body of appointed citizens than in elected representatives and as mayor he bypassed the aldermen, selecting people of his own choosing whenever he could. Then later as governor (it was his reputation as a reform-minded mayor that got him his party's gubernatorial nomination one year after his election as mayor), he consistently sided with reform groups who, far more often than not, were Protestants of wealth and social standing. When Theodore Roosevelt, a Republican assemblyman proud that he had overcome the traditional repulsion of his class for elected offices, proposed several bills which crippled the power of ward-elected aldermen in New York City, Cleveland unhesitatingly approved. Cleveland still further alienated ward politicians in Buffalo and New York City when he chocked the flow of patronage and made virtually all of his appointments based on merit.

Cleveland's actions as governor in Albany inspired reformers in his own city, and in 1889 a group of them, led by the omnipresent John Milburn, formed the Citizen's Association. By the end of the year they had drafted a new city charter which promised a revolution in the city's politics. According to the new charter, aldermen would no longer be elected by the separate wards but rather by the people in the city-at-large, and the commissioners, so long chosen by the electorate, would be appointed by the mayor.

Granted that the aldermanic system, by prescribing equal representation for every ward, discriminated against the largest and economically most important sections of the city. Granted too that it was inefficient and conducive to bribery and corruption. But the plain fact of the matter was that the ward system of representation was far more democratic than anything devised since.

Among those ward politicians who fought the new charter were the Sheehan Brothers—John and "Blue Eyed Billy" Sheehan—two Democratic leaders who built a fortress of working-class Democrats in Irish South Buffalo. Unfortunately for the Sheehans, the decision rested not with the electorate but with the state legislature in Albany, where in nothing associated with any city did Democrats, let alone Irish ones, have a chance. With the exception of a last-minute compromise which permitted the continuation of a small degree of ward representation, the charter of 1892 offered little comfort to the masses of people living in the different neighborhoods of the city. The charter was a downtowners' document and they knew it. After the passage of the charter, John Sheehan moved to New York. He became active in Democratic politics there and served briefly as the bitterly anti-Cleveland chief of Tammany Hall. His brother, Billy, continued the struggle in Buffalo, where an ever-loyal Irish constituency elected him as their assemblyman for seven consecutive terms.

When Grover Cleveland left Buffalo in 1882 for the Governor's Mansion in Albany, it was with few regrets. In spite of the success and popularity he had enjoyed in Buffalo, he never really liked the city. In 1888, at the end of his first term as president, he wrote to Charles W. Goodyear, a companion from his bachelor days in the Queen City: "I hardly think that I shall get to Buffalo very soon. I am sometimes afraid that my attachment for the place is getting a good deal lessened, but I don't know where else I can live." By 1889, he had decided to move to New York City. He never came back.

Other members of the city's WASP elite stayed in Buffalo, trying to make the best of the 1890s. It wasn't always easy. Sensing that they were in the crest of a last wave, the WASP gentry strove consciously to define and to strengthen their identity and their legacies as the bearers of a noble, yet clearly threatened New England tradition. For this generation of Buffalo's WASP patricians, the 1890s was a period of intense New England nostalgia. Biographical essays and obituaries of leading citizens were filled with idealized and nostalgic references to New England, describing one person's "hardy and heroic New England ancestors;" another in whom "the blood of New England ran vigorously;" and still another who was recorded as heralding from "ancient, honorable, New England stock, a descendent of good Puritan ancestry who behaved in the usual New England manner." Like the exclusively Protestant clubs and schools that proliferated during the 1890s—the Sons and the Daughters of the American Revolution, and the Nichols School, a private preparatory for the sons of the Protestant rich—these sentiments reflected a growing concern that the world—their world—was suddenly changing.

The many chronicles written during the nineties contained nostalgic references not only to New England but also to an earlier time in Buffalo's history, particularly the 1830s, when in fact most everybody in the city was either born in New England or directly descended from New England ancestors. Samuel Welch's *Home History*, written in 1893, was a fond and misty paean to the Buffalo of those earlier years. In a time, Welch wrote, when "the luxury and abundance of wealth did not stifle them with envious desires," Buffalo women, he said, were far more attractive and its immigrants, "though poor, were composed of the best of their class." But mostly Welch admired and longed for the "sterling and many New England virtues which planted the grace of civilization and the republicanism of our institutions upon our western frontiers."

These nostalgic references to a lost past, however, should not be taken too seriously. For despite them, the wealthy Protestants continued to dominate far more than any other group the affairs of the city. One way they did so was through philanthropy.

Philanthropy was yet another way to assert control, and it was during the late nineteenth and early twentieth centuries that Buffalo's wealthiest citizens were the most generous. Several of the wealthiest families gave enormous sums to Buffalo's public institutions. In 1900 John J. Albright, the iron manufacturer who had played such a prominent role in attracting William Scranton to Lackawanna, donated a half a million dollars for the construction of a new art gallery. Seymour Knox, who had made a fortune with the Woolworths in the dimestore business, donated a quarter of a million dollars sixteen years later to establish the College of Arts and Sciences at the University of Buffalo. Knox's gift, however, could not be made until a bitter conflict over a public system of higher education could be resolved.

Since the middle of the nineteenth century, the University of Buffalo had been a loosely-knit collection of professional schools consisting of a medical college, a law school, a school of dentistry, and a school of pharmacology. Following the appointment of Charles Norton, a native of Buffalo, as chancellor in 1905, however, a campaign was initiated to create a liberal arts college which, Norton hoped, would be subsidized by the city and would therefore serve primarily those high school graduates unable to afford a private, out-of-town college. With this in mind, Norton and his backers, who consisted of virtually every educator and community leader in Buffalo, turned to the city council for support. Promising to provide three hundred scholarships annually to deserving graduates of local high schools, Norton asked for an annual bequest from the city of $75,000. The council resisted the offer. Not only, they argued, was Roswell Park (a physician, and author of a text on the history of medicine which gave more credence to Darwin than to Genesis), a close advisor to Chancellor Norton, but also the institution was a waste of the taxpayers' money. Better to spend the money strengthening the local high schools than to throw it away to an institution where, as one First Ward priest said, "materialism, atheism, free love, as opposed to matrimony and the sanctity of the home will be taught to the children of our laboring classes." While many neighborhood-based religious and political leaders fought the proposal for a combination of parochial as well as financial considerations, most people supported it. As the struggle continued throughout the spring of 1911, countless petitions and testimonials by supporters of a city-subsidized college of liberal arts were offered to the public. All of them steered clear of the religious controversy that had been injected into the debate by certain Catholic priests and ward-based politicians, emphasizing instead the leveling influence that such an institution would have on the city's class structure: "I have seen women who work at the wash tub, men who go out early in the morn to their daily toil, mechanics, women who do sewing and other hand occupations. I have seen their eyes brighten and their faces sparkle with joy because they thought the time coming when the children they love so dearly shall have the advantages of higher education."

Most of the councilmen were not persuaded by these pleas, and refused to even consider the proposition unless they were guaranteed a majority representation on the university's governing council. When Norton and his advisors rejected this, the city, in 1911, withdrew from the negotiations.

More likely than not Norton was pleased that the talks had ended the way they had. A partnership with the parochial and easily-threatened politicians would have been extremely difficult to sustain. Realizing this, Norton turned immediately to private benefactors, and in 1916 Knox made his lavish gift for the establishment of a liberal arts college at the University of Buffalo. There would be no inter-ference from the Catholic politicians. But neither would there be scholarships for city children.

By then the common council had lost another battle. This time they had fought for their own survival. In a citywide referendum in 1914, a slim majority of Buffalo voters approved a new charter for the city that abolished the common council; the board of aldermen; the mayoralty; and all other existing city officers, departments, and courts. This sweeping change hardly came as a surprise, for criticisms of the existing government had been growing for years. Nothing was more vulnerable than the board of aldermen, the ward-based politicians who had traditionally played such a strong role in the political life of the city.

Nobody, it seemed, liked the ward system of government. It was too fragmented, too inefficient and parochial, resulting in a neigh-borhood me-tooism that made it impossible to develop policies for the city as a whole. So the reformers (a coalition of editors, businessmen, politicians, and community leaders too broad to specifically define) argued. They argued also that political power in the modern city should reflect the new economic and structural changes that had recently occurred. The old neighborhoods were dying, drained by the new central business district downtown and the new residential communities further out. And yet, despite these changes, city gov-ernment remained stagnant, dominated by the tribal politics of neigh-borhood and ward. The ward system had to go, particularly since it was also, these reformers insisted, corrupt. While Lincoln Steffens never did visit Buffalo, there were many people who swore that had he done so the corruption he would have found would have equalled, if not surpassed, that which he so effectively documented in other cities. The collapse of a water-pumping station shortly after its completion in 1911 and the resulting investigation which implicated several councilmen in a shabby affair of illegal contracts, faulty construction, and inflated budgets, convinced large segments of the electorate that something was not right. Government seemed to be getting out of hand.

Strikes, and the violence that accompanied them in 1913, suggested the same thing. For years union awareness had been mounting in Buffalo, and now union recognition, along with wage increases, became the loudest battle cry of the city's nonindustrial workers.

By 1910 teamsters, machinists, department store clerks, and the several thousand people who worked on the streetcars had all formed labor unions. Because the city's labor establishment—the United Trades and Labor Council—did not accept union recognition as a grievance worth striking over, these trade unions sought the aid and support of Buffalo's small, yet growing Socialist party. In 1913 all four of them went out on strike.

The streetcar workers' strike became violent when the National Guard was called out to protect strikebreakers. Once again, things seemed to be getting out of hand. Something had to give. This time it was the government, and in November 1914 a majority of citizens voted to abolish the present government of the city of Buffalo. On January 1, 1916, it was replaced by a seven-man commission government. Now, instead of a police department, a board of education, a mayor, a fire department, a department of the poor, and the city courts—instead, in other words, of all of the former branches, agencies and courts that had traditionally constituted the government of the city of Buffalo—there was a government of seven elected commissioners. A political revolution had occurred, and its primary effect was to radically centralize the exercise of power in Buffalo.

Some people observed these upheavals from a distance. What they saw often had little to do with the reality of life in turn-of-the-century Buffalo. Such were the amateur photographers who formed the Buffalo Camera Club.

Perhaps sensing that the people in a rapidly changing community are eager to capture themselves in those quickly passing moments of time, photographers were very early attracted to Buffalo. In 1840, only one year after the photographic process was first made public, a physician opened the city's first daguerrian studio. Before the decade was out, the studio offered sales of the latest German and American

171

cameras, plates, cases, and chemicals. The popularity of photography increased with the improvement of photographic technology and the introduction of flexible film and the hand-held camera during the 1870s and 1880s. In 1888, a group of extremely serious and talented amateur photographers formed the Buffalo Camera Club. (There were reported to be five hundred "known photographers" in Buffalo in that year.) Dedicated to the advancement "among its members of the knowledge of photography in all its branches," the club sponsored regular workshops, discussion groups, and exhibits of their own work and that of photographers throughout the Northeast.

The Buffalo Camera Club was a fascinating group of people drawn, at least at first, from among the wealthiest and most socially prominent families in the city. The founder of the club was G. Hunter Bartlett. This well-known physician, a member of the Society of Mayflower Descendents and the Sons of the American Revolution, had begun taking pictures in the seventies and had, by the middle of the eighties, become a highly skilled photographer. From the same social group was Spencer Kellogg, Jr., a director of his father's extremely successful linseed oil company. Charlotte Spaulding, the daughter of a wealthy and socially prominent lawyer, returned to Buffalo after college in the early 1900s and began a career as a photographer. Concentrating on portraits of women, Spaulding made private, dark, retreating, and haunting images of women, alone or with their children.

Rose Clark, born in Indiana, came to Buffalo in the late 1890s to teach art at a private girls academy. She was fascinated with photography, and quickly became one of the most successful members of the Buffalo Camera Club. Commenting on her mysterious and shadowy portraits displayed at Alfred Stieglitz's gallery in New York City in 1904, one critic commented that her portraits were "second only to Steichen's."

During the early twentieth century the camera club became less a purely social group, as highly skilled artisans and craftsmen, excited by photography, began to join the group. Two of the most successful were graphic designers employed by the Birge Wall Paper Company. Charles Booz and Samuel Lloyd, artistic designers of wallpaper, began taking photographs in the early twentieth century and within several years had, like other members of the camera club, begun to exhibit widely. Under the name of the Buffalo Pictorialists, members of the club were given a show at the Albright Art Gallery in 1907.

The most significant exhibition, not only for Buffalo photographers but for the art of photography itself, was the International Exhibition of Pictorial Photography held at the Albright Art Gallery in November

1910. It was initiated by gallery director Charles Kurtz and his successor Cornelia Sage, who, working with Alfred Stieglitz in New York City, mounted what was widely considered the most serious and substantial photography exhibit ever held in the United States. Rose Clark and Charlotte Spaulding were two of the three Buffalo photographers whose work was exhibited there.

The Buffalo show of 1910, however, was organized largely by Stieglitz, and consisted of images drawn primarily from his own collection. It had little to do with the state of the art of photography in Buffalo. Buffalo's photographers were pictorialists, men and women who made hazy, distant, surreal, out-of-focus images. Unlike Stieglitz and his coterie, Buffalo's artistic photographers were romanticists whose soft, transparent, vague, and highly stylized work descended directly from the mood mysticism of pre-Raphaelite paintings. While Stieglitz was consciously struggling to force photography away from painting, Buffalo's photographers rejected his notion of modernity.

The work of the Buffalo Pictorialists, as they were called, was conservative and retreative. It had a suspicious and frightened look about it, appearing at odds not only with modernism but also with the increasingly mechanized and industrialized world around it. The few images that they did make of streets and factories were idealized and abstract. Always taken at a distance or from behind a screen of billowing clouds, these pictures—bearing classic and frozen titles like *Commerce* and *Industry*—were diffident and uncomfortable attempts to come to terms with the reality of life in the modern city.

It was perhaps for this reason that the creative forces that gave birth to the Buffalo Camera Club at the end of the 1890s could not last. In 1908 Charlotte Spaulding married John J. Albright, Jr., scion of the iron and steel magnate, and the man whose money built the Albright Art Gallery. In 1910 Spaulding stopped taking pictures altogether. G. Hunter Bartlett, the founder of the club, had resigned from it even before the end of the 'nineties and never again was known to take another picture. Charles Booz never showed a picture after 1914. Rose Clark ceased her photographic activity following the exhibit of 1910. And there is no record of Samuel Lloyd after 1909. While the camera club continued in existence until 1938, something— perhaps the war, or perhaps something less tangible about the city and the artistic climate within it—brought a sudden and sad end to Buffalo's poignant, short-lived tradition of artistic photography.

Mabel Ganson Dodge Luhan was also born into one of Buffalo's wealthier and more prominent families. A writer who became involved with John Reed and his circle of radical artists and writers, Mabel

Ganson (her maiden name) wrote in 1932 a memoir of the years she spent growing up in Buffalo between 1870 and 1900. *Intimate Memories* projects a grim, bleak vision of life among Buffalo's wealthy and prominent families. Mabel Ganson's writings are filled with the imagery of emptiness and despair, loneliness, darkness, and silence. Silence was everywhere: "In the winter time there was never any sound on our streets except of peoples' voices and bells and these were muffled by snow." "The coachmen were hidden in Buffalo coats, caps and gloves," and "the streets were always dark: everybody was at home."

Mabel's home, a large, dark mansion on Delaware Avenue, was "a deathly place," where "the blinds were always drawn" and "there was never a sense of life." For, according to Ganson, "each house held its own secret, helpless shame." Behind the thick dark walls of these Victorian mansions, people were isolated from each other. Ganson wrote that "there was hardly any real intimacy between friends and people had no confidence in each other." Life was dull, predictable, and uneventful, "flowing on in an apparently commonplace way, until once in a while, something happened. Donald White would be found hanging on the gas fixture in his bedroom, naked except for a pair of white gloves. Caroline Thompson would suddenly be seen no more among her friends and no one would mention her absence."

Far more distressing to this curious and intelligent child of wealth and luxury was the "lovelessness" of her family, the cold, distant, and stilted behavior that characterized their relationships with each other. Mabel's father was "the man in my house that I called Father and who brushed by me in the hall with a look of dislike." Her mother was brusque and businesslike, a woman who spend her time in "ordering her household" and in controlling her servants and who, above all, was "proud of the appearance of her windows from the street." She recalled little closeness with her parents and remembered that she ate separately from her mother and father, "for we were allowed to be with grown-ups for a while after dinner. They would return and sit in two big chairs in the subdued atmosphere of that loveless house. They did not laugh or joke with [me] nor with each other."

Yet, Mabel Ganson did not blame these people; as if somehow she sensed that they were subject to forces too strong for them to resist. And in the end, although she left the city in the early 1900s, she dedicated her volume of memoirs to Buffalo: "We are all, inevitably perhaps, loyal to our town. I like my Buffalo as I knew it, just as I like and admire now those grown-ups who surrounded me and who endured so gallantly and with such robust courage the terrible emptiness of their lives."

CHAPTER 8

The Changing Structure of the City: Neighborhoods and the Rise of Downtown

Buffalo has always had neighborhoods. Even today, when neighborhoods have been losing population at alarmingly rapid rates, they are still characterized and depicted as being somehow indigenous to and emblematic of the city of Buffalo. To many, Buffalo remains "a City of Neighborhoods." Indeed, the legacy of the neighborhood in Buffalo is strong and long-standing, antedating its customary association with ethnicity. For well before Polish and Italian immigrants created Polish and Italian neighborhoods, before even the Germans and the Irish created German and Irish neighborhoods, Buffalo had had a tradition of separate and independent settlements. Some of them, like the First Ward, developed at the foot of the Erie Canal; others, like Black Rock, around a canal lock; others still, like Cold Springs, around a source of water supplied by a spring. Separated from each other and from the business district downtown, these communities, like medieval villages each with their own churches, markets, and water supply, grew and developed as self-contained and self-sufficient neighborhoods.

Sometimes they were separated by long distances too far to cover on foot, and sometimes by streets. No street was a more effective barrier than Main Street, which to this day marks the tacit boundary line between the East Side and the West Side. Today the East Side is virtually all black. For years it had been white and ethnic.

The East Side had an exciting, unsavory reputation. Mable Ganson, the daughter of a prominent West Side Protestant family, confessed that as a child growing up in Buffalo during the 1880s, her instinctive feeling about the East Side was one "of contempt." By the end of the nineteenth century these two sections of the city were so separate and distinct that it was possible, and in the case of the more aristocratic segment of the population probable, for one to live one's whole life in the city without ever crossing Main Street to the East Side.

By 1900, the Poles had replaced Germans as the dominant ethnic group on the East Side. No longer the despised race that Fillmore and his cohorts had railed against, Buffalo's Germans, now making up more than half of the city's poulation, had left their East Side enclave and assumed a major role in the life of the city. The whole fiber of the city had become German. There were five German-owned banks, six German insurance companies, a German hospital, scores of German churches, several turn vereins, and the nationally known Saengerbund Singing Society. But unlike the other immigrant groups in the city—the Poles, Irish and Italians—the political and financial activities of the Germans were not limited to their own ethnic group. Germans owned the largest breweries and the largest department stores. German doctors and lawyers were among the most successful in the city. German politicians, like Mayor Conrad Diehl, a former county medical examiner, determined the outcome of municipal elections, while certain German families, like the Urbans, were among the wealthiest and most powerful people in the whole community.

None were more influential than the Schoellkopf family. The founder of this prolific dynasty was Jacob Schoellkopf, who came to Buffalo in 1843 with the first wave of German migration to the city. Taking advantage of the city's location at the junction of the nation's most important commercial lines, Schoellkopf went into leather and grain, and by the end of the Civil War his tanning and flour mills were among the largest in the country. Schoellkopf was one of the first people to realize the potential of the waterpower generated by Niagara Falls, and during the 1870s he founded the first power company in the area. His two sons, Jacob, Jr. and Hugo, further developed the power company while opening a chemical company that by the turn of the century was the largest manufacturer of aniline, a chemical used in the manufacture of explosives. By the end of the century, the Schoelkopfs had become one of the wealthiest and most prominent German families in the United States.

Jacob Schoellkopf, Jr., the first member of the family born in the United States, won the respect and approbation that had hitherto been denied the city's German residents. He was admitted to the most exclusive clubs, and appointed director of two bastions of WASP control, the historical society and Buffalo General Hospital. However, Schoellkopf's success and his mobility did not isolate him from his German origins. Like his father, he sent his children to Germany for their college education, while he remained deeply concerned with the progress of the German community in Buffalo. He was gratified when the official guidebook of the Pan American Exposition, in describing the Germans of Buffalo, wrote: "There is probably not a nation in the world whose people adapt themselves more readily to all the elements which contribute to good citizenship than the thrifty, sturdy Teuton Race."

The guidebook took a different view of the fifteen thousand Italians and fifty thousand Poles in the city:

> The majority of the Italians as well as the Poles constitute the working classes of the city. The Italian residents are quite a numerous body and have their place of abode principally on the lower west side near the Canal where fruit vending, peddling and other minor occupations comprise their daily avocation. Both groups live isolated from the rest of the city each with their own markets, stores and places of worship. The docks and railroads depend almost entirely on these two classes for their labor.

It was industry and the nature of work in an industrial society that most influenced the development of neighborhood patterns in Buffalo. By 1910 over fifty percent of the city's work force worked in industry. Most of these workers were immigrants, particularly Poles. Writing in 1910, a crusading reporter and director of the Buffalo Social Survey, wrote in a local paper that "if all the Poles in Buffalo would be taken away over night many of the large factories in the city might as well go away also."

Most of these factories were on the East Side and it was here, where railroads, factories, and cheap housing converged, that the Polish immigrants made their first homes in Buffalo. Everything overlapped on the East Side, and even when in the early twentieth century a sophisticated system of rapid transit was in place, Buffalo's immigrant working class tended to live within walking distance of their work. The construction of the Belt Line Railroad reinforced this tendency. In 1883, in an effort to decentralize industrial development and to better link the factories of the city, the New York Central Railroad built the Belt Line Railroad, a freight and commuter line. This railroad, by circling the city around the unsettled sections of Buffalo, opened up whole new areas for residential and industrial development.

One such place was Assumption Parish. Located in the northwestern part of Buffalo, this area was barely settled until the 1890s. Following the completion of the Belt Line, however, this sparsely populated urban frontier began to grow, as the intertwined and inextricably linked processes of industrial and residential development proceeded apace. At first a simple stop on the Belt Line, the area quickly became a major node of immigrant settlement and industrial development. Because of its excellent connection with the rest of the city's railroad system, factories quickly located here. Settlers came too, primarily young Poles eager to move out and away fom the older Polish section on the city's East Side. Now they had the opportunity, and beginning in 1883 hundreds and eventually thousands of Poles abandoned their old neighborhood. In 1888 the Church of the Assumption was built here, and by 1900 Assumption Parish, as a result of the combined forces of immigration, transportation and industrialization, had become the second largest Polish neighborhood in Buffalo.

While railroads created new neighborhoods, they also divided and separated existing neighborhoods from each other. The Belt Line, like all railroads in nineteenth century cities, traveled along street rights-of-way at street level. Railroad lines cut through whole sections of the city, particularly in the industrialized and immigrant South and East sides. Not only were these railroad crossings extremely dangerous (the papers in the late nineteenth century were filled with gruesome details of the accidents caused to both men and beast by the street-level railroads), but by criss-crossing whole sections of the city they permanently and absolutely divided the city into separate sections that were virtually impassable. Black Rock and Assumption Parish, for example, although immediately adjacent to each other, were completely isolated and divided from each other by a fortresslike conglomeration of street-level railroad crossings. Thus lending tangible significance to the notion of "the other side of the tracks," the street-level railroads, a daily part of life in the late nineteenth century city, served to dramatically reinforce the legacy of neighborhood separatism that had already grown so strong.

Certain patterns of life in the industrial city thus served to strengthen community ties. These ties in turn influenced work choices. Indeed, it was the lure of family and neighborhood, as much as old-world taboos, that kept almost all Italian women out of the work force. For while their Polish counterparts routinely worked as domestics and sometimes as factory workers, Italian women chose to work only in their homes, taking care of boarders, or working as seamstresses and dressmakers.

When Italian women did work outside of their homes, it was in such a way that their primary domestic functions were only minimally threatened or compromised. During the summers, for example, hundreds of Italian women, along with their mothers, grandmothers, children, cousins, and aunts, made pilgrimages to the orchards and canneries in the farm areas surrounding Buffalo. Here whole families worked together, picking and canning fruit and vegetables. The influence of the family thus extended into the home and out onto the street and deep into the heart of the neighborhood. It, as much as the patterns of work or transportation, influenced the character and the quality of Italian neighborhood community life.

The communities created by Buffalo's Polish and Italian immigrants were similar in many respects. Sharply defined by class and ethnicity, identified by and named after a virtually endless litany of parish churches—St. Anthony's, St. Girard's, Assumption, Annunciation, St. Florian's, St. Stanislaus, Holy Angels, Holy Family, Corpus Christi, to name but a few—they flourished, tribelike and tightly-knit, revolving around home, family, and neighborhood. Behind the curtain of ethnicity that separated these communities from the rest of the city (contemporaries referred to them as "cities within the city"), there were great diversity. This was particularly true of the Italians. By 1910 Italians from hundreds of villages in sixteen different provinces—such as Abruzzi, Calabria, Campobasso, and Campagna—in southern Italy and Sicily lived in different parts of Buffalo. An intricate network of communication passed on the message about the New World in generaland Buffalo in particular from person to person and family to family in Italy. Migrating by villages, the Abbruzzese went to the upper East Side of Buffalo; the Campobassini to the lower East Side; the Calabrians to South Buffalo; the Campagnese adjacent to downtown; and the Sicilians, the largest group, to the lower West Side in the vicinity of the waterfront. Whole communities were thus uprooted and transplanted virtually intact in Buffalo. In 1910, eight thousand of a total population of twelve thousand in the village of Vall D'Olmo, Sicily, lived together on the waterfront on Buffalo's lower West Side. Living in two-family wood-frame houses, with a smaller unit in the rear of the lot, three-generation extended families were the norm for the Italians in this section of the city. Brothers and sisters, uncles and aunts, cousins, grandparents, grandchildren, and *paesani* living with them as boarders, all clustered tightly into these homes. No wonder the streets were crowded. Using them as an extension of their living quarters, the streets in Buffalo's immigrant communities served a public function unknown in more Americanized neighborhoods.

Migration by whole families, clans, and even villages provided strength and security, creating islands of refuge within the city where family, faith, home, and community sustained them against a new and uncertain world. For these communities were predictable, and in them the immigrants could find many of the same people and institutions that they had left at home. They knew where they were going; they had a place to stay and oftentimes a job waiting for them; and, more often than not, there were people to count on. There was always room for another *paesan.*

This intricate and inbred network could sometimes work against a transplanted villager. Rejecting a marriage that had been arranged for him, a young man from the village of San Martino in Abbruzzo migrated to Buffalo, following other villagers to Roma Street on Buffalo's upper East Side. When, several weeks after his arrival, his transplanted *paesani* discovered that the new settler had abandoned his bride in San Martino, the deserter, confronted by his priest and his irate compadres, was forced out of the Roma Street community. He moved to Toronto. Unlike this absconder, however, most people found that old village ties were strengthened by life in their new neighborhoods.

From any direction, the twin towers of St. Stanislaus Church dominated the panorama of the Polish East Side. Set on a square block in the middle of the community, the church broke the tidy line of three- and four-family homes in the community. Its massive height and breadth were somehow ungainly, like a cathedral in a prairie town. Its size, however, was not inappropriate, for in every way St. Stanislaus, like St. Anthony's on the Italian West Side and Holy Family on the Irish South Side, was the absolute center of the universe on the Polish East Side. That such poor communities were able to muster the enormous sums necessary for the construction of such elaborate facades indicates the role and influence of the parish church and the parish priest in the lives of these first-generation immigrants. The contemporary press marveled at the phenomenon. A reporter, covering the opening of Corpus Christi Church, filed this story in April, 1909:

> This is the new Church of Corpus Christi, and hither will come the people of that Polish quarter to say their prayers and return thanks that they have been able to build such a beautiful and substantial church.

181

Overwhelmed by what he saw, he described the church, which cost over $200,000, in detail:

> The exterior of the church, beyond the facts of the brownstone walls, twin towers and great tracery window, whose frame is entirely of stone, is little apparent, because the narrowness of the street precludes an advantageous view. But it is on the interior that the people have lavished their efforts. The church is after the Romanesque style, with groined arches, square columns and round arched windows. The proportions are very pleasing and the walls and roof have been done in pale, bright colors, tracing the arches and window frames in decorative border patterns. The window frames, including the divisions between panes, are all of stone, a most rare thing in Buffalo. A gallery extends along the back of the church and the view through the columns from there is most imposing, suggesting, as it does, a glimpse of an old-century church.

The symbolism may well have conjured up the Old World. The technology, however, was strictly modern. Corpus Christi was furnished with its own electrical-power generation plant in the basement so, in the words of the *Express* reporter, "it will be independent of city power." By the early twentieth century, this church, like parish churches in all of the immigrant neighborhoods of Buffalo, had become the actual as well as the symbolic focal point of community life. It was also the center of a whole range of secular activities: Needlework clubs; dramatic societies; bowling, baseball, and basketabll teams; lodges; and mutual benefit associations all used the church as a meeting place. When it came to the parish church, there was little separation between the sacred and the secular.

The tavern augmented the church as the social and cultural center of the Polish community. And on the East Side no tavern was more typical than Pasczek's. One of close to two hundred saloons on the East Side, Pasczek's was one of the most popular, making its proprietor, Michael Pasczek, a prosperous man. Michael Pasczek lived with his wife and three of his children on the ground floor of a large, two-story house that he owned on Gibson Street, just off Broadway. Upstairs, in an identical eight-room apartment, lived his two married daughters and their families. Pasczek owned three other homes which he rented to six Polish families. In addition to his tavern and real estate interests, Pasczek was extremely active in the affairs of his community. He was the treasurer of the Parish Committee of St. Stanislaus, and president of both the Society of St. Adelbert and the Young Men's Society of St. Joseph. In 1901, he became the first

Pole in Buffalo who owned an automobile. But it was the saloon that he cared most about.

On the Polish East Side, this "terra incognita where saloons often occupy each of the four corners of every street," Pasczek's tavern was on the ground floor of a two-story frame building. On two large, plate-glass windows were heavy white letters which spelled out the name of the owner. Over these were two large canvas awnings that protected the benches that Pasczek kept in front of the tavern during the warmer months of the year. Inside, a tile floor and tile walls reflected the low-burning gas light that lit the large room. The walls were decorated with religious icons, a picture of President McKinley, several calendars, and fliers announcing meetings of the Polish Cadets nd the Parish Committee of St. Stanislaus. To the right of the door was a large bulletin board reserved for announcements: the Sokol Society baseball team practice, flats for rent and houses for sale, a subscription list for the Polish Relief Fund and the Polish Army Fund, departure and arrival dates of leading steamship lines, and other news related to the life of the neighborhood. At the end of the room was a long wooden bar—"The Longest Bar in Polonia"—tended during the lunch hour and the after-work rush by both Pasczek and his wife. At other times, Pasczek's son, Michael, Jr., presided over the rows of wine, whiskey, beer, brandied fruits, hard-boiled eggs, pickled vegetables, packages of cheese, and bread all neatly arranged on the long wooden shelves. Toward one end of the bar was a cash register and a small safe. Next to it was a counter where people could buy stamps and receive their mail. To the far left of the bar was a narrow, short hall which led beyond to a closed door into a large interior office. It was here that Pasczek presided over his many diverse activities. Not only was he a ticket agent for two steamship lines, but he was also a registered real estate broker and a bona fide insurance salesman for the Hartford Life Insurance Company.

The first person in Polonia to own an automobile, by 1905 Pasczek had become the nieghborhood's most worldly and mobile man in terms of his contact with the rest of the city. As such, his most important function in the neighborhood was to serve as the liaison man with the outside world. In addition to his activities as a ticket broker and as an insurance agent, one of the more interesting services he performed was that of a local banker. In the absence of branch banks in the community, many people deposited their savings with Pasczek, and he in turn deposited the money in a trust account in a downtown bank.

Although the services which he performed on behalf of his neighbors were significant in the life of the community, as an individual Pasczek was still more important. Above all he was a model for the Polish-speaking day laborer who harbored dreams of one day becoming successful himself. The tavern, then, by serving as a social center where the workers of the area could seek the comforting company of their own kind, and the tavern keeper, who had achieved a degree of success far more visible than any other person in the neighborhood, solidified the ties that bound this peer group society together and kept alive the dreams of success which must often have been derailed by the difficulties of everyday life. By serving as a model of success while still retaining his deep ties to the community, Pasczek not only kindled faith in the future but provided a major source stability in the present.

There were well-to-do men in each of the immigrant communities who, by catering to the particular needs of their own ethnic groups, had become rich: Louis Onetto, the owner of a macaroni factory; Stanislaus Wardynski, proprietor of a large sausage factory on the Polish East Side; and Charles Borzilleri, majority stockholder in a local Italian newspaper, president of the San Vittoria Mutual Benefit Society, the first Italian graduate of the University of Buffalo College of Medicine, and the founder of Columbus Hospital in the heart of the Niagara Street Italian ghetto. Across town, Francis Fronczak, the first Polish graduate of the same school, had a thriving private practice. Because of his deep interest in public health and his excellent political connections, in 1905 Franczak became the public health commissioner of the city of Buffalo.

It was these people—men whose success reaffirmed the myths by which people lived—who quickly became the ethnic darlings of the local press, portrayed in terms occasionally patronizing as exceptional representatives of the new and strange groups of foreign immigrants. Indeed, the press in general was far kinder to the Italians and the Poles than Fillmore and his contemporaries had been to the Germans and the Irish. Rarely resorting to the mudslinging viciousness of that earlier generation, the turn-of-the-century press tended to characterize the Poles as "hard-working," "thrifty," "conscientious," and "family folks who revere hearth and home." Italians, on the other hand, were considered to be "law abiding" (although Buffalo newspapers could never quite decide if Italians were law abiding or criminals), and "neat and clean." Their community was usually seen as "picturesque." The press seemed particularly impressed with the public nature of street life in the Italian sections of town: "It's a life full of sunshine.

The houses are old, the people are crowded together, but out in the street the sun shines warm and the people really love it." With some envy, this reporter compared what he found to the pale and drab Anglo faces found in other sections of Buffalo: "How many people in our city really appreciate the joy of warm sunshine? Down here they really know what it is." Most newspapers, but particularly the *Express* and the Buffalo *Illustrated Times*, sent photographers into both the Italian and the Polish communities and throughout the early years of the twentieth century, when photographs of other neighborhoods and people were few and far between, there were often pages filled with immigrant families (particularly children) in the streets, at the market, at work, and at play. Portraits abounded too: a cobbler, a laborer, a pharmacist, a physician, a lawyer, an organ grinder, and endless young mothers with babies in their arms. The press and the people of Buffalo were clearly fascinated by the immigrants.

In turn-of-the-century Buffalo daily life, for the large number of Catholic immigrants, at least, was lived locally and revolved around the local community. Religion and politics were both rooted in geographical boundaries: the former in the parish, and the latter in the ward. Social life was rooted in the tavern and in such neighborhood organizations as the Polish Falcons, the Black Rock Cycle Club, the West Side Rowing Club, and the Humboldt Schuetzen Verein. Jobs were found in locally based, if not locally owned, factories and a degree of economic self-reliance stemmed from the neighborhood savings and loan associations which, directed by committees of businessmen and laborers in neighborhoods throughout the city, made it possible for thousands of immigrants to purchase homes. But perhaps still more important were the patterns of daily life, the constant overlapping and interconnectedness that occurred—in churches, taverns, and work places, and on the streets—providing these neighborhood communities with meaning and strength, continuity and support.

Thus it was that the neighborhood came to dominate the lives of Buffalo's immigrant groups. Cast into a strange and alien environment, Italian and Polish immigrants—all Catholic, all ignorant of English, virtually all rural with little or no experience in an urban, industrial society—struggled to survive, let alone succeed. In this difficult, often desperate effort they drew considerable strength from what they knew and from what they brought with them from their old countries. Thus relying on family and on local institutions and activities, they turned inward, seeking comfort in their families, their faith, their homes, and their neighborhood.

185

Never static, the city's neighborhoods have been subject to constant change. The greatest and most dramatic upheaval that occurred in the life of Buffalo's neighborhoods was brought about by the emergence in the early years of the twentieth century of the central business district. There had always been such a place, a "downtown." In Buffalo it developed in the vicinity of the canal terminus, at the foot of Main Street. Here, within a few densely packed blocks, were concentrated banks, marine insurance offices, sail shops, merchants, hotels, taverns, and all of the other shops and businesses that are a part of the commercial life of any dynamic city.

But this downtown was still a far cry from a central business district. Indeed, with its block after block of wood-frame and brick homes, its churches, and its marketplace, it was quite similar to the neighborhoods. For here too there was a mixture, on a relatively small scale, of commercial, religious, residential, and recreational activities. Although clearly central to the economic life of Buffalo, downtown had not yet become the indisputably dominant economic, political, and symbolic center of the city. When it did, in the early twentieth century, it altered permanently the traditional structure of the city of Buffalo.

Several factors, all coming together at the turn of the century, were responsible for the rise of downtown as the heart of the metropolitan area. Virtually every development of the period had a centralizing impact, producing a concentration of people and activities in the downtown core. Structural steel made possible the construction of skyscrapers, and changes in business procedures and organization tended to concentrate and centralize economic power into larger and larger corporations which required integrated and proximate locations. Railroads, seeking their terminals in or near the existing business center, dramatically reinforced concentration and centralization in the downtown core.

More than anything else, downtown owed its new-found power and prestige to the electric streetcar. In 1885 there were no electric streetcars in Buffalo. By 1900 there were twenty-five (along eighty-seven miles of track), twenty of which directly linked the central business district with outlying neighborhoods in all four corners of the city. Thus, for the first time, people all over Buffalo were brought within the orbit of downtown by a transit system that was far more rapid and efficient than anything we have known since.

The electric streetcar shattered the assumptions of the residents of the late nineteenth century city. In the process it created unprecedented opportunites for many. Well-known fortunes were made by hungry aldermen who, in exchange for franchise privileges, pocketed thousands of dollars in graft, by real estate developers who cornered the housing market; and by streetcar company owners who were generously compensated for the desperately needed services they provided. But beyond the personal profits that were made, for the countless numbers of middle- and working-class people who had lived in the old, confining, family-dominated ethnic neighborhoods, the electric streetcar offered a way out. For now, whole new "streetcar suburbs"—undeveloped, outlying, still relatively bucolic areas of the city—were opened to settlers. As a result, whole sections of the older neighborhoods were suddenly drained, as people in Black Rock moved further north to Riverside, east siders moved further east to Kensington-Bailey, and residents of the First Ward moved still further out to South Buffalo.

The streetcars drained the older neighborhoods in other ways too. Now, for the price of a nickel, anybody, anywhere in the city, could jump on a streetcar and ride downtown. Suddenly, thousands of Buffalonians, whose social and cultural activities had been for so long confined to the limits of their ancestral neighborhoods, could leave and go downtown. The downtown retail business boomed as new and large department stores were built to accommodate the flood. Hotels and theaters, restaurants and music halls all sought downtown locations, as the social and cultural center shifted away from the neighborhoods to the new night life downtown.

The downtown building boom was unprecedented, as giant national corporations, local banks, and developers all used the great new building material—structural steel—to create new and impressive headquarters. By 1900 the corporate office building had finally replaced the church steeple as the symbolic focus of downtown Buffalo. Nothing dominated the street-scape of downtown more than two buildings completed in 1896: Louis Sullivan's tall and sleek Guaranty Building on Church Street, and the squat but mammoth Ellicott Square Building occupying a square block on Main Street between South Division and Swan Streets. Taken together, these two buildings signalled the arrival of a new era for downtown Buffalo. Within a three-year period Church Street and the Shelton Square area were transformed into a corporate headquarters of the most modern variety. Gone were the frame houses of Church Street, the First Presbyterian Church, and the small four-story brick buildings that had stood on the site of the Ellicott Square Building.

Perhaps more jarring than the rapid change in downtown's function was the virtually overnight transformation in its scale and scope. Suddenly, within a period of less than a decade, the whole visual imagery and the physical scale of downtown Buffalo had been irreparably altered, as massive steel and stone structures replaced the more benign, simple, far less threatening environment that had characterized the area since the middle of the century. The change was swift, radical, and dramatic, and the response of the people must surely have been telling. Many naturally moved out. As their numbers grew, old downtown churches were either demolished or converted to uses more suitable to a modern central business district. With many of its congregation now living in what had been outlying areas earlier in the century, the trustees of the First Presbyterian Church, located since 1827 at Shelton Square, decided to move to a "neighborhood not so shut in by business." Following the sale of the church property to the Erie County Savings Bank, the congregation moved further north in 1889. Churches also gave way to large, garish theatres, as downtown became the entertainment center of the metropolis. In 1904, the North Presbyterian Church on Main and Huron was demolished and replaced by the Hippodrome Theatre. Eight years later the Central Presbyterian Church on Pearl and Genessee gave way to the Majestic Theatre. And in 1906 the magnificent Gothic-style St. John's Episcopal Church, built in 1846, was torn down and replaced by the Statler Hotel across from the hive of offices in the Ellicott Square Building.

When the Ellicott Square Building opened on May 1, 1896, it was the largest office building in the world. It occupied a whole square block, was sixteen stories tall, and had eight hundred separate offices. The building was designed in Italian Rennaissance style, with a cornice of immense proportions, and an open interior court—"The Grand Court"—finished in Italian marble, with a mosaic floor and a glass roof. It had Turkish, Russian, and plain baths, and a private club where the waiters wore livery consisting of blue cloth coats and trousers trimmed with gold chord. It also had Ellsworth Statler's first restaurant. Statler first came to Buffalo in 1896 on his way home to Wheeling, West Virginia, following a fishing trip in Canada. He was overwhelmed by the Ellicott Square Building and after several days of negotiations he convinced John N. Scatherd, the building's owner, to lease him space for a restaurant. Within months, however, Statler's plush retaurant failed. Scatherd had warned him that Buffalo simply wasn't a restaurant town. Businessmen, Statler was told, more often than not went home for lunch, and if people did go out in the evening they went to places in their neighborhoods.

But Statler was determined. He redesigned his restaurant for efficiency and quick turnover. First, he fired his French chef imported from New York and hired a local man in his place. Then he introduced a serving table which he had invented. It rolled on wheels and contained separate compartments for cutlery, linens, glasses, condiments, and bread and butter. The biggest change was in prices. Statler offered full-course lunches at twenty-five cents—paid in advance. (Statler was obsessed with "skippers." At his two thousand-room hotel near the Pan American Exposition he collected from his guests when they checked in. He also insisted that they purchase a meal ticket in advance.) Next, he launched an advertising campaign designed to change the eating habits of Buffalonians. Every day advertisements appeared in the newspaper: "The increase in your business has been brought about by modern up-to-date methods. You can further increase your business upon the same lines. Losing the heart out of your business day by going home to noon lunches is calculated to increase the business of your competitor who lunches downtown. Let Statler's help you." He added the notion of premium merchandising. Every day he had his chef put five-dollar gold pieces in five different servings of ice cream. Statler was revolutionizing the restaurant business, and Buffalo's downtown business district in the process.

Few things escaped the rapid course of downtown growth and development. At Main Street, a few blocks north of the waterfront, was Lafayette Park, a large square-block open space, richly planted with a variety of trees, bushes, and shrubbery. Although buildings surrounded the park on all four sides, they were small in scale and had a variety of uses. There was a library, a theatre, several churches and private homes, and a large, although not tall, structure that combined offices and an amusement arcade. While there had been some changes in the early years of the twentieth century—the church became a theatre and the arcade building a large, modern office enclave—the park itself had so far remaied intact. However, surrounded as it was by a boisterously expansive downtown business district, the park was vulnerable, threatened by electric streetcars and especially by automobiles.

Automobiles had become extremely popular in Buffalo. By 1907 there were over five hundred in the city and the Buffalo Automobile Club, founded in 1901, already had close to a thousand members. Eager to widen old roads and to build new ones, the club lobbied for the repeal of a city ordinance which said that automobiles could travel no faster then bicycles. Although their efforts failed, downtown interests became increasingly concerned with traffic flow in this vital downtown area. As they did, Lafayette Park became doomed. Only the Socialist party protested what they called "the despoilation of

MARK GOLDMAN

Lafayette Park." Citing the "continual sacrifice of park space to the needs of traffic," the *Buffalo Socialist* newspaper wrote that "this haven of rest for many a weary soul and body, the last remaining breathing spot in the downtown section of the city, is now being threatened by business, business, business, the juggernaut of today." Their protest notwithstanding, the Buffalo common council in 1912 voted to "devote to street purposes all that part of the Square except a small circle around the Soldiers and Sailors Monument." Lafayette Park had become a traffic circle.

Even residential areas on the periphery of the central business district were not immune to the expansion of downtown. Johnson Park is a case in point.

In 1900 Johnson Park was an elegant residential mall within walking distance of the heart of downtown Buffalo. Originally the suburban home of Ebenezer Johnson, Buffalo's first mayor, and developed during the 1850s as an elite, in-town residential section, Johnson Park retained many of the qualities that had for so long made it the most venerable and exclusive residential quarter in the city. Its tree-lined mall was the home of many of the families listed in the social register. Here too was the Buffalo Female Academy, the most selective school in the city. Thus, close enough to downtown to be convenient, and yet far enough away to preserve its uniqueness, Johnson Park was a well-defined and cohesive urban place. Yet the expansion of downtown was such that peripheral residential areas soon became expendable and the characteristics that had made Johnson Park a cherished corner of the city barely survived the nineteenth century.

Because it lay on an east-west axis, Johnson Park blocked movement to and from the new central business district. It was in the in the way. And despite the intense opposition of the wealthy and presumably influential residents of the park, the broad mall was cut in half in 1907 and Elmwood Avenue was extended through it to the downtown area. The park now changed quickly. A streetcar line was put on the Elmwood Avenue route and soon Johnson Park, its days as a fancy, in-town residential neighborhood over, was on the way to becoming tattered and tawdry, existing marginally on the fringes of downtown.

While the forces creating the changes that occurred in Johnson Park were, to a certain degree, inevitable, they were more often than not the result of deliberate decisions. Alternatives were being weighed and choices were being made. People got pretty much what they wanted, or rather, what they thought they wanted.

190

As downtown changed and those who could afford to moved out, whole new outlying sections of Buffalo became suddenly popular. The most desirable was in the vicinity of Delaware Park, three miles due north of the expanding central business district.

Unlike New York's Central Park, a spectacular rectangle in the middle of Manhattan, Fredrick Law Olmsted had planned for Buffalo an integrated, citywide park system. Reaching throughout the whole city, connected by arterylike boulevards and parkways, Olmsted's park system was intended to link the whole city. The center of it was Delaware Park. Consisting of acres of landscaped meadows, paths, and a lake, Delaware Park, located well beyond the center of population, had by the end of the nineteenth century become an extremely popular, quasi-suburban retreat

Olmsted's design affected residential as well as recreational patterns and had a significant influence on the physical development of the whole northern half of Buffalo. For now, in conjunction with the large grounds of the State Hospital and the extensively landscaped grounds of Forest Lawn (the latter a cemetery, the former a mental hospital), both of which flanked Delaware Park, a large greenbelt was created across the middle of Buffalo. Thus, to the divisions already separating East Side from West Side was now added one between north and south. These divisions, like the earlier ones, quickly became distinguished by class. For within several years of its completion in the late 1870s, the area in the vicinity of Delaware Park became the most exclusive residential section in Buffalo, particularly following the upheaval downtown. As hundreds of the more affluent began to escape from increasingly commercial downtown areas, the land in the vicinity of the park was quickly developed. With curvilinear streets, tree-lined boulevards, and large houses on even larger lots, it had become the refuge of the well-to-do in a fast, changing city.

It was not enough that downtown be the functional center of the metropolis. It had also to be beautiful. Led by downtown business groups, lawyer, merchants, real estate interests, the newspapers, and others, groups such as the Society for the Beautifying of Buffalo were formed with the express purpose of converting urban beauty into a business asset. Like similar groups in cities throughout the United States, the society in 1900 argued that "people must be taught to realize the advantages of a beautiful city. They must be made to understand that beauty in a city pays . . . that it is a civic asset of very great value." Lest this concern with beauty be construed as unbusinesslike and therefore unmanly, the society, whose membership consisted primarily of businessmen, was quick to point out that contrary to popular opinion, "art and beauty, far from being effeminate and enervating, are ennobling and exhalting. Yes, and useful." Drawing on concepts popularized in Washington, D.C., the society's advanced planning ideas that would bring physical order and coherence to the downtown business district. Building on Ellicott's stagnating early nineteenth century plan for Buffalo, the early twentieth century "City Beautiful" planners expanded his notion of radial order, through landscaping and the careful placement of obelisks and public monuments in central places like Niagara Square in the heart of downtown.

While the streetcar helped to create the modern central business district, the automobile helped to destroy it. Actually, though few people realized it at the time, the automobile had, by the early 1920s, begun to take its toll. Throughout the late nineteenth and early twentieth centuries, the streets and sidewalks of the city were in a constant and continuous state of upheaval, as first railroad tracks and then streetcar lines were laid everywhere and in every which way on streets all over the city. Hardly any section of the city was left untouched. Sometimes people protested. Once, during the early 1890s, when the city council had approved the construction of a streetcar line over the objections of a local alderman, residents of Hertel Avenue in the Black Rock section confronted construction crews, forcing them to abandon their work. This protest, like others aimed at the chaotic and seemingly irrational pace of change in the turn-of-the-century city, was destined to failure.

Yet nothing more dramatically altered the relationship that existed between people and their physical environment than the automobile, which by the 1920s had begun to make an impact. For years there had been a strong and active automobile lobby in Buffalo. The automobile industry, was with close to four thousand employees in 1920, and the Buffalo Automobile Club, with over three thousand members, were both forceful and aggressive proponents of the automobile. The automobile club's monthly journal, the *Motorist*, published all the latest news of the automobile world and fought all the battles dear to the heart of every motorist, particularly limits on speed which, although regularly liberalized, were always considered far too restrictive.

More significant than the particular issues which the automobile club fought for was the increasing prominence and acceptability of the vision of the future city as an automobile-oriented community, a place where the private automobile, far more than public rapid transit, would be the dominant form of transportation. Private autos, of course, meant public highways and by the early 1920s there was an irrepressible movement in the city of Buffalo for their construction.

Everybody got into the act. Oddly, considering the damage that automobiles and highways would someday do there, none were more vocal and vigorous than downtown business interests. The Manufacturer's and Trader's Bank, for example, published in 1923 a widely distributed, complimentary brochure called "Planning the City." One article, called "Highway Transportation," and written by a downtown real estate broker prominent in the budding citizen-planning movement, articulated a vision of Buffalo that was becoming increasingly popular. Since growth, the author argued, was dependent on adequate vehicular transportation, highways were essential. "The more quickly adequate highways are constructed the sooner Buffalo will arrive at the one and two million [people] mark." In addition to the construction of new highways, the bank's brochure called for the widening and extension of "all of the twenty-four radial streets entering the city." The city engineer, the official in charge of the city's streets, went still further and insisted that every street in the whole city be widened on each side by three to four feet. This should, he argued in an article in the *Motorist*, be accomplished by the elimination of trolley lines, which took up too much space and thus interfered with the free flow of vehicular movement.

Newspapers joined the outpouring of pro-automobile sentiment, printing stories of how other cities were adapting to the automobile: the widening of Park Avenue in New York City, the completion of tunnels and bridges in Boston and Chicago, the parking ramps and staggered light systems in Baltimore and Indianapolis. One scheme, adopted in Syracuse, was particularly compelling.

Syracuse, like Rochester and Buffalo, had grown up around the Erie Canal. And there, too, the canal had become obsolete by the early twenties, and was hardly used. There, however, the path of the canal passed directly through the heart of the central business district. A prime target for conversion in 1925, the languishing canal bed was filled in and paved over. On it was built a fifty-six-foot-wide highway with four traffic and two parking lanes. One local newspaper waxed poetic about this ambitious urban renewal project: "Thus out of the bed of a sluggish waterway along which sluggish canal boats were hauled by equally sluggish mules and horses, has arisen a broad ribbon of concrete where motors throb endlessly with loads of humanity and merchandise." It was this vision of massive highways built through the heart of the city that this newspaper, anyway, hoped would motivate and inspire their own city. Only recently remade for the streetcar, Buffalo was about to be overhauled for the automobile.

In 1926 the City Planning Association, a coalition of downtown business interests formed in 1919, made public their master plan for the city of Buffalo. Designed by Edward Bennett of Chicago, one in a long line of many outside experts hired to solve Buffalo's problems, the plan was monumental and truly Napoleonic in scope. The heart of it was the Civic Center, a series of public buildings grouped around Niagara Square, chosen by Joseph Ellicott in 1804 as the symbolic center of Buffalo, and already dignified, at least in City Beautiful terms, by the placement there of an obelisk dedicated to the memory of William McKinley. The gigantic, hulking City Hall, a grotesque Gothic Revival structure with a monumental classical portico for an entranceway, was the centerpiece of the Civic Center. On both its flanks were to be two large but low neoclassical government buildings. The whole mammoth project was, in the words of Lewis Mumford, architecture fit only for birds and aviators.

Then, placed at the other ends of the city, were a music hall ("as evidence of Buffalo's culture") in the east and a gigantic convention hall in the west. These two elements of the master plan were to be joined with each other and to the City Hall by what Bennett called the "Crosstown Traffic Bridgeway." The Bridgeway, a street-level, gapingly wide highway that would course throughout the downtown area, would not only free the movement of vehicular traffic but would, at the same time, achieve the lofty goals of "wiping out the artificial distinctions that seperate the East Side from the West Side and in the process benefit the whole city." More concretely, however, the purpose of the Bridgeway was clear. Like the plan to "eliminate the meanderings of Delaware Avenue through the Park," the Bridgeway was part and parcel of a whole series of proposals designed to facilitate the movement of vehicular traffic through the streets of the city.

Actually, Delaware Avenue, the tree-lined, mansion-filled home of Buffalo's rich—the city's equivalent of Commonwealth in Boston and Euclid in Cleveland—had already been widened. Because it was a major artery between downtown and the northern outlying residential districts, Delaware had become highly congested in the early 1920s. Most people agreed that something had to be done. The city favored widening the avenue. Most agreed. Others—a few—were opposed. The price—the loss of hundreds of elm trees that towered high over the streets of the city—was too high. Charles Burchfield, a painter who had moved to Buffalo in 1921, was appalled and in a painting called *Civic Improvement* protested the city's plan. Somebody else wrote a poem: "Martyred Beauties: A Sacrifice to Greed and Power: Pace, haste, destroy and lay waste." Some suggested alternative and less destructive solutions to the traffic congestion on Deleware Avenue. One person proposed a ban on parking. Another thought that if buses ran on the avenue (there had never been public transportation on Delaware Avenue before), then "many people would use this method to get downtown instead of their own cars," and the trees could be saved. Widening was the easier, tested way, however, and in 1924 Burchfield's image of hundreds of trees chopped cruelly to the ground became a reality.

The City Planning Association's master plan was the first of many grand schemes for the renewal of downtown Buffalo. Although not all of their specific plans were actually realized, their concepts and ideas about Buffalo's downtown continued to have a great deal of influence in subsequent years. While it was never built, for example, the concept of a street-level highway through the middle of the city lived on and during the late 1940s and early 1950s was, with disastrous consequences, implemented. The Civic Center was also realized, albeit in much altered form. By the end of the 1920s Niagara Square, with the exception of the Statler Hotel, was given over completely to governmental uses. The City Beautiful concept that different urban functions should each occupy their own separate urban zones have only made more difficult contemporary efforts to revitalize downtown.

The CPA was less successful when it came to the waterfront. While they had hoped that it would be developed as a public recreational area, it is, in our time, in the process of becoming a private enclave of expensive condominiums. Similarly unfortunate is the failure to build, as the CPA had suggested, a new railroad terminal in the central business district. By choosing a location in the far East Side of Buffalo instead, city planners in 1929 unwittingly made still more difficult this generation's efforts to revitalize downtown. Yet, it is perhaps not fair to blame the problems of present-day downtown on the planners of the twenties. For who at that time, given the developments that had occurred during the first thirty years of the century, could possibly have predicted that anything could ever cause damage to downtown Buffalo?

CHAPTER 9

Ethnics and the Economy During World War I and the 1920s

Except in 1812, war had been good to Buffalo. The Civil War reinforced the city's commerce and gave birth to its industry. The Spanish-American War fostered the patriotic energy that created the Pan American Exposition. It is not surprising then that by and large, the people of Buffalo greeted America's entry into World War I with fervor and gusto. Even before Wilson's declaration of war on April 2, 1917, the Niagara Defense League, similar to Fillmore's Civil War brigade, was formed to protect the presumably vital and vulnerable Niagara Frontier. And at noon on the day of Wilson's proclamation, thousands of children—the girls in grey tunics, the boys in white shirts and ties—gathered on the steps of public schools throughout the city and sang the Star Spangled Banner. (Workers at Pratt and Letchworth, Pierce Arrow, Klinck's Packing, and dozens of other companies did the same.)

These were but the first of a seemingly endless procession of public events that, lasting throughout the duration of the war, were carefully plotted and orchestrated to maintain and perpetuate a fevered pitch of patriotism. No event in the history of the city had ever before been so dramatized, so publicized, so advertised and promoted as was the war effort. Carefully calculated and controlled by a handful of advertising executives, newspaper editors, bankers, and volunteer workers, the actions on the Buffalo home front—the parades, the public demonstrations, the meatless Sundays, heatless Mondays, coalless Tuesdays, all of which culminated in the Liberty Loan Bond Drive—had all the trappings of a staged and manipulated event.

Crowds were an essential part of the hoopla. Crowds lined up around the block to see Douglas Fairbanks in *Swat the Kaiser*. Crowds inevitably gathered to greet the endless processions of federal dignitaries dispatched from Washington to promote the war. A crowd, reported to be of over fifty thousand, jammed the meadow in Delaware Park to bid farewell to the three thousand local soldiers bound for war. One local newspaper, caught up like the rest of the press in the martial excitement of the times, described the event in surreal, dreamlike terms that captured the public's sense of the happening:

A full moon climbing through the heavy clouds gave the final touch of splendor to a setting which made the Meadow a fairyland. There was a touch of awed surprise in the attitude of the great crowd that filled the meadow to overflowing when the first note of music burst forth and song and light became one harmonious whole. Paths between the trees were transformed into lantern-lined vistas. The lanterns beckoned everywhere. They pointed the way for the throngs that flowed through every entrance toward the flowing center of the celebration.

More than anything else, however, the three Liberty Loan drives best captured and characterized the temper of the times. Similar to the effort to promote and market the Pan American Exposition, the Liberty Loan drives were carefully and precisely organized citywide campaigns to sell United States Savings Bonds. The bond drive, in Buffalo as in every other city, was complexly organized, with tentacles reaching into every street, neighborhood, church, school, and workplace in Buffalo. Supervising this elaborate model of modern marketing was Walter P. Cooke, a banker and lawyer.

Better organized, more centralized, and more methodical than any local political machine or business corporation could hope to be, Cooke's citywide network represented a concentration of power unprecedented in the history of the city. Fueled by generous amounts of federal aid, the Liberty Loan drives developed a propaganda machine for the marketing of their bonds that was unique for its time. With a publicity committee, as well as an educational bureau, the Liberty Loan drive spent thousands of dollars simply marketing their product.

They made no attempts to hide the frankly propagandistic nature of their efforts: "The function of the Education Bureau was to reach as many houses in the city as possible with propaganda for the purpose of creating an informed public opinion in regard to the war and of developing and fostering patriotism." The educational bureau had four divisions. One was for "house visitations." According to their strategy, cooperating social agencies "agreed to carry on patriotic teaching in connection with family visitation." Another was "neighborhood activities," whereby the city was divided into seven settlement house districts wherein the settlement house would be used as a "center for patriotic instruction" by hosting "inspirational talks," and by sponsoring lectures, using one hundred stereopticon slides pertaining to the war and made by the Buffalo Camera Club.

There was also a women's division of the bond drive, whose members were urged to make themselves "propagandists among their own circle of friends." Great efforts were made to organize immigrant women, particularly Poles, who would act as leaders of the bond drive in their own commuities. Polish women, regarded as solid, hardworking, and unquestioning, were viewed as "naturally loyal. Their ready response offers a splendid opportunity for driving home lessons in American ideals and in good citizenship."

Even the police were brought into the campaign to market the bonds. In what was referred to as "the final combing-out process," every one of the city's fifty-five thousand homes was visited in the fall of 1917 by a member of the police department. Under the careful eyes of the police officers, each household was to fill out not only a form requesting that it be visited by a representative of the Liberty Loan committee, but also a pledge card which indicated the size of the bond they would buy.

Desperately afraid that the truth alone was not sufficient (particularly when so many of the people in the city—Germans, Irish, and even Poles—were naturally inclined to support the enemy), Cooke created fantasies. In a memo to those who wrote promotional copy for the bond drive, the banker-lawyer reminded them that "your writing must generate enthusiasm." Clearly operating under instructions of his own from George Creel and his Washington-based Committee for Public Information, Cooke insisted that they avoid "horror copy," for to give subscribers a "too vivid picture of the horrors of fighting might well chill their enthusiasm rather than increase it." They must, he concluded, "help develop a war ideal in the people of this city by appealing to certain instincts and patriotic sentiments." Cooke suggested that his writers focus on the following themes: "democracy, loyalty, gratitude and sympathy."

Nothing better epitomizes the well-orchestrated Liberty Loan drive than the organizing effort that went into the visit to Buffalo of Josephus Daniels, the secretary of the navy. In April 1917, Daniels came to Buffalo to promote the bonds. The instructions from the publicity campaign were detailed and elaborate. "Papers should feature

SECRETARY OF NAVY coming, not Mr. Daniels. Don't have a band proceed Daniels around Town for the reason that it looks like a cheap parade. The idea you want to get to the people is that the SECRETARY OF THE U.S. NAVY is here. You want to convey the fact that he needs to be closely guarded. It's supposed to look like a military maneuver; not a parade."

The memo from the publicity committee dealt with table arrangements at the banquet in Daniels' honor: "In the place of the stage, keep in mind that the PICTURE of the event is as important as the event itself." The sponsors of the event were as eager to manipulate Daniels' message as they were the environment in which he spoke:

> I think Daniels should speak last. Would it be possible for him to come into the meeting just as Roscoe finishes his speach? Roscoe can put the crowd right. All will be feeling fine. . . . The crowd will cook during Daniels' speech, but this can be brought to the boiling point by the following: During Daniels' speech, the band will leave the hall and at the instant he finishes, the band will march down center aisle followed by soldiers in columns of four. The band will move to the side of the stage; the soldiers will march on stage and go through a short manual of arms. Soldiers will stand at attention; bugler to sound colors; band to break into Star Spangled Banner and at the first strains of Star Spangled Banner, a large American Flag and Liberty Loan flag, which will be concealed in the girders of the roof, will be dropped in full view of the audience.

In this atmosphere of manufactured enthusiasm, loyalty, and patriotism, over $250 million of bonds were sold. Buffalo had "gone over the top."

This frenzied mood did more than sell war bonds. It created a pervasive feeling of paranoid superpatriotism that lasted well into the 1920s. The mayor, Charles Fuhrmann, never quite sure if, how, or when his German background might catch up with him and damage him in his campaign for reelection in 1917, was quick to jump on the bandwagon, and shortly after American entry into the war in April 1917 he formed the Committee on Americanization, consisting of fifty "leading citizens from the immigrant and native communities." Paraphrasing Theodore Roosevelt, whose growing xenophobia lent support and comfort to the Americanizers, Mayor Fuhrman said that, "either a Buffalonian is an American and nothing else or he isn't an American at all." As part of his reelection campaign he pledged to make Buffalo an "English speaking city." When coupled with his promise to "wake up Buffalo and stir the laggards to a deeper sense of duty to flag and land," Fuhrmann's message brought fear and panic to the more than 100,000 first- and second-generation Germans in Buffalo.

The pressure on the city's Germans was intense. Suddenly this long-favored ethnic group, idealized since the end of the nineteenth century as hard-working, thrifty, successful, an "American" kind of immigrant, found themselves the object of suspicion, anger, resentment, prejudice, and discrimination. While the older generation—the Schoell-kopfs, who had made millions in electrical power; the Klincks and the Dolds, the extraordinarily successful meat packers; the Scheus and the Langs, who had made their fortunes in the beer business—were beyond the suspicious glare of the Americanizers, the more recent arrivals, those thousands of Germans who had come to Buffalo since the end of the century, were constantly the object of the vigilant.

Many succumbed to the pressure. The German-language newspaper, *Der Weltburger*, published continually since the mid-1840s, faced with a rapidly declining readership and with a harsh federal law requiring that all articles containing references to the United States be translated and then read by the government prior to publication, now shut down. Names of banks and insurance companies were changed. Thousands of individuals dropped or Anglicized their German names. Cultural and community institutions, now suddenly beseiged by the changing climate of hatred and paranoia, went underground.

Many, however, were able to weather this storm, refusing to succumb to the sickening venom of superpatriotism. While German was eliminated from the curriculum in the public schools, most German cultural groups continued to meet during the war. Despite what might well be described as a state of fear, if not panic, music and singing groups—the Buffalo Orpheus, the Saengerbund, the Froshsinn Singing Society, the Teutonia Liederkranz—met, practiced, and performed throughout the war. Other community groups and institutions—the Buffalo Turn Verein, the Humboldt Club, the Emmaru Maenner Verein—remained active in their old East Side headquarters throughout the period. Many indeed seemed eager, despite the atmosphere of hostility, to express their Germanness. In late 1917, in the midst of the passionate, intensely patriotic second Liberty Loan drive, the German Deaconess Hospital announced its own campaign to raise $200,000.

Not only German institutions, but individuals too, were able to thrive during the war. Some profited enormously. Prior to 1914 most of the coal tar dyes used in America were imported from Germany. Following the Allied blockade of Germany, Americans began to turn to domestic dye makers. None benefited more from this turn of events than the Schoellkopf's National Aniline and Chemical Company, the largest dye plant in the country. National Aniline got even bigger during the war as coal dyes were used increasingly for the manufacture of high explosives and poison gases.

In politics, too, Buffalo's Germans asserted themselves. Rejecting the mayoral candidates of both Republican and Democratic parties, both of whom were German-Americans and both of whom scrambled to outdo each other's patriotic rhetoric, the majority of the city's Germans in 1917 voted for the Socialist candidate, a man named Franklin Bliss. The Socialist party, whose local newspaper had been banned, whose candidates for mayor and other local offices received no coverage in the local press, and whose demands for an end to the draft and a negotiated peace settlement were constantly characterized as disloyal, received over fourteen thousand votes and barely missed defeating the Republican candidate and thereby qualifying for the run-off in the general election. Like Socialist candidates in New York City, Chicago, and Milwaukee in 1917, Bliss, a peace candidate in an atmosphere of militarism and xenophobia, found an enormous amount of support in Buffalo's increasingly isolated and alienated German community. For, by voting for Bliss and the Buffalo Socialist party, the city's Germans rallied. Although not particularly Socialist in outlook and ideology, the German community used that party as a means of expressing their doubts about the war. In the process they risked alienating themselves from the rest of the population. It was a gamble they were apparently willing to take.

Branded during the war as the party of the kaiser and after it as the party of Lenin, the Socialist party in Buffalo, as in other communities throughout the country, quickly lost its strength during the early 1920s. This did not prevent respectable opinion from blaming the party and the principles it advocated for the steel strike of 1919.

The city of Lackawanna, the mammoth company steel town just south of Buffalo, thrived on war. Even before American entry into the war, orders from European countries for steel products of every kind sent production and employment soaring. Between 1910 and 1920 the population had grown from 14,549 to 17,918. But still Lackawanna had not really become a city. It was rather an enormous labor camp, a dormitory for the thousands of men who worked at the plant. The variety of them was staggering. There were Poles, Russians, Hungarians, Italians, Bulgarians, Spaniards, Arabs, American Indians, and a sprinkling of still other nationalities. And, there was an increasing number of blacks.

201

For years the traditional source of cheap labor for the steel mills of Lackawanna had been eastern Europe. In 1910 over half of the work force was Slavic. The war ended this, however, and in their place came a rapidly growing number of southern blacks who had begun to trek northward to Chicago, Cleveland, Lackawanna, and the other industrial centers of the Northeast.

There had always been some blacks in Lackawanna. Never a part of the regular labor force, blacks had lived on the fringes of the town, working periodically, primarily as maintenance men and as outdoor laborers in and around the mill. Their only break came during strikes when, if they could survive the bitter and brutal responses of the strikers, they found work, however temporary, inside the plant itself. This dreadful and divisive situation began to change during the war. Now, for the first time, blacks, as a result of an increasingly serious labor shortage, were entering the labor force. Now, however, they came not as janitors and strikebreakers but rather as bona fide industrial workers.

Despite their vast ethnic differences, the people of Lackawanna had a great deal in common. Most had come from rural areas in eastern and southern Europe and in the United States. Most were unskilled, with no previous experience with industrial work. And, most importantly, they were all in Lackawanna only temporarily—at least that's what they thought. Leaving their families at home and living in countless rooming houses strewn throughout the company town, most of these people planned to stay in Lackawanna only long enough to save some money and return home. The war changed that particular notion. And when it did, the impact was staggering.

The workers at the Lackawanna plant had, whether they liked it or not, become part of the war effort. Some had served in the United States Army. Others, through check-offs at the plant, had bought Liberty Bonds. Still more had been subject to intense Americanization programs of propaganda and education—English-language classes, workshops in civics, parades, rallies, flag-raisings, and group pledges of allegiance—that had taken place at the plant during the war. Nothing, however, had worked more effectively to strengthen their ties to both the town and the plant than the increase in wages. As demand for steel increased and the supply of labor shrank, average wages doubled to forty cents an hour. And, as a result of federal intervention, an eight-hour day had been imposed on the industry, and workers now earned time and a half for overtime. The war had been good to the steelworkers of Lackawanna, and as a result few of them went home when it was over. It was this sense that

Lackawanna had indeed become home that, perhaps more than any-thing else, led the steelworkers in that city to join workers in the steel centers throughout the United States in the strike in the fall of 1919.

The steel strike was also the result of changes that had been occurring within the Amalgamated Association of Iron and Steel Workers, the union that had represented workers in the industry since the end of the nineteenth century. Actually the Amalgamated had never pretended to represent all of the workers in Buffalo or anywhere else, and had instead concentrated on the skilled, predominantly American-born workers in iron and steel. The Amalgamated steadfastly refused to recognize or organize the unskilled immigrant laborers who by the early twentieth century had become pre-dominant in the mills. The Amalgamated paid for their prejudice. When they struck the Buffalo Structural Steel Company in 1903 demanding recognition for their union, the strike was broken by Polish, Hungarian, Italian, and Negro scabs. They paid in other ways too.

By the early 1900s steel production was becoming increasingly automated. Because skilled labor was more expensive than unskilled, steel companies, like other manufacturers, introduced laborsaving ma-chinery at the skilled rather than at the unskilled level. Indeed, Lackawanna would never have considered building a new plant in Buffalo in 1901 had they not been able to automate unprecedented amounts of their production. As a result the Amalgamated, with its skilled membership, suffered. Thus, faced with dwindling membership, the union began to organize among the unskilled. It was no easy chore. Not only had the union discriminated against the unskilled workers for years, but these workers had little interest in unionism. After all, they were temporary workers, or at least so they had imagined, and were basically satisfied with their earnings. With few expenses, the averge unskilled immigrant laborer living by himself could, even with his two dollar per day earnings, manage to save and even send some money back home. The Amalgamated, then, had little success—that is, until the war.

As a result of the changed status of the steelworkers, the union did begin to have considerable success during an organizing drive sponsored by the AFL in 1918. Steelworkers, both skilled and un-skilled, had joined the Amalgamated in steel towns throughout Ohio, Pennsylvania, and Illinois. They were successful in Buffalo, too. Being major centers of steel production, the AFL and the Amalgamated had made Buffalo and Lackawanna primary target areas of their organizing drive. From headquarters in Chicago, within striking distance of Judge Gary's U.S. Steel plant, organizers were dispatched to steel centers throughout the Northeast. William Griffiths, one of the original workers at the Gary, Indiana plant and since 1912 a full-time organizer for the Amalgamated, was sent to Lackawanna. He came along in the early summer of 1919. To avoid detection and recognition he registered under a succession of different names in a half dozen Lackawanna rooming houses. In June he brought a Polish-speaking organizer with him, and together they spent surreptitious hours working the mill town in its rooming houses, taverns (most were still open despite Prohibition), pool rooms, and social clubs.

Griffiths encountered enormous obstacles. The company had already fired over a hundred workers suspected of union activity. Not only did the laborers fear retaliation, but local businessmen, despite their loyalty to their customers (most of whom were workers in the plant), feared the company still more and thus lent but hesitant and reluctant support to the union drive. Government officials in Lackawanna too were kindly disposed toward the company. Not only did few of the workers vote, but the steel company, although way underassessed, still paid the great bulk of Lackawanna's taxes. Throughout August and September, Mayor Toomey, a Democrat, refused to grant parade and assembly permits to the Amalgamated.

The union also faced the overwhelming hostility of the Buffalo press, which refused to conceive of the union drive as anything more than a conspiracy fueled by Bolsheviks, Wobblies, or "displaced Russian Jews" who, according to the papers, had made their way to America following the upheaval in Tsarist Russia. One Lackawanna newspaper, however, owned and edited by Charles Ellis, who claimed to have been one of the first workers hired by the Lackawanna Company in 1901, maintained a strong pro-union position throughout the summer and fall of 1919. Ellis was an avowed Socialist. He had been against American involvement in the First World War, and now was bitterly opposed to Woodrow Wilson and his scheme for the League of Nations. He hated Wilson, and now that the war was over criticized him for touring the country, and barnstorming on behalf of the league instead of dealing with the race riots in Chicago and St. Louis and the pending steel strike. Although disavowing Bolshevism, Ellis, arguing that "the U.S. is not at war with Russia," insisted that Wilson end this "private war" and bring home American troops from their expedition on behalf of the White Russians.

Ellis was a strong pro-labor man, an unabashed advocate of the steelworkers in their struggle against the Lackawanna company which, he maintained, controlled the city as well as the mill. Perhaps fearful that he would be a victim of the growing xenophobic reaction, Ellis insisted throughout that "Solid Unionism is Solid Americanism to the Core." Indeed, he was extremely critical of the Americanization campaign that had flourished during the war. "Is it not time to quit talking about 'Americanizing the alien' when we do not permit him even to form a labor union; when armed guards with machine guns surround his meeting places; when he may not even get together to discuss conditions under which he lives without being shot or arrested on a fake false charge and thrown into prison? Who the hell owns this earth, anyway?"

In contrast with Ellis's angry and militant rhetoric the goals of the Amalgamated were reasonable and conservative. In speeches delivered in meeting halls throughout Lackawanna and Buffalo, Griffiths promised no social upheaval, no Bolshevik revolution: "We are not Bolsheviks. We do not advocate I.W.W.ism. We realize that some of us forge ahead faster than others, that there are some among us more intelligent than others. We do not contend that every man is equal and should be alike." There was nothing communistic about the efforts to organize the steelworkers, Griffiths assured the anxious outside world: "We merely demand a fair share of the profits of the producers. The steel magnates can well afford to give us more wages and still have sufficient left over to pay fancy salaries to officials and lay aside handsome surpluses."

His appeal worked. Griffiths was an extremely effective organizer. By Labor Day, four thousand of the close to seven thousand workers in the Lackawanna plant, all six hundred workers at the Rodgers-Brown plant, and over half of the two thousand production workers at the Donner Plant in South Buffalo had joined the Amalgamated Association of Iron and Steel Workers.

Despite the benign nature of Griffiths's rhetoric, the list of demands that the Amalgamated presented to Judge Elbert Gary and the other steel company owners in the summer of 1919 was long and insistent. They wanted a reduction in the work day from twelve to eight hours (after the Armistice, the companies had reinstated the twelve-hour day), company check-off of union dues, and, most significantly, official recognition of their union and with it the right to bargain collectively for the over 250,000 workers in the steel industry. Yet for Judge Gary and the other owners, the union was anathema and they refused to recognize it. The union was equally adamant on this point and in late September 1919 a quarter of a million steel workers throughout the northeastern United States went on strike.

Unlike the earlier strikes and work stoppages that had affected the industry, the steel strike of 1919 was unprecedented in its size and scope. For the first time, a strike in the steel industry represented not one or two crafts but rather the whole spectrum of labor. It was a broadly based rank-and-file movement that managed for the first time to bridge the gap that had for so long existed between the unskilled European workers and the skilled, predominantly American workers. Everybody took part in this strike (and Buffalo newspapers reported countless meetings in Lackawanna of Hungarian, Polish, Italian, Spanish, Russian, Bulgarian, and Negro workers). On the first day—September 25, 1919—close to half of the Lackawanna work force stayed away. The next day over six thousand were on strike, blocking access to the plant. The mill was forced to shut down.

There was violence on the first day when company police fired into a crowd of strikers in front of the number two gate. Several were wounded and one Casimir Mazurek was killed. His funeral, largely ignored by the Buffalo press, attracted over seven thousand mourners, who paraded behind his horse-drawn coffin through the streets of Lackawanna. A World War I veteran and a member of the American Legion (which immediately demanded an investigation into the shooting), Mazurek had "the American flag, for which he fought, wrapped around his coffin."

There was violence again in mid-October when the company, increasingly concerned about the still almost total shutdown of the plant, brought in several hundred Negro strikebreakers. This time, however, Mayor Toomey requested the help of the state militia. (This action, more than Toomey's anti-union position, was unpopular with Lackawanna's small electorate, and in the election that November Toomey was beaten by a Socialist candidate for mayor, a Lackawanna railroad worker named John Gibbons.)

There were no other efforts to break the strike, for in Lackawanna, as in the other steel towns, the company owners knew that time was clearly on their side. They really had very little to worry about. So great had been their wartime profits that they could afford to wait. They knew from the beginning that they could easily outlast the strikers.

While the strike was in effect for several weeks, by mid-October it was becoming increasingly apparent that the cause of the steelworkers was hopeless. Efforts to rally them—Mother Jones, now over eighty years old, stopped in Buffalo and Lackawanna as part of a national tour on behalf of the striking steelworkers—failed and many began to return to work. Despite the hopes of Charles Ellis locally, and

John Reed and the others nationally, who believed that the steel strike was the beginning of a national general strike, few unions anywhere expressed much sympathy. Indeed, strikers in Lackawanna, Buffalo, Cleveland, Pittsburgh, Gary, and Chicago were bitterly disappointed when railroad workers refused to join their cause. In Buffalo, only two small unions of steamship workers went out in sympathy, and then only for a day.

Even among the strikers themselves, the unprecedented solidarity that had led this broad cross section of workers to strike in the first place began by October to give way to feelings of disillusionment and defeat. Daily, workers—first a handful and then a quickly growing number—drifted back to the plant. The companies refused to budge and simply waited and the longer they did the weaker the strike became. By the end of the year steel production had returned to over fifty percent of capacity. By early 1920 it was back to normal. The workers had returned. None of their demands had been met.

Although nonviolent and easily broken, the steel strike of 1919 had a dramatic and long-lasting impact on Lackawanna and Buffalo. Eastablished interests had been threatened and frightened both by the strike and by the solidarity that had apparently existed among the largely foreign workers in the Lackawanna mills. This, combined with the imminent Bolshevik victory in Russia, the general strike in Seattle, and the police strike in Boston, made more emotional the response to the steel strike. Issues were clouded. Facts were lost sight of. The result was a sharply conservative reaction that was both anti-union and anti-foreign. Under orders from Attorney General Palmer in Washington, 158 alleged radicals were arrested in Buffalo during the winter of 1919–20. The 1920s, hard for rdicals and other pariahs, was a particularly difficult time for immigrants.

Despite the local press, whose references to Buffalo's immigrants tended to be paeans to the most successful and upwardly mobil among them, some people at least realized that success could not be achieved overnight. One of these was Niles Carpenter, chairman of the Sociology Department at the University of Buffalo and the author in 1927 of a study on "Nationality, Color and Economic Opportunity in the City of Buffalo." Carpenter's study was a meticulous account of economic mobility among immigrants and blacks. Its precise and detailed data, presented in understated, mild, hardly inflammatory prose, must have come as a shock to those who read the study (probably not too many did, as it received no attention in the local press).

Although he opened his work with a brief economic profile of the city, Carpenter's interest was not in the economy per se but rather in its impact on the nature of work and the work force. The economy being what it was, Carpenter concluded, "the Buffalo worker must expect to find his livelihood in manual as contrasted to non-manual work and in unskilled as contrasted to skilled labor." While the local economy thus worked to the advantage of the unskilled, newly arrived immigrant and the "Plantation Negro," for whom Buffalo was "a sort of occupational El Dorado," it offered little to the second immigrant generation or to the northern-born black. Barring any changes in the structure of the city's economy, Carpenter envisioned the perpetuation in Buffalo of an unskilled, uneducated, industrial proletariat. His predictions were frightening and ominous. "To the same degree that opportunities are plentiful on the lower ranges of the occupational ladder, they are scarcer on the upper reaches. By the same token, competition for these higher skilled positions is increased." Carpenter saw nothing but trouble resulting from this. "In an atmosphere of economic competition of this sort racial and nationalistic antipathies and resentments are likely to be increased."

Carpenter was particularly concerned with immigrant and black workers, and in an effort to learn more about them he did surveys of many local companies and trade unions. Everywhere he found that racial and ethnic stereotypes had created biases that invariably influenced hiring practices. He found, for example, that most employers believed that blacks were "slow thinkers" and "too easy going," and therefore "not able to assume any responsibility." Most employers Carpenter surveyed agreed that black workers "should always have a white man as foreman."

Similar prejudices informed local employers' views of eastern European immigrants. Hungarians and Poles were widely praised for their willingness to work hard, although "very few men in these races [had] any desire to become skilled workers."

Carpenter was also interested in the exclusionary practices of local trade unions. With the exception of Orientals, the city's craft unions were open to skilled workers regardless of nationality. This did not hold true, however, for skilled Negro workers. Indeed, Carpenter reported that Negroes were specifically excluded from membership in trade organizations in which they had thrived in other cities. Thus Negroes, who had traditionally worked in street construction jobs in cities throughout the Northeast, were denied membership in the Buffalo local of the Curb Setters and Stone and Asphalt Workers Union. Negro cooks (and this had long been a prestigious and well-paying occupation for black males), still managed to get some work despite their exclusion from the local cook's union. In cases where exclusion from a trade was total (the Curb Setters, for example, had a closed shop agreement with the city, thus totally barring Negro employment in that trade), there was little skilled black workers could do. At other times blacks formed their own all-Negro locals. One was the Buffalo local of the Colored Musicians Union. Another, established in 1930 after years of organizing activity in the city, was the Buffalo branch of the Brotherhood of Sleeping Car Porters.

Carpenter found the plight of the Negro female worker still worse. "The opportunity of the Negro woman worker in Buffalo is confined almost exclusively to the field of domestic and personal service." He did report that there was one Negro female office clerk and one tailor, both of whom got their jobs because they passed as white. When the National Urban League opened a Buffalo branch in 1925, one of its first objectives was to place Negro women in industry.

Some of the city's blacks had been able to enter business and the professions. They were, however, largely confined to serving the needs of their own community. There were, he found in 1927, fifteen Negro churches with Negro pastors; four Negro physicians, three dentists, one lawyer, and one architect; two Negro newspapers; two Negro undertakers; one Negro real estate company; and several Negro-owned restaurants, hotels, and cabarets, all on the black East Side. "Few Negroes," Carpenter summarized, "have achieved a measure of success in direct competition with whites."

Most striking of all was the forthright, forceful, and ominous tone with which the University of Buffalo sociologist concluded his study, as much a warning as it was a hint of things to come. He blamed prejudice for the relative failure of the eastern European laborers to become semi-skilled workers and managers: "It is hard to believe that deficient training or defective innate abilities are wholly responsible for their retarded occupational progress and that it is not in some measure due to an unwillingness on the part of certain employers to hire 'Pollacks,' 'Wops,' 'Hunkies' and 'Niggers' for other than manual labor. . . . There must have been *some* Negroes employed in these various establishments capable of rising to the rank of foreman and more than a scant handful able to do skilled labor and there must have been *some* Poles particularly those of the native-born generation, capable of doing clerical and managerial work."

While the prejudices of the period had harsh effects on the immigrants, so too did political events. For the war on the immigrant really began in October 1919 when Prohibition went into effect.

Alcohol had always been associated with immigrants, and prohibition, the culmination of close to a hundred years of temperance activities, was a direct assault on the nation's immigrant communities. Economically, it destroyed the beer business, and in the process undercut the power of the city's German Americans. Socially, it destroyed the tavern, still the focal point of immigrant community life. It is no wonder then that from the beginning Buffalo's immigrants, like most everybody in the city, were staunchly opposed to Prohibition. In 1922 Francis X. Schwab, a former beer salesman and president of the Buffalo Brewing Company, was elected mayor on a repeal platform.

Despite the magnitude of its threat, the city in general and the immigrants in particular quickly learned to live with Prohibition, persistently and defiantly violating it. While some local breweries did go out of business, a few managed to stay open, selling both legal (two percent) beer and "needle beer" in which alcohol was illegally injected. Similarly, almost unlimited amounts of bootleg liquor were available. As if it were planned with Prohibition in mind, the Peace Bridge between Buffalo and Canada opened with royal fanfare, pomp, and circumstance in 1927, and quickly became the primary pipeline for bootleg liquor trucked into Buffalo from Canada. Using either this or stuff they made in their own stills, most neighborhood tavern owners were able to keep their institutions alive and well during these times. For while there were periodic raids on the local saloons and on the speakeasies—Diamond Lil McVan's, Galdyz', Richie Roth's, Jew Minnie's, and Ann Montgomery's were the most popular— law enforcement was sporadic and relaxed. Indeed, by 1927 the Anti-Saloon League launched a campaign to "dry-up Buffalo" and the Ku Klux Klan, in Buffalo at least, was far more concerned with violations of the prohibition law than with Catholics, Negroes, and Jews.

Although at times laughable and easily circumscribed, Prohibition did not amuse the immigrant community. How much, indeed, could they be asked to take? Coming in the wake of the anti-German passions of the war years, Prohibition was not easily ignored by the German community, whose stake in the beer business was traditional and extensive. Nor could the Irish and Polish communities take comfort in this assault on what was a significant and central feature of their lives: the neighborhood saloon.

While Buffalo's immigrants might have joked about the ridiculous and futile effort to impose Prohibition, the attempt to restrict immigration in 1924 was clearly not a laughing matter. Indeed, because it, far more than the ill-fated Prohibition law, was a direct and powerful assault on immigrant life in America, it was taken extremely seriously.

World War I ended the free and relatively inexpensive access that had for so long existed between southeastern Europe and the United States. Trips between Buffalo and Warsaw, Budapest, and Palermo were everyday occurrences. Indeed, several Italian and Polish travel agents made small fortunes in this business. More significant than the contact and communication that had existed between the Old World and the New was the commonly held belief, the assumption, that this freedom would continue—that it was just a question of time before a man would be joined by his family, by his neighbors, and eventually by many of his villagers. However, the complicated and complex chain of events that had created the separate worlds of immigrant Buffalo came suddenly to an end in August 1914.

While there was a renewed flood of immigration after the war, it was stopped following the passage in the early 1920 of quotas which severely limited the number of newcomers, particularly the Jews and Catholics of southeastern Europe.

Many people tended to support immigration restriction. Particularly following the steel strike, when wild notions about Bolshevik and foreign radical conspiracies were fairly rampant in Buffalo, most everybody favored some kind of restrictions on the numbers and the kinds of immigrants. Some—citing the activities of Stella and Fredrick Koldzinski, a young couple from Black Rock who, following their arrest for robbery, swore to continue to steal as long as the poor went hungry—would "Ban The Reds." Others, like the bishop of Buffalo, who clearly stood to suffer from immigration restriction, suggested that future immigrants be channeled away from the city and into the countryside. Even some industrialists, who had for so long benefited from the plentiful supply of cheap labor, had come to advocate at least a partial restriction on the number of immigrants.

There were some who had their doubts, however. The *Courier*, for example, while advocating restriction, warned menacingly that if immigrants were to be restricted it would "result in the still greater movement here of colored workers." They, like some of the other moderates, suggested that the quotas for the number of yearly immigrants be based on the number of each nationality in the population in 1920 and not, as the hardcore restrictionists insisted, in 1890. The Ku Klux Klan, small but nevertheless increasingly active in Buffalo during 1924, had no doubts however, and through a series of wild, raucous, and vociferous public demonstrations demanded an end to "vice, corruption and immigration."

Even the immigrants seemed only mildly concerned. In late 1923 and early 1924 it became increasingly clear that the Johnson immigration restriction bill, favored by die-hards throughout the United States, would become law. The bill, more so than the legislation of the early 1920s, threatened to end completely the whole character of American immigration. The bill was a direct assault on the eastern European Catholic and Jewish communities in cities throughout the Northeast. A major source of urban vitality was ending. The number of Poles permitted to immigrate dropped from 26,000 to 9,000 a year, Italians from 42,000 to 4,000, Czechs from 14,000 to 2,000, Hungarians from 5,000 to 688, and Greeks from 3,000 to 235. Families, neighbors, and villagers would far less frequently be united on the streets and neighborhoods of America's cities. And yet, for some unexplained and mysterious reason, there was little attempt within these communities, at least in Buffalo, to fight the bill.

Of all the city's immigrant groups, the Jews were the most outspoken in their opposition to this patently bigoted legislation. It was not easy to be Jewish in Buffalo in the early twentieth century. Unlike in New York, Philadelphia, or Chicago, where Jews through sheer force of numbers had begun to play an important role in the cities' civic life, in Buffalo Jews, vastly outnumbered, were far less visible.

This changed dramatically following the large immigration to Buffalo during the early twentieth century of Russian and Polish Jews. The eastern European Jewish population (about thirteen thousand in 1920) had, with their large, Yiddish-speaking families, and their old-world ways, far more in common with the Italians and Poles than with the German Jews on the West Side who had, through success in business and the professions, become some of the wealthier residents of Buffalo. Unlike the German Jews, who blended easily into the city's social fabric, the Jewish east siders were eminently visible.

The Jewish community, particularly the Russian and Polish Jews on the East Side, had been cohesive and well organized from the very beginning, with a full range of social, religious, and cultural activities and institutions. There were close to a dozen synagogues, several newspapers, literary circles, zionist and labor organizations, and a theatre known as The Little Theatre which specialized in pacifist and socially conscious agit-prop. (During the mid-1920s, when the community was undergoing considerable turmoil as large numbers of blacks began to move in, the Little Theatre produced a play called "In Abraham's Bosom," a story about a black youth's struggle against racial prejudice.) But these activities had always functioned within the confines of the Jewish community itself. Now, for the first time, there emerged a group of young men and women, east siders and west siders, who were willing to go public as Jews, to present themselves to Jews and Gentiles alike as "Jewish Leaders." It was a risky business. One of these was Joseph Braun.

Joseph Braun, thirty years old in 1924, the year of the Johnson Immigration Restriction Act, was president of a small yet quite successful insurance business, most of whose clients were Gentiles. Born in Buffalo into a first-generation German Jewish family, Braun, who had grown up in the prosperous, Protestant social environment of the West Side, had many friends in the non-Jewish community. He belonged to an organization of downtown businessmen and a downtown luncheon club, and was an active member in the Buffalo Rotary. Although raised in a traditional Jewish household, Braun had for years belonged to Temple Beth Zion, a Reform and largely German Jewish congregation. Other than his annual attendance at High Holy Day services, Braun was casual about his religious affiliation. Being Jewish, he felt, played an insignificant part in his life; many of his Gentile friends didn't even know he was Jewish.

Life began to change for Braun after World War I. In 1918 Buffalo's first Jewish newspaper was published. In 1919 the newly organized Federation of Jewish Social Services opened its headquarters in a downtown hotel. A Jewish old people's home was built in the heart of a prosperous, Presbyterian neighborhood. Zionists like Felix Frankfurter and Chaim Weitzman came to Buffalo to talk about Zionism, a subject long frowned upon by the city's German Jewish establishment. The Jewish community was coming out.

Never more visibly than in 1924 when, more vocally and critically and more actively than any of the city's immigrant groups, Jews (much to the dismay of some of the city's German Jews, who would well have welcomed the exclusion of their scruffy, Polish and Russian Yiddish-speaking brethren) protested the Johnson immigration bill of 1924. Unlike the mild, restrained rhetoric of the *Catholic Union and Times, Everybody's Polish Daily* and the Italian *Corriere*, the Buffalo *Jewish Review* was frank and blatant in its attack, openly denouncing "these Nordic theories of racial supremacy," and calling the bill "anti-Semitic, anti-Catholic and anti-American."

Responding to the challenge of the bill, Braun, who had recently led a citywide fund drive for the Jewish Federation, now began the task of organizing the entire immigrant community of Buffalo against the bill. Working with two Polish and one Italian priest (the bishop of Buffalo refused to participate), Braun organized a citywide protest demonstration against the bill. With the support of the mayor and the common council, which passed a unanimous resolution against the bill, Braun and the others were able to attract an audience of over two thousand Jews, Poles, and Italians to Buffalo's auditorium. The *Jewish Review* noted: "The Broadway Auditorium last Sunday presented a scene that was unique and inspiring. Three groups that hitherto have been separate have united in a common protest asgainst the Johnson Immigration Bill."

Their protest failed, however, and the bill became law. Buffalo's immigrant population was now shut off from its forebears in eastern Europe. Denied rejuvenation from the outside, it was simply a question of time before these communities would begin to wither and die.

Actually, many of the older, inner-city ethnic neighborhoods had already begun to decline during the 1920s. Even though Buffalo's population was growing very quickly (it increased by thirteen percent between 1920 and 1930, to 573,076), most of the older inner-city neighborhoods had begun to lose population. There was then an enormous amount of upheaval in the city's neighborhoods, with thousands of people pouring in and thousands leaving. None changed quicker and more dramatically than the lower East Side.

The lower East Side had been to Buffalo what it was to New York City: the neighborhood of entry for every one of the city's immigrants. By 1915, the area bounded by Michigan, Jefferson, Broadway, and William Streets had lost most of its original German population and was now inhabited primarily by Jewish immigrants from Russia and Poland.

But for them, as well as for the other immigrant groups who had lived there, the East Side neighborhood was only a temporary home. While suburban-bound second-generation Americans waxed nostalgic about the old neighborhood, little love was actually lost on it. Indeed, they got out as fast as they could. During the 1920s many of the Jewish residents of the East Side, some of whom had been there for less than ten years, began to move to newer and nicer neighborhoods in more northerly sections of Buffalo. It was inevitable that these first-generation immigrants, both Jews and non-Jews, left. There were not good reasons for them to stay. The neighborgood was old; its wood-frame housing run-down and decrepit. It was a period of general prosperity, and anyway blacks, migrants from the rural south, had since the labor shortage of World War I been moving in in increasing numbers: 4,500 in 1920 and 13,500 ten years later. Virtually all of them moved onto the lower East Side, where there had been a small but consistent black community since the late 1820s.

For a while the neighborhood was integrated. Jews and blacks mixed at the public marketplace; at the public school; and at the corner of William and Jefferson Streets, where the Jewish Community Center shared the corner with the union hall of the Brotherhood of Sleeping Car Porters. But this didn't last long. As the number of blacks grew—the local grammar school had 607 black students in 1925 and only 90 in 1920—Jews left. The East Side Jewish community was dying. Interrupted by the Depression and then by the Second World War, its death was slow. But by the early 1960s it had vanished completely.

Blacks quickly filled the emptying vacuum, and as their community grew it strengthened. The surrounding white world was hostile. Segregation was accepted in every branch of the city's social, economic, and political life. And yet, there had been no violence. Buffalo, unlike St. Louis and Chicago, did not have race wars in 1919. Nevertheless, the situation was bad enough, and in response Buffalo's blacks turned inward, building a strong, yet self-reliant community of their own. Responding to the needs of the growing population, black-owned enterprises suddenly proliferated. Hotels, nightclubs, funeral parlors, cleaners, drug stores, restaurants, candy stores, saloons, and a Negro baseball team were some of them. Sherman Walker's Funeral Home, the Ruth-Patrick Drug Company, the My Cab Company, and the McAvoy Theater were substantial and successful operations. But success did not come easy. In the middle of the 1920s local banks knuckled under to pressure from white-owned cab companies and refused to extend a loan to My Cab. The effort to run My Cab out of business failed, however, when it was able to secure a loan from a New York City bank.

Self-help groups within the black community also flourished during the twenties. One of the earliest was the Colored Musicians' Union of Buffalo, founded in 1917 by black musicians who had been denied membership in the white musicians' local. In addition, there was a grocery cooperative; several Negro lodges; the Negro Businessmen's League; the American Colored Workmen's League; a chapter of Marcus Garvey's United Negro Improvement Association; the Big Brothers' Association (founded by older, established East Side blacks to help ease the settlement problems of the new southern migrants); and the Michigan Avenue YMCA, built in 1926 by a local black architect named John R. Brent. And while there was no black-owned bank, the community did boast several newspapers: *The Buffalo*

Enterprise, the *Buffalo American,* the *Buffalo Criterion* and the
Voice. Abandoned by every other ethnic group that had ever lived
there, the lower East Side has remained black to this day.

Buffalo's economy during the 1920s was going through a different
kind of upheaval. Most people knew something was happening and
most people were pleased with the course of events. The chamber of
commerce, for example, was confident that as long as the city possessed
what it called "key indusries"—according to chamber publicists a key
industry was one around which other industries would gather because
of mutual dependence on its product—the local economy would prosper
indefinitely. According to them Buffalo possessed four such industries:
steel, grain, lumber, and rubber. With these four as a foundation,
prosperity, full employment, and uninterrupted growth were absolutely
assured. There were no doubts about this. Indeed, virtually every
word spoken, every speech delivered, and every article written during
the 1920s was imbued with a total, unqualified confidence in the
future of the city's economy.

Facts tend to bear out this optimism. It is true that throughout
the 1920s Buffalo's economy was dynamic and diversified, healthy
and strong. The older industries—grain, steel, and lumber—employed
more people, and produced a larger finished product than ever before.
Meanwhile three new industries had begun to exert an increasingly
dominant role. Wartime defense contracts had turned the Curtiss-
Wright Aeroplane Company, which had moved to Buffalo in 1914
and by the mid-1920s employed over two thousand people producing
over 150 planes a year, into the largest plane manufacturing company
in the world. Buffalo, with an airport built in 1927, years before
New York and other larger cities had airfields of their own, had
quickly become the center of the nation's airplane industry.

The 1920s also saw the rise of the chemical industry in Buffalo
and nearby Niagara Falls. Within a period of a few years a whole
new industry was born. Spawning companies whose impersonal names
made no reference to either place or person—Carborundum, Niacet,
Canadium, Vanadium, and the Alox Chemical Corporation (Hooker,
named after the company's founder, was an exception)—the petro-
chemical industry, located in Niagara Falls, employed over fifteen
hundred people by the end of the decade.

They had chosen Niagara Falls because that is where the electrical
power was. Initially developed by Jacob Schoellkopf, the German
immigrant who had made his first fortune in the tanning business,
the business of producing and selling electrical power at Niagara Falls

had become a gigantic enterprise by the 1920s. Nothing, indeed, was more responsible for the accelerated development of the Buffalo region as an industrial center than the availability of cheap and plentiful electrical power.

Those who wrote about Buffalo's economy were particularly proud of what they were convinced was its healthy diversification. They considered themselves lucky that, unlike in Detroit (at times Detroit, because of its phenomenal growth rates, was also an object of envy), there was no one industry in Buffalo which monopolized the economy. Diversity, then, was a cushion against adverse cyclical swings. Afraid that people might infer that diversity meant many small businesses, the chamber of commerce used much copy to convince otherwise. Not only, they demonstrated, was there a wide range of industries in the city, but most of them were quite extensive. Fifteen thousand people worked in twelve automobile factories, 13,000 in machine and foundry shops, 2,000 in furniture, 3,000 in packing and slaughtering, and 3,000 in soap factories.

Although dominated by large-scale factories, many of which were increasingly owned by outside interests, Buffalo also maintained a vital, small-scale, largely locally owned economy that employed large numbers of skilled workers. There were a dozen shoe factories employing 228 men and 28 women; half a dozen clothing factories with 368 male and 1,386 female workers; several large machine and tool factories with over 3,000 employees; thousands of painters, glaziers, varnishers, and enamelers in the local construction trade; 2,378 electricians; 1,865 plumbers; 5,077 carpenters; and 1,180 bakers.

Manufacturing, with close to 100,000 workers, unquestionably dominated the economy. Yet, even as early as the 1920s, Buffalo's economy was quickly becoming increasingly service-oriented, and by the end of the 1920s over thirty-five thousand men and women worked in trade, primarily the retail sector.

As industry and retailing boomed, commerce and communication declined. Yet in 1930 there were still over five hundred sailors and deck hands and almost three hundred longshoremen and stevedores working on the Buffalo waterfront. More important to the daily function of the city were the five thousand general laborers and two thousand switchmen who worked in the streetcars and railroads of Buffalo.

The "Professional Services," as the census referred to them, employed over 17,000 men and women. Most of the women—over 6,000 out of a total of 8,567—worked as teachers and nurses. Of the close to 1,000 lawyers and 900 physicians, there were only 37

217

and 57 women respectively. The one job category where women were most numerous, however, was in personal and domestic service, where the overwhelming percentage of workers were black female house-keepers and servants.

The general sense of confidence and security that most people had about the local economy was reinforced by the perennial faith that Buffalo's location somehow automatically guaranteed the economic success of the city. Buffalo, whose initial rise was a result of its strategic location midway between the agricultural and industrial heart of America in the midwest and the cities of the East, had, since the completion of the Erie Canal made this nexus possible, been fixated on location. The theme was perennial and unchanging. Year in and year out professional boosters had prated about Buffalo's centrality, its excellent position between the coast and the plains, its proximity to every major market in the United States and Canada. Most significantly, it was Buffalo's location at the end of the extensive water route beginning in Lake Superior and ending in Buffalo at Lake Erie that had made the city a dominant center of commerce and now, more recently, of industry. What other city, its boosters argued in 1930 (as they had in 1900 and in 1870), was in a better position to serve as a center of assembly, manufacturing, and distri-bution than Buffalo. These beliefs were not limited to local, profes-sional boosters. Indeed, such a sophisticated outsider as the president of Bethlehem Steel wrote in 1927 that, "You have the best location in the country for the successful assembly, production and distribution of manufactured goods. There is none better, more strategically located center than Buffalo."

Belief in the excellence of Buffalo's location had become an article of faith, a community-held belief that had assumed somewhat mystical powers, as if location alone could and had somehow promised the city a perennially brilliant future. In 1927 a chamber of commerce publication confidently exclaimed: "In a nation such as ours we do not see so many examples of cities which have ceased to thrive because former advantages were lost." Did they really think it would last forever—that all of the cycles were over, or at least had somehow stopped in Buffalo?

The growth of the automobile industry during the 1920s fed the city's optimism. Buffalo was particularly proud of the Pierce Arrow Company. Unlike most other automobiles, the Pierce Arrow was handmade, produced by teams of workers, not assembly line autom-atons, who slowly and carefully, in a manner strangely reminiscent of the Roycrofters, virtually hand-crafted their automobile. Pierce Arrow automobiles were well made. The company had retired the Glidden Cup, a trophy earned for having won the annual round-trip automobile race between new York City and Bretton Woods, New Hampshire three years in a row, and its Touring Landau of 1910, with a built-in lavatory with running water, was one of the most coveted automobiles in the pre-war years.

When, during the war, the government needed fast, reliable, strong and well-built vehicles, it turned to Pierce Arrow, which began to produce trucks in the same careful, hand-crafted tradition. In 1916 they netted $5 million and George Birge, the company president, sold the company to a group of investors from New York City for $16.5 million. Local managers, most of whom had worked with the company since 1901 (Birge had boasted that there was no turnover in his company), were immediately dismissed and replaced by a new team from New York. Sensing that a dramatic increase in production was the only way to compete in the rapidly expanding automobile industry, the new owners replaced the traditional Pierce Arrow method of team production with an assembly line. The nature of work changed too, for as mechanization and the assembly line were introduced, skilled work, which comprised nearly three-fourths of all jobs in the automobile industry in 1910, declined drastically in the twenties, as the emphasis shifted to speed and efficiency in production. In 1921 the Pierce Arrow Company lost eight million dollars. In 1928, after several more years of operating at a loss, the company was bought by Studebaker.

By then Buffalo had become deeply involved in the production of automobiles. Among the twelve automobile factories that employed close to thirteen thousand people in 1930 was the General Motors Company, which had built a factory in the city in 1923. Dunlop, the tire and rubber company, came next.

Companies in other industries too suddenly became the targets of giant, national corporations searching for lucrative sources of investments. In October 1922, Bethlehem Steel, the second largest steel company in the United States, acquired Lackawanna Steel for $60 million. It was a good buy. The deal was mutually beneficial. The Lackawanna plant, already over twenty years old, had become antiquated. The company had made few improvements, and was quickly falling behind newer plants in other parts of the country. Bethlehem bought it cheap and, banking on a docile and defeated work force, spent over $40 million during the 1920s modernizing the plant. Bethlehem was interested in the growing automobile market and

Buffalo, with a significant automobile industry of its own and with easy access to Detroit and other market places, was viewed as a crucial node in the developing geography of the automobile industry. There were other acquisitions in the steel industry too, as Republic Steel, based in Cleveland, bought the Donner Steel and Iron Company, and Rogers-Brown Steel was acquired by the National Steel Company.

Buffalo's grain business was another prime target for large, national corporations eager to expand and strengthen their control over the industry. Standard Milling of New York built a gigantic elevator and flour mill on the Buffalo waterfront. Commander-Larabee and International Milling, both of Minneapolis, bought out several local operations while building new facilities of their own. Elevators, mills, and even bakeries were brought into the national network of the grain industry. In 1927 Greenan's Bakery "the largest and best equipped cake bakery in this section of the country," was bought by the Purity Bakery Company of New York City.

Similar developments sapped the vitality of the local community. Consolidations, mergers, and acquisitions doomed the *Commercial Advertiser*, a newspaper published in Buffalo since 1828. The *Enquirer* followed in 1926. In 1929 the *Buffalo Evening Times*, locally owned for fifty years, was bought by Scripps Howard. In that same year the gigantic Fox Movie Company bought up five local movie theatres.

In 1918 the Schoellkopf family of Buffalo consolidated two separate small power companies into the Niagara Falls Power Company, which immediately became one of the largest in the country. In 1925 the Schoelkopfs merged the Niagara Falls Company; the Niagara, Lockport and Ontario Power Company; the Tonawanda Power Company; and the Buffalo General Electric Company into a gigantic holding company called the Buffalo, Niagara and Eastern Power Company. Four years later this, along with the New England Power Company and the Mohawk and Hudson Power Company, was merged into yet another holding company called the Niagara Hudson Power Company. Based in Buffalo, the company dominated and controlled electrical utilities from the Hudson to the Niagara River.

Mergers and concentrations also strengthened the power and control of several local banks and bankers. In the early 1920s there were still a few small private banks, many of them neighborhood-based and immigrant-owned. Immigrants were moving out of their neighborhoods, however, and the big downtown banks were expanding. The smaller banks, caught up in these changes, were either swallowed or drowned. The Commercial Trust Company bought out Michael Lunghino's

Bank and the Ortolani Brothers Bank. Victor Szczakawoski, rather than sell to the Marine Trust, closed his business.

Far larger and more significant bank mergers were occurring. In 1919 there were thirteen commercial banks in Buffalo. In 1927 there were six. The largest was the Marine Midland. This bank had begun the decade as a major commercial bank. It ended it as the centerpiece of a gigantic holding company—the Marine Midland Corporation—whose primary goal was to acquire a controlling interest in as many banks as possible. By 1929 it owned ninety-seven percent of the capital stock of seventeen banks throughout New York State. The president and chairman of the board of directors was George F. Rand.

By the end of the 1920s Rand was the dominant figure in the financial life of Buffalo. Naturally there were others: Jacob Schoellkopf, Jr. (whose father had been the entrepreneur to first turn the water of Niagara Falls into the major power industry in the United States); Walter P. Cooke, the corporation lawyer who had presided over the Liberty Loan drive; Edward P. Letchworth, whose family had made a fortune in steel and real estate, and Cooke's law partner; and Seymour Knox, whose national five-and-dime store formed a significant link in the Woolworth chain.

The source of these men's power was their control of banking and electric utilities. Rand, president and chairman of the Marine Trust, was also a director of the Niagara-Hudson Power Company. Jacob Schoelkopf, vice-president and general manager of the same power company, was a director of the Manufacturer's and Trader's Bank (M&T). His brother Paul was an officer of both the power company and Rand's Marine Trust. Walter P. Cooke was director of both Rand's Marine Trust and the Niagara Hudson. Lewis G. Harriman, president and chairman of the M&T Bank, also served as a director of the Niagara-Hudson.

These men had other business interests too. George Rand was a director of the Remington-Rand Company, the Cleveland Transit Company, the General Baking Company of Minneapolis, and the Metropolitan Casualty Company of New York City. Schoelkopf too was a director of the Metropolitan, where Harriman was active in a variety of investment companies throughout New York State.

What is fascinating and significant about the business interests and activities of these people, men who dominated and controlled the banks and the power companies of the city, the region, and even the state, is that they had little financial stake in the industrial companies of the city. Among the men who dominated the directorships of local companies, none served on the boards of corporations involved in industry. Rather, they turned away, and local industry fell into the hands of outsiders. Why was this so? Had the city's financiers begun to dismiss Buffalo's industry and to look elsewhere for richer and more lucrative investments? What did they know about the state of local industry that the chamber of commerce either didn't know or denied knowing?

Perhaps Buffalo's economy, despite record profits and levels of production throughout the 1920 in all of the key industries, was in fact weak. Perhaps bankers were concerned about the city's slowing rate of population growth—from nineteen percent between 1910 and 1920 to thirteen percent the following decade, and worried that Buffalo's two historic rivals on the Great Lakes—Cleveland and Detroit— had by the early 1920s irrevocably bypassed it in size and industrial output. There was a great deal of talk and hand-wrinnging about this. Some members of the chamber of commerce even began a campaign to convince the census to count population density as a figure of greater significance than population size. Pehaps the bankers were concerned about this. They certainly were concerned by the statement of Eugene Grace, the president of the Bethlehem Steel Company, found buried in the back pages of the newspaper in July 1927. Grace, who had spent over $40 million at the Lackawanna plant building a new rolling mill and coke ovens, was worried. He was afraid that high railroad rates into and out of Buffalo and high production costs at the Lackawanna plant were leading to a steady increase in imported steel. Grace admitted to being deeply anxious, and told reporters that he had spoken to Secretary of the Treasury Mellon several times about it.

There were other problems too. Since the end of the war there had been much talk in Washington and in Quebec about building what was called a "seaway," an interrupted water route between Lake Ontario and the Atlantic Ocean. But for now, however, it was only talk and throughout the 1920s Buffalo's significance as a major grain and flour center—second only to Minneapolis—grew. Yet always present, almost unmentioned and unmentionable, was the possibility that someday this direct all-water route would be built, and when it was all of the advantages of Buffalo's much-vaunted location would vanish.

Yet despite the clear presence of these disturbing trends in the local economy, most people chose not to notice them. Indeed, they accepted them, thinking that what was happening was all for the good. Certainly there were tangible benefits from these developments. The mergers that created the Marine Midland system did make more money available to more borrowers. More bank branches did open in more sections of the city. Electrical power, too, was somewhat cheaper at the end of the decade than it had been earlier (some people thought that they should have been lower still and criticized the legal loophole that exempted the Niagara Hudson River Company, a "holding" company and not, according to the law, an "operating" company, from regulation). More steel was produced by Bethlehem than had been by Lackawanna, and the control of the local flour industry by Minneapolis and New York City interests had produced a larger and more profitable product than ever before.

But still, somebody somewhere—local business people, community groups, writers, educators—should have sensed something. They should have guessed that on some levels at least, the economic developments that had remade Buffalo's economy during the 1920s contained the seeds of decay.

CHAPTER 10

Buffalo Defaults: The City During the Depression and World War II

By 1930 it was too late. Buffalo, despite its vaunted economic diversity, was devastated by the Depression. Unemployment had been increasing slowly in 1928 and 1929. By the end of 1930 over twenty percent of all construction workers, cabinetmakers, carpenters, machinists, toolmakers, painters, varnishers, glaziers, railroad and streetcar workers, and factory workers were out of work. Buffalo was helpless, not knowing what to do, but trying desperately to deal with what was still generally referred to, in the newspapers at least, as "the present emergency." The mayor, grasping at straws, formed numerous committees: the Committee for the Stabilization of Employment, the Mayor's Clothing Campaign Committee, the Committee on Economic Recovery.

None of these desperate, makeshift efforts worked. Not the mayor's Committees; not the Sunday School children's drive to collect old shoes, or the Scouts' to collect food; not the Man-a-Block campaign, which pooled the funds of families on each street in order to hire unemployed men to do landscape and maintenance chores. Not even the heroic efforts by private charities to do what they had always done in times of economic crisis seemed to work. For now it was beyond their organizational ability and financial resources to have any significant impact, and at the end of 1930 the Charity Organization Society, the largest private charity in the city, announced that because of their deficit of $25,000 they would have to curtail relief work. Meanwhile, economic indicators continued to plunge. By 1932 building permits were down by 5 percent, the number of wage earners by 30

224

percent, and the average weekly earnings by 17 percent. Steel production was off by 38 percent and flour milling by 22 percent.

Relief rolls, however, mounted. In 1932 the city of Buffalo paid out six million dollars in welfare benefits to 21,706 families—more than 100,000 people. The county added close to one million dollars, while the state government reimbursed the city for forty percent of its welfare budget. Costs were enormous; benefits were small and closely monitored. Money from the city's welfare fund could be used solely for the purchase of food. Only in clearly demonstrated emergencies would welfare funds be allocated to pay for shelter and fuel. Similarly, public funds could not be used to purchase clothing, and in July 1932 the mayor, reporting that "the clothing situation is growing increasingly acute," announced the formation of an old-clothes collection campaign. Under the city's welfare provisions, a single person could receive no more than two dollars per week in food vouchers. Regardless of size, no family could receive more than the maximum weekly allotment of ten dollars. In order to most efficiently budget their money, housewives were advised that one-quarter of their food allotments be used for milk or evaporated milk, whichever was cheaper; one-fifth for vegetables such as canned tomatoes, cabbage, potatoes, and greens; one-fifth for cereals such as oatmeal, wheat cereal, cornmeal, flour, rice, macaroni, and bread, plus dried beans and pears; and one-fifth for such fat as lard, salt pork, butter, or margarine and sugars such as molasses, sugar, or corn syrup. The balance could be used to buy meat, fish, cheese, coffee, and tea.

Food allowances were cut as prices fell and a family of five, granted six dollars a week for food (ninety-five meals at seven cents each) faced further reductions. In July 1932 the mayor announced that "experts are being consulted to advise welfare workers on an absolute minimum that will not endanger health." People were losing faith. In the fall of 1930 Charles Burchfield painted *Rainy Night at Broadway and Ellicott*. The city looked dark, bleak, grim, empty, haunted, and hopeless.

The chamber of commerce, however, continued to believe in the resiliency of the city's diversified economy, and in early 1932 predicted that "no doubt Buffalo will feel the present economic crisis [yet another euphemistic reference] less than will most American cities." A local editorialist felt that it was all up to the people themselves: "If those with jobs buckle down to them; if those with properties start using them; if those with money get it to work, there will be prosperity for all." And, if all else failed, there was always the past to turn to.

Just as in 1983, when the city made a mockery of its history through self-serving pageants, boosterish books, and uninspired hoopla commemorating its 150th anniversary, Buffalo in the midst of the Depression turned to the past and celebrated the centennial of its incorporation as a city. Using the Pan American Exposition as a model, the organizers of the Centennial erected another plywood village on a downtown park overlooking the waterfront. Here—in Centennial Park—they built a stadium, a midway, aeroplane exhibits, and several large exposition buildings. Like the Pan American, the Centennial had several columned proscenium entrances. There was also a tower—a large erector-set-like structure hung with sparkling lights of different colors—called "The Tower of Jewels." There was even a fireworks spectacle which illustrated scenes from the life of George Washington. The whole community, it seemed, was looking backwards. Several newspapers featured articles highlighting "distinctive events in the life of our city," while a radio station sponsored an eight-night serial during the first two weeks of July. It was trumpeted as "a musical drama, taking eight nights to present, which will tell the story of Buffalo's progress from pioneer days to the present."

There was something pathetic about the Centennial. Not only did it mock the past and deny the present; it would, or so its sponsors believed, redeem the future. "Our Centennial," one editor wrote, "will act as an incentive for each to play his part in achieving the glorious future that lies just ahead in the second century of the history of Buffalo." Another had convinced himself that "the Centennial will give expression to the faith that Buffalo people have in the future of their city."

The rhetoric of community uplift and optimism that characterized the Centennial celebration went quickly out of style, however. For shortly after the inauguration of President Roosevelt, the massive flow of federal and state funds to the city created a real and genuine spark of hope and enthusiasm which made the boosterish hype of the Centennial seem out of place. The New Deal did not bring prosperity to Buffalo. Nor did it bring an end to unemployment and hard times. It did bring some relief however—enough, anyway, for those who remember that time to recall it in terms far fonder than it probably deserves.

New Deal benefits came slowly. It was not until early 1935 that large-scale federal relief money was spent in Buffalo. When it did finally arrive, the sums were enormous. Throughout most of 1935 and 1936 there were almost daily announcements of federally funded public works: $4.5 million for public housing, $1.2 million for airport modernization, $2 million for a downtown auditorium, $750,000 for a concert hall (and thousands of dollars for the creation of a symphony orchestra), $1 million for the modernization of the zoo, $2 million for a federal office building, $1.3 million for a stadium, $500,000 for a new police headquarters, hundreds of thousand of dollars for schools, street widenings, playgrounds, tennis courts, swimming pools. The largest single grant of all—$15 million—was for the construction of a new sewer. Between 1935 and 1937 over $45 million had been spent on permanent projects in the city of Buffalo, employing over 75,000 men and women. Although less than the initial promise of one job for every family on relief, it was nevertheless a substantial effort to provide work for those who needed it.

Although they brought relief, many people in Buffalo were disturbed by federal policies during the Depression. There was concern and confusion that despite the apparent return to some semblance of normalcy—economic indicators including wages, employment, and steel production were all up—the number of families supported by public funds continued to increase. In March and April 1936, for example, the federal government reported that for every family going off relief because of work, two families went on. During the summer of that year, 142,960 people—twenty-five percent of the city's population— still lived on relief or make work. The WPA in Buffalo was spending money at the rate of $60,000 per day, and yet it could employ only one-half of the able-bodied workers on the city's relief roles.

As prosperity slowly returned, skilled workers began to leave their public relief jobs and return to the private economy. And as relief work became increasingly dominated by the unskilled, criticism of the program mounted. There were so many people cleaning up at the airport, it was charged, that no planes could land. Articles, letters to the editor, and editorials in all of the papers began to warn about the dangers of increased public welfare, of the "opiate of relief and relief employment," of "relief and the impairment of human values," and of "welfare chiselers." Soon politicians, newspaper writers, and community leaders, Democrats as well as Republicans, began to talk seriously about "going back to private charity" in the hope of spurring thousands of workers into jobs in private industry. Only a return to private charity, the old system of outdoor relief, people argued, would, because it was so demeaning, force people back to work. At least, one paper argued, such a strategy might remedy "the servant problem," saying that "although there are thousands of able bodied girls on work relief who could support themselves by doing housework, it is impossible to find domestic help in Buffalo."

What bothered most people, however, was the sinking sense that while the Depression may well have ended, it had left in its wake a permanent and dependent class of workers forever unable to support themselves. That was a new and frightening phenomenon. The *Buffalo Evening News* drew a sombre conclusion: "It is inevitable that many thousands of families never again will become self-supporting; that a new social responsibility has been created during the Depression that only painstaking thought and far-reaching legislation can discharge."

A small yet significant element of the American Dream was going bad in Buffalo.

While not everyone liked the consequences, it had become clear by 1937 that the federal government had bailed out a bankrupt city. Local political life would never again be the same. Buffalo, like other cities at the end of the 1930s had become, to all intents and purposes, a ward of the federal government. Washington—"The Feds," as they had come to be called—was picking up an ever larger chunk of the bill and in the process was asserting an ever-growing influence on the local affairs of the city of Buffalo. Long vulnerable to the cyclical changes of the national economy, now not only was Buffalo's economy dependent on trends beyond its control but its political life too had come under the domination of Washington.

In 1937 the country once again went bad, and again the bottom of the economy fell out. At the end of the year steel production had fallen to eighteen percent of capacity, the lowest in history, and by January 1938 unemployment was back up to what it had been in 1932 and the number of families on relief was unprecedented. Depression had begun to appear inevitable and permanent.

For many in Buffalo, the Pierce Arrow Company was a beacon of hope, the symbol of the city's ingenuity and resilience, ability to survive hardship through perseverance, and dedication to excellence. In 1933 the Studebaker Company, which had acquired Pierce Arrow in the late twenties, had gone into receivership, and Albert Erskine, president of the company, jumped out of a window in his New York City office. Later that year, however, Pierce Arrow was salvaged from that wreckage by local investors willing to gamble one million dollars in cash on one last effort to save the company. Rejecting advice that they return to the manufacture of a luxury automobile, the company directors committed the company and its 3,000 workers to the mass production of a trailer known as the Travelodge, an

228

early version of the recreational vehicle. The Travelodge was luxurious, with an all-steel skeleton, aluminum-paneled exterior walls, hydraulic brakes, shock absorbers, wheel suspension, wood-paneled interior walls, dinette seats that converted into beds, and a fully equipped bathroom. Despite a massive advertising campaign, however, fewer than one thousand of the Travelodges were sold. In February 1937 Pierce Arrow went out of business. The failure of this old, prestigious, and internationally known automobile company was a blow to the city's morale, a shock and a disappointment. There were others later on in the year.

Following months of newspaper reports that the mayor, George Zimmerman, and several members of his administration, had used WPA funds to finance their payrolls, a special grand jury was created to investigate. In early 1938 a councilman was convicted of receiving fraudulent payments from the city, the streets commissioner was convicted of payroll padding, and the mayor himself was charged with the taking of unlawful fees in connection with the $15 million federal sewer project. By the end of 1938, nine councilmen and former councilmen had been indicted. Although several priests charged that the indictments were part of an "anti-Catholic plot," the charges stuck. Several of the politicians went to jail. Mayor Zimmerman died while out on bail.

Oddly enough, 1937, which saw the fall of Pierce Arrow and the investigation against the mayor, had begun as a good year for Buffalo. Not only were federal public works grants at their highest level, but the local economy appeared to be following the rest of the nation back to some semblance of economic prosperity. Steel, for example, had been coming back slowly since 1934 when, following a loss of over $8 million in 1933, Bethlehem Steel reported a profit of $5.5 million. (While people were pleased with this progress, the president of Bethlehem, Eugene Grace, was criticized bitterly in the local press when it became public that he had received a salary of $180,000 per year since 1932.) Still, at only thirty-four percent of capacity, business was slow. Part of the problem at Bethlehem was that its primary product was heavy steel sheetings used in the manufacture of railroad cars. Desperately eager to be independent of that crippled industry, Grace in 1935 invested $20 million in the construction of a new plant at Lackawanna that would manufacture the lighter steel sheets used in the manufacture of automobiles. It was a daring and dangerous gamble. It soon looked, however, as though the move had paid off. In March 1937 rumors, which had been circulating for several months, were now confirmed: For close to a year the General Motors Company had been slowly and quietly purchasing over 160 acres of waterfront land overlooking the Niagara River, just north of the Buffalo city line. General Motors, it was now announced, was going to build a $12.5 million Chevrolet plant employing between three and four thousand workers in the manufacture of automobile axles and the assembly of automobile engines.

Buffalo was ecstatic. There would be a new steel mill and a gigantic new automobile plant. The economy was changing; new directions were emerging. The Chevrolet plant had to be built. The only potential problem, involving a large parcel of waterfront land which GM wanted, was easily resolved. The Erie County Parks Commission, which owned the land and had planned to use it for the creation of a large waterfront park, eagerly complied with what appeared to be everybody's desire to turn the land over to the company. While there was some protest, most people agreed with the head of the chamber of commerce, who believed that "park development along the waterfront would be inconsistent with the industrial development that will take place there." The problem was quickly and easily resolved. GM began to build the plant in July 1937. Work proceded quickly, with no strikes or other interruptions, and the plant began production in March 1938.

GM had been looking at Buffalo as one of several places to build new plants. Ever since the Detroit and Flint sit-down strikes of 1937, the company had wanted to decentralize production and move away from the solid union towns in Michigan. Buffalo, a steel town with a nonunionized work force in its heavy industries, seemed to fit the bill. Other companies thought so too. In the spring of 1937 a local newspaper reported that the Chrysler Company was considering joining GM by moving to Buffalo. "Labor trouble in Michigan has given added impetus," the paper noted, "to the decentralization movement." The problem was, though, that labor organizers followed GM (Chrylser never did make the move), and in late 1936 and early 1937 the CIO, targeting automobile and steelworkers, began actively organizing the industrial workers of Buffalo.

It was not going to be an easy job. The economy had just begun to recover. Following Bethlehem's modernization, steel production in Buffalo, at ninety percent of total capacity, was at a record high. Factory wages, averaging $28.85 per week in early 1937, were finally back to their 1927 level. Factory employment, meanwhile, was higher than during any year since 1927. Workers were understandably reluctant to jeopardize their recently acquired status by joining a union. The Depression, while over in the minds of many, was still vivid. Besides, ever since the steel strike of 1919, the steel industry had taken severe and harsh measures to discourage and undermine unionism. Yellow-dog contracts, effective company unions, and a notorious company police force had deterred organization activities at both Bethlehem and Republic. No inroads had ever been made at local automobile plants. Workers thus were afraid of unions, afraid for their jobs and thankful for what they had.

Indeed, as had been true in Detroit and Flint, it was difficult for the CIO organizers to find workers grievances. Wages, between $12 and $15 a day in steel and autos, were far better than in other industries. There had also been vast improvements in hours. Both Bethlehem and Republic had instituted the eight-hour day and five-day work week in the late twenties. While automobile workers tended to work longer hours, most of them welcomed this as a cushion against the layoffs that occurred annually as companies shut down their plants to prepare production for the coming year. Thus, local steel and auto workers were in no rush to join the Steel Workers Organizing Committee (SWOC) and the UAW. With no help from local organized labor—the Buffalo AFL refused to cooperate with the CIO—and with fear of company reprisals keeping most of the workers away, the CIO organizing drive bogged down. When a premature and badly organized strike of steelworkers was called in April 1937, it was easily and effectively squashed by a combination of worker apathy and company policemen.

But the real problem with the disastrous steel strike of 1937, and indeed the larger problem of the CIO in Buffalo, was that its radical leadership simply did not reflect the characteristics and the ideology of the local work force. Following the strike of 1937, Marxist leadership, particularly strong among the SWOC, was now seen as an obstacle to organizing the rank and file. Realizing that organized labor needed different friends if it was to survive in Buffalo, the CIO began to purge Communists from local leadership positions. The CIO suddenly abandoned its support of the Marxist Labor Institute, which had dominated labor education in Buffalo since the early 1930s and, in a complete about-face, joined the bishop of Buffalo in sponsoring the Catholic Labor College. The CIO's campaign for respectability took yet another turn when in 1940 it stopped efforts to organize a separate labor party and made instead an alliance with local Democrats (which has lasted to this day).

With the church and the Democrats in their camp, the CIO became suddenly successful. By early 1941 organizers for the SWOC had penetrated Bethlehem and had completely undermined the company union. In February they called a strike. With the support of the bishop, who extolled them from the pulpit; the mayor, who refused to grant police protection to strikebreakers; and the president of the United States, who threatened to cancel Bethlehem's defense contracts unless the company dealt with the union, the SWOC prevailed. Later that year Republic Steel also recognized the SWOC and GM bestowed recognition on the UAW. While the CIO certainly deserved much of the credit for the triumph of industrial unionism in Buffalo, it was clear to everyone that without the support of the church and the federal governmennt, the victory would never have been theirs.

Besides, industry could afford to be in a giving mood, for by late 1939 and early 1940 the war in Europe had begun to do for the nation's economy what nothing else had been able to. Long before Pearl Harbor millions of dollars in federal contracts began to pour into what was increasingly being referred to as the "Buffalo-Niagara Falls industrial area." It had happened before—in 1936 Senator Nye's Senate Munition's Committee revealed that in 1915, two years before America had entered World War I, J. P. Morgan's banking firm had delivered a $28 million contract to Bethlehem Steel and a $30 million contract to Buffalo Copper and Brass—and was about to happen again. Preparations for war were going to bail out Buffalo's economy. In September 1939, two months before Congress repealed the Arms Embargo Act, the United States government signed a million dollar spare parts contract with Curtiss Wright. Things got better still once the ban was actually lifted. By the end of 1939 Bethlehem, making close to ten thousand tons of steel a day, was breaking all production records. There were over fifteen thousand people now employed in Buffalo's steel industry, twelve thousand of them at Bethlehem. The Buffalo *Evening News*, in an end-of-the-year wrap-up, was ecstatic:

> Business in Buffalo turned a hand-spring in 1939. But it took a war to do it; to set the stage for the swiftest advance in ten years. . . . The steel companies here hastily gathered men and materials together, took idle production facilities and made them useful again. . . . Chemical and dyestuff makers put out calls for men, raised wages . . . the railroads added men to put the transportation plant in better running order. Aircraft companies here had fifty to sixty million dollars of foreign aircraft orders fall into their laps. . . . Heavy industry has begun to shake off its lethargy. Lake commerce finished up the year with such a rush that the harbor was literally choked with boats.

The spree continued. In January 1940, with new contracts in hand, Bell Aircraft, with twelve hundred employees in their Buffalo factory, moved into a brand-new plant that the federal government had built for them in Niagara Falls. By the end of the year Bell employed 32,222 people. The expansion at Curtiss Wright, with 5,300 employees in 1940 and 43,000 three years later, was equally dramatic. In 1943, 87,000 people were working at three area General Motors plants, producing motors for engines and airplanes. By 1943 Buffalo, with over $5 billion in war supply contracts, did more war business with the federal government than all but four cities in the country. Local officials were proud that their city, "with only seven-tenths of one percent of the nation's population was producing 2.5% of all America's war goods." Bell, which produced more than one-half of all the American aircraft sent to Russia during the war, manufactured more than nine thousand Airacobras, the only single-engine pursuit plane armed with a cannon. Curtiss Wright made another pursuit plane— the P-40—and shipped over a thousand of them to England. The British Air Force was particularly pleased with the Curtiss Tomahawk, which "in one encounter attacked thirty Messerschmidts over the North African desert, destroying four and damaging many more without a loss." Bethlehem Steel produced twelve thousand tons of steel daily for tanks and railroad cars, while Republic steel was used for cannon shells, gunbarrels, tanks, and trucks. Gould Coupler made armor coatings for locomotives and tanks; Central Machine Works manufactured trucks "especially designed to be driven on the rugged terrain of China;" Spreichtool was the largest manufacturer in the world of bomb racks; and American Car Foundry was the nation's largest producers of howitzer shells. Other companies in Buffalo produced other materials for war: steel armor for ships, machine guns and ammunition, bombshells, chemical warfare equipment, diesel-powered invasion barges, tugs, parachutes, medical and hospital equipment, weather recording apparatus, rubber rafts, uniforms, marine engines, firefighting equipment, amphibious cars, army cots, pontoons, and TNT.

The war was good for Buffalo. It was the best thing, in fact, that had ever happened to the city, and everybody tried to get into the act. Whole hosts of new companies were spawned in the scramble to win war contracts. Officers for two banks formed Ships, Inc. in October 1941 and began to build ships under contract to the navy. Lake Erie Shipbuilding formed Buffalo Shipbuilding which, with millions more in navy contracts, began to produce small craft. Houdaille Industry, makers of precision auto parts, formed a subsidiary called Buffalo Arms and, employing over five thousand workers, manufactured ordnance for the British Army.

Government orders for weapons came as a pleasant and welcome surprise after the Depression. It was easy and profitable to do business with the United States government. The government was interested in output and was willing to pay for it. No longer would contracts be given to the lowest bidder. War was not the time to reward efficiency, and government contracts paid the costs of production plus a profit. The United States government had become the ultimate customer: Not only did they buy the material and equipment their suppliers produced but, in the cases of Bell and Curtiss-Wright, they built their plants as well.

For most people the war was a windfall. With over 458,000 people in the labor force (225,000 of them in war-related industries), earning a combined total of over $10 million in weekly wages, prosperity was unprecedented. With only eight thousand unemployed, crime was down, relief rates had sunk to their lowest levels since 1929, and department stores reported that the Christmas season for 1943 was the best in history. In fact, according to a spokesman for the chamber of commerce, it was "Christmas every week in Buffalo."

But if the prosperity generated by the war was unprecedented, so too were the problems. The conversion of the economy to production for war and the mobilizatin of a work force sufficiently large and skilled was a massive, extraordinarily difficult and complex task. Again, as during the Depression, local government was forced to defer to Washington.

This was bound to happen. It always does during war time. The loss of power might not have happened so quickly, however, had local government been less concerned with political spoils. In the fall of 1941 the mayor, Joseph Kelly, ignored the local branch of the Office of Civil Defense and created a civilian defense organization of his own. When a local political reporter, widely known as a friend and supporter of the mayor, was placed in charge of the new organization, the director of civil defense resigned. According to one student of the American home front, Buffalo had become "one of the chief eyesores in the civilian defense program. The town had no auxiliary police, no air raid warden, no flashlights or helmets. One practice blackout was held in December, 1941. The fire engines were brought out and the sirens turned on. The sirens promptly burned out."

With political patronage and mismanagement rife, the state stepped in and in May 1942 passed legislation which required the establishment in cities throughout the state of local war councils consisting of a diverse board of businessmen, bankers, and city officials. Buffalo's was chaired by a leading Republican judge and lawyer and administered by a stockbroker named Irwin (when Irwin resigned to become an officer of M&T he was replaced by a man named James B. Wilson, "a well-known Buffalo football coach, sportsman and attorney"). The Buffalo War Council was given vast and sweeping powers over virtually every aspect of daily life in Buffalo: "The purpose of the Council is to coordinate and make efficient utilization of every facility and every resource of the community in support of the war effort." Yet despite the breadth of its responsibility—victory gardens and child care, salvage and public transportation, subversive rumor control and recruitment of farm labor—and the size of its membership (1,700 block leaders plus over 1,000 volunteers) the council had very little power of its own. Most of the time it was simply enacting rules and regulations that had been developed in Washington. Now more than ever before—more than during World War I; more even than during the Depression—the federal government had become supreme in everyday affairs of the city.

Their most serious and difficult problem was mobilizing the work force for employment in the defense industry. Signs of a labor shortage had begun to appear almost immediately. Afraid that a critical labor shortage would lead the government to take their defense contracts elsewhere, business and political leaders willingly accepted and even called for federal manpower controls. In early 1942 the chamber of commerce demanded a government-sponsored labor draft as the only means of effectively allocating available manpower. Newspapers followed. One, reporting that local defense plants was "stymied in further stepping-up production by the scarcity of labor," joined in the call for a labor draft and cheered when in February 1942 President Roosevelt ordered that all plants with government contracts lengthen their work week to forty-eight hours and pay time-and-a-half after forty hours.

Washington imposed other measures too. Many teachers, ministers, college students, and public employees, unable to work full time, joined "Victory Shifts" and worked part time in Buffalo's defense plants. there was a "Farm Cadet Plan" whereby students under fifteen, Boy Scouts, and Girl Scouts were bused to surrounding farms, helping with the harvest. Vagrants and drunks too were enlisted by what was referred to locally as "Sunrise Courts." Here, early in the morning, men arrested for loitering, vagrancy, and drunkenness could choose between jail or work in a defense plant. Even the influx of migrants (four thousand in 1941 and thirty thousand in 1943), whose need for shelter was as pressing as was the city's need for workers, hardly made a dent in Buffalo's increasingly critical labor shortage.

Women undoubtedly helped. There had always been women in the work force—over sixty thousand, in fact, a year before Pearl Harbor. Still more were needed, however, and beginning in early 1941 the federal Work Manpower Commissin (WMC), in conjunction with the Buffalo War Council, took elaborate measures to lure more—particularly married women with children—into the work force. Despite fears that the local clergy, as self-appointed guardians of home life, morality, and the welfare of children, would interfere, women responded to the emergency and by June 1943 there were close to 200,000 women working in the city's defense industries. Women had finally joined the industrial work force in large and impressive numbers.

Women worked under a different and more intense set of pressures than men. While many had made the shift to industrial work from lesser-paying, pre-war jobs, others, particularly mothers, were not only working for the first time but were doing so under conditions of rapid production speed-up. (Many mothers chose to work the "owl" shift. Beginning at midnight, they could be home in time to help get their children to school.) Thus, the absentee rate among female workers was higher than among males. In an effort to combat it, local industries, with state and federal grants, opened day-care centers on their premises. (For some reason, however, day-care centers were never popular with working mothers of Buffalo. "Most working mothers," according to the chief administrator of the Buffalo War Council, "preferred to make informal arrangements with neighbors or relatives for the care of their children.") Despite the host of "incentives" offered to female workers, noticeably lacking among them was equal pay for equal work. Indeed, despite national policy to the contrary, women in every branch of local industry, with the exception of iron and steel, still made about thirty percent less than their male co-workers.

Despite all of these measures, however, Buffalo, over the strenuous protests of its community leaders, was declared a "labor shortage area" in October 1942. Citing the need for eighty-three thousand new workers in the forthcoming year, Buffalo's manpower mobilization program was placed under the direct control of Anna Rosenberg, the regional director of the federal government's War Manpower Commission. Functioning as a kind of industrial czar for the area, Mrs. Rosenberg's many visits to the city were greeted with a combination of anxiety and uncertainty lest her findings result in still stiffer regulations of local industry. Under her authority, WMC representatives regularly inspected all defense-related plants, reporting on a range of issues that make minute by comparison the most stringent regulations of contemporary regulatory agencies. Through detailed and extensive inspections and questionnaires, Rosenberg's investigators gathered information on wages and hours, on utilization of labor, on training programs, and on race and sex discrimination. Mrs. Rosenberg was diligent and vigilant in her work and refused to tolerate the prejudicial hiring policies that had for so long been a part of local industry. In countless speeches to community leaders, she insisted that they overcome the city's labor shortage by making "maximum use of women and other minorities." She went well beyond the problem of the labor shortage, exhorting her audiences that the "people of Buffalo must realize that minority groups just don't exist any more. There must be no closing of doors to people because they are members of minority groups."

Her constant prodding, combined with the critical labor shortage, did create unprecedented opportunities for the city's minority groups. Not only women, but blacks too, were working in places long denied them, although, according to Dudly Irwin, the director of the war council, "many were still not being used at their highest skills." Still, unprecedent progress was being made. Curtiss Wright, which had only a handful of black employees in 1942, had over one thousand by the end of the war, while over nine hundred blacks, both men and women, worked at Bell.

The physically handicapped also benefited from the city's labor shortage. In 1943 over 2,700 handicapped men and women were working in local industry. A post-war study reported that among them were footless truck drivers, one-handed machinists, one-armed engine mechanics, deaf card punchers, and several operators of overhead cranes who had artificial legs.

Still the labor shortage continued. The newspapers were filled with want ads. On just one day in June 1943, Curtiss Wright advertised for bench hands, auto mechanics, sheet metal workers, radio electricians, accountants, box makers, estimators, tool designers, template makers, and general laborers; and National Biscuit for packers, checkers, wrappers, porters, truck greasers, and salesmen; while American Optical offered to train workers to become lens grinders. Something had to be done. In June 1943 Mrs. Rosenberg implemented what was called the Controlled Referral Plan, the most sweeping federally regulated manpower mobilization plan ever used in an American city. By placing the hiring process completely in the hands of the War Manpower Commission, the Controlled Referral Plan took the hiring process out of the private sector. No longer would a company be able to do its own hiring. No longer could a worker seek work or switch jobs on his own. From now on everything would be arranged by and cleared through the United States Employment Service.

Not everyone liked the plan. Organized labor in particular was most resistant. The head of the United States Steel Workers, about to enter the service, said that "putting the plan into effect is contrary to what we're fighting for on foreign battlefields." Others questioned Mrs. Rosenberg's authority: "We feel she is putting the plan into effect over our heads." Many were bothered that "It's not a Buffalo-made plan." But Rosenberg was adamant, insisting that the plan "will become operative regardless of how the community views it."

Buffalo was being bypassed. By determining who needed how many workers and when, the USES controlled and directed almost the entire work force in the city of Buffalo. According to the plan, a company had to make its case for more workers before the WMC. The commission would then decide the merits of the appeal. Sometimes, as the Commission's deliberations over General Drop Forge's request for more workers show, they consented:

They are using quite a few women. During week prior to visit, employed 20 additional women, and are willing to employ women wherever possible. This week they are putting on 20 more women who are being employed as drill press operators, core inspection grinders, sand blasters and snag press operators, as well as working in the machine shop. They have 65 women on production.

They have lost 32 the first month.

They expect to lose a total of 22 men for the next 6 months. . . . Absenteeism, during week of 10–24, was 10%. It started declining and is about 6% a week.

Their backlog is increasing because of lack of manpower. They have a total of 631 males employed. Need 2 tool makers. They are exploring the possibility of subletting some of the die work. They need 2 machinists to work as setup men; in processing shop they want 2 grinders to fill up empty machines; need 15 machinists . . . 3 lift truck operators; 3 finish molders; 2 forge inspectors; 2 die storagemen; 1 planer; 2 shipping clerks. . . . They have three million dollars of Army and 2 million dollars worth of Navy unfinished business. Both have #1 Urgency Rating. . . . They are one hundred thousand castings behind for Cleveland Diesel Engine Company. Backlog of one hundred fifty thousand forgings for gears; two hundred thousand on engine parts. Other part of their production goes into engines which probably will go into landing craft.

They were given 25 workers just recently.

In view of the critical situation, I would recommend that they be given about 50 workers. I have a suspicion the shipping clerks will assist in loading heavy castings.

Sometimes they didn't. In late 1943 the Chase Bag Company asked for more workers:

They require eleven workers. Their male workers are utilized primarily on heavy operations. They have twenty-one males and fifty-six females.

As far as the urgency, they are low on the List. That can be made someplace else. As far as I am concerned, I think we should reserve the workers for more essential work.

We have the mills for storage, and facilities to accomplish the shipment, they need the containers.

Has this Company plants located in other towns than Buffalo? If so, I suggest this be made some place else.

Do not add to list. Advise Company to make bags in some of their other plants where there is no labor shortage.

While the WMC, through the Controlled Referral System, controlled the local work force, the Office of Price Administration, in countless regulations aimed at containing wartime inflation, monitored the price of almost every item that people ate, wore, or used. With only nine enforcement offices (the OPA never revealed how small their staff actually was), there was only so much they could do. Charged with patrolling the whole county, the Buffalo division of the OPA decided to go after only the big offenders, and all during the war meat packers, hotels, restaurants, gas stations, dairies, and other providers of food, gasoline, and tires were charged with and oftentimes sued for price gouging. Even more difficult to enforce was the statewide ban on pleasure driving. Forced to choose between giving up such favorite pastimes as going to the beach or a ballgame, playing golf, or visiting friends, and using public transportation to get there, many people chose the latter. Almost as many, rather than surrender their cars, violated the law, and in most cases received lenient treatment. Following his retirement in early 1944 the chief enforcement officer of the OPA, torn between his civic pride and the knowledge that he had gained, reluctantly admitted that during the course of the war one in every five business establishments in Buffalo and Erie County had received some kind of warning from his office.

There were other problems that the normal workings of the private economy and the local government simply could not handle. One of them was transportation. Because the federal War Production Board had ended the manufacture of private automobiles, because new tires were no longer available since rubber supplies had been cut off, and because deliveries of crude oil were drastically rationed, the burden of transporting the more than 300,000 workers to and from their place of work fell on public transportation. Under orders from the Office of Defense Transportation (yet another federal agency) the Buffalo War Council implemented a system of staggered work hours similar to that used in other industrial cities. According to it, heavy industry would operated from 7:30 to 3:30, downtown business and government offices from 8:00 to 4:00, and public and parochial schools from 9:30 to 3:30. By the end of 1943, Buffalo's streetcar and bus system was handling close to 400,000 commuters a day.

Today, when Buffalo is plagued with a seemingly endless economic decline, when unemployment is relentless, and when crime and juvenile delinquency erode our sense of social order, it is understandable that so many Buffalonians recall the war years fondly as one of the great and heroic periods of the history of the city. Production for war had become the primary measure of achievement, and by these standards Buffalo had done remarkably well. People were proud of the part that the city had played in making the United States the "Arsenal of Democracy," applauding loudly the success of its defense-related industries as they do today a sports team, boasting of these achievements as their own. One of the city's newspapers, losing its journalistic distance, extolled Curtiss Wright's P-40: "The P-40 lunged at Tojo's squadrons and broke them up. They plastered Jap ships. They escorted our bombers and when the bombers were gone heroic young Americans, British and Aussies loaded bombs into the P-40's and dropped the eggs on the Japs' advancing line." Congratulations were also extended to the Buffalo Arms Company for its success in manufacturing thirty- and forty-caliber firearms, and to Bell, Chevrolet, and Westinghouse, all of whom, along with Curtiss Wright, had won the coveted army and navy "E" award for excellence.

The city was proud of itself, too, and never tired of extolling its citizenry, diversified and yet seemingly unified, which, according to the historian of the Buffalo War Council, "had buried their vast differences and submerged all political, religious and class distinctions and had met the challenge of total war."

There was a great deal of truth to these claims. In the work place, at least, more progress than ever had been made in eliminating the racial and ethnic barriers that had for so long fragmented the people of Buffalo. (Still, in 1943, when the federal government planned to build public housing for black defense workers in South Buffalo, the outburst from that predominantly Irish community was so vociferous that the plan was dropped. It was decided to expand existing public housing on the increasingly black East Side instead.) And, perhaps because the vast majority of the German-American community were staunch supporters of the war effort, there was none of the anti-German bitterness and rancor that had existed before. Indeed, despite the war, the blackouts, the rationing, the long hours, and the unprecedented disruption in the daily life of virtually everyone, a sense of public calm, security, and confidence seemed to prevail. Even crime rates—robberies and rapes, murder and arson, fraud, counterfeiting, and juvenile delinquency—declined significantly. Brought on perhaps by prosperity, perhaps by a common sense of purpose, Buffalo did seem to be united as never before.

However, to see this as the spontaneous, somewhat mystical response of a suddenly cohesive, highly motivated community would be to miss the point. For without the strong, directing and controlling hand of the federal government it would have been impossible for Buffalo, like any other city in the country, to have risen to the occasion of war. For then, as during the Depression, it was Washington, virtually commandeering local government, leading it when possible, forcing it when necessary, to develop and implement the programs that it deemed essential to the challenge. For better or for worse then, the Depression, followed by the war, changed forever the relationship that had historically existed between Buffalo and Washington. In the years ahead Buffalo would become, sometimes as the beneficiary, sometimes as the victim, ever more dependent on programs and policies developed by the federal government.

CHAPTER 11

Paranoia: The Fear of Outsiders and Radicals During the 1950s and 1960s

Buffalo has hever been kind to radicals. Not only the WASP elite, but also the large ethnic working classes, bound by the ties of Catholicism, neighborhood, and family, have always been suspicious and afraid of radicalism of any kind. Any yet, there have always been radicals in Buffalo. Never numerous, and never a part of much of a movement, there were always some people who, despite the contumely of an outraged community, took radical and unpopular positions.

Long before the Cold War, when the memory of the crazed anarchist Czolgosz, President McKinley's assassin, was still vivid in the imagination of the community, radicals were outcast and despised. Unlike New York City, where the Communist party had, found a receptive and supportive following, in Buffalo it was different. Even during the late 1930s, when the Communist party had at last gained some degree of respectability through its advocacy of an anit-fascist Popular Front movement, Earl Browder, the American Communist Party candidate for president in 1936, could not rent a hall in Buffalo. The local branch of the party, a small cell, had furtively reserved the large assembly room of the Fraternal Order of Eagles, yet when the Eagles were tipped off about Earl Browder's politics, they reneged. There were subsequent rejections by the Dom Polski Hall, the Maccabee Hall, and the Crescent Hall of the International Order of Organized Foresters. The city too got into the act. Although unable to deny the Communist party a parade permit, they did refuse to grant them the routine request of suspending the anti-noise ordinance. They were thus not permitted to blow horns or make "other loud noises in the streets of Buffalo." Finally, several hours before his scheduled visit

242

on November 2, 1936, Browder was offered a church in Riverside. Several hundred people came to hear him denounce in mild tones the New Deal.

In the years following the Second World War, the flames of anti-Communism were fanned by a vigilant and paranoid Catholic establishment. Throughout the late forties and early fifties the Catholic hierarchy in Buffalo had its hands in virtually all of the anti-Communist activities and witch-hunting purges of the day. The bishop and his obedient priests were always present, pandering to the fear and anxieties of their eastern European flock, egging them on in their easily aroused hatred of the Communist devil. In May 1947 Bishop O'Hara spearheaded a series of anti-Red rallies in neighborhood parks throughout the city. Organized by parish priests, addressed by local councilmen, accompanied by uniformed marching bands from parish high schools, these emotional, demogogic affairs filled with poison and paranoia were a direct, though perverted, legacy of the nineteenth century parochial tradition. No wonder, one begins to understand, so many mid-nineteenth century liberals were nativists.

While much of the anti-Communist activity of these years was led by the bishop, public officials were equally involved. It was sometimes the mayor, sometimes the superintendent of education, and sometimes the chief of police, but always some higly placed representative of the administration was present at these frightening affairs. At the police academy graduation ceremonies in May 1947, the graduates were urged by Father Michael Quinn to "patrol your beats as apostles of Christianity and arrest the world's worst enemy—Communists— wherever you find them." The mayor in his remarks cemented the collaboration of church and state in the war against Communists and communism. "Affairs like this," he said, "are morale builders and mean a great deal to the community." The police learned their lessons well. By 1949 they had formed the Buffalo Police Subversive Squad and were aiding public officials in performing periodic "investigations" of Communist activities among public employees, particularly public school teachers.

Business groups, particularly the chamber of commerce, joined city and church officials in the war on what they were convinced was "Communist infiltration in Buffalo." In an article in 1947 on that exact subject in the chamber publication *Buffalo Business*, a writer expressed some concern about Communist infiltration in local industry. What bothered the chamber of commerce far more, however, was that most "Communist agitation" was among the local black population: "It is interesting and disturbing to report that a large percentage of Negroes are influenced by the Communist efforts." Unable to produce any tangible evidence or satisfactory explanation of this baffling phenomenon, the chamber surmised that it was because blacks are "usually flattered by being invited to the home of white families on the basis of equality." The chamber was not overly worried about this situation, however, and drew comfort from the knowledge that "the best of the Negro leadership have sense enough to realize that American democracy is better for the Negro than anything that Communism has to offer."

But the knowledge did not mitigate against the anti-Communist hysteria that flourished during the early 1950s. Following hearings in Buffalo in June 1954, a seventy-four-year-old British citizen, living in the city since 1907 (he had come originally to visit the Pan American Exposition in 1901), was deported as an undesirable alien. The government claimed that this man, John Hughes, had been a Communist in 1930 and 1931, and that there was "some indication" that he had belonged to the party in 1936 as well.

Senator McCarthy had been watching the city, too. Staff members of his Senate Investigations Subcommittee had been in and out of Buffalo in late 1953 and early 1954 investigating Communist infiltration into local defense plants. Westinghouse, where the radical United Electrical Workers (the UEW had been expelled from the CIO in 1949 for alleged Communist domination) had a strong following, was singled out for particularly close scrutiny. Believing McCarthy's estimates that there were 130 members of the Communist party in Buffalo (he later revised his figures to 39), the House UnAmerican Activities Committee decided to add Buffalo to their list of cities to visit. Their informers had provided them with additional information, and finally in October 1957 the HUAC came to Buffalo.

The professional informers, federal officials paid to infiltrate the ranks of the infiltrators in order to gather their names and report on their activities, testified first. They gave the names of individuals who, they said, had organized Communist cells in industries and in neighborhoods throughout the city. There was, they said, a Riverside Club, and Ellicott Club, a Polish Club, and an Italian Club, as well as clubs at Bethlehem Steel, Republic Steel, Westinghouse, Bell Aircrafts, American Radiator, Chevrolet, and Ford. Organized by "colonizers," most all of whom came to Buffalo from New York City after the war, these clubs, the witnesses told the committee, made Buffalo "a serious Communist operation." One of them, paid to say exactly what the committee wanted to hear, said that "the penetration is quite extensive in this community. We have uncovered various colonizers in fifteen to eighteen different legitimate organizations in this area." Another witness swore that there were between five hundred and six hundred of these "colonizers" in the city. The committee, however, had learned from McCarthy's histrionics the danger of bandying around false figures, and they immediately covered themselves. The actual number of party members in the city was irrelevant, Acting Chairman Edwin Willis, a Democrat from Louisiana, said. In fact, he said, "there is a fallacy in undertaking to appraise the threat of the operation on the basis of numbers." For the Communist, who are "very deliberate in seeking out nerve centers and key positions within unions and various industries themselves, have a power far greater than their numbers would ever indicate."

The "colonizers" themselves were next to testify, and over a two-day period, as their testimony became public, certain patterns emerged. The informers had done their jobs well and had caught the witnesses in an embarrassing lie. Many of them, it became clear, had in fact come to Buffalo after the war, primarily from the New York City area, and had sought positions in the city's many industries. In applying for their jobs many of them, anticipating the hostility of their prospective employers, lied about their backgrounds. Although none denied coming from "The City" (In those days before the advent of the state university and the inundation of the Buffalo area by New Yorkers, New Yorkers' accents stood out glaringly), they did lie about their education. Several of them, graduates of Queens, Brooklyn, and City colleges, had indicated at the time of their hiring that they had had no college education.

When confronted with this (the committee produced the college transcripts of the witnesses concerned), and with other questions about who they were and their motives for coming to Buffalo, most sought the protection against self-incrimination offered by the Fifth Amendment. Others took the more risky option and pleaded the First Amendment, thereby making themselves liable for a contempt indictment. Stanley Ingerman, a steelworker, was one of the witnesses who, when asked to name the names of Communists, cited the First Amendment and refused. (The committee didn't really need these names, as they already had them. Their interest was not in information but in intimidation.) He would, he said, talk about himself but nobody else. Gilbert Cohen took the same position. Cohen aggressively challenged the committee, denouncing it for attacking, not defending, American traditions. Cohen refused to talk, he said, "first, because it affects my freedom of speech and association under the First Amendment. Second, the resolution creating this Committee is too vague. Third, this inquiry is outside the Committee's jurisdiction. Fourth, the Congress did not delegate to this Committee the authority which it claims. Fifth, my rights under the due process clause are violated. Sixth, this investigation involves exposure for the sake of exposure. Seventh, I believe that this investigation is injurious to American democracy and I believe it is my duty to do what I can to resist."

Other witnesses resisted too. One woman, a Jew and a practicing lawyer in Buffalo since 1934, was a particularly sought-after victim. She had been active in radical politics for years. An early member of Buffalo's small pro-loyalist Spanish Committee during the late 1930s, a member of the Committee Against War and Fascism, a supporter of Henry Wallace's campaign for president in 1948 (she had helped to organize Paul Robeson's benefit concert for Wallace at Kleinhan's Music Hall in that year), and an ardent Zionist, this woman was a prime suspect. She too, however, refused the protection of the Fifth Amendment and used her testimony instead as an opportunity to denounce her informer as a liar and the committee as lawless and despotic.

Other women were paraded before the committee during those two days in October 1957. Several, whose husbands had been called to testify about their activities in area industries, were accused of joining local service organizations—the YWCA, the Jewish Center, the Red Cross—with the intention of spreading Communist propaganda, and still others of meeting with "young housewives in their communities" to spread the word about Communism.

After two full days of testimony, the committee concluded its hearings. While they had hoped for more pliant witnesses, Congressman Willis said, they were pleased with the "evidence" that they had acquired. "There has been confirmed," Willis said, "a pattern of Communist techniques of penetration of heavy industrial establishments of which this Buffalo area had many that are vital to our defense and economic well-being." Willis made no attempt to provide the confirming evidence, admitting that the witnesses had not helped him. But that, he said, was sufficient confirmation. "Many of the witnesses have been completely uncooperative with the Committee. But they have, in a negative way, helped to complete the factual picture which we have been trying to develop here as elsewhere throughout the nation." Their conclusions, in other words, had been foregone.

What the committee had revealed, however, was something about the nature of the Communist activities that had in fact taken place in Buffalo. The facts of the matter are that there had been a policy of "colonization," that many of the people who were indicted had in fact come to Buffalo with the expressed intention of trying to organize among the people in general and the workers in particular within the community. Operating as individuals—most of the people subpoenaed by the HUAC had never seen nor met each other until then—and never part of a centrally organized and controlled party, the activities of these people were small in scale, humble in scope, and generous in aspirations. The witnesses had become active in their unions and in their communities fighting for such progressive causes as improved work conditions, health and safety, and equal opportunity for black workers.

But the committee was threatened by these people—these Jews and blacks and women and New Yorkers—and frightened by what they stood for. Their fear was contagious, and the witnesses were treated as pariahs by the rest of the community. For two days the newspapers printed their names and their pictures, running stories with inflammatory headlines (like the one that read "Housewife Denies She's a Red Now But is Silent on Past") as if they had been convicted at a criminal trial. While the United Auto Workers protected their members who had been subpoenaed, the Steel Workers did not and refused to support those who had testified unless they signed a non-Communist pledge. The Jewish community, despite the heavy-handed anti-Semitism of the probe (The lawyer for the committee, in questioning a witness who worked at the Jewish Center of Buffalo, asked: "This establishment at which you are presently employed is under the auspices of the Hebrew Church, is it not?"), was equally silent and timid, while the Bar Association of Erie County refused to condone the action of those lawyers who cose to represent their subpoenaed clients. Even the Niagara Frontier branch of the American Civil Liberties Union refused to get involved, and issued a statement that "neither the attorneys representing witnesses nor the ACLU should in any way be identified with the views of any of the witnesses."

Not only did the committee intimidate the community, it pandered to it too. In his concluding statement at the end of the hearings, Gordon Scherer, a Republican from Ohio, assuaged the people of Buffalo. "If it is any consolation to the people of Buffalo," he said, "it is apparent from the testimony that by far the great majority of Communists in this area are not natives of the city of Buffalo. . . . Practically all of them come from the City of New York, particularly those who came to colonize the industries of Buffalo." Worse yet, Scherer concluded, "those are the individuals who have college educations." Thus, by feeding the city's fear and distrust not only of outsiders in general but of educated outsiders in particular, the HUAC hearings set the stage for the traumatic controversy that emerged in the mid-1960s between the city and the University of Buffalo.

It was easier still to blame the outsiders for the troubles at the University of Buffalo. At the time of its incorporation into the State University of New York in 1962, UB had been a medium-sized private college located on Main Street at the edge of the city's limit. "It was not," as Leslie Fiedler has written, "a great university . . . but it performed its intended functions in a way that kept the community around it happy." Fiedler, whose arrest in 1967 for "maintaining a premise on which narcotics were used" made him something of an expert on local town-gown relations, said that "what chiefly reassured the surrounding community was the prevailing sense of a school which knew and accepted its predetermined place and whose students only sought to move up to the predetermined slot next above the one into which they were born."

If the school knew its place, so too did the students. They were composed, Fiedler reminds us, not of the WASP elite, who sent their children to the Ivy League schools; not of Negroes, "who were sorted out early into technical high schools;" nor even of Poles and Italians, who, when not tracked along with the blacks, ended up at State Teachers College or at one of the many Catholic colleges in the Buffalo area. In fact, the students were primarily white Protestants and Jews "on their way to becoming dentists, pharmacists, accountants, teachers, technicians, insurance agents and real estate lawyers," who were "acting out the All-American charade called 'Bound-to-Win,' 'Onward and Upward,' 'Getting Ahead' with the promise of a degree" and, Fiedler might well have added had he written his brilliant essay on Buffalo several years later, a home in the suburbs.

UB had become then a place that could be trusted to educate the children of the city's upwardly mobile middle class without shaking them up too much; a place that could be counted on to reinforce the values and the expectations of the parents who sent their children there. For years UB had lived up to these expectations, performing ably and willingly its function, as a former chancellor has defined it, as a "training center for the defense of American integrity and the betterment of American life." It was clear, however, that the old, private, primarily commuter-oriented UB would change following its absorption into Governor Rockefeller's massive state system. Nobody realized how much, though. When they found out, the shock was traumatic.

The first change would be in the university's location. With a tenfold increase in the number of students predicted for the university by the mid-seventies, everybody knew that the old site was insufficient. Either it could be expanded—new buildings had been regularly added to the 1920s core of original buildings, and there appeared to be ample room for still more construction—or a new site could be found. The former was not the governor's way, however, and Rockefeller, who had created one of his subsequently notorious, master building, bond floating, superagencies called the State University Construction Fund, and eager to find a brand new site for his brand new campus, in 1963 commissioned a local planner named Vincent Moore to explore the various possibilities.

Even before Moore began his deliberations, the choice had been narrowed to either a large plot of vacant land on Buffalo's downtown waterfront or a much larger space in the far reaches of suburban Amherst. While Moore purported to make an objective presentation, it was clear from his conclusions that he favored the Buffalo waterfront. While the suburban Amherst site did offer larger amounts of unencumbered land (some of the waterfront was tied up in complicated urban renewal projects), Moore seemed convinced that the advantages of the waterfront outweighed these of Amherst. Besides, Moore said, the waterfront site offered a unique challenge to the university and a special promise to the city: "The situating of a university within the heart of Buffalo might provide stimulation for the solution of many bewildering problems of the urban setting by minds of latent imagination and intellecutal curiosity." The trustees of SUNY, however, felt differently, and even though they had commissioned Moore, the apparently felt no compunction about rejecting his implicit conclusion. In June 1964 they voted unanimously in favor of the Amherst site.

The question of the new site for the unversity had not yet become the critical issue that it would later. UB was growing rapidly and was otherwise occupied. By early 1966 students and faculty were becoming increasingly militant. In the spring of that year furious and frightened students entered and occupied President Furnas's Hayes Hall offices, protesting his insistence that selective service exams be held on campus. In an atmosphere of increasing dissent, it was simply a question of time before members of the university community demanded that the issues of the new campus be reopened. And in the spring of 1966 a coalition of university and community groups called CURB (Committee for an Urban Campus) was formed to fight for the waterfront site.

249

By now the site controversy had become an important local issue. CURB, chaired by a black architect, had the support not only of all the local black organizations but also of virtually every downtown business and political group, including the newspapers and the banks. In an age of increasing concern with the problems of the city in general and of the inner-city in particular, the controversy over the site of the new campus had become a prime indiction of one's "urban" credentials. An urban campus would, it was said, "add a dimension of relevance and pertinancy to the Univeristy's role and function." BUILD (Build Unity, Independence, Labor and Dignity), a Saul Alinsky–organized civil rights group, maintained that far more was at stake in the decision than the mere location of a campus. Rather, the group insisted, "the issues before the State University Trustees is whether to turn away from the critical challenges of the future or to face them squarely and deal with them creatively." In addition to the array of downtowners and black groups, a growing number of faculty members at UB began to speak out against the Amherst site where, one group felt, "the suburban location will reinforce any tendencies of the University to insulate its student body from the rest of the society."

Even Governor Rockefeller himself began to offer hints that perhaps he too had begun to reconsider. The Republican presidential convention was less than two years away and Rockefeller, still in those days before Attica considered a liberal, was counting on the support of those black and liberals who overwhelmingly supported an urban campus. The tilt toward the waterfront appeared to be gaining still more support when it was announced that as of September 1967 Martin Meyerson would become the new president of UB. An internationally known city planner, dean of the prestigious College of Environmental Design at the University of California's Berkeley campus, and a New York Jew, Meyerson would, everybody assumed, naturally favor an urban location for the campus. Indeed shortly after the start of Meyerson's tenure, Governor Rockefeller insisted on yet another report on the question. To help him and the SUNY trustees make what Rockefeller promised would be his final decision, Rockefeller, thinking that an outsider wuld be more objective, appointed the president of Rutgers University, a man named Mason Gross, to head the panel. Gross, from New Brunswick, New Jersey, in turn hired a planning firm from Cleveland, Ohio. Together they would decide on the future location of University of Buffalo.

Gross made every effort to be objective. Under his auspices meetings were held on campus, and students, faculty, and alumni were carefully and with great fanfare polled and consulted. Most of the university's constituents strongly favored the suburban site in Amherst. The staff, those hundreds of people, most of them women—the secretaries and non-teaching professionals who worked eight-hour days and really kept the university going—already lived in the suburbs and thus favored the Amherst location. The majority of the faculty, too, leaned towards Amherst. Many of them, young and hired fesh out of graduate school in the flush, early days of the university's initial growth period, had themselves grown up in the suburbs. Coming to Buffalo from all parts of the country, they had little feeling for or commitment to this particular city. Anyway they were, they thought, academic stars— on the make—whose stay here would be brief, long enough merely to build a resumé that would earn them better jobs at still better universities. For them then, the rapidly growing, highly mobile suburb of Amherst was the perfect location for the new university. The results of the faculty poll were in and had been counted: "A majority of the faculty have indicated a desire to live outside of the core city."

The alumni of UB felt even stronger than the faculty. For they, Fiedler's upwardly mobile "dentists, pharmacists, accountants, teachers, technicians, insurance agents and real estate lawyers," had already made it to the suburbs, and they wanted their children to live there, too. In a strong statement following a poll of the group, the president of the alumni association reported that "we do not feel it is incumbent upon the university to solve the urban renewal problems of Buffalo at the expense of future generations of students." They'd turned their backs on the city. Now they wanted their children to do the same.

All of these efforts to involve the university community in the decision meant nothing anyway. Indeed, all of the hearings, meetings, polls, and surveys were little more than a charade. The SUNY trustees had already made their decision, and regardless of who believed what—be it Meyerson, CURB, the faculty, students, or alumni—the Amherst site was a foregone conclusion. When Gross issued his report in February 1967, many people were disappointed but few were surprised. Gross's rationale—that Amherst offered three times the building space and twice the parking space (all of which, presumably, was required if the university was to effectively serve the forty-odd thousand students, faculty, and staff who were supposed to be there by 1975)—may well have been sound, but somehow was not convincing. Gross believed that the size of the Amherst parcel was what made the difference, and that if located on the waterfront the "university would be so limited by that site that it could not achieve its true potential." Others felt differently. The university, they believed,

251

by moving to Amherst, had rejected the city, and in the process gained a new campus while loosing its soul. Yet the decision was made. The University of Buffalo, known since 1962 as the State University of New York at Buffalo—SUNYAB—would have its new home in Amherst. While a lot of people doubted the wisdom of that decision, the riots in Buffalo's black ghetto in July 1967 convinced many of them that perhaps the governor and the SUNY trustees had been right after all.

It was always easy to blame outsiders. When Buffalo's black ghetto erupted for several days in early July, city officials and the local media were quick to blame outside agitators. Although they'd seen it happen repeatedly in other cities,, when it happened here it was too painful to bear ("young Blacks," Fiedler wrote, "in jeans and knotted bandanas, running like crazy cowboys down ghetto streets to smash store windows and steal TV sets"), and people blamed outsiders. It was they, Police Commissioner Felicetta and Mayor Sedita said (the mayor subsequently changed his rhetoric but not his beliefs), who infiltrated Buffalo's black community and incited the locals to violence.

Outsiders, real outsiders, knew differently. Writing in the *Manchester Guardian*, the English commentator Alistair Cooke suggested that Sedita and Felicetta should look elsewhere for an understanding of what happened. The size of Buffalo's black community, he told his English readers, had grown from 40,000 in the late 1950s to over 100,000 by Independence Day, 1967. In the meantime, he reported, only two hundred units of new housing had been built. As a result, he said, Buffalo's "negroes seethe in an interior desert of slums rising like war ruins from empty lots stacked with litter and garbage." The riots were thus an expression of black rage. "Hundreds of rampaging Negroes gave a grim twist to the saucy old folk song 'Buffalo Boys Won't You Come Out Tonight.' They came out in furious droves for the third night in a row to protest against their useless life in Buffalo's Negro ghetto and the civic indifference that perpetuated it."

Meanwhile there was turmoil out on Main Street, on the campus of the University of Buffalo. Enrollment had grown rapidly and steadily since 1962, not only increasing the size but dramatically changing the character of the student population. An increased number of New York Jews—the children of cab drivers, high school teachers, and civil servants who now could for the first time afford to go to college—now poured into Buffalo, bringing with them the excitement, color, and creative dynamism of their culture and their city. By 1967 UB had become the most stimulating and avant-garde cultural show-place in all of Western New York. Fiedler describes the atmosphere that he found when he came here from Montana in 1964:

> We are visited not only by poets but by successful Jewish novelists and lost Gentile ones, absurdist playwrights, underground film-makers, stand-up comedians, folk singers, mime troops, rock guitar-ists, electronic musicians, designers of geodesic domes, structural linguists, pop artists, puppeteers, defenders of mass culture or po-lymorphous perverse love, Zen Buddhists, Russians on good will tours, jazz flutists, nude dancers, Black Power organizers, pianists who play with their feet as well as their hands, and pianists who sit motionless over the keyboard, daring the audience to laugh. And before each event, there is a reception, after each a party; sometimes when visitors overlap, two or three parties combined into one: all in all a nonstop festival, a continuous ball—as the All-American Cultural Roadshow rolls into Buffalo for a one-night stand between Albany and Ann Arbor, New Paltz and Chicago.

Among the artists who appeared on campus in the spring of 1967 were three East Village Jewish inconoclastic poets and musicians who called themselves The Fugs. Announcing that they were delivering "Tomorrow's Orgasms Today," The Fugs performed at an "Angry Arts Festival" at UB in March 1967. The *Spectrum*, the student newspaper which under the editorship of yet another New York Jew, had become increasingly outrageous—at this point more culturally shocking than politically radical—reviewed the concert, printing the names of the Fugs' songs: "Jack-Off Blues," "Wet Dream Over You, Baby," "I Couldn't Get High," and a song dealing with American foreign policy called "River of Shit."

The review provoked an immediate reaction within the community, with politicians in both Amherst and Buffalo complaining bitterly and loudly. A strong anti-student stand was becoming increasingly popular in Buffalo as in the rest of the country. One local politician in Amherst vowed that when the university did move to his town he would do everything possible "to prevent such groups from appearing" there.

The *Spectrum's* editor continued to aggravate the raw nerves of respectable Buffalo opinion. Throughout the fall semester of 1966 and into the spring of 1967, The *Spectrum* had become increasingly outspoken, critical of the selective service tests administered on campus (anyone who scored a seventy or better was exempt; the rest eligible for the draft), and of a policy of dress regulations in a student-subsidized restaurant frequented primarily by administrators, while supporting such campus groups as the SDS and LEMAR, a student group that advocated the legalization of marijuana. The paper's positions, combined with its eagerness to print scatalogical material, earned it the scorn of many of the still-to-be-radicalized student body and the bitter opposition of a growing number of influential off-campus figures. (A group calling itself the Christian Family Movement had sent letters to all businesses advertising in the *Spectrum*, urging that they stop in the name of decency.) The Fugs's review set the stage for a major confrontation. The attempt several weeks later to publish an undergraduate's poem which compared Buffalo's City Hall to a "limp penis," triggered it.

Insisting that the poen was obscene, the owner of the local company that printed the *Spectrum* refused to print it. The editor, outraged by this blatant attempt to censor a paper that the printer, a man named Abgott, was paid to print, demanded that a blank page appear where the poem was supposed to have appeared. The editor had also decided to end his relationship with the printer and took his paper to another printer. (The editor, anticipating this kind of problem, had earlier urged that the *Spectrum* have its own printing presses. Although they didn't get them then, they have them now, and thus operate independently of Abgott's brand of censorship.)

The student senate, which funded the paper, refused to go along. For some time they had been critical of the editor. His budget, they said, wasn't balanced. And besides, they said, the purpose of a university paper is to represent the voice of the majority, not the radical and freaky fringe they believed the editor stood for. The three hundred–odd students who occupied President Meyerson's office demanding "Freedom of the Press" felt otherwise. Yet Meyerson's support was lukewarm at best and the editor, squeezed between the conservative student senate and a flaccid administration, resigned. The printer, meanwhile, made out fine. Awarded a medal by the American Legion for his role in "The Spectrum Case," he built a platform around his stand against the editor, ran for county office, and won handily.

Relations between the university and the community were still further strained less than one month later when Leslie Fiedler, one of the university's best known professors, was arrested on a drug charge: not for selling them; not even for using them; but rather for "maintaining a premise where narcotics are used." Fiedler's house, Erie County Sheriff Michael Amico admitted proudly, had been under surveillance for days; his phones had been tapped; and a paid undercover agent, masquerading as a hippielike friend of Fiedler's daughter, had planted a listening device in Fiedler's home. Fiedler, who had earlier incurred the rage of the community by serving as faculty advisor to LEMAR, knew throughout his three-year-long trial that the verdict would go against him. He didn't stand a chance in this venue. Subject to relentless harassment—by gawking neighbors; by his bank, which declined to renegotiate his mortgage as he sought to raise cash for the trial; and by his insurance company, which cancelled him home-owner's policy—he knew that he would lose, "since what was being judged was not my specific guilt but [our] general role in the community as outsiders and dissenters."

As turmoil on the old campus accelerated, so too did the planning of the new one. Nelson Rockefeller's appetite for architectural overkill is well known. The mall at Albany, begun during the early years of his governorship and completed barely before his death almost eighteen years later, is a wind-swept monstrosity, its superhuman scale awesome and frightening. His plans for the new UB campus in Amherst were equally distorted. One of Rockefeller's favorite architects was Buffalo-born Gordon Bunshaft. Since his truly magnificent addition to Buffalo's Albright-Knox Art Gallery in 1962, Bunshaft, the most influential partner in Skidmore, Owings and Merrill, the world's most influential architectural firm, had been designing increasingly larger and more monumental buildings. The bigger the better, as far as Rockefeller was concerned, and in the spring of 1967 he had the State University Construction Fund hire Bunshaft to prepare a preliminary master plan for the new UB campus.

In November 1967 Bunshaft's plan appeared on the front pages of Buffalo's newspapers. It defied description. What was pictured was a single "building" (the local press, not knowing quite what to call it, put the word in quotations) nearly one mile long and one thousand feet wide. It was, a spokesmen for the SUCF said, "to be the largest single architectural undertaking in the country and possibly the world." It would, the SUCF said, "dwarf the Pentagon." Within this enormous structure (later buildings like this would be called "megastructures") would be housed all of the academic departments of the university, all classrooms, all libraries, all research facilities, all offices and laboratories, and all recreational facilities. It would even contain a hospital. Surrounding this mind-boggling mega-thing were to be thirty colleges—"centers of identification," Meyerson called them—where one thousand students and faculty would live and learn together. Bunshaft's new campus would serve a university community of forty thousand people and would be built at a cost of between $600 million and $650 million. (When questioned about the enormity of the budget the chancellor of SUNY replied that since most of the funds were coming from the state and federal governments, the question of costs was "academic."

The plan was too much for most people to swallow. Even the sophisticated Meyerson thought that it was inappropriate, and soon the chorus of criticism questioning the scale and the scope as well as the cost of Bunshaft's distorted vision was such that the plan was withdrawn. (The University downplayed the significance of this and said that Bunshaft plan was but one of many being considered.)

Meanwhile, a group of engineering students, fearing for their campus lest the likes of Bunshaft and the others have their way, proposed a plan of their own. While based on the requirements for the new university, their model had a completely different form than what had emerged from Bunshaft's office. Using a variation of the quad-rangle, the design that had typified Ameriċn and European colleges for several hundred years, the engineering students suggested that the buildings of the university should be small in scale and located around the preimeter of a large circle. The effect of this then, unlike Bunshaft's mile-long horizontal shaft, would be to contain the activities of the university in a linked enclosure traditionally characteristic of campus designs.

The final plan revealed by the SUCF in June 1968 was much closer to Bunshaft's original plan that to the student's alternative. While the mile-long mall had been trimmed considerably, the plan still centralized and concentrated virtually all of the university in a single structure referred to as "The Spine." In order to scale down the size of the original megastructure, the "Health Sciences," as they were called, were removed and placed instead in twenty-four separate towers. Lest anyone suspect that these revised and seemingly more humble plans represented a concession by the university, a compromise of their bloated dreams of giganticism, Robert Ketter, the officer in charge of campus construction (his official title was vice-president for facilities planning) and the man who two years later became the president of the university, specified the support system that this new campus would require. It would need, Ketter said, a new highway system capable of carrying thirteen thousand cars per hour (four times the existing capability), a rapid transit system joining the campus to the city, a seventy-five-acre park for research activities, seventy-five acres of commercial property, thirty-five to forty thousand units of new housing, and parking for over five thousand cars.

Meanwhile, back on the Main Street campus upwards of twenty-five thousand students, faculty, and staff continued to live in cramped, overlapping, yet somehow satisfactory and pleasing quarters. The university was expanding rapidly, every year hiring dozens of new faculty members at a time (in the spring of 1967 over 120 faculty were hired for the coming fall semester). Thus, with more students, more faculty, more radicals, and more reason to be angry than ever before, UB, like campuses throughout the United States, became increasingly involved in anti–Vietnam War activities. For several years there had been a small yet continuous stream of anti-war protests, but by the fall of 1967 these were galvanized by the march on the Pentagon in October. Now, with frequency and ferocity, significant numbers of students and faculty were becoming involved in protests at the UB campus.

Anti-war activities continued throughout the winter and spring of 1967–68. Recruiters for Dow Chemical and other companies involved in war production were harassed, Department of Defense-funded campus research projects were constantly trashed, and draft cards were regularly burned. As long as these activities were confined to the campus itself, there was little trouble from the community. While the common council of the city of Buffalo had voted overwhelmingly in favor of a motion objecting to the use of state facilities for anti-war activities, there was little, politicians realized, that they could do about what happened on the campus. But it was a different matter when the protests spilled over into the rest of the communtiy.

In the summer of 1969 anti-war activities were taken directly into Buffalo's residential West Side, where several students, already found guilty of draft evasion, sought asylum in a Unitarian church on Elmwood Avenue. Finally, after several tense days of efforts by the minister to mediate between the students and the federal agents outside the church, the Feds stormed the church and forcibly arrested the students within, who at that point became known as "The Buffalo Nine."

The trial of the Buffalo Nine, charged with assault and resisting arrest, occupied the attention of UB's anti-war movement throughout the fall, and when in February 1969 one, a student named Bruce Beyer, was convicted on two of three counts, the university exploded. Unlike the other irritants, there was something about the trial of the Buffalo Nine, the seriousness and commitment of the defendents, and the violent assault on the church by the federal officials, that captured the imagination and ignited the energy of a large proportion of the student population. Meeting at the gym the next night to express their solidarity with Beyer, 2,500 students demanded an end to American involvement in the war and an end to UB's participation in defense-related research. Meyerson, whose flexibility with students (deemed patronizing by them and permissive by the community) had helped to earn his job as president, agreed on this latter point and expressed his hope that no such projects would be permitted in the future. He agreed also to cancel classes temporarily so that teach-ins on the war could be held.

His attempt to mollify the growing student anger failed, however, for when on March 19, 1969, Beyer was sentenced to two concurrent three-year terms, real violence broke out as several hundred students (local papers referred to them as "rampagers") set fire to several buildings that were part of a navy research project. From there they jubilantly entered administration offices at Hayes Hall, where several climbed to the bell tower of that hundred-year-old building and began to clang uproariously the bells of the University of Buffalo.

Meyerson's reputation in the community as a capitulator to the students grew still more when he, choosing to avoid confrontation, allowed them to leave Hayes at their leisure. He further outraged the community (there had already been formed in Buffalo an organization called Mothers Against Meyerson) when, the very next day, he expressed his support for a cause that had become increasingly important to many in the university community. Now, only six months after ground for the new campus had been officially and ceremoniously broken, Meyerson publicly urged that Governor Rockefeller stop all work there until the labor force was equitably integrated. (Rockefeller subsequently complied, imposing a moritorium on all campus construction. A year passed before the integrated construction crews were in place and work resumed.) On the next day—March 21, 1969— a handful of Buffalo councilmen demanded that Meyerson be fired for his "weak" action as president of the University of Buffalo.

Meyerson's troubles with the community were exacerbated by his educational philosophy. For Meyerson did not want to duplicate in Buffalo the worst aspects of the California system, a large and lonely "multiversity" that had somehow managed to lose sight of the personal as well as the educational needs of the individual student. Thus, he supported enthusiastically the creation of separate colleges—those "centers of identifiction"—where faculty and students would live and learn together according to their particular interests. By late 1969 and early 1970, however, several of these colleges had taken on lives and identities of their own well beyond the range of possibilities that anyone had ever imagined. Several of them, committed to a nontraditional education in which students and people within the community-at-large would somehow learn with and from each other, had leased office space in storefronts off campus, on Main Street. College A, as it was called, had become a particularly nettlesome problem. Dedicated to social change and student activism as much as it was to nontraditional education, College A, with its bevy of dishevelled, bearded students and faculty walking around and hanging out in their Main Street storefront, made a lot of the local people very angry. Offering courses—and for credits, too—for subjects that few people had ever heard of, let alone understood (subjects like "Conflict and Change in the Local Community" and "Social Change in America"), College A was an outrageous affront to what most people in Buffalo regarded as sound eduation. As had happened once before, earlier in the century, the content of the university's education again became the legitimate subject of political discussion, with Buffalo councilmen hearing witnesses, and debating and resolving questions that had most always remained beyond the pale of the prejudice of politics. One member of the Buffalo Common Council, reflecting the views of more than a few of his colleagues, said that "we are concerned over this—the kind of program at College A—and I feel that the University needs a definition of education which excludes this sort of aimlessness. Education should have more concrete goals."

It was bad enough that public funds were being wastefully spent on such ill-conceived notions of education. It was much worse when those notions began to ooze out into the rest of the community. (One college, an off-shoot of College A called Rosa Luxemburg after the notorious German Communist, was concerned primarily with taking radicalism directly into the community. Their brochure said: "It does little good to know abstract theories of racism and imperialism if one cannot impart this knowledge to a high school student, or a young housewife, in your neighborhood.") This, more than the content of the courses offered at College A, was what most concerned the people in the surrounding neighborhood who now formed the Concerned Parents Group to deal with the question. Located directly across the street from a parochial school, the college, the Concerned Parents argued, was luring neighborhood children there and encouraging them to "drop-out of school and church." It was, many charged, harboring runaways and initiating them into a world of sex, drugs, and radicalism. When a local politican revealed that ten of the instructors in the Social Change in America courses were facing prosecution on criminal charges ranging from assault to vandalism and anti-war activities, it heightened still further the anger and anxiety of this particular neighborhood as well as the community at large. The events of February 1970 made the situation worse still.

It was easy to create a crisis at UB in the early spring of 1970 and, like the events that have triggered cataclysms throughout history, the spark that ignited the confrontation between police and students on the night of February 27, 1970, was quickly forgotten. It all started at a demonstration against the allegedly racist practices of UB's basketball coach. At the end of a freshman game between UB and a local Catholic college called Canisius, students took to the floor chanting "Power to the People," "Ho-Ho-Ho Chi Minh," and "Serfustini [the coach] is a racist."

While campus security, which had been alerted that a demonstration migh occur, was able to peacefully disperse the crowd, the game, already much delayed, was now postponed. Meanwhile the demonstrators, increasingly aroused, joined other students coming out of yet another rally in yet another building, and together this group of approximately one hundred people made their way to Hayes Hall, where at 9:30 at night Acting President Peter Regan (Meyerson had taken a year long leave absence in September 1969) was working in his office. After entering the building and then the lobby in front of Regan's office, the students saw approximately twenty unarmed (though fully outfitted in riot gear) university security police approaching the building. Upon seeing them coming their way, the students quickly dispersed, breaking several windows in Regan's office as they left. Sensing that this time they would be pursued, the students ran to Norton Union, several hundred yards away. They entered it and, hastily gathering tables and chairs, barricaded the doors, blocking the campus police who were indeed on their heels. Now, however, they had been reinforced by officers from the Buffalo Police Department (to this day, despite extensive testimony and depositions, nobody seems to know for sure who called the Buffalo police) who, without any hesitation, smashed through the doors and began to violently chase the students through the halls of the union. Within less than an hour the policemen had gone, leaving behind them the wreckage of several badly beaten students, a badly damaged student union, and a bitterly hurt and angry student body.

While there was tension, anxiety, and a great deal of uncertainty following the police raid, the union was relatively quiet, and activities were soon back almost to normal. Acting President Regan, however, now holed up in security headquarters at the other end of the campus, thought differently and even though he had apparently received information to the contrary, he acted on the assumption that the violence in Norton had continued. Once again the Buffalo police were dis-

260

patched to the student union. A report prepared ten days after the night of February 25 narrates the events that followed:

Two students who had walked around the quiet campus from Norton to Hayes and Acheson and then across to Capen report seeing the police vehicles arrive along the roadway between 10:10 P.M. One witness recalls counting fourteen vehicles including at least two K-9 trucks and one or two campus police cars. The cars and trucks proceeded along the roadway with some vehicles entering the loop between Norton and Tower. The procession stopped, and some cars parked on the grass near the postal kiosk. These same witnesses observed the police and security officers immediately dismount from their cars.

Some of the officers moved to the Tower side of Norton. Another group of officers crossed the footbridge over the service drive to Norton and moved into the fountain area, followed by the two witnesses who saw the police proceed directly up to stairs and through the doors into Norton. Some persons leaving the building at that point apparently turned before the oncoming officers and moved back into Norton. Several reports indicate that this group of officers proceeded through the foyer into Haas Lounge, clearing these areas of people. There are several reports of punching and shoving by police officers during this first operation, and a report that police officers used their nightsticks in clearing Haas Lounge.

Police officers entered the Tower doors of Norton at about 10:10 P.M. A witness observed several persons hurrying through the Tower doors followed shortly thereafter by policemen. Persons in the foyer area, upon seeing the police approach, began moving rapidly down the hallway. Apparently, some shouts of warning were raised by those who had observed the police enter through the Tower doors. A wave of people moving from the Tower side entered the foyer near Haas Lounge just as the police entered through the Fountain doors. In the resulting crush, some people spilled into Haas Lounge. The crowd was so dense in this area that a severe injury to the right hand was sustained by a university staff member as he was pressed against a glass showcase. He reported that as he left Norton to seek medical attention he was clubbed by a policeman standing in the doorway of Norton. This report was corroborated by another person present at the scene.

While quiet returned to Norton some time after midnight, student outrage could not be contained. The next day—Thursday, February 26—several thousand students marched vigorously to Hayes Hall shouting "We Want Regan." From there they continued on to the building housing the campus security where, linking hands across the street, they sang endless choruses of the National Anthem and "America the Beautiful." With over four thousand students "on strike"

261

there were no classes held anywhere on the campus. Nobody seemed to care. How could they? The University of Buffalo—now the State University of New York at Buffalo—was under siege. By Sunday, sensing that another outbreak of student anger was imminent, Regan again summoned the Buffalo police. By midday, as three hundred fully armed and leather-jacketed police officers, with highly polished, knee-high leather boots and Darth Vader–like riot helmets, patrolled the grounds of their campus, hundreds of faculty members and students marched in silence round and round the perimeter of the campus, mourning the death of their university.

This time the police stayed. Indeed, they were still there despite an overwhelming faculty vote demanding that Regan have them removed. When he refused to comply, forty-five members of the faculty, on March 15, 1970, peaceably entered the lobby in front of his office, sat down on the floor, and vowed not to move until the police left the campus. They were arrested several hours later.

The events of the spring of 1970 were traumatic for everyone involved. Indeed, none of the participants—students, faculty, police, and administrators—will ever be able to forget what happened. While students risked their lives (although none were killed, at least twenty-one were hospitalized) and faculty their careers, the police and the members of the administration were better protected—the former by their strength and equipment, the latter by an agile instinct for survival. President Meyerson, away from the campus on a year's leave of absence, had already announced that he would not be returning to UB. He had, he said, accepted a new job as president of the University of Pennsylvania. Acting President Regan, meanwhile, overwhelmed by the events of the spring of 1970, also announced his resignation later that year. He was, he said, resuming his position at the University of Buffalo medical school in the Department of Psychiatry.

Most of the lessons learned from that breakdown of the university in the spring of 1970 were abstract and difficult to identify, having to do with the nature and function of institutions of higher learning. In some cases, however, the lessons were clear-cut and easy to surmise. Such was the case for those people who were planning the new campus in Amherst.

Actually, it was far more than a new campus that Rockefeller, the SUNY trustees, Meyerson, Ketter, and all the others wanted to build. It was, rather, in the phrase increasingly popular among those expectant master builders, "Brasilia in America;" a whole new environment filled with monumental and dramatic structures that would capture the imagination of the world. The planners were thrilled by the magnitude of the challenge:

> The scale, complexity and coordination of this project [the Director of the SUCF wrote in 1970] require that the State University Construction Fund create an organizational framework and develop new techniques to augment the traditional planning process. More than twenty planning firms are working in a coordinate effort to ensure that the resultant facilities not only satisfy the University's program, but also realize the potential of the site and the atmosphere of activity envisioned there to bring new life to the land. Never [he concluded] has the development of a single university been more potent with possibility.

Only the best, the brightest, and the most expensive architects would be permitted to work on the major buildings of the new campus: from New York came I. M. Pei, Ullrich Franzen, and the firm of Davis, Brody; from Chicago came Harry Weese; and from Cambridge came Sasaki, Dawson, and DeMay. Although Bunshaft's mile-long megastructure had been rejected (Miffed, Bunshaft had withdrawn from the project. He got revenge on his hometown, however, when, hired by the Marine Midland Bank to build their Buffalo headquarters, he erected a vertical version of his mile-lone monstrosity at the foot of Main Street.), his concept of a spine or, as the architects liked to call it, a "central activity corridor," remained the dominant feature of the plan for the new campus. The primary differences was that Bunshaft's megastructure was now broken into two smaller spines, each of which contained three linked buildings. In the first were all of the administration offices, three specialized libraries, fifty-two classrooms, several "food service areas," and a conference theater. In the second spine was the law school, a gigantic building with office space and classrooms for over twenty-five hundred people; and the library, an enormous structure which, with its one-million-volume capacity and over thirty miles of shelves, was three times larger than the library on the Main Street campus it had replaced. Although not a part of this second spine, a ten-story office building housing the English and Modern Language Department was directly linked to it by a pedestrian overpass. A half-mile away from these two spines was yet another megastructure, a place called the Ellicott Complex. It was, in the words of the SUCF, "an environment which, though massive in scope, consists of a series of smaller, intimate spaces designed to combat the vastness and impersonality frequently associated with large universities"—Meyerson's antidote to the "multiversity."

Other than its enormity, what most distinguished the design of the new SUNYAB campus from the old UB campus was its sudden and dramatic departure from the idea of centrality and enclosure that not only had dictated the form of the Main Street campus, but indeed had been the dominant concept in the design of universities throughout the world since the Middle Ages. For, on the new SUNYAB campus, there were no quadrangles, no fountain areas, no plazas, no enclosed courtyards—no places and no spaces, in other words, where the individuals who composed the college community could come together.

It did not have to happen thay way either. Indeed, no other campus of the state university system was so designed. At Potsdam an existing quadrangle was reinforced and expanded by adding several L-shaped clusters. Similarly, there, as at the campus of the State University College at Buffalo on Elmwood Avenue in the heart of the city of Buffalo, two structures, usually considered the core buildings of any campus—the student union and the library—were placed in classic juxtaposition on either side of a clearly defined, enclosed public square. Even at the state campus at Albany, where the scale was monumental, the arrangement of buildings and the spaces between those buildings follows traditional notions of how universities should be built.

The absence of contained and clearly defined spaces that characterizes the exterior of the new campus is also true of interior spaces. Even the Ellicott Complex, allegedly designed to foster feelings of closeness among students and faculty, is a maze of incomprehensible, interconnecting, unrelated spaces which more than eight years after its completion continues to baffle even those who use it on a daily basis. The main dormitory, too, is a lonely and isolating environment. Located on a wind-swept plateau, cutoff from the other buildings on the campus and miles away from the city, Govenor's Residence Hall is despised by the over eight hundred students, most from the New York City area, who live there. It is little wonder that alcoholism has become such a serious problem on this campus.

The most alienating interiors are within the two spines. For while there is ample provision for classrooms, offices, and conferences and library needs, there are few places within these spines which make possible the relaxed, causal, and serendipitous gatherings that have always been an essential aspect of life and learning on a university campus. For here spaces are linear, and linear spaces, like the mall in downtown Buffalo where all the benches have been removed, tell us to move on, to go about our business quickly, without dawdling.

But the people who use these long, interior corridors—the students and faculty who spend so many hours of every day in them—have, on their own, without the aid of architects and designers, carved meaning out of otherwise banal and alienating environments. At first they began to sit on the banquettes that extended out from the walls that lined the endless halls, talking and drinking coffee that they had bought out of food machines tucked under staircases and behind alcoves. Then gradually, rather than walk the length of the halls to the one central dining area that exists within these spines, they began to bring their lunches here. Finally, recognizing that the needs of faculty and students had led them to use these corridors in ways that were new and different from those originally contemplated, the administration responded. A cafeteria was installed and tables and chairs were set up. A long and cold corridor had, long after it had been built, evolved into a community.

But that was much later—in 1981—almost ten years after this spine was originally designed. Times had changed and the student uprisings of 1970 had since long been forgotten, a source of nostalgia among once-active professors and a subject of term papers for undergraduates in history, sociology, and education. But for those people who had designed these buildings, the campus disorders of the late 1960s and of 1970 had been critical. Indeed it seems, as many people have suggested for years, that security and the containment of student uprisings were the paramount concerns in the design decisions of the SUCF and the architects they hired. This is particularly evident in the design of the president's office on the new campus.

The president's office at Hayes Hall was on the ground floor. Surrounded by windows which rounded off the corner of the building where he worked, and accessible by any number of doors, the office was extraordinarily vulnerable. For, as we have seen, it was occupied by demonstrating students and faculty on at least five different occasions between 1966 and 1970. This could never happen at the president's office on the new campus. Indeed, it is difficult for an outsider, with no prior knowledge of its location, to even find it. Unlike the old Main Street campus, where Hayes Hall was located on "Administration Road," there are no signs or any other indications pointing to it. While there is one large billboard map on the campus which does include "Central Administration" as one of the activities housed in a place called Capen Hall, there is no way of knowing where within Capen the president's office actually is. Only after asking does one learn that it is on the fifth floor. (The only place listed as being on the fifth floor is the Capen Gallery.)

It is impossible to get to the fifth floor of Capen without using the elevator. While there are interior stairs, these are emergency fire stairs that are locked and accessible only from the inside. The only stairs leading directly to the president's office is a one-flight staircase connecting the fifth floor only with the fourth floor, where other administrative offices are located. They do not connect with the outside. Thus, other than the elevators, which can be locked as easily as a bridge over a moat can be raised, there is absolutely no way for anybody to get to the president of the university. He is shut off completely from the life of the campus. Here, five mysterious floors above the ground, no windows can be broken, no students can demonstrate, and no faculty members (let alone forty-five of them) can sit down on the floor of the president's office demanding action.

While the design of the president's office clearly reveals a paranoid preoccupation with security, a conscious effort to shield him from his constituents, the design of the rest of the campus reveals contempt not only for the students and faculty but, even more serious, for the true function of a university campus. For by failing to provide the necessary spaces where a sense of social well-being can ferment, the university can, at best, be little more than a think tank.

But by 1970 anyway, university officials in Buffalo and in Albany distrusted students and faculty, and felt threatened by the changes implicit in their challenge to the traditional sources of campus authority. Frightened by what they saw happening on the old campus of the University of Buffalo, they tried, through their plans and designs, to guarantee that it would not happen on the new campus too.

CHAPTER 12

Praying for a Miracle

The boom times that had begun during World War II couldn't last. And, as they had after the First World War, Buffalonians began to worry about economic collapse. They were concerned that the federal government, a generous customer during the war, would prove fickle in peacetime; that the prosperity and full employment generated by federal contracts would quickly vanish as the government withdrew the hand that had for years fed the city. They were right to worry. For hardly had the war ended when abrupt and complete cutbacks in all aspects of war production were made. The economy could not adapt to these drastically changed conditions.

Most vulnerable was the aircraft industry. During the war Buffalo had become the center of that industry, the Seattle of its day. With millions of dollars in federal contracts, and thousands of its workers involved in the production of planes, engines, and their component parts, Buffalo prospered as long as the war continued and the government bought its planes. The end of the war signalled disaster. In 1943 there were over 40,000 people working at Curtiss-Wright. By September 1945 the number had been reduced to 5,500 and the ripple was felt throughout the whole economy. By Christmas, 1946 there were over 80,000 people, close to fifteen percent of the area work force, without work. Then, in early 1946, Curtiss-Wright announced that it was closing down almost all of its Buffalo operations. They were moving to Columbus, Ohio. They claimed they had nothing against Buffalo itself. The city, a spokesman for the company said, had been a "swell place in which to operate." It was simply a matter of space; they didn't need so much of it anymore, and in

Columbus they would be able to scale down and consolidate their operations.

City officials and the chamber of commerce were hurt. They felt betrayed, believing that they should have been told of Curtiss's decision ahead of time and given a chance to work things out. They rationalized it as best as they could, reassuring themselves with dated verities. "There is nothing in these factors to cause concern to civic leaders or industrialists in Buffalo," the president of the chamber said of the Curtiss Wright move. It was, he said, "a combination of circumstances such as will probably never arise again." As other leaders had done in the past and still more would do in the future, he drew support from increasingly obsolete considerations. "Buffalo still has the tremendous advantage of cheap power, excellent water and transportation facilities and a highly responsible group of skilled and unskilled workers." As if saying it somehow made it true, he said that "Buffalo is still a desirable place for industry."

Industry did in fact continue to flourish in Buffalo. But it was not easy. The economic upheavals of the post-war years were extremely traumatic. Strikes in virtually every industry, the continuation of price controls, the shortages of raw materials and consumer products that continued into the late forties, and the high unemployment (particularly among women, who left their jobs as the men returned from the war), created continued instability and havoc. Only war seemed to help. Indeed, conditions improved steadily during the Cold War years and reached a peak during the Korean War. Speaking of its role in that conflict, one local newspaper editor wrote that "Buffalo's industrial machine once again packs a mighty war punch. Like a trim front-line soldier, it is geared to shoulder any job which it may be assigned to. Buffalo is a bigger arsenal for democracy than ever."

But, these conditions couldn't last forever. Times were quickly changing. Buffalo's industrial infrastructure—its factories and railroads—was aging, and its work force, as the result of a series of crippling yet successful strikes, was deeply entrenched. Its population too was beginning to decline, as that of places further west was growing. And, beginning in 1952, a small yet significant number of Buffalo's industries began to leave. Spencer-Kellogg, the largest maker of linseed oil products in the United States, announced in January 1952 that it was closing its Buffalo plant. It was, the owner said, fifty years old and out of date. Others followed. Dupont decided that it would build a ten million dollar plant in Ohio to manufacture a product—mylar—that they had developed in Buffalo. National Anilene, now owned by Allied Chemical, had also lost its loyalty to the local community, and announced that it was moving its plant to Virginia to process coal tar products, while Hooker Chemical choose Mississippi over Niagara Falls as the site of a new chlorine plant. The reason, they said, was "a combination of circumstances including cost of land, the labor situation and the cost of doing business in New York State."

Most people, unable to face the reality of the dramatic upheavals that were occurring within the community, failed to grasp the significance of these events. Commentators remained boosterish in the face of discomfitting facts. One newspaper editor, responding to the rash of corporate departures in 1952, remained optimistic. "Buffalo's economic position, with its low cost of power, its skilled labor and its shipping advantages is far too secure to bring about any wholesale dislodgement of industry here." While they may have been able to convince themselves that all was indeed well, the economy continued to unravel.

Commerce was in even more trouble than industry. Commerce had made Buffalo, and despite the dominance of industry and of railroads for almost a century, Buffalo's self-image was still rooted in trade. The city's symbol—a lake boat, floating on the rippling waters of Lake Erie, a canal boat moving slowly down the still waters of the Erie Canal, and the lighthouse of the Buffalo harbor—still served as the seal of the city. In 1950, as in 1850, Buffalo was still (or so people liked to think) "The Queen City of the Lakes."

The facts of course were different. The city had long ago lost its historic function as a port of transshipment, and by mid-century most of the processing industries that had at one time provided a diversified and stable economic base had all but disappeared, with lumber, tanning, and soap among them. Even the beer industry was in trouble.

While the number of breweries had been reduced during Prohibition (there were seventeen in 1919, but only five in 1933), and the number of brewery workers was down from two thousand to twelve hundred, production remained steady. After the war, however, sales and production began to decline precipitously. The problem was that while Buffalonians were drinking more beer than ever (per capita consumption was estimated at twenty-two gallons per year), they were drinking less local brew. National companies—Schlitz, Budweiser, and Miller—in a concerted effort to destroy home-based breweries in cities throughout the country, were invading local markets and successfully undercutting local breweries (Annheuser-Busch, for example, opened a local distributorship in Buffalo in 1953).

MARK GOLDMAN

The local industry staggered under this intense pressure from the large national companies. They simply could not compete. Not only did they lack the cash to mount more than regional sales campaigns, but their plant facilities were old and obsolete. As much as anything, it was their failure to modernize that had done them in. While breweries in other cities had introduced automated processes in virtually all aspects of the industry, Buffalo's family-owned breweries continued to operate largely by hand. Workers still poured all of the ingredients, washed the gigantic kettles, and uncorked, cleaned, rinsed, and stacked the returned kegs by hand. In 1964 one Arthur Newman, a business representative for Brewery Workers Local No. 4, went on a national tour of modern breweries. When he returned to speak to the few local brewers still remaining in Buffalo about the new automated processes that he had seen, he got little response. Newman told the papers: "People didn't care. They never believed it would happen." Buffalo's last brewery, the Iroquois, closed in 1972.

Failure to modernize, to reinvest profits in new plants and equipment, had destroyed Buffalo's breweries. Had the local families who owned these companies made different decisions they may well have been able to alter the results. They had the ability to do differently but chose not to. The St. Lawrence Seaway offered no such choices.

By the early 1950s the battle against the construction of the St. Lawrence Seaway had like the Pan American and the War Bonds drive, become the kind of a communitywide cause that the people of Buffalo seemed so fond of. Although hopeless, the effort was justified, for the stakes were extremely high. The relentless lobbying effort against the Seaway had begun in the 1920s, and continued through the subsequent decade. By the mid-1950s, as passage of the St. Lawrence Seaway legislation seemed inevitable, local opposition reached a climax. Virtually every interest group in the city—businesses and banks, labor, politicians, newspapers, social and civic clubs—joined the campaign to prevent what everyone knew meant disaster to the local waterfront economy. (The common council approved funds for a special lobbying effort that carried a message to Washington: The Seaway, they said, would be vulnerable to Soviet air attacks and therefore should not be built.) Everybody had a stake in defeating the bill and everybody did what they could to fight it. (Realizing that electrical power along the route of the Seaway was going to be developed by public authorities, none fought harder than local power interests.) But the cause was lost and in 1954 the legislation was enacted. Five years later, President Eisenhower and Queen Elizabeth ceremoniously opened the St. Lawrence Seaway.

The impact on Buffalo was immediate. Ocean-going vessels carrying goods both to and from the midwest now bypassed Buffalo. After stopping at all the Great Lakes ports—Duluth, Chicago, Detroit, and Cleveland—they would exit Lake Erie, well before they even got to Buffalo, pass through the Welland Canal into Lake Ontario, then continue across that lake and onto the Seaway to Montreal. Buffalo's long-dreaded nightmare had finally come to pass. With no reason for ships bound either for the ocean from the West or from the ocean to the West to ever come to Buffalo, the city sat bypassed at the end of a long dead-end street.

Suddenly a whole range of waterfront industries—boat companies, ship chandlers, ship repairers, and shipbuilders—began to go. In 1962 the American Shipbuilding Company closed down, the last vestige of an industry which had been in Buffalo since 1812. The grain industry, consisting primarily of grain storage and the manufacture of flour, suffered more than anything. Since the middle of the nineteenth century Buffalo had been the grain storage capital of the world, harboring millions of tons of midwestern grain in its internationally renowned grain elevators. But now, as increasing amounts of grain were shipped to Montreal via the Seaway, Buffalo's significance as a port of storage was sharply and quickly eroded.

Flour milling also faced hard times, and mills and elevators were closing throughout the 1960s. In 1966 alone five flour mills were shut down and in 1981 Standard Milling, a Kansas City–based company, closed its Buffalo mill, the largest in the city. Still, Buffalo, with its daily capacity of ten million bushels, remained the leading flour production center in the United States. Employment in grain was down though: from 4,800 before the St. Lawrence Seaway opened to under 1,000 today.

The construction of the St. Lawrence Seaway was not the only occurrence that doomed grain storage and flour milling in Buffalo. There were others that were equally harmful. One of them involved freight rates. For years the Interstate Commerce Commission had maintained artifically low rates for the shipment of grain by lake boats. By the mid-1970s the ICC revised its rate structure and it now became far cheaper to ship grain on railroads directly from the Midwest to ocean ports on the East Coast. Thus squeezed between a new rate structure on the one hand and the St. Lawrence Seaway on the other, Buffalo's grain industry, once the foundation of the city's prosperity and the source of its pride, struggled desperately to survive.

Or did it? By the 1960s Buffalo's grain storage and flour industries completing a trend that had begun early in the century, were completely owned and controlled by outside interests. The national corporations that owned the local mills—Cargill, International Milling, Standard Milling, and Pillsbury—had little stake in or commitment to the local economy. The struggle to maintain the local grain industry, then, was left to organized labor, the chamber of commerce, and the local political establishment. The grain interests themselves were aloof from this struggle. Without their support, wrote one newspaper in 1966, Buffalo had no chance of winning the rate restructuring case. Angered and frustrated by the increasingly apparent weaknesses of an economy dominated by outsiders, the paper concluded that the grain companies really didn't care, that "big companies with nationwide or worldwide operations have told their local executives to steer clear of the problems of an individual city." This they did, and Buffalo suffered for it.

Meanwhile, there were equally dangerous, if more subtle trends at work slowly but surely undermining the industrial sector of Buffalo's economy. By the mid-1950s the nexus of steel and automobiles had become the backbone of the city's economy, employing between them close to sixty thousand workers. Despite high wages, productivity, and profits in these industries, Buffalo's rate of unemployment remained consistently high throughout the period. Indeed, with the exception of the years between 1964 and 1970, Buffalo's average rate of unemployment has, every year since 1954, been above the six percent figure that the federal government considers "acceptable." Sometimes, as during periods of national recession, it was much higher. Sometimes, it was lower. But always it was worse here that in the rest of the nation, and almost always it was worse here that in the rest of the state.

The peak years were during the Vietnam War, when the economy expanded, purchasing power increased, defense spending boomed, and local unemployment rates (3.8 percent in 1968) were at a record low. Everybody was optimistic. The steel industry was enjoying a period of unmatched profit and productivity, "in step," as one spokesman for the industry put it, "with the quickened pace of progress in Buffalo." The industry still had compelling allure, as newspapers, in the mid-1960s as they had at the turn of the century, still described it with heroic, almost magical imagery. In a two-page supplement on the steel industry, one paper, in copy describing several majestic, powerful, and awesome color photographs of the steel-making process, wrote: "men who make steel are dwarfed by their surroundings and the titanic machines they control." Another picture illustrated "men releasing great torrents of fluid iron from volcano-like furnaces." And, later on, another reference to a volcano: "This night shot of a blast furnace resembles a volcano."

The automobile industry also looked indomitable at the end of the 1960s. With over twenty thousand people employed in two Chevy plants, a Ford plant, and a radiator plant, industry and UAW spokesmen forecast more of the same for the future. They had great hopes that increased production of such small-sized cars as the Ford Falcon and Chevy Vega would create still more demand for the engines, axles, radiators, tires, and windshield wipers that had become a mainstay of the city's economy. "If you've got any faith in this country at all," the president of Bethlehem Steel said in 1970, "you can't help but believe that a tremendous decade lies ahead. There are so many things that have got to be done."

The tide turned quickly, however, and within a year or two industry in Buffalo, particularly steel and automobiles, entered a period of deepening economic crisis from which it will never recover.

Steel felt it first. In 1971 half of the eighteen thousand–man work force at Bethlehem was permanently laid off. Suddenly and shockingly people began to say that soon the entire plant at Lackawanna would be permanently closed. So extensive were the rumors to this effect that in January 1972 Bethlehem Steel felt compelled to explain itself in a half-page advertisement in one of the local newspapers. The first question Lewis Foy, Bethlehem's president, dealt with was the issue of plant closings. He did not want, he said, to close any plants. But, he continued, certain features tend to make certain plants "sick." There were, he outlined, "oppressive taxes" and "unrealistic environmental control laws." Most damaging of all, according to Foy, was "an uncooperative labor force." Placing the onus on the workers and not on management, Foy concluded that "it is quite obvious that we're in deep trouble unless all of our employees improve their productivity."

Indeed conditions worsened during the 1970s. Unemployment rates, fueled by continued layoffs at Bethlehem, reached close to nine percent in 1974 and hit a post-war peak of twelve percent a year later. With close to seventy thousand area workers out of work, the press began to pay more attention to the problems of unemployment. Noting that manufacturing jobs in Buffalo had fallen from 180,000 in 1954 to 154,000 in 1967, the *Courier Express*, in a front-page article in the summer of 1975, asked, "Has high unemployment become a way of life for the Buffalo area economy?" Descriptive rather than prescriptive, the story went on to explain what had happened: why corporations were leaving; why Rochester, with a more diversified economy, was more successful; and why high wages and high taxes contribute to industrial decline.

Even the Sunday *New York Times* covered the story of unemployment in Buffalo. There, on February 9, 1975, on the cover of the most widely read Sunday magazine in the world, was a photo montage of the faces of Buffalo's unemployed men and women. The quotation on the front of the magazine was from one of the people interviewed for the story, "Down and Out in America." It said: "I Didn't realize it was this bad." Inside were a series of interviews with men and women, factory workers and academics, clerical workers and professionals. Accompanied by sad-faced and sombre pictures of the subjects, resembling the social documentaries of the Depression era, the article painted a picture of devastation and hopelessness.

Surprisingly, Buffalo's press welcomed the article. Local thinking about the economic crisis was beginning to change as newspapers and politicans were both, for the first time, ready to deal openly and nondefensively with the problem. The article, one paper said, was not "a slam piece, another one of those shots of bad national publicity about Buffalo." The mayor too, a Polish-American named Makowski, agreed that the local economy was "extremely depressed" and hoped that the article would generate help and understanding for the people of Buffalo.

But the problems only worsened. Nineteen seventy-seven was a particularly bad year. The American steel industry as a whole and the older factories in the industrial Northeast in particular faced financial collapse. Despite a $417 million tax credit from the federal government, Bethlehem Steel reported a fourth quarter loss of $477 million, the largest quarter loss in history. Thirty-five hundred more workers were laid off at the Lackawanna plant. With only eighty-five hundred men left there (there had been close to twenty thousand in 1965), half the plant would be "mothballed" and its capacity reduced by forty percent. Meanwhile, the list of local corporations that were leaving grew longer. Citing high state income taxes, high wages, a unionized workforce, bad weather, and a declining population, an evergrowing number of companies left Buffalo. Some, like National Gypsum and Houdaille, went to the Sunbelt; others, like Carborundum and Western Electric, to the Midwest. A story in the *Courier Express* on why companies were leaving showed a picture of an executive of the Houdaille Company seated comfortably with his family in the air conditioned sun porch of his Ft. Lauderdale home. This man, a second-generation Italian-American who like his mother and father before him had been raised on Buffalo's West Side, told the reporter that a job candidate "would accept a job with a Buffalo company and go home and tell his wife. Then he would call back later and say he's sorry, he can't take the job."

The economic decline was relentless throughout the late seventies and early eighties. For now added to the problems of steel were those of the automobile industry. Mismanagement had brought the American automobile industry to the brink of ruin, crippling its ability to compete with its rivals in Europe and Japan. Now, faced with dwindling sales, the auto companies joined Bethlehem Steel in drastically slashing even the more senior members of their labor force. Thousands were laid off and by early 1982 barely skeleton work crews maintained General Motors, Ford, and Bethlehem. Automobiles and steel, steel and automobiles, automobiles and steel . . . crumbling together. The whole city shook. The list of closings, like schools on a stormy winter day, now mounted: Whole chains of retail and wholesale department stores, restaurants, shops, and service organizations were going out of business, while venerable institutions like the Philharmonic Orchestra, the art and science museums, and the Buffalo Historical Society teetered on the brink of bankruptcy.

These events had a traumatic and shocking effect on the community and left no one and nothing untouched. Most affected, naturally, was the industrial worker, the man who had grown up fully expecting that if all else failed, there was always a job at Bethlehem or at Chevy. Indeed, these were not last-resort jobs but rather, because they paid well and were highly unionized, were considered worthy, secure, and estimable forms of employment. In 1954 one paper waxed poetical writing about steel work and steelworkers: "Once a steel worker always a steel worker. Perhaps the roar and clangor and blistering heat hammer such a respect in a man that he never can become bored with his job. Perhaps that is why a steel-maker never can be content except in the arduous toil and sweat that goes with the fabrication of hard metal. For here everything tells him that he is part of something stumpendous, that he is doing something worthy of a man."

That attitude had changed by the early 1980s. It was hard for these people, raised in the belief that work was manly, to accept the realities of Buffalo's economy. A laid-off worker at Harrison Radiator told a reporter (By 1980 the newspapers had become almost morbidly obsessed with traumas of unemployment. Revealing a Depression mentality, there were countless articles on handling stress, alcoholism, child abuse, and other behavioural problems that the newspapers now generally attributed to unemployment) that "I loved my job. I loved the pay, with two days off a week what more could anyone ask for. I was helping to build a good product [automobile and truck radiators] and I went in there with the attitude that I was going to give those people the best damn eight hours I could. It made me feel like a man. Sitting around the house knocks your masculinity right down the drain. . . . Day after day, it's the same old thing. Nothing but stress. . . . I'm thirty-five years old and I've never felt so insecure in my life."

By the early 1980s Buffalo was a city in search of a function. Its location, once crucial, had become inconsequential, as the city was now bypassed by new transportaiton routes. Its industrial economy, rooted in steel and automobiles, was increasingly nonproductive and obsolete. What had happened? What had gone wrong? There can be no question but that the decline of Buffalo's economy was related to the decline that was affecting all of industry during the late 1970s and early 1980s. For the whole industrialized world had suddenly found itself in the midst of a major, worldwide economic transformation. From now on industry, if it were to survive, would have to be highly automated, relying more that ever on a highly skilled work force. Unfortunately, Buffalo's industrial economy was not automated nor was its work force particularly skilled. Indeed, everything about the city's economy worked against its survival in the new post-industrial age. Its physical plants were antiquated, its work force old and overpaid, and its management shortsighted and greedy. Indeed, it was this, far more than the proverbial scapegoats of high taxes, high wages, the high cost of environmental legislation, and "the Japanese," that was the real problem with Buffalo's industrial economy. Certainly foreign competition in both the steel and the auto industries was partly responsible for the local decline. But in blaming the Japanese, few people stopped to wonder why that nation had been successful while we had failed.

For unlike steel and automobile companies in Japan, these industries in the United States in general and in Buffalo in particular were slow to adopt new technological means of cutting costs. They took minimal steps to reduce energy consumption and air and water pollution, and did little to increase productivity and still less to improve the quality of their products. Worse still, the industrial corporations with plants in Buffalo simply refused to modernize their local factories, concentrating most all of their resources instead on newer facilities in different parts of the country. The steel and auto industries in Buffalo, as in the rest of the country, were bound to fail. What is so tragic is that they took so much with them as they went under.

There are few places to walk in Buffalo. The automobile has been permitted to invade the city. The streets have been widened and the sidewalks narrowed. Since few people use the pavements anyway, they are rarely repaired, and thus are cracked, broken, and uneven. The diversified city street of overlapping stores and homes has been replaced by parking lots: Some of them are large, square-block lots; others small, "vest pocket" lots. Even in the densest, potentially most urbane places, streets where people want to and still try to walk, an endless string of gas stations, drive-in fast food restaurants, and parking lots impede pedestrians, chasing them away and off the streets.

The detritus of the automobile is everywhere. Streets, gutters, and even the parks are filled with the remains of emptied ash trays, and littered with beer bottles, soda pop cans, and plastic and paper remnants of countless meals at McDonald's, Wendy's, and Burger King, thrown aggressively out of fast-moving cars and into the human environment.

Why have the people of Buffalo allowed this to happen? After all, Buffalo is not, like Los Angeles and the other awesome cities of the "Sun Belt," a product of the automobile mania of the post-war years. Why have we been willing to sacrifice the most decent and humane aspects of the city to the ravages of the automobile? This process is, as we have seen, nothing new. It began long ago. Indeed, had it not been for the fifteen-year hiatus of first the Depression and then the war, most of the destruction of the city that we have come to witness in our own time would have occurred years ago.

Although it started in the twenties, the worst of it happened during the second automobile age, which began with the end of the war. Buffalonians could not wait to throw off the controls that had so specifically and precisely regulated the use of their cars during the war. They had had enough of gas rations, of limits on when they could and could not drive, and of jam-packed rapid transit, and they began to plan well before the war was over for what everybody fully expected would be the new golden age of the automobile. And indeed, by the war's end the mechanism for bringing it about—a sweeping plan for the construction of a whole new system of city wide highways and arteries—was in place. New York State had passed a thruway bill in 1943, and in 1946 the state, in conjunction with planning officials in Buffalo, made public their *Report on the New York State Thruway and Arterial Routes in the Buffalo Urban Area.*

This report, which became Buffalo's basic transportation planning document for the next thirty years, was rooted in the belief that the city's survival required that it take dramatic and immediate steps to accommodate the projected enormous increase in private vehicles. The vision of the city articulated in this document was that of a large, downtown business district surrounded by evergrowing numbers of suburban residential communities (few people realized then the extent to which the suburbs would become virtually self-sustaining and independent). Since, the planners argued, more and more people would be leaving the city for the suburbs, the city would have to develop strategies for handling the private automobile. "Surburban traffic," the report said, "must be given high consideration in the logical treatment of any conditions within the city." Given this notion then, local streets could no longer serve their traditional function of being local paths of movement and transportation, relatively small routes linking neighborhoods to each other and to downtown. They would rather have to become large arterials on which fast-moving vehicular traffic would be able to travel quickly between suburban residential areas and the downtown business district.

The plan was expensive and ambitious. According to it, a system of highways would be built around the city—"a cordon virtually encircling the city"—which would be linked to the downtown area by a series of connecting arteries. Since the main concern of the plan was to handle, distribute, and disperse downtown-bound suburban traffic, streets would have to be widened considerably so that they could, in the words of the planners, "intercept traffic on all the main arteries leading into the city and to carry that traffic freely to the downtown area." At all costs congestion and bottlenecks would have to be avoided as cars approached downtown. Traffic, the report emphasized, must be free-flowing, uninterrupted, and unburdened. "Unless provision is made for the uninterrupted flow of vehicles from the Thruway [the major highway intended to link the city to the suburbs] onto the streets, and they in turn have the capacity to receive this concentrated flow, there will be blocked intersections and heavy congestion at every point."

The first link in the citywide system of highways was the Niagara section of the thruway. Built along the banks of the Niagara River at the end of the Erie Canal, the Niagara section, completed in 1949, connected Buffalo with Niagara Falls, twenty-three miles away.

The problem was, however, that while the Niagara section of the thruway linked Buffalo with areas in the north and west, it was to the east of the city that the greatest suburban growth was occurring.

What was needed, it was felt, was a highway from east to west within the city. Not only would this provide a direct link between the city and the new eastern suburbs, but it would bring the airport within direct and easy reach of downtown Buffalo. Thus in 1953 state and city planners outlined their proposals for the construction of five highways which would cut through the city along five different east-west axes. Thus, superimposed upon the street system of the city of Buffalo would be a monstrous gridiron consisting of five super-highways whose purpose would be to join the rapidly growing surrounding suburbs with a rapidly declining central city. The price they paid for this plan was enormous; the damage irreparable.

It didn't look that way at first. In elaborately illustrated and documented brochures, these expressways were presented to the public in 1953. The views of these neighborhood- and street-obliterating highways was always from the air, and from a distant, bird's eye view they looked clean and benign. Sprinkled here and there with cars, lined with rows of thickly planted trees, the highways looked small, harmless, and almost bucolic. The reality was far different.

The first link in the system of east-west highways was the Scajaquada Creek Expressway. It began at the thruway on the west side of the city and then made its way east, where it connected with the Kensington Expressway, the second link. The Kensington carried the system directly to the eastern suburbs on one spur and into downtown Buffalo on the other. The Kensington bulldozed through a neighborhood; the Scajaquada through a park. Both areas were expendable.

The neighborhood was known as Humboldt Park, named after the Olmsted-designed park it was near. Like Buffalo's lower East Side during the 1920, the Humboldt Park area was in a state of transition. Still predominantly Jewish and German, it was quickly becoming black. But for now, at least, it was an integrated, stolid, substantial middle-class community of one- and two-family homes on tree-lined streets, the best black neighborhood in Buffalo and, though not the best, still a desirable Jewish neighborhood. Yet located as it was directly in the middle of the proposed route to the suburbs in the east, few planners questioned the wisdom of building a major highway through it. After all, there was a parkway already there, and if by converting that into a six-lane grade-level highway (depressed on part of its route) the airport and the suburbs would become suddenly accessible, the price was worth it. What's more, there was little opposition. The Jewish residents had already begun to abandon the community, and while many of the incoming blacks opposed the plan, they, among whom were many professionals and business people, had not yet acquired the political power that they would have at a later time. The Kensington had far more proponents than opponents, and in the early 1960s construction on it began. In 1967, the year of Buffalo's ghetto riots, the Kensington Expressway, coursing through the middle of Buffalo's only middle-class black community, was opened to traffic.

When it was built several years earlier, the Scajaquada Creek Expressway met with even less resistance. The people of Black Rock and Riverside, however, did, at least for awhile, try to fight it. These riverfront communities had already suffered irreparable loss at the hands of the state highway planners. For by then the New York State Thruway, built on the bed of the Erie Canal along the edge of the Niagara River, had become a vast ribbon of concrete obliterating forever the easy access to the river that the people of these communities had long taken for granted. The Scajaquada, whose construction required the demolition of the Black Rock market, was an additional affront to the neighborhood and they tried, however futile their effort, to stop it.

The Scajaquada Creek Expressway passed not only through parts of Black Rock but through Delaware Park as well. It was necesary, the planners said, in order to connect the west and east sides of the city. For the same reason, they said, it was necessary to build the expressway through Delaware Park. But even this proposal which, in bisecting Lincoln Parkway, one of the most exclusive residential streets in the whole city, proved that not even the wealthy were protected from the damage that automobiles and their advocates were causing the environment, brought little opposition. For it seemed that people had become used to and had even accepted the notion that urban park space was expendable; that it was a luxurious and even wasteful use of land that could and indeed should be put to more practical purposes. In fact, when they first released their plans for the Scajaquada Expressway, the planners (who, because they were from Buffalo and not the state, might have been expected to feel differently) referred to the land in the park as "vacant."

This view of urban park space was not the result of the post-war era of automobiles and highways, but rather of a notion that evolved during the first automobile age in the 1920s. At that time local planners had advised that Delaware Avenue, the long north-south roadway that extended the whole length of the city, be widened as it passed through Delaware Park. For the park, like the cemetery that bordered it, was considered a "barrier to traffic" and therefore, these gentlemen-planners argued, "should willingly contribute enough of its little used lands to provide another roadway to relieve traffic." Thus, it came as neither a shock nor a surprise when it was announced in 1953 that the Scajaquada Creek Expressway, a four-lane highway, would be built through Delaware Park.

This absurd and destructive view of Buffalo's most magnificent park did not stop with the completion in 1957 of the Scajaquada. For throughout the fifties and sixties city planners continued to conjure up still more schemes in an effort to keep the relentlessly growing flood of commuters moving between downtown and the suburbs. Indeed, the construction of the Scajaquada and the Kensington through and near the park only increased the demands for further use of parkland for vehicles. One proposal, advanced in 1958, called the "Delaware Park Shortway," would have taken a large chunk of parkland on the north side of the Delaware Park meadow and built there yet another divided highway, across the park and parallel to the Scajaquada.

It is no wonder then that even today, presumably a period of disillusionment with the automobile and greater sensitivity to the park needs of city dwellers, there are still plans to turn parkland, if not into highways, at least into parking lots. In 1958, as part of their never-built shortway, planners in city hall called for the construction of six parking lots in the park to accommodate a total of one thousand cars. In 1978, as part of their master plan for growth and expansion, the Buffalo Zoo, which is located in the park, planned to build one giant five-hundred-car parking lot in the middle of the largest playing field in Delaware Park. Following the opposition of outraged park users, the zoo backed down. Its attack on the park was relentless however. Now the zoo insisted on building a new main entrance, replete with snack bar and gift shop, directly facing the same meadow it had planned on destroying with its parking lot. The city went along with the zoo, and this once safe and quiet park area has become traffic-clogged, dangerous, and unsightly. Thus, Delaware Park remains fair game for road-happy planners and a car-crazed public. Despite fences which limit access and signs which limit speed, people continue to violate Buffalo's parks with their automobiles. Whether parking on the grass or speeding along narrow roadways reserved for pedestrians, bikers, and skaters, large numbers of Buffalonians, wedded to their cars, continue to despoil the physical environment of their city.

When not planning highways, city planners have lavished their attention on downtown. Since the early twentieth century Buffalo's downtown business district has been the object of numerous studies, proposals, and master plans. The earliest plans dealt with traffic flow and the construction of a civic center. More recently, planners have stressed economic revitalization. These differences, however, have more to do with strategies than with ultimate objectives, and from this point of view all of the plans for downtown, spanning a period of over sixty years, have in common the assumption that downtown Buffalo was and still is, despite years of delcine and decay, arson, abandonment, and crime, the symbolic center of the metropolitan area. While this understanding of the function of downtown may well be held by many, particularly those with a business investment there, most Buffalonians, raised in the thirties and forties in cohesive, largely self-sustaining ethnic neighborhoods and living today in equally self-sustaining suburbs, never had any real interest in or use for downtown. It is perhaps for this reason that all of the plans for its revitalization have failed.

Historically, planners' visions of downtown have never been consistent with the way the majority views and uses that section of the city. In 1938 the University of Buffalo, in conjunction with the City Planning Association, brought to Buffalo one in a long line of outside architects and planners to help them remake the city. The man was one of the great exiled Bauhaus masters—("The Great White Gods," Tom Wolfe has called them)—a German-Jewish refugee named Walter Behrendt. Behrendt was greeted enthusiastically by the downtown business establishment and the academic community, and touted lavishly in the press as the man who would bring order and beauty to Buffalo's downtown. Afraid to reveal what they thought was their lack of sophistication, Buffalo's leaders registered neither anger nor hurt when Behrendt told them how disappointed he was with their city. After all, he was, as the papers had said, "an internationally known architect and planner" whose advice should be heeded.

He wasted few words and minced none. Behrendt did not like what he found in downtown Buffalo. Walking around downtown behind the recently completed City Hall, searching for what he thought was a "suitable approach to the waterfront," he was dismayed when he stumbled on an Italian immigrant neighborhood: "I found Court Street continued on a rather dilapidated form, bordered on both sides with poor residential structures—most strikingly contrasting to the architectural dignity of Niagara Square. And, about one or two blocks from the City Hall—at its back door so to speak—was a rather rural scene. I saw, believe it or not, a goat nibbling at some weeds along the curb." Looking for "beauty, not ugliness" and "splendor not squalor," Behrendt was appalled. As if to threaten his already humbled audience, Behrendt concluded: "In a German city there would have been issued an order forbidding any encroachments of this kind."

Behrendt didn't like Buffalo. It offended his Germanic sense of design, order, and discipline. But here he was, hired by the university and by prestigious citizen's organizations, and he would try to make the best of it. He would try, he said, to remake the city. He would do it, he said, by bringing order out of the chaos that he found. In one of the many speeches that he delivered throughout the city in 1938, Behrendt argued for conformity and uniformity in urban design: "People in our time seem to be afraid of using uniformity as a means of architectural design. They obviously hold that uniformity proves lack of originality. They are mistaken. . . . Uniformity certainly secured a much better effect than is achieved in present times in the streets of our modern cities when everybody thinks he must differ from his neighbor in order to prove his personal taste." Fortunately, Behrendt's stay in Buffalo was short, as plans for the renewal of downtown were delayed until after the war. Had he been given the chance, however, he would surely have done more harm than good. With his vision blurred by the automobile—Behrendt's favorite activity in Buffalo was to walk along the Humboldt Parkway in the morning, "enjoying the pulsating life of the city revealed in the uninterrupted flow of traffic"—and skewed by a sense of architectural scale and uniformity out of character with the city, Behrendt had little feeling for the workings of the pluralistic, multi-faceted city of Buffalo. He left in 1939.

After the war the problems of downtown were more serious than ever. For, as the rise of the suburbs began to have an increasingly depressing effect on downtown, planners and downtown business groups began to launch major programs for the revitalization of the central business district. Now, in 1959, a group calling itself the Greater Buffalo Development Foundation hired a planner named Arthur D. Little from Cambridge, Massachusetts (while European architects and planners were preferable, an occasional one from Cambridge would always suffice). Little's mandate was nothing short of making downtown competitive with suburbia.

He was not overly optimistic, for despite the presence of several large retail stores in the central business district, Little noted that a growing amount of retail business was being lost to suburban malls. In its place, he said, there had been an influx of "marginal retail establishments" (a euphemistic reference to the increasing number of specialty shops catering specifically to the rapidly expanding black community east of Main Street). These had, Little said, created "an unsightly appearance," and had caused a sharp decline in pedestrian traffic. The task was difficult, and the odds against its success long. But, Little argued, downtown Buffalo might survive if it could develop a new retail core of its own by building just what downtown business interests had most come to fear—a mall. Thus, only by copying the tactics and strategies of the suburbs, Little concluded, could downtown hope to compete with them.

The key to a dynamic retail district, Little realized, was pedestrian traffic. That's what, above all, distinguished the best streets—Charles in Boston, Madison Avenue in New York, Hertel Avenue and Grant Street in Buffalo—making them active, busy, and alive. Shocked by the small amount of pedestrian traffic that he found in downtown Buffalo, Little urged that only by building an enclosed mall—a large weather-protected retail spine—of its own, could the area hope to "restore much of the pedestrian environment that prevailed before Poppa" and therefore survive. The goal then was the resurrection of the street, the return in a new form of the crowded, dense, diversified immigrant street in the modern city. Little offered other strategies too. One was a gigantic development "similar," Little said, "to Rockefeller Center with high rise office buildings enclosing a public park." There would also be a new governmental center and acres of new underground parking. While much of the Little plan was actually implemented—a mall was built, and three banks, with generous amounts of city, state, and federal loans and guarantees, erected three duly impressive modern office towers—the effect on downtown was minimal at best. For the flight to the suburbs accelerated during the 1960s, fed by relative prosperity and a growing fear of blacks. By 1970 Buffalo's population had sunk to 462,000 from its 1950 high of 532,000. The decline of downtown deepened during the seventies despite the belief that the high cost of automobiles, gasoline, and home mortgages would lead to the area's revitalization. In 1980 Buffalo's population had shrunk to 357,000 people. Downtown Buffalo was dying quickly now.

The decline of downtown Buffalo was not reversed or even slowed by government policies. With the same generous cost write-down benefits that city officials had provided for developers willing to participate in schemes for the renewal of downtown, suburban municipalities provided for developers willing to participate in similar developments in the surburbs. As a result, by the end of the 1970s the city was surrounded in every direction by enormous, enclosed, weather-controlled, landscaped, and elaborately designed shopping malls that filled the same role in the life of teenagers cruising there after school,mothers with infant children, and senior citizens with nothing but time, that the neighborhood street had once performed for an earlier generation of city dwellers.

Downtown was similarly undermined by other disastrous planning mistakes. When forced to choose between a downtown and a suburban location for such major public developments as a new university campus or a new sports stadium, public officials invariably chose the latter. Confronted with a rapidly deserting population as well as public officials willing to abandon the area for the new frontier in the suburbs, it was impossible for downtown to survive, let alone compete.

Still, the late 1970s and early 1980s saw even more ambitious plans for the revitalization of downtown, including the construction of government-subsidized hotels and office buildings and a new rapid transit system. (The heavy-handed and slow pace of building the six-mile-long system caused more financial hardship and losses to downtown businesses than anybody had ever imagined.) Thus, increasingly insignificant as a retail center, surrounded by desperately poor communities of blacks, hispanics, and whites, downtown, now hardly more than a besieged daytime fortress of office buildings, stood at the brink of total disaster.

Public policy had done equal damage to the neighborhoods that surrounded the central business district. None had suffered more than the Ellicott District.

Despite the ghettoization of blacks that was occurring on Buffalo's East Side, the area was still integrated as late as 1950. While one section of it, the Ellicott District, had become overwhelmingly black, others (places with names like the Fruit Belt, Hamlin Park, and St. Lucy's Parish) were still white. Within ten years, however, all of them had become part of a vast East Side ghetto. How do we explain this sudden and dramatic transformation?

For one thing, whites in Buffalo, like those in cities all over the country, were taking advantage of generous federal subsidies and moving into the suburbs. Between 1950 and 1960 over eighty thousand white Buffalonians—close to twenty percent of the 1950 population—moved out of the city. At the same time the city's black population was mushrooming; from 36,645 in 1950 to over 70,000 ten years later. Even the oldest, most cherished neighborhoods in the city experienced this population turnover.

The ghettoization of the old East Side was to a large extent the result of demographic patterns beyond the control of local policymakers. To stop here, however, would be to pass the buck, to absolve local politicians and bureaucrats of the critical role that they in fact did play in the making of a ghetto on the old East Side.

More than anything else, it was the housing policies of both local and federal governments during the 1950s that destroyed the existing white communities in the Fruit Belt, Hamlin and Humboldt parks and St. Lucy's Parish, creating a black ghetto in their place. Ever since the federal government first entered the housing business in 1935 with the creation of the Federal Housing Authority, discrimination in housing had been written into law. Until the late 1940s the underwriting manual of the FHA sanctioned what one critic of their policy has called "the Racist Theory of Value." According to this, neighborhoods in which there had been an "infiltration of inharmonious racial or nationality groups" would receive lower credit ratings.

Local housing policy was equally racist in intent. In 1939, for example, the Buffalo Municipal Housing Authority, in conjunction with the federal government, built the Willert Park low-income housing project on Jefferson and William Streets. Despite strenuous opposition from both black and Jewish residents of the area—who claimed there were sufficient vacancies in other projects—the city, eager to cordon off blacks within the existing boundaries of the black community and to preserve the racial purity of existing low-income housing, went ahead with the project.

Racism imbued not only public housing policy but the private real estate market as well. By steering blacks into the old East Side and whites away from it, the city's real estate industry aided and abetted the ghettoization of Buffalo's blacks. Just as blacks were not shown property in white neighborhoods, brokers—with few exceptions—refused to sell homes to whites in remaining integrated neighborhoods. It was only a matter of time before the streets of the old East Side that still were integrated in the 1950s became part of the black ghetto.

Like their predecessors during the 1920s, blacks on the old East Side thirty years later still could not rent in white neighborhoods. The great majority of rental units are now, and were then, in two-family owner-occupied homes. To this day there is no local law that forbids discrimination in this type of housing.

There is perhaps no better example of how both the public and private sectors reinforced the ghettoization of blacks on the old East Side than the Ellicott Redevelopment Project. In early 1952 the city of Buffalo, again with the support of the federal government, announced that it was going to demolish twenty-nine blocks in the Ellicott

District. The area was to be cleared and replaced with new residential and recreational facilities.

While there was little question that the housing in the Ellicott District was old, often decayed and beyond repair, the communities on the site—the blacks to the north and the parishioners of St. Lucy's to the south—were stable. Most of the residents of St. Lucy's had been in the parish since the early twentieth century, while the great majority of blacks in the redevelopment disrict had been there for fifteen to twenty years. Indeed, ten percent of the black residents on the site were homeowners who had lived there for over twenty years.

Despite the communitywide opposition, residents were given no choice. Some of them had suggested something called the "Baltimore Plan," whereby the funds would be used for renovation and restoration of existing homes—but the city would have not of it. The clearance of the area and the removal of the residents were never negotiable issues.

Beginning in January 1959, sixteen hundred black families and over seventy black-owned businesses, over one thousand Italian-American families and well over a hundred Italian-owned businesses began the search for new locations. For the residents of St. Lucy's Parish, the process was painful. Many had paid up their mortgages long ago and now found it extremely difficult to enter the housing market. However, within a year most had moved: some to other neighborhoods in the city, others to the suburbs. In late 1960, the Rev. Msgr. Carl J. Fenice held the last mass at St. Lucy's. Urban renewal had destroyed in one year what it took fifty-six years of neighborhood building to create. Msgr. Fenice remembered that: "We were bewildered by the whole operation. It all happened so fast. There was such good, solid brick housing in the parish. That money could have done a lot of rehabilitation—but the city wasn't thinking along those lines. What most galls me is that the plot of land where our church stood still is vacant."

Ellicott District blacks, in the meantime, had a much more difficult time. Given the discriminatory housing policies in existence, they had no place to go. Tenants could be legally kept out of one- and two-family homes while homeowners, even had they received a fair market price for their homes, were denied access into areas other than those within the old East Side. To a degree it was easier for the black renters, many of whom had already begun to move into homes left behind, but still owned, by white former residents of the Fruit Belt. Homeowners had far less flexibility. The city told them they could go into the existing projects until new housing became available in the redevelopment area. But for people who had owned their own homes, this was not a viable solution.

Thus, with most realtors unwilling to show homes in white neighborhoods and with no banks or federal lending agencies willing to lend money, blacks dispersed by the Ellicott project had no choice but to resort to blockbusting. Working with realtors, sometimes black and sometimes white, black homeowners quietly but steadily began to purchase homes in all-white areas along Humboldt Parkway, Hamlin Park, and other sections in the northern part of the old East Side. While many blacks were able to buy new homes, the price they paid was dear in more ways than one. For with the exception of the realtors nobody benefits from blockbusting. The white homeowner is sacrificed, the black homeowner pays an exorbitant amount and gets the blame—and the realtor makes the money. Fear and panic spread, neighborhoods were abandoned, race relations were poisoned, and the ghetto grew.

Not only housing policy was segregative in Buffalo during the 1950s. Indeed, as the Buffalo school desegregation case has shown, it was in 1954—the year the Supreme Court ruled segregation in public schools was unconstitutional—that the Buffalo school board, by changing the boundaries of East High School, took the first of many steps whose eventual result was the creation of a virtually segregated school system.

By the early 1960s then, the old East Side had become a black ghetto. It didn't have to happen that way. Indeed, had the neighborhood been allowed to follow its own patterns of historical development, blacks and whites might well still be living there together. But the tremendous growth of Buffalo's black population during the 1950s provoked white fear and anxiety. As this happened, private prejudice was not dealt with but was rather translated into public policy in such critical areas of urban life as housing and education. And, in a desperate effort to contain the spread of blacks, a ghetto was created on the old East Side.

While Ellicott was the worst area, others were almost as bad. By 1980 Buffalo, "The City of Neighbors," had become a city of failed neighborhoods. For despite the best efforts of hard-working community groups in every section of the city trying desperately to hang on, the obstacles were proving too great. Whole districts were bleeding to death. Wracked by arson and crime, plagued by a wrecked economy, eroded by a sinking population, battered by the destructive policies of public officials culminating in the Reagan administration, the city's neighborhoods, long the dominant and most significant element in the life of the city—Black Rock and Riverside, South Buffalo and the West Side, North Park and Hamlin Park, Kensington-Bailey and Grider-Delevan—seemed destined to failure.

Nothing seemed to be working right. The built environment—the streets, neighborhoods, homes, and parks—was crumbling. Now too the natural environment seemed to be giving out as well.

"The Mighty Niagara," that magnificent and majestic body of water that runs rapidly from the bottom of Lake Erie at Buffalo, due north to the city of Niagara Falls where it crashes indescribably over the falls, had been polluted for years. It was, the United States Public Health Service said in 1949, one of "the most seriously polluted rivers in the United States." Polluted also was the air along the Niagara Frontier, particularly over Lackawanna and at the concentration of chemical industries in Niagara Falls. For awhile it seemed that considerable progress was being made, as state and federal anti-pollution laws were able throughout the sixties and seventies to control, to some extent anyway, the manner in which the industries and municipalities in the area disposed of their waste. But by the late 1970s people in the Buffalo area became suddenly aware that the issue of industrial wastes was far more critical than anybody had ever imagined.

For years manufacturers had disposed of their waste products, however toxic they were, in a haphazard and almost random manner. Hooker Chemical Company, for example, began dumping thousands of gallons of highly toxic chemicals in a place called Love Canal near their Niagara Falls plant in the early 1940s.

William Love came to Niagara Falls in 1892 in order to build a model industrial community centered around the electrical power generated by the falls. Within a year he had bought close to twenty thousand acres of land and had begun to dig a canal which would connect his hoped-for community of 600,000 people to nearby markets. The depression of the nineties, however, ended his scheme and the land he had purchased and the canal he had begun to dredge lay fallow. Because the canal was lined with clay presumed to be impermeable, the Hooker Chemical Company of Niagara Falls bought the property in 1942. It began to use it as a dump for chemical wastes.

Meanwhile, the canal area, for some reason zoned "General Residential," began to develop, as homes were built and several hundred families moved in. Now the Niagara Falls school board, looking for a site for a new school for the area, and thinking that the canal was a suitable location, approached Hooker. Hooker was at first reluctant to deed the property to the school board. Reminding the board that the canal had been used as a dump site for chemical wastes, Hooker argued that it was not a suitable site for construction. Despite these warnings, however, the board was insistent and in 1953 the deed to the land was transferred.

Following the construction of the school the area grew still more and in 1958 the city of Niagara Falls began the construction of two avenues through the canal property. In the process part of the canal cover was broken, some chemical wastes were exposed, and children playing in the area received skin irritations.

There were no major incidents for several years. Indeed, it was not until 1976, when several homeowners reported that strange-looking and foul-smelling chemical wastes had seeped into their basements, that the people of Love Canal were reminded of just how hazardous their neighborhood was. In August 1978, as reports of migrating chemicals became still more frequent, the New York State Health Commissioner declared that a health hazard existed there, ordered the immediate closing of the school, and advised that pregnant women and children evaculate. Two years later, following the initiation of court proceedings that will last the better part of the next decade, President Carter declared that a state of emergency existed at Love Canal and that the federal government would fund the evacuation of the 710 families still living there.

In the wake of the Love Canal tragedy it became known that there were at least 153 known contaminated sites in the Buffalo area where toxic wastes had been stored. But the increased knowledge and vigilance of the public did little good, as people throughout the community wondered when and where the poisons would next appear. One day it was in a residential neighborhood near the factory of Union Carbide; another near the plant of Hooker Chemical's Durez division. There was something terrifyingly unknown about seeping underground wastes. Where would they go? Would they migrate into the Niagara River? Into underground water supplies? Into the water that people drank and swam in?

Added to the anxiety caused by toxic wastes was the fear of radioactive wastes. Between 1963 and 1975 an area known as West Valley, thirty-five miles south of Buffalo, had been a state-licensed burial ground for radioactive wastes. During that time 550,000 curies of radioactive waste materials were dumped into dirt trenches approximately thirty feet deep and six hundred feet long. "The trenches were not," the Sierra Club reported, "lined with concrete, plastic or any other medium. Radioactive garbage was dumped directly into the ground in a 'pussy-cat' approach: a little earth was scratched away, material dumped in and then, recovered by scratching back the original earth."

People were angry; people were afraid. Several accidents and derailments involving trucks and trains carrying radioactive materials, and the revelation that a shipment of over one hundred pounds of plutonium had been shipped secretly through the suburbs of Buffalo on its way to the Ginna power plant near Rochester, led the common council of the city of Buffalo to try and ban the transportation of hazardous toxic and radioactive products through their city. But area industrialists were too strong and, lobbying against the ban, were able to defeat it.

The people of Buffalo were vulnerable. Would they be safe in their homes, their streets, and their neighborhoods? What would happen to their health and to the health of their children? Nobody really seemed to know.

Conclusion
The Rise and Decline
of Buffalo, New York

Cities, caught up in the continuous sweep of momentous historical events, are always changing, sometimes growing and sometimes shrinking. The invention of agriculture, the rise of commerce, the development of industry, changing technology, immigration and migration, war, famine, and disease, are but a few of the long list of overlapping and interacting historical phenomena that have been at work shaping the destiny of the world's cities. In this book I have tried to chart, analyze, and interpret these changes and their impact on the city of Buffalo, New York.

We have seen that for many years historical developments created a set of circumstances that led to the continuous growth of Buffalo. Superbly located at the mouth of the Great Lakes, Buffalo quickly assumed a place of importance in the developing national network of trade and transportation. Tied to the cities of the East Coast and of Europe by the Erie Canal, and linked to the rapidly expanding Midwest by the chain of the Great Lakes, Buffalo by 1850 had become the most significant inland port in the United States. The seemingly endless flow into Buffalo of products from the Midwest led quickly and naturally to the creation of a highly diversified manufacturing economy. Buffalo's flour industry was the largest in the country and its breweries, tanneries, iron shops, and furniture factories made it a significant and rapidly growing center for the production of a wide range of manufactured products. The city's population grew too. Luring thousands of people from central New York and still more from Germany, Ireland, and Canada, Buffalo's population increased dramatically, at times doubling during the middle years of the nineteenth century.

Because of the strength and vitality of Buffalo's commercial economy and the diversified manufacturing to which it was intimately connected, the shift to heavy industry occurred gradually. But the confluence of several powerful historical forces at the end of the nineteenth century was such that the transition was inevitable. The creation of an integrated national network of transportation based on the railroads, the movement to the city of thousands of immigrants willing to work long hours for little pay, the development of electrical energy, and the marshalling of millions of dollars for investment together led to the creation in Buffalo of a large and growing industrial economy by the early years of the twentieth century.

In the years following World War I Buffalo emerged as an industrial giant, a major center for the production of steel, railroad cars and engines, airplanes, and automobiles. While this may well have worked to the advantage of the enormous numbers of unskilled black and white workers who comprised a growing percentage of the city's population, these trends were ominous as far as the long-term economic well-being of the city was concerned. For, while few realized it at the time, it was during the 1920s that the patterns that have come to characterize the contemporary economic crisis in the city of Buffalo first became apparent. For now, added to the insecurity of an economy whose well-being had traditionally been dependent on the cyclical swings of the national and even international economy, was the fact that the increasingly industrialized economy was owned increasingly by outsiders. By the end of the 1920s Buffalo had lost practically any ability to control its own economic destiny.

These trends were accelerated during the Depression, a decade which saw the demise of still more small-scale, locally owned operations and the continued rise of such large-scale outsider-owned industries as automobiles and steel. Given this orientation toward heavy industry, the economy of Buffalo fared well during the Second World War. Indeed, the war years were the halcyon period of urban industrial society, a time when everybody worked and most everybody felt good about their community. While local leaders talked proudly about the city's industrial strength during the post-war period, the city's commercial position suffered irreparable damage. For when in 1959 the St. Lawrence Seaway opened a direct all-water route between the Great Lakes and the Atlantic Ocean, it destroyed the remnants of the once thriving commercial economy of the city. With commerce now drying up rapidly, the city became ever more dependent on industry.

But industry was fickle, and few seemed to realize that the post-war prosperity that characterized the steel and auto industries was temporary. With the rest of the industrialized world devastated by the war, the United States, and with its cities like Pittsburg, Detroit, and Buffalo, had been able, for a time anyway, to dominate the industrial markets of the world. It couldn't last, however, and by the end of the 1960s Germany and Japan had emerged as serious rivals of America's industrial metropolises. By the early 1970s American industry was suffering badly and American industrial cities appeared to be dying.

Change also affected Buffalo's population. Moving during the 1950s and 1960s to the suburbs and then later even further away to the South and the West, Buffalo's population has dropped precipitously since the end of the war. To the older, poorer, and more dependent people who stayed behind were added thousands upon thousands of southern blacks whose predominantly rural backgrounds equipped them with few of the skills necessary for survival in post-industrial urban America. The impact of these population shifts may well have been mitigated had it not been for the restrictive immigration policies which had remained relatively unchanged since 1924. Denied for over fifty years the vigor, energy, and intelligence of several generations of foreigners, American cities in general and Buffalo in particular have withered and decayed.

While there is perhaps little that could have been done to modify the historical forces that have so altered the economy and the population of the city during the years since the war, there is much that could have been done to ease the transition so that the changes which have occurred would not necessarily have created decline. After all, several times during the course of the city's history conscious efforts by local leaders and entrepreneurs had been made to purposefully alter the direction of the city, to better adapt it to the changes that were occurring in the larger world. Yet, while some people in some places saw that the days of industrial domination were numbered (Boston's conscious effort during the post-war period to restructure its economy from one based on industry to one based on high technology is the most famous), little effort was made in Buffalo to reorient the economy of this city to the changing realities of an increasingly post-industrialized world.

While little has been done to nuture new economic developments, still less has been done to foster a new generation of political leaders.

Long dominated by a tribelike Democratic party suspicious of and hostile to new ideas and individuals, a party that effectively rewards its own and punishes outsiders, Buffalo has been governed by lackluster machine politicians with little vision and imagination. Thus, the city stagnates and declines, ensnared by historical forces that have made its traditional economic function increasingly obsolete and exacerbated by a local business and political establishment bent on perpetuating itself rather than trying to encourage creative possibilities and dynamic leaders for the future.

What, if anything, can be done about the cycle of decline and stagnation that has afflicted this city? Is there any way to confront the forces of change and channel them in directions that could lead not to decline and decay but rather to creativity and ingenuity? Is there some way to avoid the bleak future that the present scenario suggests?

If there is, it is absolutely essential that the people of Buffalo accept that the glory days of industrial growth are long gone and that they will never return. While there may well be hope for the future of the city, it must not be based on antiquated and obsolete visions of a great and growing industrial city. Buffalo has not been a growing city for almost half a century and will never be again. Once we have discarded this image of growth we must begin to think in terms of trying to create a vital community within the contexts of a shrinking population. This is perhaps the greatest challenge for local leaders in the years to come, far more difficult and complex than the challenge of planning with growth in mind ever was. It is not easy. It may even be impossible. We do not have any models of graceful decline. Is it possible, for example, to mitigate that hurt that the less skilled and the poor automatically suffer in periods of decline? Is it possible for a declining city—a place where newspapers close and art galleries, historical societies, and art and cultural groups are threatened with daily extinction—to be an innovative community, an incubator for new ideas, energies and enterprises?

These are the kinds of questions that the people of Buffalo must begin to deal with if they are to ease the pain that inevitably accompanies decline. There are answers. In the interests of all the people who make Buffalo and other declining industrial cities like it their home, I have posited an agenda which would help to make the future of this city brighter.

1. Buffalo will need a coherent program of federal economic planning that would equalize and distribute economic growth and development based on regional needs.

2. There must be a major commitment by both private and public sectors to job training so that workers locked into obsolescent industrial production will be able to make the transition to the news forms of work available in a changing, post-industrial economy.

3. There must be a program of federal manpower planning that will provide greater occupational choice for those workers willing to relocate to other places.

4. The local financial and political establishments must become more open and begin to reward inventiveness, new entrepreneurial activity, and new ideas.

5. There must be a commitment by all parties to strengthen the University of Buffalo based on the understanding that the life of the mind is a vital and absolutely essential part of renewing the city.

6. There must be a commitment by all parties to purposefully and energetically seek to rebuild the local economy; to use the resources of a revitalized university as well as the imagination and talent of the people in the city-at-large to find a new direction and function for the economy of the city.

7. There must be a program that would facilitate the transfer of ownership of operations from people who want to leave the city to people within the community willing and able to assume that responsibility.

8. There must be a humane system of public support that will enable those unable to move or to retrain to survive the dislocations of the current economic transition.

9. There must be an unlimited immigration into America.

10. Based on the assumption that the richer and stronger local community life is—the more control, responsibility, and involvement people have in the life of their communities—the better life in the city will be, we must do more to strengthen the fabric of the local communities that exist within the city.

Thus, by adopting programs that would soften the blow of decline by strengthening the quality of local life, Buffalo could well avoid the most painful side effects of decline, and enable in the process those people who will continue to live in the city to have a chance for a decent future.

Notes

Chapter 1

There is virtually an endless amount of information on the Pan American Exposition. Indeed, there is more material and information on this than on any other event in the history of Buffalo. I have relied primarily on the great many guide books to the exposition that are housed in both the Buffalo and Erie County Historical Society (hereafter cited as BECHS) and the Buffalo and Erie County Public Library (hereafter cited as BECPL) as well as the large scrapbook collections that both these repositories contain.

Chapter 2

For a general background on Buffalo in the early nineteenth century see John T. Horton, *Old Erie: The Growth of an American Community* (New York, 1947); Henry W. Hill, *The Municipality of Buffalo: A History*, 4 vols. (New York, 1923); H. Perry Smith, *History of the City of Buffalo and Erie County*, 2 vols. (Syracuse, 1884); and J. L. Larned, *History of Buffalo*, 2 vols. (New York, 1911).

For Buffalo during the War of 1812 see William Dorsheimer, "Buffalo During the War of 1812," *Publications of the Buffalo Historical Society*, vol. 1 (1879), 185-211 (hereafter cited as *PBHS*) and "Papers Relating to the War of 1812 on the Niagara Frontier," *PBHS*, vol. 5 (1902), 21-111.

For Thayer Brothers see N. Witgus, "Execution of the Three Thayer Brothers," *PBHS*, vol. 1 (1879), 179-185.

Most of the material written about the Seneca Indians and their leader Red Jacket dates from the late nineteenth century. The best source is

William Stone, *The Life and Times of Red Jacket* (New York, 1871). Alexis de Tocqueville's comments on the treatment of the Indians can be found in George Wilson Pierce, *Tocqueville in America* (New York, 1959), 149. The speech made at the ceremony in Red Jacket's honor in 1884 is from *PBHS*, vol. 3 (1884), 62 ff. The 1889 quotation on the Senecas is from Samuel Welch, *Recollections of Buffalo Fifty Years Since* (Buffalo, 1893). For Tocqueville's statement see George W. Pierson, *Tocqueville's America* (New York, 1961), 32. Indian Agent Granger's letter is from David Usick, *Ancient History of the Six Nations* (Lockport, New York, 1961), 183.

The material on the growing class divisions in Buffalo was developed from the *Workingman's Bulletin* and the *Commercial Advertiser*. The former newspaper represented the nascent workingman's movement while the latter spoke for the established, commercial interests in the city. The information on the *People v. Fischer* was found in Horton, *Old Erie*, 92. Many of the descriptions of day-to-day life in Buffalo were found in Welch, *Recollections*. For more information on the role of Joseph Ellicott and the Holland Land Company see William Chazenof, *Joseph Ellicott and the Holland Land Company* (Syracuse, 1970).

For the names of those born again during the Finney Revival see the Records of the First Presbyterian Church in the BECHS. For Noah's Grand Island fantasy see L. F. Allen, "Founding the City of Ararat," *PBHS*, vol. 1 (1879), 305–29. For information on government in the early city see the charter for 1832. For information on the Patriot's War and Buffalo's role in it see Welch, *Recollections*, 274 ff. For the crusade against sin see the *Buffalo Emporium*, October 18, 1828, February 2, 1829. The comment about the weather is from the *Emporium*, March 15, 1828. For more on Finney see Whitney Cross, *The Burned-Over District* (Ithaca: Cornell University Press, 1950) and Paul E. Johnson, *A Shopkeeper's Milenium: Society and Revivals in Rochester, New York 1815-1837* (New York, 1978).

For information on Wilkeson and the building of the Erie Canal see J. C. Lord, "Samuel Wilkeson," *PBHS*, vol. 4 (1896), 85–93 and A. Bigelow, "The Harbor Maker of Buffalo," *PBHS*, vol. 4 85–93.

For the impact of the cholera epidemic see L. F. Allen, "The Cholera in Buffalo," *PBHS*, vol. 4 (1896), 245–75 and Welch, *Recollections*, 264 ff.

There is an enormous amount of material on the Rathbun case in the collections of the BECHS. See particularly, Welch, *Recollections*, 197–203 and "The Case of Benjamin Rathbun as Told by Himself," *PBHS*, vol. 17, 227–70.

There is a great deal of material on the Patriot's War. My ideas were drawn primarily from Welch, *Recollections*, 274–93, in addition to material in Horton, *Old Erie*.

Chapter 3

For an account of Buffalo in 1825 see S. Ball, "Buffalo in 1825," *PBHS*, vol. 1 (1879), 139–151. For more on the grain trade see J. G. Clark, *The Grain Trade in the Old North West* (Chicago, 1966). See also Joseph Dart's own account in his "The Grain Elevators of Buffalo," *PBHS*, vol. 5 (1902), 211–82. For more on the Erie Canal see Hill, *Municipality of Buffalo*, vol. 1, 207–45. The progress of the New York Central Railroad is taken from D. Wentworth, *Annual Review of the Trade and Commerce and Manufactures of Buffalo for the Year 1854* (Buffalo, 1855). The description of Hart, Ball and Hart's stove is from a publication called *The Manufacturing Interests of Buffalo, 1855* (Buffalo, 1856), 20. The description of the Jewett stoves is from that company's catalogues in the BECHS. The description of the puddling process is from John Fitch, *The Steel Workers* (New York, 1911). The quotation describing Forbush and Brown's is from the *Commercial Advertiser*, November 7, 1854. The description of Pratt's Iron Works is from *The Manufacturing Interests of Buffalo, 1855*. The information on the impact of the panic of 1858 is from R. Edwards' *New York's Great Industries: Buffalo and Vicinity* (New York, 1884), 74. For similar efforts in other lake cities to diversify a commerce-based economy see Bayard Still, "Patterns of Mid-19th Century Urbanization in the Middle West," *Mississippi Valley Historical Review* (September 1941): 187–206.

For more on Fargo see Henry P. Smith, *History of Buffalo and Erie County*, vol. 2, (Syracuse, 1884), 295. Information on Ketchum's machine is in *Manufacturing Interests of Buffalo*, 82. For size of factories and for wages see the New York State Manuscript of the *Census of 1855*. The description of the iron factory environment is from the *Commercial Advertiser*, August 22, 1863. Inventions and their inventors are found in *The Manufacturing Interests of Buffalo*. Hill, *Municipality of Buffalo*, vol. 1, 297 ff. discusses founding of mid-nineteenth century banks.

Chapter 4

For mid-century population data see Laurence Glassco, "Ethnicity and Social Structure" Irish, German and Native born of Buffalo, 1850–1860." University of Buffalo PhD diss., 1973. Mabel Dodge's description of the East Side is from the first volume of her autobiography entitled *Intimate Memories* (New York, 1932). The Irish view of the German East Side is from Roger Dooley's novel, *Days Beyond Recall* (Milwaukee, 1949). The quotation from the *Courier* was printed on April 19, 1954. Klatz's sentiments were printed in the *Catholic Sentinel*, August 24, 1860. For information on the German language question see Horton, *Old Erie*, 146 ff. For the quotation from Democracy see *Buffalo Und Sein Deutschen* (Buffalo, 1898), 117–18. The letter from Germany is in the Manuscript Collection of the BECHS. For more on the '48ers see Carl Wittke, *Refugees of Revolution: The German 48ers in America* (University of Pennsylvania, 1952). The concerns about the state of the economy are found in the *Commercial Advertiser*, June 15, 1857. The *Express'* views on the poor are from the *Express*, July 29, 1957.

The biographical information of some of the leading Germans is from a scrapbook of clippings compiled from the *Buffalo Times* over the last quarter of the nineteenth century. The scrapbook, with no title nor date, belongs to the BECPL. Timon's descriptions of his tenure in Buffalo are taken from his handwritten journals in the archives of the Chancery of the Diocese of Western New York. There is much material on the St. Louis controversy ranging from early accounts such as C. G. Deutcher's *The Life and Times of John Timon* (Buffalo, 1870), to more recent accounts in Horton and Hill, to still the most recent and most scholarly work done by David Gerber, "Modernity in the Service of Tradition," *Journal of Social History* 15, no. 4 (Spring 1982): 655–83. The information on the Irish community and on Bishop Timon is from the *Catholic Sentinel*, published sporadically throughout the late 1850s and early 1860s. The March 17, 1857, edition is the source of the quotation dealing with the production of inferior goods. The medical information on cholera is from the *Buffalo Medical Journal* 9 and 10, published in 1854 and 1855. Valuable information can also be found in "The Cholera Journal" in the Manuscript Collection BECHS. Timon's sermon was printed in the *Sentinel*, September 22, 1854. For information on Blacks in Buffalo during this period see the *New York State Manuscript Census*; (1855), Glassco and H. Graff, "Abolitionism and Anti-Slavery in Buffalo and Erie County," a State University of New York at Buffalo Master's Thesis, 1951. For details of Wilkeson's scheme see Horton, *Old Erie*, 131. The information on black schools is from the *Seventh Annual Report of the Superintendent of Schools* (1843), 7.

Christy's lyrics are from Meade Minnegerode, *The Fabulous Forties* (New York, 1924). The anti-draft speech was quoted in the *Morning Express*, August 8, 1863. There is much material on the Fenians. I have relied primarily on newspaper accounts and an unpublished student paper in the archives at State University of New York at Buffalo by Terry Luthart written in 1966 called "The Fenian Movement in Buffalo." For Timon's cathedral-building activities see C. G. Deutcher, *John Timon*.

Chapter 5

Burwell's reactions are found in the papers of Bryant Burwell in the Manuscript Department of the BECHS. The views of Buffalo's medical fraternity are from the *Buffalo Medical Journal* 10, 1855, 184–85. Hamilton's lecture appeared in that journal, 428–31. The phrenological "data" are from Vol. 8 of the *Journal*, 1854, 152 ff. For more on the kinds of work the Buffalo legal fraternity did see the Papers of the Erie County Court in the Manuscript Collection of the BECHS. For the background material on Buffalo's WASP physicians see the New York Manuscript *Census*, 1855. For biographical material on Thompson and Tift see

Smith, *History of Buffalo*, vol. 2, 204, 210–11. The Merwin Hawley Papers are in the Manuscript Collection of the BECHS. The *Commercial Advertiser*'s view of the city are from that paper, March 18, 1955, June 19, 1955. The anonymous minister's letter appeared in the *Commercial Advertiser*, November 2, 1854.

For information on the public schools see the *Annual Reports of Buffalo Public Schools, 1839–1858* at the BECHS. For temperance material see *The Christian Advocate*, 1855–1857. The views of the Catholic establishment are found in the *Catholic Sentinel*, 1858–1860. For the information on Lord see Charles Brooks unpublished paper in the University of Buffalo Archives (hereafter cited as SUNYBA): "John C. Lord and Old School Presbyterian Thought in Buffalo, 1837–1864." Nov. 1981. There is a fascinating Anti-Sabbatarian pamphlet in the Manuscript Collection of the BECHS. The information on the 1854 and 1856 elections are from Lawrence Glassco, "Ethnicity and Social Structure: Irish, Germans and Native-Born of Buffalo, 1850–1860" PhD. Diss. in the SUNYBA, June 1973, 255. For anti-Fillmore feelings among the Irish see the *Catholic Sentinel*, October 2, 1956. For Brunck's views see Horton, *Old Erie*, 179–81.

Chapter 6

For industrialization of Buffalo in the mid-nineteenth century see Richard Ehrlich, "The Development of Manufacturing in Selected Counties in the Erie Canal Corridor, 1815–1860." Unpublished dissertation in the SUNYBA, 1967. For the information on particular industries see the Industry Scrapbooks, particularly vols. 1–3 in the BECPL. The description of Goodyear's furnace is from the Buffalo *Evening News*, August 17, 1903. For the industrial accidents see the Buffalo *Times*, April 17, 1967, February 24, 1908.

For Goodyear Brothers see a family history called *Goodyear Family History* written by George F. Goodyear and printed privately in Buffalo in 1976. Also, there is a good deal of information on the Goodyear business activities in the Industry scrapbooks in the BECPL. The quotation from the *Morning Express* was from a paper of July 13, 1891. Information on the acquisition of lake steamers by railroads was taken from newspaper clippings in the several volumes of clippings on Buffalo industry in the BECPL. The quotation from the Buffalo *Evening News* dealing with Goodyear's blast furnaces is from August 8, 1903. Material on the size of the companies locating in turn-of-the-century Buffalo is from *Twentieth Century Buffalo*.

There is much material on John Milburn. In addition to the standard texts, newspapers of the early twentieth century are filled with references to this man who was something of a folk-hero in turn-of-the-century Buffalo. The information on the coming to Buffalo of the Lackawanna is found primarily in a scrapbook on the subject in the collection of the

BECPL. The *Courier*, June 8, 1900, has the story of Milburn's Albany dealings while the information on the Vanderbilt's involvement with Lackawanna is from the *Courier*, April 17, 1900. The *Courier*, September 4, 1904, has the heroic description of the plant site while the *Times*, January 18, 1903, includes the statement about the size of the establishment. On the percentage of the work force from Scranton, see the *Express*, October 15, 1904. The number and the description of foreign laborers appeared in the *Courier*, December 19, 1904. The biographical information on the white collar workers at Lackawanna is from the clipping scrapbook on the company in the BECPL. See the *Courier*, September 9, 1904, for the record-keeping efforts of management. For the information on the incorporation of Lackawanna as a city see the many clippings on this subject in the Lackawanna Scrapbook mentioned above. Fitch's article, "The Human Side to Large Outputs: Steel and Steel Workers in Six American States," appeared in *The Survey*, vol. 27, October 1911 - March 1912. For information on steel production in the early years of the twentieth century see the clippings in the Lackawanna Scrapbook.

Chapter 7

For port clearings in September 1910 see the *Courier*, September 15, 1910. For developments in flour industry see Hill, *Municipality of Buffalo*, vol. 2, 748. Goodyear's death is recounted in *the Goodyear Family History*. The material on the diversity of Buffalo's manufacturing economy is taken primarily from Hill, *Municipality of Buffalo*, vol. 2. The best material on the Larkin Company can be found in the vertical files of the BECHS. While there is a great deal of information on the automobile industry in early twentieth century city (see, for example, *Twentieth Century Buffalo*), the best material is in the Vertical File Collection at the BECHS. The specifics on the city's labor force in 1910 are taken from the Federal Census for that year. For material on the rise of the railroads and the decline of the canal see the *Annual Report of the Board of Trade*, 1869, 71. These reports are an invaluable resource for learning about the specific ups and downs of the city's economy. The quotation on the problem that the railroads posed is found in Mark Hubbell, *Our City and Our Police* (Buffalo, 1893), 191. The material on the trade unions of the late nineteenth century is found in Central Trade Union, *The United Trades and Labor Council Handbook*, (Buffalo, 1897). The account of the striking railroad workers in 1877 is from Hubbell, *Our City*. Horton, *Old Erie*, contains a good, detailed description of the strike and the response to it. While there is a good deal of information on the grain scooper's strike of 1899 the best is Brenda Shelton, *Reformers in Search of Yesterday* (Albany, 1976), 173–93. The Wilcox correspondence is in the Manuscript Collection of the BECHS. For the work of the COS during the late nineteenth and early twentieth century see the Annual Reports of the Charity Organization Society in the BECHS. For the comment about Buffalo accents see the Annual Reports of the Superintendent of Schools, 1897. The quotation on the education of newsboys is from the Buffalo *Evening News*, April 15, 1896. For Dold's claim see Hill, *Municipality of Buffalo*, vol. 2, 821. For more on the Buffalo Honduras Company see Industry Scrapbooks, vol. 1. For street addresses of Hager and Miller see the *City Directory*, 1905.

There is an enormous amount of material on Grover Cleveland. The best work on his early Buffalo career is in Allen Nevins' award-winning biography *Grover Cleveland: A Study in Courage* (New York, 1932). For more on the ward system see Goldman, "Buffalo's Black Rock: Neighborhood Identity and the Metropolitan Relationship," PhD diss., SUNYBA, October 1973.

Material on Buffalo's WASP gentry is from Welch, *Home History, 1893*. The information on the early days of the University of Buffalo is part of the collection of the SUNYBA. The material on the Commission Charter is from the local newspapers of 1914. It was a major issue that received much attention throughout that year. The electric streetcar strike is well covered in the *History of Erie County*, (BECHS, 1976). The best information on the Buffalo Camera Club is Anthony Bannon's *Buffalo Photopictorialists*, a catalogue for an Albright-Knox Art Gallery exhibition of the same name held at the gallery in the fall of 1981. The quotations from Mabel Dodge are from her memoirs entitled *Intimate Memoirs* (New York City, 1932).

Chapter 8

There is a wealth of material on the Germans of Buffalo. This material comes from a book put out by the Germans themselves called *Buffalo Und Sein Deutschen* (Buffalo, 1898). Material on the Belt Line and the growth of Assumption Parish is from Mark Goldman, "Buffalo's Black Rock: Neighborhood Identity and the Metropolitan Relationship," PhD diss., State University of New York at Buffalo, September 1973. The best material on Italian family and community structure is in V. Y. McGlaughlin's *Family and Community: Italian Immigrants in Buffalo, 1880-1930*, (Ithaca: Cornell University Press, 1977). Information on Val D'Olmo is from the scrapbooks on "Buffalo's Foreign Population" in the collection of the BECPL. The description of Corpus Christi is from the *Buffalo Times*, April 19, 1909. Pasczek's biography is taken from an album on leading members of the Polish community called *Album Painiatkowe* (Buffalo, 1906). The journalistic accounts of the immigrants are culled from the articles contained in the above-mentioned scrapbooks on Buffalo's immigrants. Data on streetcar rides is from Roger Simon, "The City Building Process: Housing and Services in New Milwaukee Neighborhoods, 1880-1910" in the *Transactions of the American Philosophical Society* 68:5, 1978. For a description of Poles in the work force see articles by John Daniels in the *Buffalo Express*, February-March, 1910. Successful immigrants like Fronczak and Onetto have been written about so much by local writers eager to chronicle the upward mobility of turn-of-the-century immigrants that they have become local lore.

Much of the information on the rise of downtown was drawn from a close study of Buffalo city atlases which trace changing land use over time. Extremely helpful is *"Picture Book of Early Buffalo" PBHS*, vol. 16, (1912). The best information on the Ellicott Square Building can be found in the Vertical File Collection of the BECHS. There are a few scant editions of the *Buffalo Socialist* for 1912-1913 in the BECPL. The city atlases which were most helpful in charting the changes that occurred on Lafayette Square. For changes in Johnson Park see the scrapbook on the Elmwood Avenue Extension in the collection of the BECHS. There is as much information available on Olmsted as on any other subject in the city's history. Most of the ideas here were suggested by the city atlases. The Society for the Beautification of Buffalo deposited its minutes in the BECPL. The *Buffalo Motorist*, the publication of the Buffalo Automobile Club, is housed in the BECPL. The quotation on the Syracuse highway is from the Transportation Scrapbooks in the collection of the BECPL. The plans of the City Planning Association were publicized in *City Facts* (1926), in the BECPL.

Chapter 9

The material on the Liberty Loan Drive is from that collection in the Manuscript Department of the BECHS. The event in Delaware Park is described in the *Buffalo Evening News*, June 24, 1917. Information on the changing of German names was garnered from the City Directories during the war period. The material on Deaconess Hospital is from the Buffalo *Times*, March 16, 1918. For a general background on the steel strike of 1919 see David Brody, *Labor in Crisis: The Steel Strike of 1919*, (Philadelphia, 1965). For material on the strike in Buffalo during the fall and winter of 1919 see local newspapers. For the view from Lackawanna see the Lackawanna *Daily Journal* for this period.

Carpenter's study on ethnicity and work is in the BECHS. For material on the response of the Jewish community to the immigration restriction bill see the *Buffalo Jewish Review* during the spring of 1924. Information on Braun is taken from a personal interview with the real man involved who has asked that his name be withheld from this publication. For information on the ghettoization of the black East Side see Mark Goldman, "Buffalo's East Side" in the *Sunday Magazine* of the *Buffalo Courier Express*, June 29, 1980. For Jewish community in general see S. Adler and T. Connolly, *From Ararat to Suburbia* (Philadelphia, 1960).

For general information on the economy in the 1920s see Horton, *Old Erie*, 409-417. For employment breakdown in 1920 see the Federal Census for that year. The quotation from the President of Bethlehem is from *Buffalo's Text-book* published by the Board of Education in Buffalo, 1927, 38. The best material on Pierce Arrow is in the Vertical Files of the BECHS. For changing nature of work in automobile factories see J. S. Peterson, "Autoworkers and their Work, 1900-1933" in *Labor History*, Spring 1981. For information on the steel industry during the

1920s see Horton, *Old Erie*. Horton is also the source for the acquisition by outsiders of local companies during that decade. For information on corporate executives see Standard and Poor's *Register of Corporations, Directors and Executives* (New York, 1929). Information on Niagara Hudson is from Horton, *Old Erie*, 389–417. For banks in Buffalo during the 1920s see Horton, 410–12.

Chapter 10

Economic indicators are from an annual Chamber of Commerce publication called *Buffalo Business* in the BECPL. For information on relief efforts see the scrapbook on "Welfare Work Projects" in the BECPL. Chamber's optimistic quotation is in the *Evening News*, November 21, 1933. The *Courier* on April 28, 1932, was equally optimistic. The material on the Centennial is taken from a Centennial Scrapbook in the BECPL. The New Deal activities are taken from the above-mentioned scrapbook on relief in Buffalo. Quotations on "welfare cheats" are from the *Courier*, August 11, 1936, and the *News*, November 16, 1936. Information on the expansion of Bethlehem is from the *News*, February 1, 1935, and the move of GM to Buffalo is discussed in the *Courier Express*, March 19, 1937. The hint that labor difficulties had something to do with the move is found in the *Courier*, April 4, 1937. Information on SWOC is from James McDonnell, "The Rise of the CIO: Buffalo, 1936–1942." PhD diss., University of Wisconsin, 1970.

The *News'* year-end wrap up is found in the Buffalo *Evening News Almanac*, 1940, 179. Information on expanding economy is from Dudley Irwin, *The Buffalo War Council* (Buffalo, 1945). The local companies producing for the war were mentioned in the *News*, December 4, 1943. See the *News*, January 19, 1944, for the quotation about Christmas. The failure of Buffalo's initial civil defense program is detailed in R. R. Lingeman, *Don't You Know There's a War On? The American Home Front, 1941–1945* (New York, 1970). For the workings of the Buffalo War Council see Irwin, *War Council*, 10 ff. For the local manpower story see Leonard P. Adams, *Wartime Manpower Mobilization: A Study of World War II Experience in the Buffalo-Niagara Falls Area* (Ithaca: Cornell University Press, 1951). Mrs. Rosenberg's visit to the Buffalo area is mentioned in the *Courier*, October 2, 1942. The testimony before the War Manpower Commission is from Adams, *Wartime Manpower*. The twenty percent warning figure is from an interview with former OPA administrator in Buffalo, Milton Friedman, on April 6, 1982. The number of commuters was found in *Evening News*, December 28, 1943.

Chapter 11

For Browder's hard times in Buffalo see *Courier Express*, November 1–2, 1936. The Mayor's red-baiting speech is in the *Courier*, May 12, 1947. The article on Communist infiltration is from *Buffalo Business* September

NOTES

1947. The testimony before the HUAC is from *Investigation of Communist Activities in the Buffalo, New York Area. Herings Before the Committee on UnAmerican Activities. House of Representatives.* The hearings were held in Buffalo on October 2–3, 1957. The position of the ACLU is from the *Courier* October 3, 1957. For an interesting fictional account of radical activities in Buffalo during the middle years of the twentieth century see Harvey Swados, *Standing Fast* (New York, 1970). For Quinn's speech see the *Courier Express*, May 12, 1947.

For Fiedler's views on Buffalo and his terrifying account of his trial see his *Being Busted* (New York, 1969).

Much of the material on the site selection controversy is from David McDonald, "Waterfront vs. Amherst: A Study of the Campus Site Controversy," a student paper written in February 1971, in the SUNYBA. The Archives contains a wealth of material on this subject. This includes back copies of the student newspaper, the *Spectrum*, letters, and reports, as well as newspaper clippings dealing with the subject.

Cooke's report was reprinted in the *Spectrum*, September 3, 1967. The pages of the *Spectrum* are the best source for the temper of the times on the campus.

Again, there is extensive material on the question of the design of the new campus in the SUNYBA. For community reaction to the events of the time see the clippings in the Archives. The report on the events of February 25, 1970 is from a special edition of the *Spectrum*, March 10, 1970.

For the goals of the SUCF see their 1970 report on the new campus in the Archives. For what the other SUNY campuses looked like see the *Architectural Record*, August 1972, 85 ff.

Chapter 12

Curtiss Wright's decision to move is covered in the local papers of September 1945. The Chamber's blind optimism is taken from the *News*, September 18, 1945. The buoyant Korean war-time economy was noted in the *News*, November 18, 1950. The editorial on the economy following the early corporate exodus is from the *Courier*, August 19, 1952. The decline of the beer industry is taken from stories in the *Courier*, May 20, 1952, and January 17, 1972. There has been a great deal of material written on the St. Lawrence Seaway. The best sources are the indexes to the local papers found in the BECHS and the BECPL. The local reaction to the lack of concern shown by international corporations is from the *News*, September 11, 1966.

For unemployment data see the *Employment Statistics* provided by the New York State Department of Labor, 1958–1978.

The heroic images of steel making are from the *Courier*, June 21, 1964. The optimism of the President of Bethlehem Steel was recorded in the *News*, January 3, 1970. The interview with Foy is in the *Courier*, January 17, 1972. The story on unemployment in Buffalo was printed in the *New York Times*, February 9, 1975. Stories on the decline of Buffalo's economy were found in the *Courier*, August 18, 1977, January 15, 1981, August 16, 1981, and December 13, 1981 and the *News*, July 17, 1954. The problems of the automobile industry in general are well described in Emma Rothschild, *Paradise Lost: The Decline of the Auto-Industrial Age*, (New York, 1973). For the steel industry see Robert Crandall, *The U. S. Steel Industry in Recurrent Crisis* (Washington, 1981).

For highway planning within the city see the City of Buffalo's *Report on the New York State Thruway and Arterial Routes in the Buffalo Urban Area, 1953*. For road building ventures in the 1920s see Chamber of Commerce, *Live Wire*, January 1925. For Behrendt's views on Buffalo see the *News*, December 4, 1937. Little's plans for downtown are contained in A. D. Little, *Downtown Survey*, December, 1960. For decline of the Lower East Side see Goldman, "Buffalo's East Side" in the *Sunday Magazine* of the *Courier*, June 29, 1980.

For information on the Love Canal see the index to the local newspapers in the BECHS. The West Valley issue is well covered here, too. The Sierra Club quotation is taken from the *Sierra Club Radioactive Waste Campaign Fact Sheet*, nd.

Bibliography

Books

Adams, L. P. *Wartime Manpower Mobilization: A Study of World War II Experience in the Buffalo-Niagara-Falls Area.* Ithaca, 1951.

Adler, S., and T. Connolly. *From Ararat to Suburbia.* Philadelphia, 1960.

Bannon, Anthony. *Buffalo's Photo-Pictorialists.* Buffalo, 1981.

Brody, David. *Labor in Crisis: The Steel Strike of 1919.* Philadelphia, 1965.

Buffalo Und Sein Deutschen. Buffalo, 1898.

Chazenof, William. *Joseph Ellicott and the Holland Land Company.* Syracuse, 1970.

Clark, J. G. *The Grain Trade in the Old North West.* Chicago, 1966.

Crandall, Robert. *The US Steel Industry in Recurrent Crisis.* Washington, 1981.

Deutcher, C. G. *Life and Times of John Timon.* Buffalo, 1870.

Donahue, Thomas. *History of the Catholic Church in Western New York.* Buffalo, 1904.

Dooley, Roger. *Days Beyond Recall.* Milwaukee, 1949.

Dwyer, Charles. *The Economic Cottage Builder: Or Cottages for Men of Small Means.* Buffalo, 1856.

Edwards, R. *Great Industries of Buffalo, New York.* New York City, 1884.

Evans, C., and G. H. Bartlett. *History of St. Paul's Church, 1817–1903.* Buffalo, 1903.

Fiedler, Leslie. *Being Busted.* New York, 1969.

Fitch, John. *The Steel Workers.* New York, 1911.

Goodyear, C. W. *The Bogalusa Story.* Privately printed in Buffalo, 1950.

Goodyear, George. *The Goodyear Family History.* Printed privately in Buffalo, 1976.

Graham, Lloyd, and Frank Severance. *The First Hundred Years of the Buffalo Chamber of Commerce.* Buffalo, 1945.

An Illustrated History of the United Trades and Labor Council of Erie County. Buffalo, 1897.
Irwin, Dudley. *The Buffalo War Council.* Buffalo, 1945.
Hill, Henry H. *The Municipality of Buffalo: A History.* 4 vols. New York, 1923.
Horton, John T. *Old Erie: The Growth of an American Community.* New York, 1947.
Hunt, S. W. *Methodism in Buffalo.* Buffalo, 1893.
The Industries of Buffalo: A Resume of the Mercantile and Manufacturing Progress of Buffalo. Buffalo, 1897.
Johnston, J. J. *The Poets and Poetry of Buffalo.* Buffalo, 1904.
Larned, J. N. *History of Buffalo.* 2 vols. New York, 1911.
Lingeman, R. R. *Don't You Know There's A War On?: The American Home Front 1941-1945.* New York, 1970.
Nevins, Allan. *Grover Cleveland: A Study in Courage.* New York, 1932.
Pierce, George Wilson. *Tocqueville in America.* New York, 1959.
Rayback, R. J. *Millard Fillmore.* Buffalo, 1959.
Rothschild, Emma. *Paradise Lost: The Decline of the Auto-Industrial Age.* New York, 1973.
Shelton, Brenda. *Reformers in Search of Yesterday: Buffalo in the 1890's.* Albany, 1976.
Smith, H. Perry. *History of the City of Buffalo and Erie County.* 2 vols. Syracuse, New York, 1884.
Standard and Poor. *Register of Corporations, Directors and Executives.* New York, 1929.
Stone, William. *The Life and Times of Red Jacket.* New York, 1871.
Sweeney, P. J. *History of Buffalo and Erie County in World War I.* Buffalo, 1919.
Townshend, J. B. *Buffalo Fine Arts Academy, 1862-1962.* Buffalo, 1962.
Twentieth Century Buffalo: An Illustrated Compendium of Her Municipal, Financial, Industrial, Commercial and General Public Interests. Buffalo, 1903.
Welch, Samuel. *Recollections of Buffalo Fifty Years Since.* Buffalo, 1893.
Yans-McGlaughlin, V. *Family and Community: Italian Immigrants in Buffalo, New York, 1880-1930.* Ithaca, 1977.

Journals

Buffalo Arts Journal. Published periodically during the 1920s by the Buffalo Arts Club.
Buffalo Medical Journal. 1845-1898.
Buffalo Motorist. Published by Buffalo Automobile Club, 1908-1948.
Clean Clothes: An Illustrated Magazine Devoted to Cleanliness, Sanitation and Sound Textiles.
Buffalo Saturday Night. 1921-1923.
Publications of the Buffalo Chamber of Commerce appeared under different names. They are:
The Live Wire. 1910-1927.
Chamber Contacts. 1924-1933.

BIBLIOGRAPHY

Buffalo Business. 1933-1963.
City Facts. Published by the City Planning Association, 1922-1933.
The Gospel Advocate. An evangelical weekly published during the 1820s.
Niagara Frontier. 1953-
Ourselves. Published by the Larkin Company, 1906-1937.
Publications of the Buffalo Historical Society. 1879-1930.
Town Tidings. 1927-1937.
Weeds, Trees and Turf. Nov. 1980.

The Public Record

Atlas of the City of Buffalo. 1854, 1872, 1884, 1891, 1894, 1915
Buffalo *City Directory.* 1828-
Dept. of Public Works. *Index to Streets, 1814-1896.* Buffalo, 1896
Manuscript of the New York State Census. 1855, 1875, 1905, 1915, 1925
Proceedings of the Common Council of the City of Buffalo. 1854-

Annual Reports

Buffalo Board of Trade (later the Chamber of Commerce) *Statistics
of the Trade and Commerce of Buffalo,* 1853-1925.
Annual Reports of the Department of Education, 1837-1938.
. . . . . . .Buffalo Fire Department, 1868-
. . . . . . .Buffalo Parks Department, 1869-
. . . . . . .Health, 1886-
. . . . . . .Police, 1887-
. . . . . . .Public Works, 1894-
Annual Message of the Mayor. 1874-1909.
Annual Reports of the Charity Organization Society. 1877-1937.

Manuscript Collections (Buffalo and Erie County Historical Society)

Bryant Burwell Papers
Merwin Hawley Family Papers
Cholera Records from 1849
The Liberty Loan Drive

Newspapers

The Early Period

Buffalo Emporium, 1824-1829
Buffalo Patriot, 1829-1837
Workingman's Bulletin, 6/5/1830-5/28/1831
Black Rock Advocate
Black Rock Beacon

General Newspapers

Commercial Advertiser, 1/1/1835–11/30/1918
Morning Express, 1/15/1846–6/13/1926
Daily Courier, 11/1/1842–6/13/1926
Courier Express, 6/14/1926–
Buffalo *Evening News*, 4/11/1881–
The Lackawanna Daily Journal, 1919–1920

Neighborhood Newspapers

The International Gazette, 12/31/1885

Ethnic Newspapers

The Criterion, a Black newspaper
The *Buffalo American*, a Black newspaper published between 1920–1926
Der Weltburger, 12/2/1837–11/24/1852
Daily Buffalo Demokrat, 1/8/1863–7/17/1918
Il Corriere Italiano, 3/25/1904–12/1/1950
Buffalo Jewish Review, 11/9/1917–
The Catholic Sentinel published periodically throughout the late 1850's and early 1860's.

Unpublished Papers

For a general listing see the *Bibliography of Unpublished Papers, Theses and Dissertations*, a guide to holdings in all local libraries. I have made particular use of the following:
Bay, Harriet, "Social Conditions in Early Lackawanna." Student paper, University of Buffalo, n.d.
Binkowski, John. "Pan Americanism and the Original Pan American Exposition Company." Student paper, University of Buffalo, 1968.
Borowiec, George. "A Comprehensive Site Survey of Lower Main Street, 1804–1925." Student paper, University of Buffalo, 1969.
Buczkowski, C. "St. Stanislaus Church: Nucleus of the Polish East Side." Student paper, University of Buffalo, n.d.
Dindeman, T. C. "The Rise and Fall of the Pierce Arrow Motor Company." Student paper, University of Buffalo, 1973.
Ehrlich, Richard. "The Industrial Development of Buffalo, 1880–1900." Student paper, University of Buffalo, 1967.
Fleischman, R. K. "Labor Unrest in Buffalo in 1913." Master's thesis, University of Buffalo, 1966.
Gerson, Leonard. "The Buffalo Park Movement in the 1870's." Student paper, University of Buffalo, n.d.
Graf, Henrietta. "Abolitionism and Anti-Slavery in Buffalo and Erie County." Master's thesis, University of Buffalo, 1951.
Luthart, Terry. "An Examination of the Fenian Movement with an Emphasis on Buffalo." Student paper, University of Buffalo, 1966.

BIBLIOGRAPHY

Mancuso, Susan. "The Larkin Company of Buffalo, New York." Student paper, University of Buffalo, 1973.

McDonald, David. "Waterfront vs Amherst: A Study of the Campus Site Controversy at SUNY at Buffalo." Student paper, University of Buffalo, 1971.

McDonnell, James. "The Rise of the C.I.O. in Buffalo, 1936–1942." University of Wisconsin, Ph.D. diss., 1973.

Powell, Elwin. "News from Aceldama: Black and White Relations in Buffalo as Revealed by the Journal of G. W. Johnson, 1832–1868." University of Buffalo, 1976.

Rapp, Marvin. "The Poor of Buffalo, 1825–1880." Ph.D. diss., Duke University, 1968.

Sorrell, Richard, "Life, Work and Acculturation Patterns of Eastern European Immigrants in Lackawanna, New York, 1900–1922." Student paper, University of Buffalo, 1969.

Stern, Alan. "The Red Scare in Buffalo, 1919–1920." Student paper, University of Buffalo, 1971.

Sweeney, Paul D. "Locational Economics and the Grain Trade and the Flour Milling Industry of Buffalo." Ph.D. diss., University of Buffalo, 1941.

Miscellaneous

Scrapbook Collection (Buffalo and Erie County Public Library). These scrapbooks contain clippings covering all of the twentieth century and even parts of the nineteenth century on a wide range of subjects. Among those consulted were scrapbooks on "Transportation," "Housing," "Industry," "Railroads," "Buffalo Harbor," "Charities," "Welfare Work Projects," "Buffalo's Foreign Population," "City Planning," "Parks," "The Pan American Exposition," "Aviation," "Buffalo Centennial," and "The McKinley Monument."

School Yearbooks

Masten Park Chronicle. 1899–1920.
Lafayette Oracle. 1903–1921.
The Seminarian. 1905–1922.
Bennett Beacon. 1926–1935.

Catalogues

Jewett & Root's Catalogue of Stoves, 1856.
Catalogues of the Firm of Hart, Ball & Hart Company. 1855.
Catalogue of the Architectural Design of the Buffalo Eagle Iron Works. 1859.

Reports

House Unamerican Activities Committee. Investigation of Communist Ac-

tivities in the Buffalo, New York Area 10/2–3/1957. House of Representatives.

Arthur D. Little, *Downtown Study.* Dec. 1960

City Planning Department. *Report on the New York State Thruway and Arterial Routes in the Buffalo Urban Area.* Buffalo, 1953.

Index

RELATED TITLES FROM SUNY PRESS